OVERCOMING NECESSITY

THOMAS P. CROCKER

Overcoming Necessity

EMERGENCY, CONSTRAINT, AND THE MEANINGS
OF AMERICAN CONSTITUTIONALISM

Yale

UNIVERSITY PRESS

NEW HAVEN & LONDON

Yale University Press books may be purchased in quantity for
educational, business, or promotional use. For information, please e-mail
sales.press@yale.edu (U.S. office) or sales@yaleup.co.uk (U.K. office).

Set in Scala type by IDS Infotech, Ltd.
Printed in the United States of America.

ISBN 978-0-300-18161-6 (hardcover : alk. paper)
Library of Congress Control Number: 2019951388
A catalogue record for this book is available from the British Library.

This paper meets the requirements of ANSI/NISO Z39.48-1992
(Permanence of Paper).

10 9 8 7 6 5 4 3 2 1

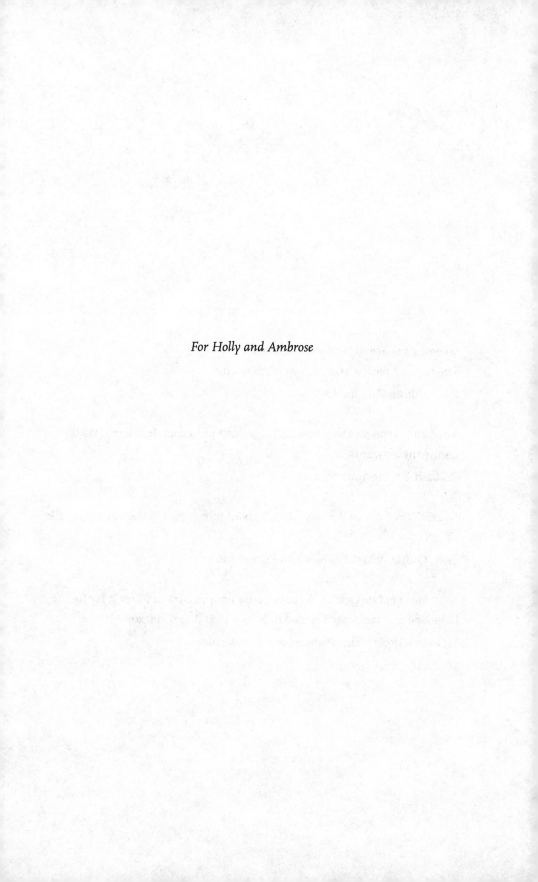

For Holly and Ambrose

So spake the Fiend, and with necessity,
The tyrant's plea, excus'd his devilish deeds
John Milton, *Paradise Lost*

Necessity is the plea for every infringement of human freedom. It is the argument of tyrants.
William Pitt the Younger

Necessity resides in the way we talk about things, not in the things we talk about.
W. V. Quine, *Ways of Paradox and Other Essays*

A picture held us captive. And we could not get outside it, for it lay in our language and language seemed only to repeat it to us inexorably.
Ludwig Wittgenstein, *Philosophical Investigations*

CONTENTS

ACKNOWLEDGMENTS

I HAVE WRITTEN THIS BOOK OVER A number of years and with the generous support of a number of institutions and colleagues. I received generous support from the American Academy of Arts & Sciences in Cambridge, Massachusetts, where I spent a year on a fellowship as a Visiting Scholar; the Forschungskolleg Humanwissenschaften at the Johann Wolfgang Goethe-Universität, Frankfurt am Main, where I spent time as a Fulbright Senior Research Scholar; and the University of Edinburgh, where I spent time both as a MacCormick Visiting Fellow at the School of Law and as a Visiting Research Fellow at the Institute for Advanced Studies in the Humanities. At each of the institutions, I benefited from wonderful feedback and intellectual engagement. I also spent a year as a Visiting Scholar at Vanderbilt University in Nashville, Tennessee, revisiting my roots in philosophy with old friends and intellectual influences. Very many thanks to all these institutions and my colleagues at each. I also received generous feedback from audiences and hosts at Frankfurt, Edinburgh University, the University of Chicago, Boston University, Boston College, and Vanderbilt University, where I presented various portions of this project.

Many people have been very generous with feedback, friendship, conversation, inspiration, and help along the way, for which I am most grateful: Bruce Ackerman, Scott Aikin, Cormac Mac Amhlaigh, Bob Barsky, Christine Bell, Jay Bernstein, Bob Brinkmeyer, Rebecca Brown, Amy Cohen, Debra Rae

Cohen, Bob Eaglestone, Jordan Factor, Richard Fallon, Rainer Forst, Brian Galle, Bernard Harcourt, Tony Jarrells, Michael Hodges, Zak Kramer, John Lachs, Sandy Levinson, Darrel Moellendorf, Aziz Rana, Nathan Richardson, Caprice Roberts, Wadie Said, Christian Schemmel, Bill Scheuerman, Andy Siegel, Chris Slobogin, Kevin Stack, Rob Talisse, Stephen Tierney, Clint Wallace, Brad Weidenhammer, Asanga Welikala, Shelley Welton, Steven Winter, Gretchen Woertendyke, Andy Wright, and Marcia Zug. Any such list I can make will be incomplete, for the conversations and influences are too many.

Dean Jack Pratt and Provost Michael Amiridis provided invaluable institutional support at the University of South Carolina in helping me to jump-start this project. Also thanks to Pat Spacks and my fellow scholar-patriots at the American Academy: Austin Graham, Coleman Hutchison, Amy Lippert, and Tracy Steffes. Vanessa McQuinn provided invaluable assistance with the manuscript. I benefited greatly from outstanding research assistance on this project over the years from Kristina Cooper, William McKinney, and Zach Horan. I am very grateful for their assistance. Two anonymous readers for the press provided invaluable feedback, for which I owe thanks. I am grateful to Kate Davis for terrific copyediting. And I am very grateful for the editorial patience and guidance of Bill Frucht.

Portions of chapters 4 and 5 draw from material first published as "Torture, with Apologies," in *Texas Law Review* 86 (2008): 569; "Overcoming Necessity: Torture and the State of Constitutional Culture," in *SMU Law Review* 61 (2008): 221; and "Who Decides on Liberty?" in *Connecticut Law Review* 44 (2012): 1511. Portions of chapter 6 draw from material first published as "Presidential Power and Constitutional Responsibility," in *Boston College Law Review* 52 (2011): 1551. In every case, the arguments presented here represent much-revised versions and rearticulations.

Holly Crocker helped in so many ways, not the least of which was keeping in perspective those things that are most necessary because most important. And Ambrose exercised wonderful constraint in sharing valuable writing time with me. I dedicate this book with love to them.

OVERCOMING NECESSITY

Introduction

CHOOSE YOUR OWN NATIONAL SECURITY catastrophe. Another one is almost certainly inevitable. For present purposes, let us imagine some future day when a third major attack within a year occurs, this time in the American heartland. A radioactive dirty bomb explodes from a truck parked outside the Willis (Sears) Tower in Chicago. Fatalities number in the thousands, and the seriously injured and ill run into the tens of thousands. Each of the prior attacks was perpetrated by persons of Pakistani, Yemeni, or Saudi national origin. Some of the previous attackers were naturalized U.S. citizens. Anxiety and fear dominate the public landscape, with widespread calls for the president to do more to protect the American people.

Sensing growing public panic, and facing declining political prospects for his party, the president takes bold emergency actions, issuing an executive order empowering the attorney general to detain any person with national ties to a list of Middle Eastern states, and to establish tribunals whose purpose would be to ascertain whether each individual posed a security threat to the United States. Liberally interpreting a statute making it a crime to provide material support to terrorists or terrorist organizations, the order empowers the attorney general to examine all associations of those already sharing national ties to terrorists or terrorist organizations. The president further authorizes the attorney general to commandeer public lands and buildings for the indefinite internment of individuals he determines pose a national security threat. Potentially impacting hundreds of thousands of persons, the order invokes national necessity, and cites Franklin Roosevelt's executive order in 1942 authorizing the military exclusion of Japanese Americans from the West Coast, which was judged constitutional by the Supreme Court in *Korematsu v. United States*.[1] In determining who is a security threat, no citizen need be convicted of a crime. A federal appeals court has already held that the president has power to detain indefinitely citizens he designates as unlawful enemy combatants in the ongoing "war on terror." Congress enacted a law empowering the president to strip those U.S. citizens he deems to have been "involved in a foreign terrorist organization" of their citizenship. These stateless persons are then subject to indefinite detention if no state is willing to take them. Moreover, any non-U.S. person is subject to deportation as well, merely on a showing by the administration that the individual poses a security risk.

Justifying these drastic measures, the president claims a prerogative duty to preserve and protect the security of the United States. In view of the situation of ongoing deadly attacks within the nation, the president claims that necessity justifies his need to take decisive action. Deflecting concerns about civil liberties, the president intones that the Constitution is "not a suicide pact," and asks, in the words of Thomas Jefferson, whether it would be better "[t]o lose our country by a scrupulous adherence to written law."[2] Recognizing his duty to "take care that the laws be faithfully executed," the president again cites Jefferson to support his claim that "[t]he laws of necessity, of self-preservation, of saving the country when in danger, are of higher obligation."[3] Are the president's actions justified? Do they violate core constitutional commitments?

This fiction might seem far-fetched, even outrageous, but we already have elements of this scenario in play today. President Trump began his term in office by issuing an executive order that banned entry into the United States by individuals from seven majority-Muslim countries, citing the need to "protect the American people from terrorist attacks by foreign nationals admitted to the United States."[4] Having promised a "total and complete shutdown of Muslims entering the United States" as a candidate, Trump moved immediately after inauguration to implement a related policy.[5] The president's claim to unreviewable authority to institute this ban was rejected by a U.S. court of appeals, which noted that "the Government has taken the position that the President's decisions about immigration policy, particularly when motivated by national security concerns, are unreviewable, even if those actions potentially contravene constitutional rights and protections."[6] When faced with judicial checks on his travel ban, President Trump turned to his favored social media platform to excoriate the judiciary, exclaiming, "Just cannot believe a judge would put our country in such peril. If something happens blame him and court system. People pouring in. Bad!"[7] He also proclaimed, "What is our country coming to when a judge can halt a Homeland Security travel ban?"[8] The president issued this order, and levied these unprecedented attacks on judicial independence, when no national security emergency was at hand. Moreover, a five-justice majority of the Supreme Court eventually upheld a revised version of the ban in *Trump v. Hawaii*, citing the broad "deference traditionally accorded the President in this sphere," thereby also rejecting claims that the ban violated constitutional protections against religious discrimination.[9]

In light of this background, what can the American people expect from a president—the current or a subsequent one—if a future emergency of the scale imagined in these pages were to occur during his term? How can American constitutionalism's commitment to protecting fundamental rights and principles withstand a president who claims exclusive and unreviewable authority to do whatever he deems necessary to protect the nation? Given the fact-specific nature of claims about what might be necessary in light of the circumstances, what role can a constitution play for a president who lacks a commitment to truthful assertions?

This imagined drama exemplifies the conditions under which constitutional theory confronts practice—often under pressure from an emergency. The cycle is readily discernible: a national security crisis leads to assertions of executive power to follow policies and practices that exceed preexisting constraints. The response to this dynamic, by contrast, is less clear. Americans take pride in their constitutional form, except when it interferes with function. Why not simply round up people who look Middle Eastern? Why not torture terrorist suspects, because somewhere a bomb could be ticking? Why not conduct widespread surveillance without particularized suspicion? After all, if you have nothing to hide, then why would it matter?[10] If events similar to those imagined here were to unfold—and similar events

are not at all unlikely—how would we articulate the moral, legal, and political implications of these presidential actions? What role are we willing to
allow necessity to play in justifying national policy? In the imaginary situation, necessity provides both reason and rhetoric—reasons to deviate from
constitutional form and the rhetoric to make deviation seem inevitable. But
in either capacity, when should we allow necessity to justify actions taken in
conflict, or at least in significant tension, with prevailing constitutional
commitments? These are the central questions this book seeks to answer.

Any attempt to answer these questions takes us to the heart of American
constitutionalism and its unsettled relation to necessity. On the one hand,
American constitutionalism prioritizes order, providing principles and structures to guide and constrain everyday governing practice. James Madison's
solution to the problem of factional strife was to align persons with offices,
seeking to channel disorder into institutional structure. Our written Constitution created the sole foundation for structuring enumerated, separated,
and limited federal powers. On the other hand, American constitutionalism
permits disruption, licensing policies and practices that respond to unfolding circumstances, sometimes in the absence of, or even in conflict with,
prevailing legal rules. Alexander Hamilton sought to preserve "an indefinite
power of providing for emergencies as they might arise."[11] The foundation
for such an "indefinite power" remains unclear. American constitutionalism
therefore embeds an ambiguity between constraint and necessity. This ambiguity is amplified by the responsibilities of executive power.

There is a tradition in constitutional theory that recognizes the prerogative power of the executive to act on necessity in times of emergency. Drawing on a theory of prerogative power articulated by John Locke, scholars and
officials allege that the president has "Power to act according to discretion,
for the public good, without the prescription of the Law, and sometimes
even against it."[12] Alexander Hamilton advocated strong executive power
under our Constitution, urging:

> The authorities essential to the common defense . . . ought to exist without
> limitation, Because it is impossible to foresee or define the extent and vari-
> ety of national exigencies, or the correspondent extent and variety of the
> means which may be necessary to satisfy them. The circumstances that en-
> danger the safety of nations are infinite, and for this reason no constitu-

tional shackles can wisely be imposed on the power to which the care of it is committed.[13]

Although committed to the idea of "[t]he necessity of the Constitution . . . to the preservation of the Union,"[14] in Hamilton's words, James Madison recognized that "[i]t is in vain to oppose Constitutional barriers to the impulse of self-preservation. It is worse than in vain; because it plants in the Constitution itself necessary usurpations of power."[15] Following Locke, self-preservation is the prerogative of the executive, just as it was of the royal sovereign.

American constitutionalism contains within it both a commitment to the necessity of a written constitution empowering and limiting governing officials and institutions, as well as a recognition that national security may fall outside the governance not only of "parchment barriers," but also separation of powers. Seeking to preserve the Union, President Lincoln rejected a singular constitutional meaning in times of both war and peace, proclaiming that "the Constitution is not, in its application, in all respects the same, in cases of rebellion or invasion involving the public safety, as it is in time of profound peace and public security."[16] Moreover, Lincoln "felt that measures otherwise unconstitutional, might become lawful, by becoming indispensable to the preservation of the constitution, through the preservation of the nation."[17] These arguments arise from the different attitudes Americans take toward their Constitution and the constraints it imposes.

What is at stake is both fundamental and intractable. Madison's concern that the Constitution not be opposed to impulses of self-preservation can be matched by a contrary concern that claims of necessity not be allowed to undermine principled constitutional commitments. Few would doubt that actions may be compelled by circumstances, that preservation of national security is a duty of the highest order, or that scrupulous adherence to the letter of particular laws may actually produce greater public harm during emergencies. Agreement on these propositions guides us little in deciding whether, and to what extent, the executive is empowered to act against established laws, to change laws and their execution unilaterally, or to reshape settled principles and practices that touch on the liberty and dignity of persons. The problem is further complicated by a common-law tradition of embedding necessity as an exception or defense to the violation of legal rules; for it might therefore seem normal to claim a prevailing necessity exception to constitutional principles. The necessity about which this book is concerned is not the common-law or international doctrines of necessity, but a family of justificatory arguments that arise within liberal constitutionalism to the effect that "necessity knows no law."

What is at stake is also theoretically vexed. The German political theorist Carl Schmitt, writing in the early twentieth century, criticized liberal democracies for being incapable of directing responses to emergencies through law. As he explained, "The precise details of an emergency cannot be anticipated, nor can one spell out what may take place in such a case, especially when it is truly a matter of an extreme emergency."[18] Instead, the unpredictability of emergencies opens up a state of exception in which "[t]he most guidance the constitution can provide is to indicate who can act in such a case."[19] Because liberal constitutions cannot anticipate the precise states of emergency, the most they can do is assign decisional authority to act beyond, or outside, the law. Popularizing Schmitt's idea that emergencies create "states of exception," the Italian philosopher Giorgio Agamben takes this problem to entail an ambiguity over what is the law. In the state of exception, executive officials suspend the law to preserve it while maintaining "the force of law without law."[20] Official edicts are still to be obeyed—they have force—even though they lack the proper form of law. Other contemporary legal scholars, such as Paul Kahn, focus on the point that law cannot determine exceptional decisions, arguing that "[t]he exception, accordingly, can only be recognized in the decision. More precisely, it is constituted in the decision itself. The truth of the matter is not something apart from the decision."[21] Because even during the best of times law creates gray zones, where it is unclear what the law in fact is, executive officials have discretion on this view to claim that their actions are in accord with the law upon which they decide.[22] When exceptional circumstances arise, gray zones can become law-free zones, according to liberal constitutionalism's skeptics.[23] Political actors do what they must, checked only by what citizens will allow.

Although these views correctly identify the fact that emergency complicates constitutional constraints, none account for how a liberal democracy sustains other forms of legal constraint. Law constitutes, and thereby constrains, the very offices of those charged with responding to crises. Even during an emergency, where executive officials might exercise discretion that exceeds, or even violates, existing law, the president will not vote in the legislature and will not sit as a Supreme Court justice. Thus, more than naming the authority "who decides on the exception," constitutional government also constrains by constituting the governing office and embedding normative expectations about how that office may function.[24]

Although constraint is never complete, it being the nature of rules to be always partial, officials are not licensed to do anything at all, no matter the law. Normative boundaries define the settled grammar of each office. More than a puzzle of exception, we discover that during emergencies constitutional constraints work through a different grammar, spurred by the urgency that necessity creates, but curbed by the normativity constitutionalism embraces. Recognition of this fact absolves us of lawlessness but does not yet explain how we relate legal form to emergency function. In ordinary constitutional governance, Chief Justice Marshall, in *McCulloch v. Maryland,* articulated a relation between necessity and applicable rule that emphasized the normative role of appropriateness: "Let the end be legitimate, let it be within the scope of the Constitution, and all means which are appropriate, which are plainly adapted to that end, which are not prohibited, but consist with the letter and spirit of the Constitution, are Constitutional."[25] So while emergency may complicate the function of legal form, there is no reason to think that constitutional norms altogether fail to guide and constrain choice of action through analysis of what is appropriate, even if thought necessary. This idea motivates the approach this book takes: since constitutional norms always apply, the questions we must ask and answer—even during emergencies—are unavoidably normative constitutional questions.

How to check claims to necessity and emergency has become a particularly salient question after the events of September 11, 2001, and now spans the actions of three presidential administrations. It will span more administrations in the future, because the fundamental issues at stake—how constitutional commitments relate to claims of necessitarian exception—are perennial. Thus, although the examples this book focuses on include post-9/11 counterterrorism practices of surveillance, detention, interrogation, and targeted killing, the scope of the argument transcends these specific practices to encompass the structure of constitutional thought out of which policy choices arise. Because future responses to emergencies will depend upon the ideas we have on hand, it is important to analyze and criticize a way of thinking about necessity and presidential power ascendant since 9/11. Claims that necessity relieves us of our constitutional commitments are ever present.[26]

Biological and political necessity provide strong motivations to act. Yet, as Franklin Roosevelt realized, "necessitous men are not free," for the need to obtain food, shelter, and other life necessities can overshadow other political concerns.[27] Just the same, citizens under physical siege are not free, either, for the need to secure the polity's physical safety can supersede all other political objectives. Necessity may well be part of the human condition, as chapter 1 explores.[28] But so too is the aspiration to political liberty obtained through constitutive commitments made possible by overcoming the conditions of necessity. Action chosen by matching conceptions of the good life with current practices and projects requires reason and reflection, not surrender to the tyranny of events. Thus, another piece of the puzzle requires recognition of sociological fact: necessity compels both the biological and the political body. Constitutionalism pulls in a different direction, ordinarily requiring commitment to principles and plans irrespective of present preference. Indeed, what can count as a present preference is partially constructed from the strength and content of prior principled commitments. This conflict between necessity and constraint unfolds most clearly during emergency and crisis, when necessity is most salient and constraint most fragile. Let's look further at how this tension unwinds in relation to the idea of unwritten law.

In exceptional times, as Jefferson went on to state in the same letter the president cited in our imagined crisis, "the unwritten laws of necessity, of self-preservation, and of the public safety, control the written laws of meum and tuum."[29] Placed in Schmitt's philosophical idiom, the unwritten law has priority because "[t]he state suspends the law in the exception on the basis of its right of self-preservation."[30] During emergencies, on this view, the sovereign's prerogative is to suspend ordinary law in order to preserve it. Necessity therefore becomes the condition that enables the executive to choose which methods to employ in the pursuit of self-preservation. Unwritten imperative sets the conditions for choice. Like the problem of free will that dominated eighteenth-century philosophy, which featured the opposition between necessity and liberty, necessity stands in some tension with the idea of political liberty's protection through commitment to a written constitution. And like its freewill counterpart, to cite necessity as a justification for acting is to eschew voluntary choice and consent. Potential confusion abounds here. Causal necessity, for David Hume, to mention one eighteenth-century philosophical source, if it existed, would imply no freedom of action, whereas only a proper understanding of practical necessity can explain free action taken in light of rationally chosen ends.[31] The upshot of such debates is that the more theorists rely on a claim that an action is necessary—for it arises from the natural necessity to self-preservation—the less they can speak of "the decision" as a product of will rather than causal determinacy. But if we are to preserve the liberty of choice, then necessity cannot determine political and legal decisions, and thus cannot alone provide a justification for action. Necessity, so understood, is inconsistent with choice.

If necessity occupies a space of "unwritten laws," as Jefferson suggests, it is presumably still a form of law, controlling the written laws. Americans place great importance on their written Constitution and its role in sustaining an intergenerational conversation about who they are and what they believe. We cannot simply throw out the Constitution because a president claims necessity. Everything that is written is not all that matters, for perhaps the "unwritten laws of necessity" are like the unwritten and retained rights and powers of the people expressed in the Ninth and Tenth Amendments. They form an unwritten framework within which the written Constitution applies.[32] Executive authority might therefore be both conferred by text and controlled by necessity. This last claim—the authority of necessity— is difficult to place. Whereas we have a tradition of reading our Constitution in the context of retained substantive human rights, we have no similar tradition of conversing about both unretained *and* unwritten law. But if necessity were to have some continuing legal relevance, would it justify actions that supersede our considered constitutional commitments?

Officials in the Bush administration certainly thought so, combining the compulsion of self-preservation with a robust assertion of executive prerogative. Lawyers working in the Department of Justice Office of Legal

Counsel produced a string of memos providing legal justification for "coercive" interrogation techniques, indefinite detention, and warrantless electronic surveillance of Americans. As one such memo urged, "In wartime,
it is for the President alone to decide what methods to use to best prevail
against the enemy."[33] Because ordinary written law is everywhere bounded
by its absence in the state of exception, executive action is free on this view
to operate on the basis of an "unwritten law." Even then, necessity, sourced
in unwritten law, must respond to articulated legal norms, even if antecedently unscripted.

But who decides when the unwritten laws of necessity prevail over extant
law? According to Schmitt, "For a legal order to make sense, a normal situation must exist, and he is sovereign who definitely decides whether this
normal situation actually exists."[34] Translating this theory into American
practice, a president asserting prerogative power would decide to act on the
laws of necessity in the name of the sovereign people. And, indeed, in some
situations the president *is* the decider, as George W. Bush memorably proclaimed.[35] But are decisions based on necessity constitutionally legitimate?
Do the "unwritten laws of necessity" provide a legally cognizable basis for
official action? President Richard Nixon thought so, as he claimed to David
Frost regarding his ability to decide to "do something illegal": "Well, when
the President does it, that means that it is not illegal. . . . If the President, for
example, approves something, approves an action because of the national
security . . . then the President's decision in that instance is one that enables
those who carry it out to carry it out without violating a law."[36] Going well
beyond a claim of necessity, President Trump asserted a power to self-
pardon, effectively proclaiming that he could never be held responsible for
illegal acts—an assertion that would presumably be stronger when made on
national security grounds.[37] On Trump's Nixonian view, a president can decide whether or when to comply with the law, being unaccountable to ordinary legal norms and constraints. Abraham Lincoln also claimed authority
to violate otherwise operative laws by suspending habeas corpus to preserve
the Union: "By necessary implication, when Rebellion or Invasion comes,
the decision is to be made, from time to time; and I think the man whom,
for the time, the people have, under the Constitution, made the commander-
in-chief . . . is the man who holds the power, and bears the responsibility of

making it."[38] President Barack Obama claimed an unreviewable authority to target U.S. persons abroad for lethal aerial attacks, proclaiming that constitutional protections are satisfied by whatever "due process" a president chooses to afford through internal processes.[39] But claiming the power does not make it legitimate. Such claims fall within a broader constitutional tradition extolling the principles on which governing officials may act.

In the American tradition, legitimacy rests in part on consent of the people. If the people consent to lawless practices, then they grant an important form of legitimacy to those practices, even though their consent comes at the expense of unsettling strict adherence to the Constitution. Consent presupposes limits on actions in accordance with the fundamental dignity, autonomy, and liberty of persons—the constitutive substance of due process. When persons are not afforded these protections, official action undermines the very conditions of legitimacy. Official practices are historically replete with failures of this kind. Legitimacy cannot be all or nothing, but admits of complex relations between executive practice and popular acceptance.[40] For example, by contesting practices such as racial discrimination, popular conceptions of equality can alter constitutional meanings that better align respect for individuals with the legitimacy of governing practice. Consent also flows from a self-conception of who we are as a constitutional community and culture. As chapter 7 argues, a self-conception embedded in constitutional culture is not fixed and final, but responds to the circumstances, perceptions, and priorities we give to our current situation in light of our constitutional commitments. Nonetheless, a community is accountable for the character of its choices. Thus, constitutional equilibrium is always fragile. A constitutional community's shared responses to crises can always legitimate actions that, in turn, change constitutional culture by changing constitutional commitments. These considerations reveal the underlying fragility of any particular priority of constitutional meaning. Constitutional practices may change in light of external conditions and popular consent. Practices can in turn change constitutional meanings. Necessity may therefore become the occasion and the basis for altering the priority and content of constitutional meanings and national character.

What are these priorities that operate contrary to the unwritten laws of necessity? What are our sources for saying the Constitution does more than govern the ordinary situation, that prerogative does not prevail over commitment? For one thing, we have a strong tradition of upholding separation of powers principles, even in the face of presidential assertions of unilateral power. Rejecting President Bush's unilateral claim of power to detain U.S. citizens indefinitely without due process, the Supreme Court said in *Hamdi v. Rumsfeld,* "Whatever power the United States Constitution envisions for the Executive in its exchanges with other nations or with enemy organizations in times of conflict, it most assuredly envisions a role for all three branches when individual liberties are at stake."[41] Presidential unilateralism is not settled practice, even in times of claimed military necessity. We often look to the federal courts, particularly the Supreme Court, to articulate our shared constitutional values and vision. Constitutional commitment, even in the face of claimed necessity, has a fundamental place in our tradition, as Justice Hughes wrote concerning the scope of congressional power during economic crisis: "Extraordinary conditions may call for extraordinary remedies. But the argument necessarily stops short of an attempt to justify action which lies outside the sphere of constitutional authority. Extraordinary conditions do not create or enlarge constitutional power. . . . Those who act under these grants are not at liberty to transcend the imposed limits because they believe that more or different power is necessary."[42]

Separation of powers, as the Supreme Court repeatedly reminds us, exists to protect liberty. The immediate aftermath of a national security emergency always produces fear and trauma, challenging us to act on our own best principles. Claiming an emergency is therefore one way to achieve legal changes unavailable in more reflective times and circumstances.[43] In this way, necessity remains the adversary of liberty; for when it grounds claims to unchecked and expanded power, liberty often becomes its object. Internment of Japanese Americans, designation of others as "enemy combatants," interrogational torture of terrorism suspects, or widespread electronic surveillance are all ways that basic liberties can become the objects of claimed necessity. We have lived through the clash between liberty and necessity before, from Lincoln's suspension of habeas corpus during the Civil War to enactment of the Alien and Sedition laws during World War I, to the worst abuses of the Cold War "red scare" and the surveillance of citizens during the civil rights and anti–Vietnam War eras.[44] In many of these occasions, what necessity justifies at one moment liberty demands as grounds for recompense at another. Reparations were later paid to Japanese persons forcibly removed to "War Relocation Centers," for example.[45] To avoid this cycle of constitutional unsettlement and later constitutional adjustment, Justice Hughes argued that governing officials should stay within constitutional limits, despite any contrary claims to necessity. Justice Jackson dissented from the Supreme Court's opinion in *Korematsu v. United States,* which upheld the order excluding Japanese Americans from the West Coast during World War II, arguing that altering the Constitution to accommodate what is said to be necessary can be a "more subtle blow to liberty" than the policy itself, for if necessity becomes a "doctrine of the Constitution . . . it has a generative power of its own."[46]

Necessity's presumed salience during exceptional times creates a potential paradox for constitutional commitments. Constitutional principles function most clearly as constraints on official action when officials are tempted to exceed principled boundaries. Without temptation, there is no felt constraint. If, however, necessity trumps principle when circumstances tempt officials to violate the Constitution, then constitutional principles offer no constraints precisely when they most apply *as constraints.* Necessity therefore circulates in the political imagination not only as a justification—executive officials could not have done otherwise in light of their commitment to achieving a compelling end—but also as an excuse vitiating antecedent constraints designed to limit the means available for achieving national security.

Circumstances can indeed make the temptation to transcend constitutional and legal limits at times seem overwhelming. Soon after the events of September 11, talk turned to the possible necessity of torturing terrorism suspects, and practice quickly followed. We now know that Khalid Shaikh Mohammed was repeatedly waterboarded, that other suspects were subject to brutal treatment, and that Department of Justice (DOJ) lawyers—arguing on behalf of presidential prerogative—provided legal justifications for these and other practices.[47] Bush administration actions were supported by some in the academic community by claims like this: "A view holding that coercive interrogation is sometimes permissible need not deny that coercive interrogation is a grave moral evil; of course it is. But sometimes evils, even grave ones, are also necessary."[48] As chapter 4 will explore, to resort to torture is not to resort to just any quotidian practice. Torture is the very paragon of unprincipled and unconstrained governing power that recognizes no limits marked by human dignity. Although not explicitly embedded in constitutional text, the prohibition against torture plays a foundational role in assigning priorities and establishing commitments to the dignity and liberty of persons as well as the constrained powers of government.[49] These commitments are further embedded as core features not only of domestic law but also of regional and international human rights instruments, such as the Covenant on Civil and Political Rights and the Convention Against Torture.[50] The latter even makes clear that "[n]o exceptional circumstances whatsoever . . . may be invoked as a justification for torture."[51] It might have seemed obvious to claim that torture is not only illegal and immoral, but that it is bad policy as well. But what the ocular sense readily sees may depend too much on what is now contested constitutional meaning. As chapter 4 explores in depth, the Bush administration's resort to torture was reversed by the Obama administration, only to be made vulnerable to President Trump's claims that "torture works," leaving a fundamental disposition toward torture subject to future contingencies.[52] My task here is not to explore the counterterrorism policies in which these practices occur for their own sake, but to examine the constitutional meanings that make them possible. These meanings have made America out of constitutional text and unwritten script, through both liberty and necessity, in a process of creative civic engagement.

Constitutionalism seeks to overcome the challenges and temptations necessity creates. This book explores the background constitutional principles and values that support available policy choices, especially during perceived emergencies. This book confronts a certain way of thinking about constitutional practice that retains the idea that "necessity knows no law," which creates an opposition between what circumstances appear to make necessary and what the law might otherwise require. Commitment to constitutional principle, as well as constitutive practices providing public justifications, are conditions that make American constitutionalism possible. Without a clear understanding of the importance of constitutional commitment, we shall struggle to answer affirmatively Alexander Hamilton's question in *Federalist* No. 1: "whether societies of men are really capable or not of establishing good government from reflection and choice, or whether they are forever destined to depend for their political constitutions on accident and force."[53] In Hamilton's challenge, I understand "accident and force" as a different way of referring to necessity. Thus, a key contrast to which I will return throughout this book exists between actions taken on the basis of "reflection and choice" and those taken on the basis of necessity—or "accident and force." I start with the premise that as the product of democratic self-government, American identity is constituted through extended reflection and choice. "Our" Constitution is not something achieved in a moment but is the product of an intertemporal contestation over meanings and values, subject to contingent change and choice. Our political constitution manifests commitments to deliberation and self-determination, each of which depends on more than following the dictates of perceived necessity. In this way, "good government" is a process of overcoming necessity. This process leads to constitutional conflict.

This book's central claim is that the meanings of American constitutionalism depend on a continuing process of overcoming necessity. But far from seeking to overcome necessity, in both historical precedent and current practice, executive officials often seek to harness its power. Events, not deliberative reflection, are said to compel responses to real national security threats. On this view, the choice of priorities and perspectives is obscured behind the overriding imperative of necessity. As I argue throughout, this view is not only mistaken, but perilous for the future meanings of American constitutionalism and practices of democratic self-governance. Despite the seeming inevitability of the unwritten legal commands of necessity, even when confronting extraordinary situations, such as those we can imagine and those we have experienced, we must choose our responses and establish our commitments. What policy choices we make and which constitutional commitments we uphold depend on the contested political worlds we both imagine and inhabit. From within these sometimes inchoate and unarticulated worlds, we seek to establish narrative priorities to articulate for ourselves, as well as for others, our political and constitutional meanings. How we envision our Constitution—what role it plays in our lives in structuring the content of a continuing conversation across generations—is not already determined by past or present events, but is a matter of continuing choices among contested priorities, practices, and principles.[54] Necessity creates the false impression that things could not have been otherwise.[55] We imperil the legitimacy of political consent when we hide our responsibility for choosing our constitutional meanings behind the compulsion of circumstance. The task of choosing is not easy, and one cannot guarantee success.

I write of a "we" here because the responsibility for constitutional meaning is widely dispersed. No doubt, Supreme Court justices since *Marbury v. Madison* have asserted that it is "emphatically the province and duty of the judicial department to say what the law is."[56] But that duty does not preclude the obligation of the people's representatives and for the people themselves to carry on the conversation about the Constitution's meaning in their lives and the shared world it constructs.

This book participates in a deliberative constitutional tradition, exploring the conceptual resources Americans have available to shape their responses to future emergencies. We are all implicated, but the president's voice carries further than others because it can have the most immediate impact in directing policy and practice. Presidential vision shapes the national community—its priorities and practices. The plebiscitary president also relies on popular participation in his proffered vision, for he is indebted to as much as empowered by public opinion. Even when engaged in ordinary politics, the people can consent to, or dissent from, presidential vision.

Despite the rule of constitutional principles, the enumeration of powers among the branches of government, and the function of constitutional norms, the American Constitution leaves much everyday governance to discretion—even regarding fundamental matters. This discretion—whether the presidential power to conduct foreign affairs, set policy priorities, or direct national security—is subject to the contingency of an administration's prevailing attitudes and vision. It is this discretion that leads critics in the Schmittian tradition to be skeptical of law's ability to constrain unfettered executive decisions. In the wake of the events of September 11, the question of the relationship between constitutional commitments and extraordinary action occupied a central place both in public discourse and official rhetoric. The very meanings of events and commitments seemed up for grabs. Nothing short of an entire "civilization's fight" had begun in which President George W. Bush imposed an absolute disjunction: "You are either with us, or you are with the terrorists."[57] The scope of this "war on terror" would be virtually limitless: "It will not end until every terrorist group of global reach has been found, stopped and defeated."[58] In his address to the nation on the fifth anniversary of September 11, President Bush articulated a transformative view: "For America, 9/11 was more than a tragedy—it changed the way we look at the world."[59] This changed way of looking was intended to reverberate across a wide spectrum of social and political practices, providing organization and legitimation by its acceptance and repetition throughout the polity. And reverberate it did, for a time at least, as politics and everyday practice changed to match the new world.[60] A new Department of Homeland Security, citizen vigilance, war, arrests, detentions, and political rhetoric all worked in concert to establish features of this changed world. As the twenty-first century unfolds, we live in this world—one that is simultaneously the same and transformed.

The official narrative of September 11, as articulated by President Bush, was that "[t]he attacks of September the 11th, 2001 also revealed the outlines of a new world."[61] In the wake of future deadly attacks, such as the hypothetical one described earlier, pundits and officials will have all the more reason to claim that we live in a different world, one where the very meaning of America may have shifted in relation to real and perceived threats. Since contingencies enable narrative choices, a lot rides on the ideas and principles that animate such choices.

According to President Bush's September 11 narrative, "We've entered a great ideological conflict we did nothing to invite. . . . Yet the destination of history is determined by human action, and every great movement of history comes to a point of choosing."[62] We must choose to accept an invitation to enter into a "great conflict" requiring a new articulation of purpose and a new way of viewing history. The "destination of history" does not befall by mere "accident and force." Yet President Bush's claim was of a kind with commentators who saw a historical rupture through which old concepts and understandings would no longer apply to American political experience.[63] A cornerstone of this new way of seeing is reliance on necessity to justify official practice.

Choice of narrative has consequences for constitutional meaning and government practice. Until September 11, criminal law enforcement was the

predominant way of confronting terrorist activity. After September 11, however, both the narrative and the way of thinking about terrorism threats
changed.[64] The new, alternative "war on terror" narrative offered expansive
presidential power. President Bush described this new narrative in broad
terms: "The war against this enemy is more than a military conflict. It is the
decisive ideological struggle of the 21st century, and the calling of our generation."[65] Moreover, President Bush emphasized the insufficiency of ordinary law: "After the chaos and carnage of September the 11th, it is not
enough to serve our enemies with legal papers. The terrorists and their supporters declared war on the United States, and war is what they got."[66] Echo-
ing this theme, John Yoo, a scholar and author of DOJ memos justifying
actions that constituted official use of torture, explained that the new narrative framework would be permanent: "The days when society considered
terrorism merely a law enforcement problem and when our forces against
terrorism were limited to the Federal Bureau of Investigation, federal pros-
ecutors, and the criminal justice system will not return."[67] According to this
"war on terror" approach, ordinary criminal law cannot address the exceptional threats posed by international terrorist organizations.[68] This narrative
was used to strengthen presidential power to protect national security, to
limit the operation of civil rights constraints on counterterrorism policy, and
to evade institutional mechanisms of accountability.

What gets framed as necessary depends on prior normative commitments. Contingent on the content of those commitments, what necessity
requires, and what necessity excludes, will differ.[69] Illustrating this point
of choice, President Obama changed the narrative, eliminating the central
place of "war" rhetoric in relation to terrorism. Viewing terrorism as
only one among several threats to national security, the Obama administration's new strategy provided that "[w]e will always seek to delegitimize
the use of terrorism and to isolate those who carry it out. Yet this is not a
global war against a tactic—terrorism or a religion—Islam. We are at war
with a specific network, al-Qa'ida, and its terrorist affiliates who support
efforts to attack the United States, our allies, and partners."[70] Describing
the new strategy, John O. Brennan, deputy national security advisor to President Obama, stated, "Terrorists may try to bring death to our cities, but it
is our choice to either uphold the rule of law or chip away at it . . . to either

respond wisely and effectively or lash out in ways that inflame entire re-
gions and stoke the fires of violent extremism. That is our choice."[71] Because it is a matter of choice, the narrative changed, animated by a different
overall vision of America's identity, values, and place in an international
community.[72] The future meanings of American constitutionalism await
further articulation.

Since September 11, 2001, necessity has taken on a positive power that has
not been subject to sufficient scrutiny. During the current and previous two
administrations, necessity has been normalized as a way of justifying actions taken on behalf of national security in ways that risk undermining
important constitutional commitments to constrained power and respect for
fundamental rights. Because arguments made by one administration can be
invoked by later presidents, if Americans do not address the conceptual and
practical work that claims to necessity do, then they risk silently and unreflectively turning away from key constitutional commitments in pursuit of
greater security. The commitments this book is most concerned with are
about the scope and constraints that exist on executive power. The arc of
American constitutionalism does not bend toward justice of its own accord.

The president in our hypothetical national security emergency has choices to make. If something like this occurs under President Trump's—or a
future—administration, how will he balance the felt necessities of the situation with a tradition of constitutional constraint? How much does he call
upon Congress to assist in setting policy and making law? Does he limit his
actions to temporary measures, or does he make more lasting changes in
policy and practice? In deciding to take the drastic step of claiming broad
powers of seizure and detention, how will he articulate what this means for
the American polity and its commitment to liberty? Answers to these and
other questions will all depend on what prevailing vision of constitutional
commitments guides the president's decisions. These visions do not follow
deductively from established axioms, though they lead us to hope that "enlightened statesmen" will "always be at the helm," for institutional checks
and separation of powers can only do so much.[73] At the point of decision,
the sometimes unarticulated and inchoate social imaginary contributes as
much to the practice of American constitutionalism as any court opinion or
constitutional law treatise.[74]

To claim that an action is necessary, in the sense that it was unavoidable, is an attempt to hide responsibility for the underlying choices. One of the background choices not often made explicit is the decision to view a situation through a securitarian or a libertarian normative framework—a choice that will create substantive differences in policy. The former view focuses on the state's obligation to provide security above all other values, and the latter emphasizes the state's formative purpose to preserve civil rights and liberties. And then there is the ever present possibility of emergency manipulation—of claiming a state of emergency to generate exceptional executive authority. If necessity entails greater presidential power, then there is a real temptation to find necessity, a task made easier from a securitarian viewpoint. The problem of this possibility is as old as the Republic, as James Madison warned Thomas Jefferson in 1798: "Perhaps it is a universal truth that the loss of liberty at home is to be charged to provisions against danger, real or pretended, from abroad."[75] And the problem of this possibility is as recent as President Trump's declaration of emergency to fund a border wall between the United States and Mexico.[76] After Congress refused to provide additional funding for his long-promised border wall, President Trump declared a national emergency in February 2019 and reallocated funds that Congress had authorized for other military purposes. Yet in the same public statement in which he announced these actions, the president also admitted that there was no real emergency. With extraordinary candor, he explained to the American people that "I didn't need to do this, but I'd rather do it much faster," thereby exemplifying Madison's caution regarding cynical manipulation of emergency claims.[77]

Because, as Madison warned, a claim of danger can always be made—truthfully or not—a president's commitment to truthfulness, constitutional principles, and rule-of-law norms are especially important. Having already signaled a level of disregard for the values of separation of powers by denigrating the "so-called judge" who blocked his travel ban, Trump also made clear his disregard for the constitutional value of due process.[78] In a series of public statements related to his border detention policy of separating children from their parents, Trump lashed out against the judicial process the Constitution affords detainees.[79] Invoking a claim to unreviewable and unilateral power, he complained that he was "no longer able to say who can, and who cannot, come in & out, especially for reasons of safety &.security

[*sic*]—big trouble!"[80] Amplifying this claim, he further claimed on social media that "[w]e cannot allow all of these people to invade our Country. When somebody comes in, we must immediately, with no Judges or Court Cases, bring them back from where they came."[81] Charged by the Constitution's Oath Clause with upholding the Constitution, Trump should know that the Supreme Court has made clear that "[a]liens, even aliens whose presence in this country is unlawful, have long been recognized as 'persons' guaranteed due process of law by the Fifth and Fourteenth Amendments."[82]

President Trump's actions and statements illustrate how claims to necessity can also produce another outcome—disregard for constitutional values and principles. And, just as Madison warned, the loss of liberty at home can arise from presidential claims of "safety &.security," especially when governing actions are chosen with an absence of constitutional commitment. A loss of liberty can also accompany a presidential disavowal of responsibility. By attacking judicial power—and the principle of separated and balanced powers—Trump lays the foundation for disclaiming responsibility and thus blaming judges if another attack, such as the one imagined at the outset of this introduction, were to occur. The president can then claim that further deprivations of liberty are necessary to fulfill his responsibility to protect the nation—an obligation with which the judiciary unduly interfered. This dynamic is dangerous for American constitutionalism.

Necessity does not emerge like a phoenix born anew from the ashes of a prior state of affairs. How we understand events is shaped by the narratives in which the events appear *as* events. Hannah Arendt captures the fragility of this relation between facts and meaning: "Facts and events are infinitely more fragile things than axioms, discoveries, theories—even the most wildly speculative ones—produced by the human mind; they occur in the field of the ever-changing affairs of men."[83] Facts and events—subject always to notions of truthfulness—exist inside particular normative and narrative worlds. History and past precedent are relevant to our understanding of both what might be necessary as well as what can be justified as proper in relation to our constitutional commitments.

This book aims to defend processes of choice based on reflection and subject to public justification according to constitutive principles that arise from within the polity's normative order. Relying on necessity to trump

constitutional meanings grounded on written text and living tradition creates a different, and more perilous, world than its alternative. In either
world, necessity is often opposed to liberty. In both worlds, the impulse toward self-preservation raises questions about the identity of that self to be
preserved. Whose preservation claims overriding importance with what
values and practices? From a self-generating people who called their political world into existence with words, that self is one secure in the blessings
of liberty.[84] Prioritizing necessity means that we will continue to react to
"accident and force" rather than establish "good government from reflection and choice."[85] Good government secures liberty first before creating
national security policy. When policy is dictated by circumstance, necessity
always risks normalization by expanding outward from the confined emergency to operate in diverse legal domains. Deliberative choice, by contrast,
ensures that our commitments to civil and political liberties will not get lost
in the urgency of the situation.

Constitutional meanings are contingent both on the ideas to which we
give priority and the content of our commitments. Transformations in how
we see the world are always possible through reinterpretation of past precedents and events. When based on unreflective and episodic responses to
necessity, there is a real concern about relying on accident and force to decide matters fundamental to a polity's identity. As Harold Lasswell warned
when it came to the threats to liberty inherent in what he called the "garri-
son-police state" during the Cold War, "An insidious outcome of continuing crisis is the tendency to slide into a new conception of normality that
takes vastly extended controls for granted, and thinks of freedom in smaller
and smaller dimensions."[86] When a narrative of constitutional exception
takes political priority, to change the world we must change the narrative.
With words, we create our constitutive worlds.

As the argument of this book unfolds, two chapters will explore the
ways that American constitutionalism overcomes necessity through incorporating it into justificatory frameworks and governing institutions. Three
chapters will explore how American constitutionalism, properly understood, rejects claims to necessitarian exception and excess. The first and
last chapters will explore points of theory, settling on the question in chapter 7 of why consideration of necessity is important and pervasive, for

claims about what Americans must do arise out of a constitutive character—a diachronic identity forged through reflection and choice—subject to
change if they yield to unreflective claims about what is necessary. Throughout the argument, consideration of four counterterrorism policies will provide concrete examples of how necessitarian logic produces policy
consequences. Detention, surveillance, interrogation, and targeted killing
are aspects of American counterterrorism practice that implicate the meanings of American constitutionalism. In each case, I argue that reliance on
claims of necessity push away from the deliberative and reflective structures of justification constitutive of "good government." By arguing against
necessitarian logic, I defend processes of public justification that make coherence with applicable constitutional values and principles central to any
defense of counterterrorism policy. Real differences follow. There is no justification for torture. Pervasive surveillance under a claim of exigency is too
unbounded. Detention policies require Congress and the president to agree
on practices subject to review by courts for whether they are consistent with
constitutional protections for liberty. Expanded reliance on targeted killing
raises questions about American values, as well as separation of powers
principles. In every case, the focus of this book is on the constitutional powers and constraints that justify executive actions.

We begin an account of necessity's story in chapter 1, in a moment of re-
ceding crisis in American life that produced Franklin Roosevelt's warning
that "necessitous men are not free." Necessity can produce dictatorship, because the people are willing to allow whatever it takes to solve their immediate needs. In theory, a president might suspend the constitutional order like
a Roman dictator, subject perhaps only to post hoc political accountability.
As chapter 1 argues, a misguided belief that constitutional systems can function in these so-called "states of exception" exists, for it misconstrues the
relation between rules and exceptions and thereby fails to understand how
legal constraints operate. "Rule skepticism" results from believing that if
rules do not determine responses to new applications—if choice and judgment must be exercised—then rules cannot function as constraints. Anything would then be possible—extralegal, illegal, or legal suspension. If we
reject these skeptical beliefs, then we have good grounds to reject versions
of the "do whatever is necessary" claim. And if we reject this claim, we can

better understand how constitutionalism overcomes necessity through incorporating it into justificatory frameworks.

Necessity can arise within constitutional practice in multiple ways. In the post–September 11 world, counterterrorism policies of detention and surveillance are continuous with ordinary law enforcement practice as well as extraordinary situations. As chapter 2 explores, the American Constitution embeds authority to suspend the writ of habeas corpus in extraordinary times, "when in Cases of Rebellion or Invasion," freeing executive officials to detain individuals without judicial oversight during emergencies.[87] This provision functions as a temporary "emergency constitution," but does not license anything like a complete suspension of the constitutional order. Recognizing how the Suspension Clause works, and what it does *not* authorize, sheds light on how to incorporate necessity—and thereby overcome it— through ex ante constitutional means. As Chief Justice Marshall explained in *McCulloch*, necessity has an ordinary governing relation to normative constraint. As a normal part of governing decision-making, necessity is subject to review—and to justification—in proportion to how much it invades protected constitutional rights and liberties considering the degree of governmental interest at stake. As chapter 3 explores, the greater the governmental need, the better the justification for intruding upon baseline rights and liberties. A legislature, for example, may have license to pursue a compelling need by means claimed necessary even while deviating from strict protection of a constitutional right. Closely related, necessity can enhance or diminish the scope of preexisting powers of a defined government office, for example, granting a president confronting a military emergency wide discretionary latitude to act with enhanced executive powers without having to claim new ones. Moreover, channeling executive discretion into a judicial doctrine of "exigency" enhances the scope of government action in relation to a protected right. Focusing on counterterrorism surveillance practices, I argue that the existence of exigency doctrines, in addition to other Fourth Amendment search-and-seizure doctrines, provides ways to normalize necessity in everyday governing practice through constitutional norms of reasonableness subject to judicial review.

If necessity can be normalized into constitutional practice in some situations, for others, most particularly in cases of emergency, there remains a family of claims that "necessity knows no law." In chapter 4, I consider a family of constitutional theories that advocate for an internal principle of necessity, that argue constitutional constraints can become a "suicide pact," or that promote acting illegally first and asking forgiveness later. These theories fail both as interpretations of the Constitution and as pragmatic solutions to a paradox of constitutionalism—that constitutions might be harmful if we follow them too faithfully. As a limit case, justifications for such emergency measures often rely on extreme cases of potential "ticking bombs" to justify the use of torture. I argue that such theories cannot justify torture while remaining theories of constitutionalism. They are internally incoherent theories. A key feature of American constitutionalism is the existence of limits to the means available to achieve security ends. Crossing these limits in the case of torture undermines the dignity of persons and the conditions of consent upon which the legitimacy of constitutional institutions is built.

One way of justifying extreme counterterrorism policy—such as the interrogational use of torture—is to argue that necessitous circumstances require us to trade off liberty for greater security, and that we must defer to the measurements the president makes. In chapter 5, I argue that the trade-off thesis is fundamentally flawed and that deference to the president is inconsistent with a constitutional tradition that preciously guards decisions about liberty. Even if the president has special expertise in matters of security, no such expertise extends to liberty, or to the accurate weight and measurement of the relative value of each. Moreover, the very idea of constitutional trade-offs is fundamentally flawed, lacking a conception of how to compare the two values or how to describe what specific liberties must give way for which particular gains in security. To the extent that there are gains and losses to be made in liberty or security, processes of democratic deliberation—reflection and choice—comport with American constitutionalism, rather than reflexive claims that necessity requires a trade-off.

Necessity enables presidential discretion. In the aftermath of September 11, the president argued that because he has great responsibility to protect national security, he must have all the powers needed to fulfill his obligation. On this view, with great responsibility comes great power, enabled by claims of what necessity requires. Thus, in chapter 6 I respond to arguments that the president has all the power necessity confers. One version of this view is that there is an implied "necessary and proper" power that applies to the president, analogous to the Article I Necessary and Proper Clause enumerated for Congress. I accept the invitation to reconsider the scope of implied presidential power—including its obligation to "take care" to faithfully execute the laws—in light of such a view, arguing that even if there is power to do what is necessary, it is constrained by conceptions of what is proper. Propriety becomes a way of incorporating Marshall's argument in *McCulloch* that constitutional principles constrain necessitarian discretion. Thus, there is no independent hook upon which a claim empowers necessity, or that "necessity knows no law" within American constitutionalism, because any claim that an action is necessary must be justified according to its consistency and coherence with other constitutional values and principles.

Commitment to constitutional values is also a constitutive feature of political identity in American constitutionalism. As the final chapter argues, we choose our character—as well as the actions that constitute our character. Even if the "affairs of men" are "ever-changing," as Arendt suggests, some can change substantially without affecting the meaning of the whole, while others are more central to the entire enterprise. After the Reconstruction Amendments, reinstatement of a constitutional basis for slavery, for example, would alter the very fabric of American constitutionalism and the identity of the American people. So too, I argue, would reinstituting torture as an official means of criminal process. A long history of constitutional understandings has woven a fabric of rights protections in both domestic and international law that stand against the use of cruelty as a means of criminal procedure. Even if the events of September 11 revealed the outlines of a new world, as President Bush asserted, we must examine how this world is chosen and justified through arguments appealing to constitutional fit and coherence, not through arguments relying on unreflective claims to necessity. In the end, we must choose our commitments and actions—whether by affirming or overcoming necessity—which will not only create constitutional meaning, but also constitute our character as "We the People."

1

Can "Necessitous Men" Ever Be Politically Free?

NATIONAL EMERGENCIES TAKE MANY FORMS. Natural disasters, climate change, economic collapse, international incidents, and terrorist attacks are all extraordinary events that shake us from our ordinary lives. These events, while not ordinary, are not entirely alien, either. We cannot predict very far in advance when a devastating hurricane might hit or swift flood-waters might rise. But we do know that these kinds of events happen, and we often know the conditions under which they occur. Even if we wanted to, we are powerless to prevent natural disasters, knowing they are an inevitable feature of our world. When we add human intentionality to unpredicted events, we fare little better. We are often unable to predict when and where the unexpected terrorist attack will occur. Those we predict, we seek to prevent. For those attacks we think probable or possible, but for which we lack knowledge of where, when, or how, we are nearly as powerless as we are when facing the forces of nature. We are forever vulnerable to emergency events, because as disruptive as they may be, they remain the unwanted "extra" appended to the ordinary we expect.

Because we know that ordinary life is vulnerable to interruption by extraordinary events, we plan in advance, empowering ourselves with knowledge and tools to address the emergency situation.[1] In the United States, Congress has empowered the president with a number of "emergency powers" to invoke when extraordinary events occur.[2] Variations on such approaches proliferate across liberal democracies.[3] Lest the impulse to

prioritize the necessity generated by violence and terror mislead, emergency powers also abound for addressing the unpredictability and uncertainty
attending economic crises.[4] Legislation carefully crafted in advance of potential unexpected events can provide the resources, authoritative framework, and processes necessary for rapid responses to emergency situations.

Sometimes, however, legislation may not be enough. Foresight may be
too hazy. There is a tradition, exemplified in the political philosophy of John
Locke, of claiming the existence of prerogative powers for discretionary executive action. "[B]ecause also it is impossible to foresee, and so by laws to
provide for, all Accidents and Necessities, that may concern the publick,"
the executive has prerogative "Power to act according to discretion, for the
publick good, without the prescription of the Law, and sometimes even
against it."[5] Because the factual particularity of any specific emergency may
be too difficult to predict in advance, Locke's view suggests that executive
officials must retain discretion and flexibility in responding to the urgent
needs of the situation. Law has only limited foresight in a world of unfettered variation.

How far executive discretion extends is a vexed question. Officials under
President Trump's administration claim broad unilateral and unreviewable
executive power, falling into a tradition of ever expanding assertions of
presidential power. Especially in the immediate wake of September 11,
President George W. Bush's administration claimed unrestricted executive
discretion to respond to national security emergencies, vindicating the out-
er limits of Locke's theory of prerogative by claiming legislation to be null
or invalid that would govern executive power in the emergency situation.
As John Yoo—an author of the infamous "torture memo"—wrote in another Office of Legal Counsel (OLC) memo, "Just as statutes that order the
President to conduct warfare in a certain manner or for specific goals would
be unconstitutional, so too are laws that would prevent the President from
gaining the intelligence he believes necessary to prevent attacks upon the
United States."[6] These claims are controversial, and ones this chapter contests. They are of a kind with the claim that "necessity knows no law."

Even with the possibility of some prerogative discretion, it is not at all
clear that the framework of an emergency situation is so alien as to foreclose advance notice of the powers the president may exercise. Nor are they

ever so unexpected, urgent, or dire as to liberate executive officials from all normative constitutional constraints. We do not jettison the Constitution in an emergency, nor do we need to do so. Emergency preparedness is possible because we know that the ordinary always entails the extraordinary, and therefore what we call an "emergency" or what we construe as necessity may often compel urgent action but need not be politically so very unordinary. To arrive at these conclusions, however, we must first understand the reasons why some claim that emergencies undermine the commitments and constraints that define liberal constitutional order. I will call those who make such arguments "constitutional skeptics."

That an emergency is a type of event expected to interrupt ordinary life does not resolve the question of how a legal order can or should respond to necessity's claims. How a political body relates to "Accidents and Necessities," as Locke calls extraordinary events, is a fundamental issue of constitutional governance. Liberal constitutional democracies in particular appear susceptible to emergencies. Events challenge liberal political order by seeming to require flexible, discretionary, and immediate responses that might supersede or even conflict with existing laws and legal norms. Events also challenge institutional allocations of power between executive, legislative, and judicial bodies by shifting power to the decisional capacity of executive officials. Human rights and liberties are said to receive a lightened measure when balanced against the needs of national security. After all, we are told, a constitution is "not a suicide pact"—a claim often used to assert the priority of security over liberty.[7]

These are challenges this book confronts throughout. Despite these necessitarian claims to limit the constraints constitutional principles might impose during emergencies, I argue that thinking about executive power—and constitutionalism more generally—in terms of a residual Lockean prerogative power is misguided. Whether arguments about the role of necessity appear in the negative (constitutionalism fails to account for emergencies), or in the positive (executive officials can appeal to prerogative powers or "constitutional dictatorship"), this chapter rejects the threshold idea that constitutionalism comes to an end when crisis begins. We are never left to the episodic vicissitudes of necessity absent the normative guidance constitutional commitments provide. This overarching principle is valid in its own right. But, to see how, we need to first understand how "necessity knows no law" claims are both incoherent and fail to provide the relief and security they seek.

Although committed to the rule of law in normal times, constitutional skeptics claim that liberal democracies founder when unexpected events seem to require exceptions to the legal order. Not simply a claim of a retained executive prerogative, this critique, in its strongest form, claims that liberal democracies are incapable of addressing emergencies. This constitutional incapacity, according to the influential German theorist Carl Schmitt, means that "[t]he most guidance the constitution can provide is to indicate who can act" to decide "whether there is an extreme emergency as well as what must be done to eliminate it."[8] Functioning as states of exception to the ordinary legal order, such decisions are themselves ungoverned by legal norms. "The decision frees itself from all normative ties and becomes in the true sense absolute."[9] In this claim, Schmitt's challenge to liberal constitutionalism is more radical than the problem of "Accidents and Necessities" Locke contemplates. For Locke, the problem is resolved by the prince's legal power "to provide for the publick good, in such Cases, which depending upon unforeseen and uncertain Occurrences, certain and unalterable Laws could not safely direct."[10] For Schmitt, recognizing prerogative power does not adequately address the nature of the exception, which consists in "principally unlimited authority, which means the suspension of the entire existing order."[11] Similarly, law professors Adrian Vermeule and Eric Posner argue that modern executive discretion is unbound from legal constraints, particularly when emergencies arise.[12] On this view, liberal constitutional orders cannot account for emergencies as exceptional circumstances. This critique has the consequence, according to Paul Kahn's neo-Schmittian view, that because "[t]he exception is exactly that which does not stand under any rule," then "[t]he rule of law is the will of the sovereign," which equates to the will of the executive decider.[13]

On the one hand, Schmitt's challenge might lead to a theory of republican dictatorship—the need for a political actor to assume unlimited temporary authority to resolve the crisis. Following the Roman model, a legal order can be suspended in order to preserve it until a normal situation is restored. Indeed, Clinton Rossiter advocated for constitutional dictatorship on the Roman model, embedding the thought within mainstream American academic discussion.[14] On the other hand, Schmitt's critique is more radical, suggesting inherent weakness and instability in liberal constitutional systems. Such a view gives rise to more pervasive advocacy for the unbounded power of executive officials to act free from legislative or judicial checks. For both possibilities Schmitt relies on a distinction between rule and exception, in which the domain of the one is excluded from the other. In this appraisal of constitutional governance, he is joined by the Italian philosopher Giorgio Agamben, who defines a state of exception as "the opening of a space in which application and norm reveal their separation."[15] These views attracted much attention in the wake of the "war on terror," and seem to call for a reappraisal of the role constitutional commitments play in liberal democracies. These calls are misplaced.

These challenges to liberal constitutionalism present necessity as a problem that arises from outside a legal order, creating what Agamben labels "zones of indifference," where legal norms, or their absence, become indistinguishable. In this way, emergencies threaten to undermine the foundations of existing constitutional systems by showing that they remain unavoidably vulnerable to extralegal pressures.[16]

These views are grounded in a fundamental confusion. I take the constitutional view that a state of emergency is not a problem that arises among "zones" demarcated inside or outside the law. Rather, emergencies pressure the ambivalent and unsettled relation between norms and necessity within constitutional orders. Constitutional practice requires commitments to principles embedded in foundational legal forms and realized through institutions responsive to democratic processes and limited by substantive rights and obligations. Necessity does not create a problem whose solution exists beyond constitutional governance, but rather a problem whose contingent solutions are constitutive of constitutional practice. Necessity creates dilemmas—as in, who has power to act under what constraints and in light of which commitments?—but these do not demonstrate that liberal constitutional practice and institutional form are inherently inadequate to meet the challenges emergencies present. Instead, when we examine these dilemmas we find situations suffused with norms. There may be an absence of rules that tell us how to respond in a mechanical fashion, but the absence of determinate answers to emergency circumstances produces the skepticism of "undecidability" or "zones of indifference" that constitutional skeptics such as Agamben embrace only if one thinks the rule of law is the rule by determinate rules. If constitutional practice inhabits a "zone of indifference," then it becomes easier to affirm the Schmittian challenge that liberal constitutional practice is inadequate and to conclude that the executive should be unbound.[17] Necessity becomes "the stuff of which dictatorships are made," as President Franklin Roosevelt warned, and as this chapter will explore.[18] If, by contrast, we recognize that choices in responding to emergencies (in terms of "emergency" powers) depend on background commitments to constitutive values as well as institutional forms and practices that normatively constitute governing offices, then we are in a better position to contest the claim that necessity requires an unbound executive authority empowered by sovereign prerogative.

In sum, this chapter rejects this threshold theoretical challenge about the nature of constitutionalism, which argues that it lacks resources to address emergencies. If constitutionalism fails during emergencies, then according to this challenge, we must abandon constitutional commitments and seek recourse to extraconstitutional ideas about the nature of sovereignty to resolve the dilemma. But if the extraconstitutional ideas are incoherent, as I argue, then so too is the claim that constitutionalism fails. As my argument unfolds we see that natural necessity provides a basis on which we form governments—to overcome biological and physical necessity—and national necessity is something we overcome through processes that establish good government based on reflection and choice.

Natural and National Necessity

Necessity is the central concept challenging constitutional commitment. As the adage states, *necessitas legem non habet*, or "necessity knows no law." Ambivalence about legal commitments has a venerable genealogy. But genealogy is not justification. Apart from creating ambivalence about law's jurisdiction, necessity names the political and physical conditions under which a polity chooses and justifies actions.

The conditions of necessity can arise within a political body in two significant ways. First, the material conditions of basic biological life must be satisfied. A polity lacking material sustenance for its members will do little more than labor under the constraints of natural necessity. Confined to satisfying biological need for food, shelter, health, and the basic necessities of daily life, a polity would have no opportunity to pursue comprehensive policies and projects designed to fulfill broader aspirations for human happiness.

Insecurity regarding basic human provisions will produce political insecurity. Necessity's relation to human freedom is vexed, for "liberation from necessity, because of its urgency, will always take precedence over the building of freedom."[19] Hannah Arendt's insight is important for understanding how natural necessity interacts with the possibility of political life. Analyzing three fundamental human activities she labels labor, work, and action, Arendt defines "[l]abor [a]s the activity which corresponds to the biological process of the human body,"[20] and for Aristotle, as Arendt explains, "[t]o labor meant to be enslaved by necessity."[21] Because the products of labor are to be immediately consumed to satisfy the bare conditions of biological life, humans bound entirely by necessity are "incapable of freedom."[22] For Arendt, the ability to initiate new projects, to construct a common world of artifacts, and to disclose who we are in a shared political space are all aspects of freedom unavailable to persons unable to do more than attend to the demands of natural necessity. With work one can fabricate a world, and with action one can create the conditions of human political plurality. But with labor one remains bound by the conditions of immediate biological necessity.[23] For the conditions of labor to occupy the political realm means that politics remains insecure, bound to the changing circumstances of satisfying immediate needs.[24] To have a commitment to realizing human liberty requires that we attend to the conditions of choosing our goals, our individual and collective conceptions of the good, and our projects and pursuits through which we each constitute a self in intersubjective interaction. If the most basic necessities of biological life forever beckon our urgent attention, then we will fail to realize our potential of political liberty, remaining focused instead on satisfying basic life processes. We will remain insecure.

A second way that necessity arises for a polity is through its need to maintain its own security against external threats. Under external threat and struggling to maintain basic security, a polity will be tempted "to resort for repose and security to institutions which have a tendency to destroy their civil and political rights. To be more safe, they at length become willing to run the risk of being less free."[25] As Alexander Hamilton framed the problem, physical insecurity creates the risk that political institutions may be unable to withstand the temptations of expediency. Constitutional design seeks to channel these impulses into institutional and legal frameworks.

Once established, legal norms ordinarily apply without incident, as Schmitt argued. But during emergencies, by contrast, necessity will often compel unconstrained responses that would have the "tendency to destroy" civil and political rights. In blunt overstatement, Schmitt writes, "There exists no norm that is applicable to chaos."[26] If Schmitt is right in claiming that resorting to exceptional measures is inevitable and that norms cease to apply during emergencies, what role is envisioned for legal norms in the first place? Legal norms become most salient as governing constraints when officials are tempted to transgress them. If legal norms cease to apply when extraordinary events occur—those most likely to tempt—it becomes unclear in what sense legal norms ever constrain official conduct—which is precisely Schmitt's critique. For Schmitt, exceptions reveal the failure of liberal constitutionalism at all times.[27] As the argument of this chapter unfolds, we will see that Schmitt's argument is false: legal norms unavoidably apply even in extraordinary situations.

In response to the forces of national, or political, necessity brought about by insecurity, there is a rich history of political theory that urges episodic flexibility as an ineliminable condition of political life, limiting the temporal applicability of constitutional norms. For example, considering the basis of political life in the early modern period, Niccolò Machiavelli observed that "where one deliberates entirely on the safety of his fatherland, there ought not to enter any consideration of either just or unjust, merciful or cruel, praiseworthy or ignominious; indeed every other concern put aside, one ought to follow entirely the policy that saves its life and maintains its liberty."[28] Similar sentiments echo throughout the writings of British political theorists, giving rise to the claim of executive prerogative by Locke, and claims like the following by David Hume in the eighteenth century:

> Suppose a society to fall into such want of all common necessaries, that the utmost frugality and industry cannot preserve the greater number from per-

ishing, and the whole from extreme misery; it will readily, I believe, be admitted, that the strict laws of justice are suspended, in such a pressing emergence, and give place to the stronger motives of necessity and self-preservation. . . . Or if a city besieged were perishing with hunger; can we imagine, that men will see any means of preservation before them, and lose their lives, from a scrupulous regard to what, in other situations, would be the rules of equity and justice? . . . but where the society is ready to perish from extreme necessity, no greater evil can be dreaded from violence and injustice; and every man may now provide for himself by all the means which prudence can dictate, or humanity permit.[29]

Under extreme necessity, where the preservation of self or state is at stake, Hume's claim is that other constraints give way and that one's responses are to be ordered by circumstances. Where "order in society" is threatened from without by "extreme necessity," virtues such as "scrupulous regard" to law can become grave vices. In such situations, normal order in society no longer governs one's actions. We hear Thomas Jefferson question whether it would be better "to lose our country by a scrupulous adherence to written law" in this passage from Hume.[30] Jefferson added that "[t]he laws of necessity, or self-preservation, of saving the country when in danger, are of higher obligation."[31] In this way, the necessity of national self-preservation is the political analogue to the problem of individual natural necessity. Both produce insecurity.

If we combine Locke's claim of institutional executive prerogative with Machiavelli's and Hume's claims of circumstantial necessity, we derive the view that in times of emergency, or "extreme necessity" occasioned by external threat, the executive is authorized to pursue any and all means to save lives, preserve liberty, and maintain the state. These views are significant because they demonstrate that an ambiguity about the role of law during emergencies is imbedded within the heart of republican and liberal constitutional theory. This ambiguity is ripe for exploitation that would compel us to turn away from constitutional commitments.

It may be the case that protecting security is a necessary condition for the enjoyment of other rights. Henry Shue makes the point clear: "No rights other than a right to physical security can in fact be enjoyed if a right to physical security is not protected. Being physically secure is a necessary condition for the exercise of any other right."[32] The very point of establishing the state is to provide security against physical threats—as Thomas Hobbes argues, "if there be no power erected, or not great enough for our security; every man will and may lawfully rely on his own strength and art, for caution against all other men."[33] If we connect the foundational role of security with its functional priority, we begin to see how important security is to political order. In this way, security may function as a condition for the possibility of enjoying any other civil and political right. For as Shue suggests, "No one can fully enjoy any right that is supposedly protected by society if someone can credibly threaten him or her with murder, rape, beating, etc., when he or she tries to enjoy the alleged right."[34] The right to security "is desirable as part of the enjoyment of every other right."[35]

Extended to national security issues, the claim is that threatened terrorist attacks undermine the ability to fully enjoy other rights. Even if terrorist attacks do not implicate sovereign control over physical territory, they challenge effective sovereignty through the fear of insecurity they produce.[36] As Bruce Ackerman argues, repeated challenges to a state's effective control over violence can undermine the political standing of liberal institutions, producing a specific problem of emergency power. And as Ian Loader and Neil Walker argue, "security is a valuable public good, a constitutive ingredient of the good society," which a democratic state is obligated to provide.[37] We cannot enjoy the Constitution's "Blessings of Liberty" without securing them against political and physical necessity.

On the basis of security's role as a necessary condition for the possibility of enjoying other liberties constitutionally protected, constitutional skeptics make a further claim: security therefore has ordinal priority over liberty. When confronting political necessity, some claim that national security requires us to recalibrate the balance of liberty and security, where increases in the one require depravations of the other.[38] If security is a basic right held alongside, or even as a condition of, rights to due process and equality, it has a particular salience in emergencies. It may require adjustment to the protections afforded other rights when necessity requires. Rights are traded off for the benefit of another right of at least equal, if not prior, importance— a dynamic I examine in detail in chapter 5. These thoughts about priority and trade-offs provide the rationale offered after September 11 for increased surveillance, curtailment of due process, indefinite detention, and other practices and policies affecting rights said necessary to preserve security. These counterterrorism measures arise because of security's priority, justifying in turn the existence of a residual prerogative power to do what is necessary, no matter the applicable normative order.

If achieving security proves difficult, then a political body will be continually thwarted in its pursuit of national projects, shared prosperity, and the civic life in which other rights and liberties are enjoyed. Developmentally, if securing the state is a necessary first step to a rights-flourishing polity, then a state under constant threat never moves beyond the need to provide security to take the second step. A state that never wants to take the second step will always cite security concerns as reasons for denying the existence or application of other rights. Even for mature democracies such as the United States, prioritizing expenditures for security comes at a cost to provisions for other public goods under conditions of scarcity. In this way, both national and natural necessity can thwart more comprehensive projects of constitutional governance and policy, undermining the conditions of human and political freedom that Arendt identifies.

Thus, to give some kind of priority to security requires us to better understand what security is. If it stands for no more than a low likelihood of any individual being harmed by a terrorist attack, then even with the events of September 11, most Americans are perfectly secure. If providing security means that a state should devote appropriate resources to minimize the risk of terrorist attacks, then the fact that nations such as the United States spend considerable sums on defense and counterterrorism should likewise lead to the conclusion that most citizens are perfectly secure. Security has both of these meanings. But it also means more than what it seeks to achieve. Security names one form in which necessity appears in politics.

Like the urgency of biological need, necessity appears in politics under the urgency of action aimed to quell threats by expedient means. In this approach, attention to the forms of legality may wane as achieving security takes precedence in setting governing priorities. This thought defined the American approach to counterterrorism after September 11. Vice President Dick Cheney claimed that government needed to "work through, sort of, the dark side. . . . A lot of what needs to be done here will have to be done quietly, without any discussion, using sources and methods that are available to our intelligence agencies, if we're going to be successful. That's the world these folks operate in. And so it's going to be vital for us to use any means at our disposal, basically, to achieve our objective."[39] The political appearance of the right to security—to use any means available to protect it—can crowd out consideration of the duties owed to other rights. Under the Bush administration, concern for security did displace duties toward the rights of due process, as well as those against torture and against cruel, degrading, and inhuman treatment.[40] Al-Qaeda leaders were waterboarded, for example, because the administration claimed it was necessary to find out what they knew. The priority of security, on this view, also means that neither courts nor Congress can interfere with the president's unilateral and unfettered responses to necessity. Curiously, the proposition that we must trade off security and liberty never seems to lessen the priority of security over liberty.[41] The trade-off often works in only one direction— more security, less liberty, as chapter 5 explores. In the context of national emergency, and with evocation by some of a "constitutional dictatorship," or the sovereign decider who lies beyond constitutional governance, what remains unquestioned is the meaning and scope of "security" that occasions the calls for constitutional deviation.[42]

Necessity appears in politics in these two ways—natural and national. When it appears, it does so either as a way of overcoming the insecurity of basic biological needs or as an emergency interruption to normal political process. Taking the Hobbesian approach, the commonwealth is formed to overcome the necessity of both material and political insecurity.[43] But the paradox is that security has an irresolvable nature, subject always to new risks and predictably unforeseen events. To turn to Arendt again, our biological needs prove irresistible at times, interrupting settled social arrangements, for "[a]ll rulership has its original and its most legitimate source in man's wish to emancipate himself from life's necessity"—a wish that can never be fully fulfilled under conditions of scarcity.[44] Human needs for both forms of security—against biological need and against physical threat—break through the normality of everyday political life. About this much, Schmitt is undoubtedly correct. But skepticism about constitutionalism does not follow from the existence of these challenges. The central issue then is how commitment to governing through constitutional principles and practices—both those that already exist and those we might create—provides resources to address the needs necessity creates.

"Necessitous Men" and a Second Bill of Rights

Security, like the necessity to which it is linked, produces its own ambivalence. Security can have different meanings and involve multiple values, such as protection from physical harm, safeguards against illegitimate economic loss, provision of basic necessities, maintenance of a political community, and others.[45] Necessity presents circumstances whose meaning within the political realm is insecurity. Insecurity in turn requires a response. Ambivalence arises in determining the occasion for and the nature of the response.

In the midst of a national security crisis in 1944, this dynamic relation between necessity and security led President Franklin Roosevelt to propose what remains an unrealized second Bill of Rights. The timing and topic are significant. With the United States at war on two fronts, necessity would seem to have prescribed focused attention to the conditions of physical security—those defining the first duty of the state. Yet Roosevelt examined the meaning and implications of natural necessity for national security, blending the two forms of necessity as partner political projects.

President Roosevelt claimed that "[t]his Republic had its beginning . . . under the protection of certain inalienable political rights—among them the right of free speech, free press, free worship, trial by jury, and freedom from unreasonable searches and seizures. They were our rights to life and liberty."[46] These are important political rights, but on their own they would seem to be incomplete, Roosevelt reasoned, if we are to achieve "equality in the pursuit of happiness."[47] Recognizing the state's role in ordering the demands of natural necessity, Roosevelt asserted that "[w]e have come to a clear realization of the fact that true individual freedom cannot exist without economic security and independence."[48] Human freedom requires the ability to pursue independent projects that rely on basic economic security. In other words, the conditions of biological necessity must be met as a matter of security itself.

Roosevelt makes the link between freedom and necessity explicit. He warned, "Necessitous men are not free men."[49] They are not free because the conditions under which humans exercise liberty presuppose the ability to satisfy biological necessities. Economic depression foregrounds these basic necessities, showing the fragility of political life where unsatisfied urgent need can deflate comprehensive life projects. The danger is not simply a matter of unsatisfied natural necessity. Roosevelt's speech recognizes how necessity can undermine the possibility of human liberty in multiple ways, creating insecurity in everyday political life just as it can during states of emergency. Roosevelt also invoked solidarity as a basis for security. "We cannot be content," Roosevelt argued, "if some fraction of our people" is "insecure."[50] If we import Henry Shue's description of the right to security from physical harm, then security from biological necessity also becomes a necessary condition for the possibility of enjoying civil and political rights. If we cannot get beyond step one—the provision of security against natural necessity—then we never achieve enjoyment of "our rights to life and liberty" that motivated the American Republic's founding.[51] The political and institutional risk entailed more than a failure to realize the fruits of civil and political rights.

Roosevelt continued: "People who are hungry and out of a job are the stuff of which dictatorships are made."[52] Unaddressed natural necessity can produce a particular kind of politics at odds with liberal constitutional practices and ideals. Insecurity that arises from severe economic hardship can create political insecurity, making politics a function of circumstance—what Locke calls "Accidents and Necessities"—that renders authoritarian dictatorship possible, the very political systems against which the United States was in the midst of fighting.

Roosevelt's proposals for recognizing new rights to a job, adequate food and clothing, and adequate medical care, among others, provide, as he states, "a new basis of security and prosperity."[53] If the state has a duty to provide the conditions for realizing these rights to economic security, then human freedom can be achieved only by making natural necessity a matter of political necessity. Insecurity, and with it the prospect of dictatorship, arises from a failure to address both natural and national security. Regarding the right to a remunerative job, the right to earn enough for both food and recreation, the right to adequate medical care, the right to a good education, or the right to a decent home, Roosevelt claims that "[a]ll of these rights spell security."[54] Moreover, "Security . . . means not only physical security which provides safety from attacks by aggressors. It means also economic security, social security, moral security."[55] Connecting domestic rights to security to the nation's global leadership, Roosevelt admonished that "America's own rightful place in the world depends in large part upon how fully these and similar rights have been carried into practice for our citizens. For unless there is security here at home there cannot be lasting peace in the world."[56]

Overcoming necessity requires providing security. Both necessity and security introduce ambivalence because what counts as necessity and what satisfies security will remain undetermined, yet politically and legally significant. As Roosevelt's speech indicates, we solve the problem of "necessitous men" through institutional life as a matter of political beginnings. Roosevelt's proposal has an implied connection to Hobbes: the first duty of the state is to provide basic security for the polity as a condition for the possibility of political life. What Roosevelt further recognizes is that security requires more than protection from physical harm. And like the institutional allocations of rights and powers that gave rise to the polity's constitutional formation, Roosevelt proposes a similar higher-order lawmaking—a second Bill of Rights that announces a new beginning within an old institutional setting. Through constitutional transformation, he sought to secure the polity against the risks of political tyranny "necessitous men" make possible. His speech echoes the U.S. Declaration of Independence, which held certain political "truths to be self-evident." For Roosevelt believed, perhaps more optimistically than was found to be warranted, that "[i]n our day these economic truths have become accepted as self-evident."[57]

Truths that become self-evident to a political community give rise to new institutional and legal beginnings. In the Declaration of Independence, when it became "necessary . . . to dissolve the political bands" that bound the American colonies to their political masters, the outcome was not a state of exception. Instead, "necessity . . . constrains them to alter their former systems of government," not to abolish their government or to resort to dictatorship or decisionism. Having "warned" of their political grievances, "reminded" the British Crown of their circumstances, "appealed to their native justice," and "conjured" common ties to be met only by deafness "to the voice of justice," only then does "necessity . . . denounce[] our separation." Far from a situation of unreason and urgency, necessity here is invoked within a process of political justification, but one whose rupture makes possible the formation of a new legal order. The revolutionary spirit meant that actors could implement new legal and political orders through reflection and choice, not merely on the dictates of immediate necessity. But in so doing, political innovation carried forward already existing values, and truths held self-evident, into new political and institutional formations. Where the conditions of necessity faced by the Declaration of Independence led to a new political foundation, the necessity that Roosevelt's proposed second Bill of Rights addressed would have radically transformed many practices of the American polity. Each arose out of a condition of necessity, and both propose (ultimately) to solve the problem of "necessitous men" through institutional and constitutional formation.

Far from imposing a problem that inevitably ruptures the institutional and legal orders in the direction of lawlessness, necessity motivates constitutional formation and amendment. A condition for the enjoyment of rights—even rights to security—is that we establish a political order to free ourselves from circumstantial vulnerability and thereby overcome necessity. Roosevelt shares with Arendt the insight that those subject to the dictates of necessity will remain unfree. The world of necessity is one of caprice. Rights, by contrast, overcome necessity.

Whether generated out of biological need or external threat, necessity is a condition that establishes a normative order. If "necessitous men" are to become free, they must resolve their social insecurity through institutional form and political formation. The problem then is not that decisions must be made that exceed law, but that law must constitute the power to govern.[58] Constitutionalism answers one problem of "necessitous men" by providing the governing form to respond to future exigencies and emergencies. "Necessitous men" are not only a possible cause of dictatorship, but also the source for constitutional transformation.[59] Responses to necessity can therefore either harness constitutional processes of higher lawmaking to transform the polity (to provide a New Deal and a second Bill of Rights, in Roosevelt's case), or appeal to the charismatic leadership of a "decider" who claims authority to do whatever it takes to resolve a crisis. Because political action could foreclose the possibility of dictatorship, Roosevelt demonstrates that the choice of how to respond to necessity is not antecedently determined. And once made on behalf of constitutional processes, the choice lays the foundation for future responses to unforeseen events.[60]

Our problem is that necessity seems to name a set of conditions that demand immediate responses from a "decider" ungoverned by ex ante laws and norms. Two paradigm cases present themselves. One is the biological need for life sustenance, satisfaction of which becomes a condition for the possibility for fulfilling comprehensive life plans within a polity. The other is the political or national need to secure members of the polity against threats from outside as well as from each other. Each of these cases finds resolution not in an ungoverned state, but in the formation of political and legal orders capable of addressing the ongoing insecurity that arises from basic need and physical threat. The fact that constitutional systems arose out of revolutionary acts does not undermine the importance of the continuing commitment to govern within constitutional form and on behalf of shared constitutional norms. Thus, an initial state of necessity that bridges the divide between the prepolitical and the political does not raise a fundamental problem for liberal constitutionalism. Instead, it highlights the importance of choice, responsibility, and commitment to constitutional processes.

It may seem, however, that I have ignored the real challenge Schmitt and others have levied against liberal constitutionalism. The issue is not whether a polity can constitute institutional and legal forms to forestall the everyday urgency that necessity imposes, but whether constitutional forms can address dire emergencies that interrupt already existing legal orders. Interruptions will occur. Once established, a constitutional polity lacks resources to avert an irresistible slide into dictatorship or decisionism. Even if a polity can provide initial institutional security against biological need and economic loss, it will remain vulnerable to systemic shocks or external threats. This vulnerability can be resolved, according to the constitutional skeptic, only by recourse to a unitary executive empowered to act independently of governing legal norms.[61] Lest this view seem historically and theoretically distant, recall that two law professors recently defended Schmitt's views, arguing that "the Schmittian view supplies a better account of institutional capacities and behavior in these crisis episodes than does the liberal legalist view stemming from Madison."[62] Constitutional formation may be effective for a time, but it will remain vulnerable to exogenous events demanding a decision that exceeds both governing form and its legal norms. This view presents a skeptical challenge.

Alexander Hamilton's Question and the Impossibility of Dictatorship

The challenge raised at the end of the prior discussion leaves us with a puzzle. Necessity is said to know no law. But as we have seen, necessity gives rise to law and legal processes. In that case, necessity knows law, for law is a means for achieving shared moral aims by overcoming the immediate claims of necessity. We must commit to the formation of a constitutional order for the possibility of deviance and dictatorship to arise as a possible exception. But if necessity can be bound by higher lawmaking in the case of constitutional beginnings—it being the self-constituting task of people to bind themselves to legal form—then how can extreme necessity render decisions free from all legal norms in the case of interruptive emergencies, when neither beginnings nor endings need be at stake? If the interruption is of such a nature that new beginnings are possible, then the issue is not about decisions freed from legal norms, but the establishment of new norms and new forms of governing power. If the interruption is of such a nature as to constitute localized necessity—a terrorist attack, an earthquake, an economic crisis—then something so radical as new beginnings are not at stake. And absent revolutionary rupture, it is puzzling how a state of exception could trigger decision-making authority unbound by legal norms, as Schmitt claims. On closer inspection, as Kim Scheppele argues, law is everywhere during and in relation to emergencies.[63] Many statutes authorize many different kinds of executive authority during emergencies large and small. Moreover, the Constitution created the very presidential office that would claim a Schmittian decisional authority. This is not to say that unlawful action is not a continuing temptation for public officials. But illegal tendencies do not mean that actions spin free from the legal mechanisms to which they are attached.

The resolution of Schmitt's puzzle—that liberal democracies are unable to address the urgency of emergencies—requires examining how the temporal dynamics of constitutionalism contextualize potential emergency ruptures within existing norms. Interruptions cannot be addressed without implicating political origins.

As we first encountered in the introduction, Alexander Hamilton asks the key question of political origins in the first *Federalist* paper: "It has been frequently remarked that it seems to have been reserved to the people of this country, by their conduct and example, to decide the important question, whether societies of men are really capable or not of establishing good government from reflection and choice, or whether they are forever destined to depend for their political constitutions on accident and force."[64] The dilemma is between the material conditions and external constraints of "accident and force," or necessity, and the internal imperatives of "reflection and choice." The one is circumstantial in nature, the other rational. The one is reactive, the other proactive. To be governed only by "accident and force" is to be governed by the despotism of circumstance. Whereas to be governed by "reflection and choice" is to manifest both reason and liberty. Reflection and choice requires political actors to identify with self-constituting decisions regarding political forms and practice. What is necessary leaves little room for choice, and where choice is not possible, it would appear that neither human reason nor moral responsibility has a significant opportunity to play a sustaining role in a political constitution. By contrast, what is freely chosen sustains a participatory political body, requiring individuals to take responsibility for the reasons and practices they advance and pursue.

Framed like this, why would anyone *choose* to establish government on the basis of "accident and force"? The very contrast between necessity and liberty would seem to resolve the matter. Because Americans established the framework for a "good government" on the basis of an extended period of deliberation, reflection, and choice, Hamilton's dilemma would seem to be decided. Because the Constitution was forged in crisis, it is all the more capable of taming and overcoming necessity. But perhaps the real dilemma is temporal. How should an organized political body relate to inevitable "Accidents and Necessities" as a matter of their everyday "political constitution"? And when they arise, don't "Accidents and Necessities" present urgent and dire situations to which we must give utmost and immediate attention? Having made a political start, a polity must determine its continuing commitments and its practices of governing. What will be the relation between principle and practice when security challenges arise? A constitution can be no more than a "parchment barrier," as James Madison warned, without the commitments of citizens and governing officials to constitutional principles and practices. Understood in this way, Hamilton's question is about origins as well as diachronic identity.

Why would a polity risk the possible despotism of circumstance by giving priority to necessity rather than committing to practices of "reflection and choice"? Perhaps a political body could do no more than respond seriatim to each emergency and crisis as it emerges, treating any existing rules as technicalities to be overcome or adapted through the discretionary prerogative of a sitting executive. Embracing "accident and force" in this way, however, seems an unpropitious approach. Alternatively, a polity might prioritize a process of decision-making that relies on rules and accumulated wisdom when useful but opts for maximum flexibility as circumstances warrant. Such a view normatively embraces Schmitt's challenge—that liberal legalism cannot constrain executive power—by making a virtue of residual prerogative powers. Flexibility solves the problem of emergency interruptions. This flexibility is said to entail a claim both that the president is the official empowered to act, and that normal constitutional constraints do not apply.

Because emergency situations require urgency, the temporal constraint demands governing officials to take decisive and swift action, diminishing the role for interactive "reflection and choice." Emphasizing the unilateral role of executive decision-making, Hamilton writes in *Federalist* 70, "Decision, activity, secrecy, and dispatch will generally characterize the proceedings of one man in a much more eminent degree than the proceedings of any greater number; and in proportion as the number is increased, these qualities will be diminished."[65] There is a small chorus of academics who make a similar point, that a "unitary executive can evaluate threats, consider policy choices, and mobilize national resources with a speed and energy that is far superior to any other branch."[66] Both dispatch and decisiveness imply that necessity has an unavoidable and continuing role to play in processes of governing.[67] To respond best to necessity, a polity might prefer the decisive-ness strong presidentialist government offers as one interpretation of con-stitutional structure, undeterred by risks of authoritarianism or tyranny that separated powers seek to avoid.[68] A polity might be ambivalent about com-mitting to principles established through "reflection and choice" out of fear that negative consequences could follow from emergency. Here we return to the Schmittian challenge—because normal constitutionalism is incapable of governing emergencies, flexible decisionism results. But this potential incapacity would not be caused by a failure of constitutional norms, but by a polity's failure to adhere to its own constitutional commitments.

According to this challenge to constitutionalism, the priority of security therefore entails the priority of presidential power, linking emergency to de-cision, as Schmitt suggests. Writing as a lawyer for the Department of Jus-tice Office of Legal Counsel under the administration of President G. W. Bush, John Yoo offered the view that "[t]he text, structure and history of the Constitution establish that the Founders entrusted the President with the primary responsibility, and therefore the power, to ensure the security of the United States in situations of compelling, unforeseen, and possibly recurring, threats to the nation's security."[69] If the president has power to ensure security, Jay Bybee working with Yoo further claimed regarding statu-tory prohibitions against torture that "[a]ny effort to apply . . . [them] in a manner that interferes with the President's direction of such core war mat-ters as the detention and interrogation of enemy combatants thus would be unconstitutional."[70] Together these two claims, repeated over a number of Department of Justice memos, each contextualized to the "massive destruc-tion and loss of life caused by the September 11 attacks,"[71] make the com-bined claim of executive prerogative to preserve not simply the order of society, but its security, and in so doing to "follow entirely the policy that saves its life and maintains its liberty," as Machiavelli suggested.[72] The events of September 11 became the occasion for applying political theory to practice.

Yoo's articulation of executive power both invokes the founding as "en-trusting" responsibility and power in the president, and appeals to "unfore-seen" and "recurring" circumstances that become the occasions for the exercise of this power. Both political origins and constitutional persistence figure prominently in the memo's conclusions. On this view, our political constitution is such that we stand ready to confront "recurring" emergency circumstances with extraordinary powers "entrusted" to the president. We can disentangle two versions of the prerogative claim here: one is that there is a superseding law based on the necessity of circumstance that empowers the executive, and the other is that legal constraints cease to apply and circumstance governs. The former means that the executive is constrained both by circumstance and by the rules and norms that attach to the superseding legal authority (for example, the commander-in-chief power). The latter means that the executive may "every other concern put aside," as Machiavelli directs, in pursuit of state preservation.[73]

The memo's claims on behalf of the executive are ambiguous regarding this distinction until we consider the nature of the statute he claims would be illegal if applied to the president. That statute is one enacting the standards applicable under the Convention Against Torture.[74] The convention very importantly states that "[n]o exceptional circumstances whatsoever . . . may be invoked as a justification for torture."[75] If the president is unconstrained by law in ordering torture as circumstances dictate, then it seems clear that the administration intends to invoke a version of prerogative unmediated by legal constraints. Seeking an executive unbound, the memo subverts long-standing commitments against torture as a means of achieving political objectives. As was widely recognized in the late eighteenth century, it was a foolish and cruel practice to expect that through the infliction of torture one might discover that "the criterion of truth lay in the muscles and fibers of a poor wretch."[76] Declarations of the rights of man were made, and laws against cruel punishments followed, foremost of which were laws against imposition of torture. So vilified is the idea of official torture in U.S. legal practice that federal courts have declared that the "torturer has become like the pirate and the slave trader before him *hostis humani generis*, an enemy of all mankind."[77]

We thus have a deeply embedded moral and legal norm that prohibits the practice of torture, as chapter 4 explores in greater depth. We also have an executive-branch legal opinion that authoritatively constitutes presidential prerogative "with complete discretion in exercising the Commander-in-Chief power"[78] and that includes the authority to torture captured terrorist suspects.[79] Add to this conflict the state of emergency that continues in the wake of September 11, and we see the potential for sustained deviation from core established limitations on the exercise of governing power.[80] Here we have executive action taken in violation of law, yet retaining the force of law—a candidate for the kind of state of exception Agamben describes as having the quality of undecidability, for it is taken under color of law (under the Constitution's grant of commander-in-chief power) while violating statutory and treaty law.[81] Such deviation from normal constitutional constraints is said to follow from the interruption imposed by national necessity.

In short, the response to *Federalist* 1 that Yoo's argument exemplifies is that "reflection and choice" is fine for normal times, but that unfettered flexibility governs the exceptional. If the "good government" model is insufficient, it is not enough for the skeptical challenge to press a purported shortcoming, but it must also provide further political theory advancing an alternative. Yoo's memo reconstitutes executive powers and embeds as an authoritative legal opinion an articulation of executive power during an emergency to which the label "constitutional dictatorship" might apply. Within American legal thought, Clinton Rossiter developed a comprehensive normative theory of "constitutional dictatorship."[82] Where President Roosevelt, as we have seen, sought to foreclose the slide toward dictatorship, Rossiter finds dictatorship not only inevitable during national security crises, but normatively desirable. Because of the prominence of this idea— appearing in Schmitt and Agamben, and recently resuscitated in academic circles under various guises—it is worth pausing to examine at some length what it means, and more importantly, what it obscures, particularly given the sweeping claims of unilateral executive discretion urged by the OLC.[83]

A primary goal of constitutional dictatorship, according to Rossiter, is "the preservation of the independence of the state, the maintenance of the existing constitutional order." To accomplish this goal, the dictator must aim to "end the crisis and restore normal times."[84] To defend this imperative, Rossiter identifies a number of "fundamental facts" regarding dictatorship in a constitutional system. Two of these are particularly significant, because they are demonstrably false for instructive reasons.

The first supposed fact is about the design and purpose of a liberal constitutional state. Rossiter claims, "[T]he complex system of government of

the democratic, constitutional state is essentially designed to function under normal, peaceful conditions, and is often unequal to the exigencies of a
great national crisis."[85] Whether this is possibly true depends on the inflec-
tion intended by "exigencies of great national crisis." The United States
Constitution was written and ratified following a period of unprecedented
revolutionary action and achievement. It seeks to empower governing bodies to address the problems and exigencies that arise with both internal and
external problems and threats, granting authority for war-making, calling
forth the militia, economic regulation, revenue raising, suspension of laws
during invasion or rebellion, and powers "necessary and proper" to fulfilling constitutional purposes. As Chief Justice Marshall observed in *Mc-
Culloch v. Maryland* during the early Republic, the power to do what is
necessary and proper "is made in a Constitution intended to endure for
ages to come, and consequently to be adapted to the various crises of human affairs."[86] Thus, it is not at all clear that the American constitutional
state is fixed by its function in normal times alone, nor would it be likely
that any constitutional state would neglect to assign powers and jurisdiction to address both the normal and the extraordinary circumstance.

Regarding the second fact, and the ultimate goal of his project, Rossiter is
simply mistaken as to both fact and value. "[I]n time of crisis a democratic,
constitutional government must be temporarily altered to whatever degree is
necessary to overcome the peril and restore normal conditions. This alteration invariably . . . [means] the government will have more power and the
people fewer rights."[87] As a factual matter, what is restored, the new "normal
conditions," will be unavoidably altered as a consequence of the suspension.
The political world looked very different at the end of the American Civil War
than it did before, especially after passage of the reconstruction amendments. Reconstruction was hardly a return to the "normal," outlawing as it
did slavery, imposing civil rights limitations on the states, and protecting
rights of franchise, all through military occupation. Likewise, the world after
the New Deal was a very different political world than the one before, even
without the passage of a second Bill of Rights. And, as President G. W. Bush
explicitly stated, we may live in a different political world after the events of
September 11: "For America, 9/11 was more than a tragedy—it changed the
way we look at the world."[88] How much more change might have occurred if

any of these restored "normal conditions" happened after explicit use of a "constitutional dictatorship"?

In each of these pre–September 11 "emergencies," after circumstances no longer compelled urgent or deviant action, there was no restoration of prior "normal conditions," even if what emerged was a newly constructed normal. Without a reversion, political actors cannot "restore normal conditions" to an unaltered prior state of affairs, but can only create a new normal condition.[89] Rossiter recognizes this fact, but not its consequences, claiming that "[n]o constitutional government ever passed through a period in which emergency powers were used without undergoing some degree of permanent alteration, always in the direction of an aggrandizement of the power of the state." Restoration becomes alteration.[90]

If emergency generates unilateral power exercised with temporal urgency, then the problem from the perspective of Hamilton's question is that legal reordering will not involve multilateral "reflection and choice." Emergencies come in many sizes and shapes, each inviting deviations from present legal rules, institutional arrangements, or legal practices. Contingency and choice will define the nature of governing officials' responses, as we see in the case of both beginnings and interruptions. But the primary goal of any deviation has to be the resolution of the problem provoking the emergency, not the preservation or restoration of a precise normal order. Normal or abnormal, constitutional deviance produces constitutive change. Recall that Hamilton's question requires a polity constituted through "reflection and choice" to have a continuing commitment to the processes of intertemporal self-constitution.

Given the multifaceted possibility for emergency, Rossiter's normative imperative that the "constitutional government must be temporarily altered . . . [so that] the government will have more power and the people fewer rights" is also implausible.[91] If the point is to resolve an emergency, not to aggrandize power, how do we know ex ante that government must be altered in this manner? We may know that there will be pressure to increase government power and to diminish the force of civil rights, but pressure alone is not enough. We must choose to adjust the distribution of power and liberty, a choice not fully determined by circumstance. In everyday political life, governing practices and policies change as new problems and agendas arise, sometimes by increasing the power of particular officials. Because it does change, it "must." But the precise nature of any deviations from legal norms during emergencies will depend on normative commitments and pragmatic considerations, not ex ante imperatives. In fact, if we can anticipate problems and their needed legal framework, we can legislate both power and oversight. For example, because we can anticipate that an executive may seek to detain terrorist suspects without probable cause in the aftermath of future attacks, it is possible to enact framework statutes that better guide a president's actions within structures of oversight and constraint.[92] Even without such guidance, a decision to deviate from settled legal limits is an imperative only for one bound to the necessity of circumstance, not to the processes of "reflection and choice." Because it rationalizes the despotism of circumstance, talk of "dictatorship" during a national crisis tends to obscure the institutional and ethical issues at stake, both with specific deviant practices in law and with broad assertions of unchecked discretionary power.

The factual and normative grounds for advocating a "constitutional dictatorship" are not sound. What is more, the very idea of embedding a dictatorial structure within constitutional practice contradicts the continuing commitment to "reflection and choice" that defines a liberal democracy's political constitution and "good government" aspirations. No doubt, as a pragmatic matter, the presidential office confronting crises may have considerable discretion in deciding how to respond—an *initiative power*. Even so, the imagined dictatorship must function within the normative values that constitute the very office of the president, the institutional context in which the office possesses power, the roles of other institutions with incentives to ensure that policy stays broadly within prescribed frameworks, as well as the broadly conceived constitutional culture that provides the values and principles in which a response must be justified. A constitutional government is an unwieldy system in the best of times, which is why executive initiative and discretion within liberal constitutionalism are not usefully conceptualized as dictatorship. Not usefully described, that is, if one wants either to provide an accurate description of institutional practice or if one wishes to provide a useful contribution to legal theory. But if one's purpose, by contrast, is to use the rhetoric of dictatorship to clear more space for more unfettered executive power, checked only by the limits of what electoral politics will allow, then "dictatorship" may resonate for some within constitutionalism—though the term itself has normative limitations to constitutional ears.

In addition to these normative and conceptual failings, other considerations undermine the coherence of "constitutional dictatorship." Importantly, an initiative power runs into a problem of choice. Under conditions of unsatisfied basic biological need, humans lacking the capacity to make genuine choices will always be subject to necessity. By contrast, humans who have reasons compelling them to act, but who retain the freedom to choose, realize the full capacity of "reflection and choice" in their actions.[93] A president who claims to have no choice but to detain indefinitely terrorist suspects, or who claims that circumstances compel his choices, would likewise seem to be subject to necessity. And in being subject to necessity, a president would disclaim responsibility for choosing, because no choice was possible.

In this way necessity also relates to political responsibility, not just for the security government is obliged to provide but for the framework in which events might appear as having the character of necessity. Because necessitous men are not free, paradoxically we are faced with a dilemma. Necessitous dictators would also be unfree. To embrace necessity is to admit to a lack of governing vitality, to be subject to the caprice of "accident and force," in Hamilton's words, or "Accidents and Necessities," in Locke's. But to admit choice is to become responsible, possibly for illegality. Inverting John Yoo's claim that the "Founders entrusted the President with the primary responsibility, and therefore the power," the appeal to necessity asserts the power to act without taking responsibility.[94] The executive would plead, "I had no choice but to act. Circumstances dictated my choice of action." Tyranny of circumstance would undermine all governing freedom. Roosevelt's solution—reliance on recommitment to constitutional ideals and forms—would equally apply here. If "necessitous" presidents are unfree, then we avoid the "stuff out of which dictatorship is made" by adhering to the constitutional constraints and values that constitute our normative order.

Because a president gains statutory and discretionary power during emergencies, there is a real temptation for a president to choose to govern in crisis mode as much as possible—a dynamic that the practical or theoretical availability of a "constitutional dictatorship" would amplify. What constitutes a crisis warranting urgent attention does not come already defined by the nature of things. Crises require articulation within a governing practice. Floods are emergencies that create policy priorities, for example, but not existential threats requiring a "constitutional dictatorship." No doubt, events like September 11 are clearly emergencies requiring attention, but the force, scale, and meaning of the crisis awaits articulation. People look to the president to shape what may be a traumatic narrative, explaining what has happened and what the response shall be. For example, President G. W. Bush addressed the nation after September 11: "This is not, however, just America's fight. And what is at stake is not just America's freedom. This is the world's fight. This is civilization's fight. This is the fight of all who believe in progress and pluralism, tolerance and freedom."[95] That we are engaged in an ongoing fight for civilization where freedom is at stake not only for the United States but for the world is not self-evident from the events alone. This narrative required an author. The new edition of Rossiter's *Constitutional Dictatorship*, reissued in paperback in 2002, features a picture of the twin towers ablaze with an image of the Constitution obscured in the background. The narrative meaning and implications of the crisis must be created, and the cover illustration could not be clearer in its representation that the events of September 11 supersede constitutional commitments. The overlay obscures how "emergency" becomes more malleable the more a polity embeds a conception of presidential prerogative or "constitutional dictatorship." Rather than a descriptive claim that constitutions fail to apply in exceptional circumstances, "constitutional dictatorship" embraces an unwarranted normative position that constitutions should not apply.

Because "emergency" has a contingent relation to emergency powers, presidents are able to exploit the political ambiguity between "emergency" as existential threat and "emergency" as policy priority to bypass deliberative processes. The president must act—he has no choice but to respond to the exigent circumstances. Bruce Ackerman calls this "government by emergency," and sees this trend toward unilateral presidential practice as a democratic pathology.[96] It is pathological to democratic practice because it substitutes unilateral decision processes for the reflective deliberative practices proper to governing through "reflection and choice." Government by emergency is more likely to rely on decisions made with asserted pressing urgency and without institutional or wider democratic deliberation.[97] If in the wake of pressing emergencies, as we have seen, there is no return to the "normal," then lasting legal changes can occur outside of deliberative processes.

Urgency undermines deliberation. Unilateral discretion exercised outside of emergency preparedness eschews deliberation as well. Such decisions have a greater likelihood of error. Social cascades might develop in which early decision-makers are given deferential ratification by later actors, entrenching a position that might have begun in error. Group polarization can result when executive officials all think alike and reinforce each other, without adequate critical input. These and other rationality failures become possible when the executive branch relies on its own insularity to make decisions in haste.[98]

We have seen the problems urgency presents to deliberative rationality in other national security contexts during the First World War and beyond, for example, with results that were for many years constitutionally deficient. In order to assure uninhibited conscription and to minimize opposition to the war effort, Congress passed the Espionage Act of 1917 and the Sedition Act of 1918, curtailing speech to promote national unity in the name of security. A series of Supreme Court cases, authored by Justice Holmes, acknowledged the temporal and security needs while downplaying the interests of personal liberty. Revolutionary fervor evoked images of rapidly developing situations for which to wait to act could be too late to act: "A single revolutionary spark may kindle a fire that, smoldering for a time, may burst into a sweeping and destructive conflagration."[99] Or, as the Court understood the right to speak during the second "red scare": "Obviously, the words cannot mean that before the Government may act, it must wait until the putsch is about to be executed, the plans have been laid and the signal is awaited."[100] States of emergency call for swift action, not reflective delay. Eventually the Court came to realize that the antidote for dangerous ideas is more speech, not censorship—that is, "reflection and choice," not "accident and force."[101] But more speech takes time, it requires reflection within the "marketplace of ideas," and choice among contending viewpoints. Governing by emergency does not take time. Governing in the shadow of emergency also has effects within the overall constitutional culture, reflected in how rights such as those to free speech might function.

If, as we have already seen, the right to security has a certain kind of priority in our thinking and in our governing practices (because one cannot enjoy other rights without security), it does not follow that the exercise of other rights does not have effects on what constitutes security. A right to free speech helps create a political climate in which the ambiguity of "emergency" will be manifest in ways different than in a political context lacking robust public deliberation. In light of the ambiguity of the status of emergency and security, it is not enough simply to say that necessity gives priority to security without acknowledging that the means of addressing interruptive emergency events are already conditioned by prior decisions to govern within constitutional principles and constraints. Talk of "constitutional dictatorship" obscures these complexities.

Whether described as a "constitutional dictatorship" or a sovereign prerogative power located in "he who decides on the exception," the relationship between necessity and the liberty of choice and reflection is one that brings us back both to constitutive beginnings (How do we address natural necessity to constitute a polity, and what will the character of that polity be?) and to sustaining commitments (How do we reconcile new claims of national necessity with our constitutive comments within a practice of constitutionalism?). In neither case do we enter a space devoid of constitutive values and principles that can guide and constrain our choices. No decisions occur outside a normative order. The Schmittian challenge we have been considering was that interruptions to a constitutional order would reveal its emptiness, for it would be unable to govern during emergencies, relying instead on presidential prerogative or "constitutional dictatorship." What we have found instead is that a conception of "dictatorship" is not only antithetical to processes of "reflection and choice" that define American constitutionalism's aspirations to "good government," but it is also internally incoherent. Its many shortcomings demonstrate the impossibility of "constitutional dictatorship" within American constitutionalism.

Conclusion

John Yoo and others tracing a genealogy of prerogative powers to Locke or Hamilton's contributions to the *Federalist Papers* are quick to seize on the language of exception and empowerment. Sources of power to raise revenues discussed by Hamilton in *Federalist* 36 become justification for emergency power generally, as Yoo quotes: "There are certain emergencies of nations in which expedients that in the ordinary state of things ought to be forborne become essential to the public weal. And the government, from the possibility of such emergencies, ought ever to have the option of making use of them."[102] What "ought to be forborne" or not is a question of priorities within existing governing structures, and the "emergencies" at issue might occasion use of enumerated powers to raise revenues, but it is not a question of exception. But to determine what "ought to be forborne" requires reason and reflection, a matter of deliberation over the common weal. Yoo is quick to trace a genealogy to purported sources justifying "assumed" and unenumerated powers but is blind to the existence of accompanying responsibilities for reflection and choice in the same genealogy.

It is difficult to prescribe generally about particular circumstances, which is what creates the possibility of emergency government in the first place. The French philosopher Jean-Jacques Rousseau, for example, recognized this, writing, "A thousand cases can arise for which the Law-giver did not provide, and it is a very necessary foresight to sense that one cannot foresee everything."[103] Hamilton elaborates on this problem, claiming that particular national powers "ought to exist without limitation, because it is impossible to foresee or define the extent and variety of national exigencies, or the correspondent extent and variety of the means which may be necessary to satisfy them."[104] What follows from the impossibility of foresight is a key question. In choosing to establish a constitutional government through "reflection and choice," the polity makes a commitment to acting within prescribed limited powers and with respect to the civil and political rights of others even when addressing future contingencies we cannot foresee.

In the end, as we see from Arendt and Roosevelt, natural necessity always lingers in the background, and, as made more salient in theory and practice after September 11, emergency can always interrupt the flow of ordinary politics. What happens next depends not only on institutional ordering but also on constitutional commitments and the values and virtues they reflect. Our response to emergency depends on political attitudes— our relationships with each other, our institutional organization, our constitutive commitments. Because our political reality is contingent, we are always vulnerable to the historical dependency of the political constitution of "We the People." "We" can change who we are through what we do. In theory and practice, history gives us ample warning that necessity will reappear in the future. Hannah Arendt sums up a response: "Man cannot be free if he does not know that he is subject to necessity, because his freedom is always won in his never wholly successful attempts to liberate himself from necessity."[105] Knowing that we are subject to necessity requires our commitment to "reflection and choice" not only in founding principles and institutions but in continuing practices of constitutional governance. Knowing that we are bound by necessity allows us to seek our freedom through constitutional forms and practices.

2

Constitutionalizing Necessity
Through Suspension

ABRAHAM LINCOLN RAISED A DRAMATIC QUESTION about suspending habeas corpus at a time when Southern secessionists had split the nation apart and "[t]he whole of the laws which were required to be faithfully executed were being resisted and failing of execution in nearly one-third of the States." He asked, "Must they be allowed to finally fail of execution, even had it been perfectly clear, that by the use of the means necessary to their execution, some single law, made in such extreme tenderness of the citizen's liberty . . . should, to a very limited extent, be violated?"[1] Lincoln's question encapsulates a central problem of constitutional governance. On the one hand, governing officials derive their authority to act from a constitution that simultaneously empowers and constrains. Empowered officials must decide how to prioritize and organize a complex legal web within a constitutional structure that itself limits what can be done. Constrained officials must govern within structural and principled limits in order to preserve the constitutional order no matter the pressing, sometimes vexed, situations requiring public action. Yet, on the other hand, circumstances may sometimes require decisive action that exceeds both enumerated powers and settled constraints. The complex legal web might lead to ruptures and discord in ways that make consistent execution of all the laws, and respect for principled limitations, no longer possible. Governing form and function may sometimes fail to fit emerging crises. Preserving the whole, Lincoln suggests, might require violating the one, or the few, specific laws. But the real emphasis is on the converse—that it may be necessary to violate some law or laws to preserve the whole. Explaining his actions to Congress months later, Lincoln asserted that his choices, "whether strictly legal or not, were ventured upon under what appeared to be a popular demand, and a public necessity; trusting, then as now, that Congress would readily ratify them."[2] Whether "strictly legal," Lincoln found another source of authority in "public necessity," suggesting that circumstance can be met and justified by necessity, even when law runs out.

The questions Lincoln raised go beyond the ones we encountered in the first chapter. Our primary concern there was with the argument that constitutional systems are incapable of governing according to law during emergencies. The weakness of this criticism, as I argued, is that it contains a false view of the relation between governing form and function, thinking that political decisions during emergencies must arise from outside the constraints of a constitutional order. The idea that a constitution could be suspended in order to preserve it proved unavailing. Preserving presidential prerogative might be a tempting idea, but it is a dangerously misleading one that flirts with normalizing an idea of "constitutional dictatorship" that would undermine the foundational commitment to "good government" justified through "reflection and choice." Even though we seek security against the forces of natural necessity only to be subject to episodic emergencies that challenge constitutional governance, we remain free only by seeking to overcome the necessity that would bind us to circumstance. Rather than appeal to political theory, an alternative step is to look internally at how the Constitution provides its own means for resolving crises. Lincoln sought to justify emergency action, not on the basis of prepolitical prerogative, but upon a principle of "public necessity," bound within a constitutional structure of public justification, which Congress had the authority to constrain. With this example, our attention is drawn away from the challenges of political theory toward the more particular issues that arise within American constitutionalism.

As we saw in the previous chapter, what makes the appeal to prerogative so tempting is that it would give priority to a different kind of commitment—a prepolitical, or at least preconstitutional commitment, to self-preservation. Political theorists such as Thomas Hobbes emphasized the role that fear plays in organizing commitments to governing powers and institutions that promise security and stability.[3] In order to alleviate fears about self-preservation and therefore about security, the individual gives up liberty to the sovereign who possesses the power to do whatever is necessary to provide that security. This prepolitical form of commitment, however, is merely another way of articulating the tension between necessity and constitutional commitment. For the necessity of survival and security pulls against the formal constraints law places on the appropriate actions that may be taken on its behalf. The state grounded on an individual fear of self-preservation merely politicizes this tension between necessity and law without resolving it. Appeal to prerogative as the sovereign power to decide without constraints does not explain how and when legal and constitutive commitments might otherwise function.

"Public necessity" attempts to be both prior to and constitutive of political actors and communities, creating confusion over the source and scope of its authority. It claims to be both required on behalf of the "public" and justified by prepolitical prerogative. But even if necessity claims cannot properly invoke residual prerogative powers to consider the consequences of actions for national security without regard to other constitutional limitations, then many questions arise over how necessity works within, or in relation to, constitutional forms and practices.

Lincoln's questions draw us deeper into issues of constitutional governance within the American system. Closer examination of the structure of Lincoln's appeal to "public necessity" as a source of governing authority reveals the tension that exists between constitutional commitments and claims of necessity. Commitment is a precondition for constitutionalism. A constitution is nothing more than a "parchment barrier" without the political and moral commitments that give it meaning within the political lives of citizens and officials alike. For James Madison, who introduced "parchment barrier" into the American constitutional lexicon, the worry was that commitments needed institutional embodiment in ways that tied individuals to offices that could check and balance the concentration of power.[4] Constitutional commitments, whether to office or principle, require participation in a practice of justifying and conceptualizing the framework of governance through a foundational, albeit contingent, assignment of powers and constraints. Even though we begin a discussion about American constitutionalism with our written Constitution and a series of framework statutes that define many of the basic features of American governing practice, both the present and future of American constitutionalism are grounded on governing commitments to procedural and substantive principles.

This chapter begins our exploration of the ways that American constitutionalism internalizes necessity. If we reject the idea that emergencies invite a "constitutional dictatorship" that suspends, in the name of preserving, a constitution, is there some functionally similar provision embedded in the U.S. Constitution? The first place to look is the Suspension Clause, which provides, "The Privilege of the Writ of Habeas Corpus shall not be suspended, unless when in Cases of Rebellion or Invasion the public Safety may require it."[5] Because the writ of habeas corpus is a guarantee against arbitrary and cruel detention, it is a fundamentally important constraint on executive power. With the writ, courts can check executive power, requiring that arrests and detentions be made in strict accordance with the law. Contemplating its suspension invites emergency government. In this chapter, I explore how the U.S. Constitution's Suspension Clause and the U.S. government's post–September 11 detention policy seem to exemplify the possibility of a power akin to prerogative—that constitutionalism internally fails to tame claims that necessity requires responses unmoored from constraining norms and principles. Even if there is no broad prerogative power, the existence of the Suspension Clause, combined with the precedent of President Lincoln's unilateral suspension of habeas corpus, might appear to be a way of internalizing prerogative and thereby legitimizing actions justified by appeal to necessity. On closer inspection, however, we see how American constitutionalism constrains the availability and salience of claims to a prerogative power nominally justified by the Constitution. In response to necessity, deviant practices will remain possible. The task is therefore to confine them within constitutional justificatory frameworks while acknowledging an unavoidable contingency born of the background attitudes and priorities that shared social imaginaries make salient.

Necessity Inside the Constitution:
The Suspension-Clause Challenge

In the circumstances Lincoln faced, "public necessity" led to his suspending the writ of habeas corpus in some jurisdictions. Southern rebellion provided the substantive trigger for suspending habeas, but the Constitution is ambiguous regarding whether Congress or the president has authority to invoke the clause. It simply states the conditions under which it is permissible to "suspend" the writ. Relying on his own authority to confront the growing crisis of Southern militarism, Lincoln determined that he could exercise the constitutional power to suspend the writ. Lincoln's appeal to "public necessity," combined with a case of rebellion threatening "public Safety," also functioned as a claim about emergency, about the exigencies of the situation. It posits a type of threat, one that we can call "existential," because the "whole of the laws" might fail to be executed because of an "attempt to destroy the Federal Union," the prevention of which requires that "a choice of means to that end became indispensable."[6] Pressing the justification of "public necessity," Lincoln asked, "Must a government of necessity be too strong for the liberties of its own people, or too weak to maintain its own existence?"[7]

In justifying his actions in private correspondence, Lincoln appealed to "indispensable necessity" under which "measures, otherwise unconstitutional, might become lawful, by becoming indispensable to the preservation of the constitution, through preservation of the nation."[8] His attorney general, Edward Bates, provided a justification in light of the necessity of the situation Lincoln faced, which reasoned, "In such a state of things, the President must, of necessity, be the sole judge, both of the exigency which requires him to act, and of the manner in which it is most prudent for him to deploy the powers entrusted to him, to enable him to discharge his constitutional and legal duty—that is, to suppress the insurrection and execute the laws."[9]

To suspend the writ of habeas corpus is no small matter. Tracing its lineage back to the Magna Carta in 1215, habeas corpus has a long tradition of protecting against arbitrary arrest and detention, playing a central role as the "bulwark of our liberties," according to William Blackstone.[10] It enforces a legal norm of separated powers with a judicial check against unwarranted and arbitrary deprivations of a person's liberties. In this way, it is a core value of due process of law.[11] Without the legal obligation to produce the body of the detainee before a court, executive actions risk the prospect of abuse and tyranny. The power to suspend the very legal obligation that checks against its abuse is a potentially dangerous power. As Attorney General Bates admitted, "This is a great power . . . said to be dangerous in the hands of an ambitious and wicked President, because he may use it for the purposes of oppression and tyranny. . . . Still it is a power necessary to the peace and safety of the country."[12] Regarding this point, Chief Justice Taney was surely right in *Ex parte Merryman* to be concerned that if the power to suspend habeas did not reside in Congress, it would be difficult to avoid the prospect of self-serving justifications about what was necessary. Lincoln's actions, however, fulfill a constitutional obligation that mitigates this concern: he publicly justified his decision to suspend habeas. Suspension was necessary, he argued, so that he could be temporarily relieved from the burdens of judicial oversight concerning the legal basis for each individual act of detention in light of the conditions of "rebellion or invasion" that persisted.

Suspension is also a limited-occasion power. It can only be invoked in cases of "rebellion or invasion," even if the parameters of what counts remain subject to interpretation and circumstance. Lincoln's suspensions did not go without political opposition. In a June 1863 letter written to Erastus Corning in response to public resolutions criticizing him for unconstitutional deprivations of civil liberties, Lincoln argued first that "suspension is allowed by the constitution on purpose that, men may be arrested and held, who can not be proved to be guilty of defined crime."[13] And second, the necessary and limited triggering conditions precisely represented "our present case—a case of Rebellion, wherein the public Safety does require the suspension." Because this letter was in part a justification for arresting an Ohio politician, Clement Vallandigham, Lincoln articulated reasons why "public Safety" required preventing the extension of the rebellion by individuals "warring upon the military." He further explained that an implication of the Suspension Clause is "that the Constitution is not, in its application, in all respects the same, in cases of rebellion or invasion involving the public safety, as it is in time of profound peace and public security."[14] With such justifications, Lincoln does not make broad arguments about internal principles of necessity no matter the kind of exigency. Rather, he justifies a particular constitutional power (the power to make arrests free from judicial oversight by suspending the writ of habeas corpus, ambiguously assigned as it is) exercised in a particular kind of circumstance ("rebellion or invasion") against particular individuals (those "warring" against the Union).

In *Ex parte Milligan,* a case immediately following the Civil War, the Supreme Court articulated the logic of the power to suspend the writ as follows:

> In the emergency of the times, an immediate public investigation according to law may not be possible; and yet, the peril to the country may be too imminent to suffer such persons to go at large. Unquestionably, there is then an exigency which demands that the government, if it should see fit in the exercise of a proper discretion to make arrests, should not be required to produce the persons arrested in answer to a writ of Habeas Corpus.[15]

Though it is important to add that the Court also explained that "the theory of necessity on which it is based is false; for the government, within the Constitution, has all the powers granted to it, which are necessary to preserve its existence."[16]

Suspension responds to the immediacy of circumstances and the practicalities of security when dangerous persons remain at large. In his letter to Erastus Corning, Lincoln hypothesized that it was within the power of the government, once the war began, to detain generals such as Robert E. Lee now occupying "the very highest places in the rebel war service" who were known at the time to be traitors. "Unquestionably if we had seized and held them, the insurgent cause would be much weaker."[17]

Lincoln's authority to suspend habeas corpus was, and is, much in doubt—not because of any general political theory, but because the clause is located in Article I, which is largely devoted to enumerating the powers of Congress. When ordering suspension, Lincoln could stand on firm ground in asserting a "rebellion or invasion" was at hand imperiling public safety, but he could do no more than assume a power the text failed to assign. Who has the power to suspend the "Great Writ"? The Constitution does not say, though one might reasonably infer it is a power assigned to Congress given the Suspension Clause's placement in Section 9 of Article I, among other provisions limiting Congress's powers. For example, Section 9 disables Congress from prohibiting the slave trade until 1808, and forbids Congress from making ex post facto laws or granting titles of nobility. Indeed, Chief Justice Taney made this inference in 1861, reasoning in *Ex parte Merryman* that the clause assigns Congress, not the president, power to suspend habeas corpus. Such a striking rebuke of the president's assumed powers had no immediate effect, because Lincoln ignored the ruling. But in his July 4, 1861, message to Congress, Lincoln provided a constitutional argument to justify his actions: "But the Constitution itself is silent as to which, or who, is to exercise the power; and as the provision was plainly made for a dangerous emergency, it cannot be believed the framers of the instrument intended that in every case the danger should run its course until Congress could be called together."[18] The public necessity that a dangerous emergency creates, according to Lincoln, justified constitutional deviation from the Constitution's silence regarding the precise question of who has the power of suspension.

Lincoln had authorized military detention of persons such as Lieutenant John Merryman on the grounds that such action was a "public necessity" in light of the threat to the Union's security. Merryman was accused of acting on behalf of the Confederate cause in Maryland at a time when it was possible that Washington, D.C., could be cut off from the rest of the Union. After declaring martial law in Maryland, President Lincoln also authorized the suspension of habeas corpus because of continued local resistance. Merryman was arrested for his activities on behalf of the Confederacy and sought the protection of the writ before Chief Justice Taney sitting on the circuit court.[19] General Cadwalader, who held Merryman, answered that the president had authorized suspension of the writ of habeas corpus "for the public safety." In response to Cadwalader's refusal to produce Merryman before the court, Chief Justice Taney's opinion struck high notes regarding the writ's role in protecting liberty, the danger of the president assuming both legislative and judicial powers denied to the English Crown, and the resulting failure of the rule of law over the rule of executive officers. Taney explicitly rejected the verity of arguments "drawn from the nature of sovereignty, or the necessity of government, for self-defence in times of tumult and danger" to justify the president's unilateral suspension of habeas.[20] Necessity, on Taney's account, does not justify extralegal deviation from established constitutional forms. These forms required a legislative suspension of habeas, not an executive proclamation.

We need not resolve the controversy over who has the power to suspend the writ to see that the formalities of constitutional governance can be challenged by the necessities of circumstance. Congress was not in session, and the president needed to act. "Public necessity," as Lincoln called it, took priority over the strictly legal. Lincoln's attorney general, Edward Bates, issued an opinion arguing that the president has the power of suspension, for it "undeniably belongs to the Government, and therefore must be exercised by some department or officer thereof."[21] Because the president has the responsibility to lead the effort to "put down the insurrection," Bates argued, he is a constitutional officer authorized to make warrantless arrests and to suspend judicial review of them.[22] Such an argument, however, ignores the placement of the Suspension Clause in Article I, which is focused on congressional powers, and thus where it might more naturally be read to empower Congress.

Nonetheless, Lincoln did not ignore the Constitution altogether. Nor did he ignore the obligation of public justification. He went before Congress and provided constitutional and practical arguments to justify actions already taken. He submitted to Congress's "better judgment" the question "whether there shall be any legislation on this subject."[23] Congress eventually obliged, providing legislation to authorize suspension. As a minimal, but important, point to observe, even where one aspect of constitutional structure might be temporarily displaced, such as who has power to suspend habeas corpus, others remain in operation—congressional oversight of executive action and the obligations of public justification.

If suspension is a limited-occasion power, its scope is of more contested breadth. The power to suspend the writ is at minimum the power to avoid judicial review of decisions to arrest and detain individuals, eliminating the principal due-process check on discretionary executive authority—at least for a time. Debate exists, in the absence of an authoritative Supreme Court ruling, as to whether the suspension power might extend much further. On the expansive view, the suspension power authorizes the president to arrest and detain individuals when it would otherwise be illegal to do so.[24] Because the *remedy* of habeas corpus is removed, the *rights* the writ protects are suspended as well. Because of the extraordinary power suspension entails, Blackstone admonishes that "this experiment ought only to be tried in cases of extreme emergency; and in these the nation parts with its liberty for a while, in order to preserve it forever."[25] On this view, when circumstances make suspension of the writ an absolute necessity, the president can arrest and detain persons on mere suspicion, holding them for a limited period without indictment, trial, or access to judicial review. But even on the expansive view, the suspension power is confined by law and circumstance. All other rights and powers unrelated to arrest and detention remain unchanged. A detainee, for example, may not be subjected to torture.[26]

As the core value of due process, habeas corpus might have a more robust substantive meaning. On the narrow view of the Suspension Clause, executive officials are relieved of the burden of justifying their arrest and detention practices before a judge but remain bound by their oath to support all other constitutional rights and values.[27] What they could not do under the Constitution before suspension, they may not do after. Executive officials are merely insulated from the immediate pressures of litigation and accountability, and if Congress so desires, it can immunize them from liability later. But neither the president nor Congress may invoke the Suspension Clause to suspend other constitutional obligations and constraints. Arrest and detention, though not reviewable in court, must nonetheless satisfy legal criteria and do not authorize other unlawful actions. As a result, the executive must take responsibility for upholding the core habeas value by providing due process of law, even in the absence of an external institutional check.

As the Supreme Court reasoned in a later case involving preventative detention by a state governor during an insurrection in Colorado as authorized by statute, if use of deadly force is authorized to contest armed insurrection, then the lesser use of force entailed by detention is all the more justified. Justice Holmes reasoned for the Court, "When it comes to a decision by the head of the state upon a matter involving its life, the ordinary rights of individuals must yield to what he deems the necessities of the moment. Public danger warrants the substitution of executive process for judicial process."[28] Appealing to a seemingly broader principle of necessity, Holmes suggested that "what is due process of law depends on circumstances. It varies with the subject matter and the necessities of the situation."[29] Read for all it is worth, such a statement of constitutional principle could imply that necessity is its own authorization for executive action responding to circumstances. But relevant features of the circumstances in this case are both the presumed existence of state constitutional authorization for the governor's action as well as the federal Militia Acts, which authorized calling forth the militia to suppress insurrection and, by implication, to detain those standing in the way of restoring peace.[30] If we view Lincoln's actions through the lens of statutory authorization as well as Holmes's reasoning, then it follows that although motivated by "public necessity," they also hewed closely to explicit legal justifications, and congressionally delegated powers, rather than amorphous appeals to naked principles of necessity.

On either view regarding the power's scope, a primary purpose of suspending habeas corpus is to loosen the immediate restraints on executive action during times of particularly acute crisis. The Civil War provided such a case of rebellion and dire national crisis.[31] Even under tremendous public necessity, President Lincoln and Congress worked together to establish the legality and limits of the president's arrests and detentions, and the Court was willing to establish further constraints on continued detention and use of military commissions against individuals such as Lambdin Milligan. Past practice and current understandings demonstrate how partial—though momentous—the decision to suspend the writ is.[32] Necessity does not foreclose the "reflection and choice" that allows for adopting flexible legal forms to meet pressing public necessity. Lincoln's precedent illustrates the appeal to legal and practical arguments that justify the deviations he claimed "public necessity" required. Claims about necessity are channeled through arguments about constitutional text, structure, and practice and do not appear as claims about prerogative triggered by circumstances said to require constitutional forbearance.

Precedential Use

It is important to be clear what precedent Lincoln's actions and their justifications might plausibly set. Does internalizing necessity through the Suspension Clause provide a way to justify a form of unfettered executive prerogative? Is "public necessity" combined with the power to suspend habeas a way out of constitutional constraints? This issue is pressing going forward, because Lincoln's precedent is used by some scholars and presidential administrations to justify claims to extraordinary executive power. Seeing in his actions a "historical gloss" that constitutionally justifies giving priority to "public necessity" over constitutive commitments and constraints to principles other than security, advocates of unbounded presidential power appeal to Lincoln's resolve.

Yet Lincoln did not propose complete suspension of the constitutional order, despite the existential threat to the perpetual union that Southern succession presented. But he did appeal to necessity as a justification for significant constitutional deviation in taking actions without prior congressional authorization and in suspending habeas corpus. Systemic suspension is not a viable way to think about constitutional orders, even for Lincoln. "Constitutional dictatorship" is not a viable conceptual option. As we saw in chapter 1, it is difficult to make sense of such a situation ungoverned by any norms applicable from everyday life—legal or otherwise. Where specific rules give way to action judged necessary, other rules and norms must remain in place, for one cannot choose to act ex nihilo, as if from a moral and legal view from nowhere. And Lincoln's precedent does not serve as grounds for such complete suspension. Lincoln did not act irrespective of law but instead provided post hoc justifications for actions that were not "strictly legal" by appealing to "public necessity." But this appeal to "public necessity" was also a constitutional appeal.

Lincoln's example demonstrates how constitutionalism normalizes claims of necessity by placing them within justificatory frameworks in which they play a role in both directing and assessing the legality of governing practices. Constitutionalism overcomes necessity by establishing means for addressing the underlying circumstances appropriate to the constitutional order, thereby guiding and constraining both the understanding of what is at stake and the availability of particular responses. The means established, like the arguments Lincoln presented in his defense, cohere with other relevant constitutional principles while minimizing disruption to the normal constitutional order. If deviation is unavoidable, along with the risk of altering baseline constitutional attitudes, commitments, and practices, then actions must be both reflectively chosen and publicly justified. The availability of habeas establishes a normative constitutional order that ensures the availability of judicial review of executive detentions as a way of checking against tyrannical abuse. Necessity, however, does not justify stepping outside of processes of constitutional decision-making. Necessity is at home within constitutionalism.

The problem with using the Lincoln precedent as a basis for defending a general principle that the Constitution can be suspended by executive decree when public necessity requires it is that constitutional constraints exist to solve the temporal problem of passion, not to license unreflective decision-making.[33] Lincoln's precedent provides a model of public reason-giving that justifies the chosen constitutional deviation in terms recognizable within the grammar of constitutional discourse. He provides more than conclusory statements about how the president's powers and responsibilities justify constitutional deviance. He argued in terms of constitutional theory applied to the exigencies of his circumstances. Because other responses were, and are, possible, liberal constitutionalists face a continuing contingency in the choice and application of constitutional theory and practice.

The Supreme Court also stood ready to check the president's power to suspend habeas in locations, such as Indiana, where rebellion was not at issue, admonishing that "troublous times would arise when rulers and people would become restive under restraint, and seek by sharp and decisive measures to accomplish ends deemed just and proper, and that the principles of constitutional liberty would be in peril unless established by irrepealable law."[34] Despite the executive's appeal to a "theory of necessity," the Court reasoned that "The Constitution of the United States is a law for rulers and people, equally in war and in peace, and covers with the shield of its protection all classes of men, at all times and under all circumstances."[35] In this way, Lincoln's precedent must also include what the Supreme Court said of its limits and of the limits placed on the theory of necessity said to justify unilateral and unfettered claims to executive power.

Lincoln's precedent should be confined to Lincoln's precise circumstances. Lincoln engaged interbranch dialogue, not secret decision-making. Although the president was the first mover, he did not have the last say. And even though Lincoln admitted to Congress that his actions were not "strictly legal," he justified them by appeal to the particularity of the situation he faced and to their consistency with the spirit of the laws more broadly. Saving the Union was a unique situation. Adhering to the body of laws while deviating from exclusive congressional authority to suspend habeas was not an example of using a pervasive prerogative power to do whatever was said to be necessary. Nor is it a complete suspension of the legal order. Suspension is one way—an extraordinary one—to internalize necessity within the Constitution.

Can We Switch the Constitution On and Off?

One power that the Suspension Clause authorizes is detention outside of normal judicial checks. Might there be other occasions, short of suspension, when a president would be authorized to detain individuals on a claim of "public necessity," free from judicial oversight? In his "Military Order of November 13, 2001," authorizing detention of any noncitizen whom the president concludes is a terrorist, President G. W. Bush personally "determined that an extraordinary emergency exists for national defense purposes, that this emergency constitutes an urgent and compelling government interest, and that issuance of this order is necessary to meet the emergency."[36] Claiming that his actions were necessary under the circumstances, President Bush further determined that these terrorism detainees could be held at the U.S. naval base at Guantánamo Bay, Cuba, outside the reach of any Article III court. Department of Justice (DOJ) lawyers justified this conclusion, reasoning that Guantánamo lies outside the territorial extension of habeas jurisdiction, and further asserted that any doubt about the detainee's status should be resolved by deference "to the executive branch's activities and decisions."[37] If courts lack jurisdiction to hear habeas petitions from Guantánamo Bay, then executive officials could face no other institutional restraint on their decisions about whom to detain and how to treat them.

President Bush's November 13 military order also declared that detainees would be prohibited from seeking judicial remedies in U.S. courts or in international tribunals. What is more, the president determined that al-Qaeda and Taliban detainees were not protected by the Third Geneva Convention because they were not parties to the convention, nor did they fall within the class of persons it protects.[38] Thus, no substantive constraints applied to the president's authority. In this context, the White House counsel notoriously referred to protections of the Geneva Conventions as "quaint."[39] Appearing before the Supreme Court to defend these views, the Bush administration argued that even if federal courts had jurisdiction over Guantánamo detainees, they lacked any legal basis for interfering with executive authority to declare individuals unlawful enemy combatants and detain them for the indefinite duration of hostilities. As the government argued, "A commander's wartime determination that an individual is an enemy combatant is a quintessentially military judgment, representing a core exercise of the Commander-in-Chief authority."[40] As a result, the Bush administration urged that the "customary deference that courts afford the Executive in matters of military affairs is especially warranted in this context."[41] Moreover, John Yoo wrote an internal memo for the DOJ arguing that "The President's power to detain enemy combatants, including U.S. citizens, arises out of his constitutional authority as Commander in Chief. . . . Congress lacks authority under Article I to set the terms and conditions under which the President may exercise his authority as Commander in Chief to control the conduct of military operations during the course of a campaign."[42] In the Bush administration's view, the president had plenary detention authority, unchecked by courts or Congress to detain individuals, including U.S. citizens, whom the president designated as unlawful enemy combatants.[43]

By 2004 the Supreme Court began considering the legality of the Bush administration's detention policies. Relying on Supreme Court precedent from a World War II–era case, *Johnson v. Eisentrager*, involving German soldiers detained abroad, the government argued that courts lacked jurisdiction to consider any claims made by aliens detained pursuant to the president's war powers who are held at Guantánamo Bay, which is outside the sovereign territory of the United States.[44] One implication of this reasoning was that no court—Cuban or American—had jurisdiction. This fact, indeed, was its very charm from the administration's perspective. It was also part of its downfall. The Supreme Court rejected the government's reasoning in *Rasul v. Bush*, holding that "the federal courts have jurisdiction to determine the legality of the Executive's potentially indefinite detention of individuals who claim to be wholly innocent of wrongdoing."[45] For the other consequence of the government's position was that the government asserted authority to hold those it detained indefinitely without any judicial review of its determination.

Once the Supreme Court established jurisdiction to hear claims from Guantánamo Bay detainees, the next question became: Were there limitations on the president's power to detain persons he declared to be unlawful enemy combatants? In *Hamdi v. Rumsfeld,* the Supreme Court answered affirmatively, holding it to be necessary that "a citizen held in the United States as an enemy combatant be given a meaningful opportunity to contest the factual basis for that detention before a neutral decisionmaker."[46] Finding statutory authorization for the president's assertion of power to detain persons like Yasser Hamdi who were captured on the battlefield in Afghanistan, the Court did not affirm the broader claims to unchecked unilateral executive power to detain individuals deemed unlawful enemy combatants. A plurality of the Court found convincing the claim that Congress had authorized detention of persons captured on the battlefield when it passed the Authorization to Use Military Force (AUMF) against those persons, nations, or organizations that played a role in the attacks of September 11.[47]

But the plurality also made clear that unilateral executive power has limits, even in times of purported military emergency. "Whatever power the United States Constitution envisions for the Executive in its exchanges with other nations or with enemy organizations in times of conflict, it most assuredly envisions a role for all three branches when individual liberties are at stake."[48] Moreover, the Court emphasized that "[w]e have long since made clear that a state of war is not a blank check for the President when it comes to the rights of the Nation's citizens."[49] The Court provided the check's value: the executive must afford detainees minimal due process, guaranteed by the Constitution's Fifth Amendment, to contest their statuses as enemy combatants. The Court was careful not to draw too heavily on the executive's accounts, claiming that due process requires some independent appraisal, even if the evidentiary burdens and processes required fall far short of regular trial procedures. As a result, the administration established Combat Status Review Tribunals to review the case of each detainee and to grant them a forum to contest their status with the assistance of counsel. Illustrative of the contrast between the assertion of unilateral unreviewable authority and the nature of the evidence justifying detention,

Hamdi was released shortly after the Supreme Court decision in his favor in 2004, on condition that he renounce his U.S. citizenship.

War criminals require prosecutions. Proceeding on his own commander-in-chief power supplemented by Congress's AUMF of September 2001, President Bush's November 13 military order also established military commissions to try unlawful enemy combatants. In *Hamdan v. Rumsfeld* the Supreme Court recognized that Congress had granted the president power to establish military commissions through statutes establishing the Uniform Code of Military Justice. This power came with limitations, however. The Court held that the Geneva Conventions applied to the Taliban and al-Qaeda detainees whom the administration held at Guantánamo. According to the convention, rules for courts-martial and rules applicable in military commissions must be "uniform insofar as practicable." The military commissions President Bush established deviated from courts-martial in significant evidentiary and other procedural processes. Moreover, military commissions must also comply with the laws of war, which include the treaty obligations imposed by the Geneva Conventions. A key provision of Common Article 3 of the Conventions is that trials of detainees must be held before "a regularly constituted court affording all the judicial guarantees which are recognized as indispensable by civilized peoples."[50] The government could not plausibly argue that the president's military commissions either were uniform with courts-martial or were sufficiently similar to regularly constituted courts for purposes of Common Article 3. Thus, the Court concluded that the president exceeded his power in establishing military commissions inconsistent with the requirements of federal statutes and the Geneva Conventions.

Although constitutionally protected, the writ of habeas corpus is also subject to congressional authority over federal court jurisdiction. Because in *Rasul* the Supreme Court relied on the congressional habeas corpus statute to claim jurisdiction over Guantánamo detainees, Congress also attempted to facilitate executive power by depriving federal courts of jurisdiction to hear cases brought by Guantánamo detainees. When the Court held in *Hamdan v. Rumsfeld* that the Detainee Treatment Act (DTA) did not deprive federal courts of jurisdiction over pending litigation because it did not provide a clear statement of congressional intent to do so, Congress enacted the Military Commissions Act of 2006 (MCA), which made crystal clear its wish to deprive federal courts of general habeas jurisdiction.[51]

In response to these efforts, the Court recognized Congress's power both to grant and withdraw statutory jurisdiction, but it found no similar power to withdraw the Constitution's grant of habeas jurisdiction. In *Boumediene v. Bush* the Court reasoned that the Constitution requires federal courts to have jurisdiction to hear habeas petitions, unless Congress exercised its power to suspend the writ in times of rebellion or invasion, as provided in Article I, Section 9 of the Constitution. Since neither condition obtained, the Court retained its minimal constitutional jurisdiction. Matching its striking language in *Hamdi* that the Constitution confers no blank checks, the *Boumediene* Court explained, "Security subsists, too, in fidelity to freedom's first principles. Chief among these are freedom from arbitrary and unlawful restraint and the personal liberty that is secured by adherence to the separation of powers."[52] Despite the claims made throughout the course of detainee litigation that the executive must have power to do what is necessary to keep the nation secure, the Court responded by claiming that "[t]he laws and Constitution are designed to survive, and remain in force, in extraordinary times. Liberty and security can be reconciled; and in our system they are reconciled within the framework of the law."[53] To allow suspension of habeas corpus under claimed necessity in this circumstance, the Court argued, would be tantamount to saying "the political branches have the power to switch the Constitution on or off at will."[54]

Switching the Constitution on or off would be an extraordinary power. As we have seen, suspension of judicial review is one way the Constitution incorporates claims of necessity. No matter how one interprets the scope of what can be done under the Suspension Clause, in no case does it grant or imply a power to suspend all aspects of the Constitution's allocation of powers, imposition of constraints, and protections for liberties. It is not a general emergency power. Lincoln's precedent might seem to establish unilateral executive authority to act during an emergency, but this brief history of litigation over the detention of enemy combatants illustrates how the power of the president is more circumscribed. The president cannot act unilaterally, nor can he ask Congress to turn the Constitution on and off as a means of addressing claims to necessity.

But the scope of what they can do together is quite broad. In a pair of cases heard before the Fourth Circuit Court of Appeals, but never reviewed by the Supreme Court, the Bush administration obtained rulings that permit the president to subject citizens and noncitizens alike to military detention on his claim that they are unlawful enemy combatants. This claim was made in part on the basis of the authority Congress conferred through the AUMF. President Bush's theory was that in the war on terrorism, the battlefield was everywhere—even in Peoria, Illinois. Although the factual circumstances recited several times by the plurality in *Hamdi* concerned individuals detained on the battlefield in Afghanistan who had taken up arms against the United States, the president claimed expanded detention authority in the "war on terror" beyond these circumstances. For example, he detained José Padilla, a U.S. citizen, at Chicago's O'Hare Airport, eventually placing him in military custody for more than three years, under solitary confinement, and subjecting him to various sensory deprivation techniques designed to break down his will and make him a more compliant interrogation subject.[55] Because terrorists could strike anywhere, and demonstrated their intent to attack the homeland, then, on the president's view, any domestic location could be part of the battlefield in the "war on terror."[56]

As if the "everywhere battlefield" claim were not broad enough, President Trump in January 2018 reversed President Obama's executive order that prohibited any further transfers to Guantánamo Bay. Trump's order gave a broad statement that "the United States may transport additional detainees to U.S. Naval Station Guantánamo Bay when lawful and necessary to protect the Nation."[57] With the favorable Fourth Circuit rulings, President Trump could claim the ability to pick up U.S. persons on U.S. soil, and transport them to Guantánamo Bay for military detention, under a claim that such detention is "lawful and necessary." The Fourth Circuit authorized detention of those designated as unlawful enemy combatants, but President Trump's wording is broader—"additional detainees," opening up the possibility to claim authority for broader use of the facility, even absent additional congressional approval.

At stake regarding Guantánamo is both the scope of detention authority as well as the degree to which necessity can justify deviation from ordinary legal processes. The Suspension Clause is one kind of deviation that is constitutionally authorized under the appropriate circumstances and with the correct procedures. We can regard the Bush administration detention policies as a version of suspension—an attempt to detain persons outside the review of courts and on the basis of exclusive presidential power. The president was not authorized to act alone on the basis of what he claimed was necessary because judicial review applied and congressional authorization existed. These detention policies failed to create the legal black hole they sought to achieve, though they did get judicial authorization for flexible due process. Nonetheless, this flexibility recognizes the role of necessity outside the formal procedure of suspension, opening up a basis on which further future legal deviation is possible.

The scope of the president's detention powers beyond those authorized through exercise of the Suspension Clause is therefore malleable and contingent on the constitutional views of whoever anchors the current administration, as illustrated by the opposing views of the Obama and Trump administrations. This problem of contingency highlights the importance of the background attitudes and ideas we might have on hand at the time of the next terrorist attack.

Genesis and Danger

What ideas do we have on hand now? Since it is nearly certain that Americans will confront future crises, it is vital to consider the role of necessity in our legal thinking in advance. Necessity can be generative—the mother of invention—in circumstances not always conducive to proper constitutional creation. Lincoln's example supports the continued function of law in the midst of crisis, even if the form of due process is flexible. In seeking to control the danger inherent in the unreflective pull of a less fettered principle of necessity, can we establish congressional directives to control future acts of preventative detention? Giving priority to necessity in determining policy in the midst of crisis risks not only unreflective action that is less effective, but unreflective action that needlessly tramples on the existing constitutional order through deprivations of rights and liberties.

One example of this flexible dynamic is Bruce Ackerman's proposal for an "emergency constitution."[58] In the wake of a devastating terrorist attack and in the face of public pressure, politicians will be tempted to provide greater security by repressing more liberties. The temporal urgency of necessity does not lend itself to proper "reflection and choice," with the consequence that what extraordinary actions necessity appears to demand today will become normal practice tomorrow. To forestall such dynamics, Ackerman proposes a framework statute that works much like a suspension of habeas—yet far more constrained and limited in scope and duration—that empowers the president to detain individuals on mere suspicion after a triggering terrorist attack occurs. The power comes with a catch. To sustain the detentions past an initial sixty days, the president must return at regular intervals for congressional authorization, with escalating demonstrations of need and escalating supermajoritarian demands for approval. In addition, those detained must be treated decently and receive subsequent compensation for their detention.

This proposed "emergency constitution" enables executive flexibility in the immediate wake of an attack, while retaining institutional oversight with increasing intensity over time. Moreover, because those detained in effect pay a tax for their involuntarily contribution to the nation's security, they must be compensated by the political body they aid. Far from a legal black hole, as many charge the Bush administration with seeking to create at Guantánamo Bay for the detention of terrorism suspects, this proposal contemplates continuing legal oversight of temporarily suspended civil liberties. Linking passions with necessity, this proposal seeks to place the fear and alarm likely to ensue in the wake of a devastating attack under a framework requiring sustained "reflection and choice" in both the substance and procedure of possible detention policies.

Critics like David Cole charge, by contrast, that such an emergency-constitution framework would be ripe for abuse and does not properly secure civil liberties against the demands of necessity.[59] History is replete with examples of unnecessary use of preventative detention. The internment of about 110,000 persons of Japanese ancestry living on the West Coast after the attacks on Pearl Harbor is perhaps the most notorious instance.[60] In *Korematsu v. United States*, the Court confronted an executive decision to exclude persons of Japanese ancestry from the West Coast, citing military necessity as the justification. Justice Black accepted that "pressing public necessity may sometimes justify the existence of such restrictions."[61] In practical effect, the move from curfews to exclusion and finally to internment was a case of suspended rights on a massive and programmatic scale, justified by appeal to the "pressing public necessity" circumstances imposed. There was also a ratcheting process whereby curtailing civil liberties to a lesser extent (curfew) led to vastly greater violations (internment). But "pressing public necessity" when articulated as a kind of "military necessity," given the overriding end to win the war, led to a relaxed institutional oversight of the substance of the necessity claims. By giving credence to "military necessity" justifications, the Court altered the scope of constitutional rights and their application in light of the claimed circumstantial need. The Court's willingness to constitutionalize necessity led Justice Jackson to warn in dissent against legitimating naked claims of necessity: "[I]f we cannot confine military expedients by the Constitution, neither would I distort the Constitution to approve all that the military may deem expedient."[62] Although exclusion and internment were not accomplished through suspension of habeas, the effect was to legitimate executive actions justified by necessity that constitutionalized the invention of new executive practices.

A suspended habeas corpus, or an emergency provision, only highlights the care and responsibility actors and institutions have to the grounded Constitution. The problem with both suspension and Ackerman's "emergency constitution" is that the courts have no immediate ability to check executive abuse, and that during times of national crisis Congress has a record of complicity, not resistance. This pattern is little changed after the events of September 11, even if the specific factual circumstances differ. Neither an "emergency constitution," nor a temporarily suspended constitution, nor even a constitution unaltered, can forestall the temptation for illegal action if the circumstances incite the passions enough.

It is relevant to note here that, in a prescient argument, Justice Jackson warned in *Korematsu* that the Court's opinion licensed a "principle [that] then lies about like a loaded weapon, ready for the hand of any authority that can bring forward a plausible claim of an urgent need."[63] Such an eventual presidential authority campaigned for office in 2016 by calling for "a total and complete shutdown of Muslims entering the United States,"[64] because he believed that "we can't allow people coming into this country who have this hatred of the United States."[65] As a candidate for president, Donald Trump had favorably cited President Roosevelt's actions underlying *Korematsu*: "what I am doing is no different than what FDR—FDR's solution for Germans, Italians, Japanese, you know, many years ago."[66] Urging national security necessity upon taking office, President Trump instituted a travel ban, initially against seven Muslim-majority countries, a version of which the Supreme Court eventually upheld against constitutional challenges. In upholding the change in immigration policy, the Court took pains to defer to presidential authority over matters of national security, explaining, for example, that "[a]ny rule of constitutional law that would inhibit the flexibility of the President to respond to changing world conditions should be adopted only with the greatest caution, and our inquiry into matters of entry and national security is highly constrained."[67] In response to Justice Sotomayor's dissenting claim that the Court's opinion has "stark parallels" to *Korematsu*, Chief Justice Roberts went out of his way to try to revoke the license the opinion might grant, and to which the president had appealed, writing that "*Korematsu* was gravely wrong the day it was decided, has been overruled in the court of history, and—to be clear—'has no place in law under the Constitution.' "[68] What is troubling about Trump's pursuit of a Muslim travel ban and his campaign invocation of *Korematsu* is the way of thinking it embraces, prioritizing claimed necessity over reasoned constitutionalism. The ability to suspend normal constitutional protections on claims of "pressing public necessity" persists in ways that caution more ex ante reflection, congressional foresight, and judicial vigilance.

Whether we adopt emergency measures or not, both Ackerman and Cole agree that actions taken pursuant to necessity can alter our understandings of proper constitutional limits and practices that further work to normalize these practices that necessity makes available. Whether and to what extent such transformations occur depends not upon whether we choose to adopt an emergency-constitution framework or to rely on strengthened commitments to present understandings of civil liberties. Rather, they depend on the "reflection and choice" by which we govern. These are matters internal to the practice of constitutional governing and involve officials and citizens alike.

Institutional reform of the kind Ackerman proposes reshuffles how necessity plays within and in relation to new institutional arrangements, but it does not change the pressures that necessity exerts on the discretionary, normative, or expressive aspects of the actors working within governing institutions. For *that* we need a normative understanding of constitutional commitment embedded in practice. New framework statutes that realign institutional balances must be inhabited from the inside, with commitments to norms and priorities that always go beyond what can be expressed by the letter of the law.[69]

Although I think that Ackerman's proposal is a helpful approach to controlling the temptation for presidents to act illegally, my aim here is not to take sides in this debate, but rather to make a related point. No amount of institutional reform and reflection will work if we do not control how we think about necessity. If our governing and constitutional discourse does not take care to avoid a fallacy of hasty generalizations—because necessity can be used to justify invoking the Suspension Clause, it can justify *any* kind of legal deviance—then as Cole rightly suggests, no amount of advance preparation will forestall illegal action. We have to do the normative constitutional work of affirming the content of our commitments in order to be prepared for the next attack.

This affective contingency is in play with every change in presidential administration and with every crisis that occurs within an administration. There will be an ever present claim that a president is empowered to do whatever is necessary to protect national security. Such claims most often lead not to formal invocation of the Suspension Clause, but to informal constitutional deviation. Necessity arises as both a claim about political action and as an occasion for shaping action in light of background attitudes and commitments. Because claims about necessity can both create and destroy commitments to rights, liberties, and institutional balances, they have unavoidable effects on a polity's normative ordering.

A possible security paradox looms.[70] For in the name of preserving security, constitutional principles and practices can be made insecure. This contingency in constitutional theory and practice can produce different outcomes, depending on how a polity practices constitutionalism in the midst of emergency disorder. For example, future contingencies can challenge the wisdom and consequences of rigid compliance to constitutional rules, thereby altering the constitutional meanings through nonreflective processes.

Accretionary constitutional change can occur because one deviant practice, subsequently normalized through new constitutional understandings, can lead to another. Another possibility might lead governing officials and members of a polity to abandon their broader constitutional commitments altogether. In addition, prior reflection and choice, of the kind that Ackerman envisions, could lead a polity to take proactive steps to provide for both flexibility as well as a recommitment to constitutional values protected through governing institutions. Because of the unreflective deviation possible through the alternative approaches, Ackerman is right to insist that we need further ex ante reflection on how we might fashion an "emergency constitution"— no matter what plan we adopt. For a presidential administration committed to "taking all actions necessary to protect national security"—as the Trump administration claims—it is all too easy to threaten security in the name of protecting it.[71]

Constitutional form provides no handy field guide to navigate emergency terrain, telling us what other norms and values apply to situations that exceed particular rules. When they are at their best, legal rules can never determine their own applications. For each application, we must always exercise "reflection and choice," even when the experience is routine. When rules are at their most uncertain, the exercise of will becomes more pressing. The attitudes we adopt toward necessity are therefore particularly important because, with the power to deviate from constitutional baselines that the Suspension Clause contemplates, necessity can both create and destroy.

What makes the problem of how necessity fits within constitutional frameworks so intractable is that we often find ourselves of two minds about constitutional principles and rules. For on the one hand, we are committed to the rule of law, not the rule of governing officials. We govern ourselves through adherence to legal principles and processes established in advance. On the other hand, we recognize the contingency of future events, our limited foresight in planning for such contingency, and the importance of preserving governing flexibility to address future crises. The very idea of a constitution, Chief Justice Marshall wrote in *McCulloch v. Maryland,* is that it is "to be adapted to the various crises of human affairs."[72] In this way, how we think about necessity in relation to future contingency shapes how we think about constitutional governance.

How we think about necessity is not simply a matter of an isolated belief about a feature of constitutional principle or legal rule. How we view the contingency of the future and the risk of harm that might flow from mindless adherence to constitutional rules is a product of our broader social and political imagination, how we envision the way our political lives should be.[73] Finding ourselves of two minds, we also can distinguish between two different and opposing ways of envisioning constitutional practice: the national security lens and the liberty lens, each of which operates within what we might call either securitarian or libertarian logics.[74] The former gives priority to the value of security, seeing in it the basis for state action relying on claims about what is necessary to do in order to address ever present threats. The latter, by contrast, gives priority to protecting the liberties by which a polity might enjoy the benefits of security. The priority of one vision over another is not prescribed by constitutional rules themselves, but instead relies on citizens and government actors to give them life within the polity in a way that is inescapably contingent.

In light of this possible paradox of security, I want to conclude this chapter with some considerations for how we might best understand this internal constitutional contingency. First, constitutional contingency, especially as it is manifest in the security paradox, produces a problem of asymmetry. The security lens, tethered to the strong form of necessity, has a natural tendency to tug in the direction of flexibility and away from constraint. Less fettered, or even unfettered, power to respond makes politics the only check, uninformed by deeper constitutional commitments. Contingency here is most risky, for the possibility of political accountability is itself subsumed by the necessity that generates presidential power. In short, security's greater immediacy—the need to respond to an emergency situation—means that flexibility bends more easily in the direction of claims of necessity than toward the requirements of constitutional constraints.

Second, fear of insecurity tends to excite the passions more than fear of tyranny. Both are themes in our constitutional history, but the former can have more salient manifestations in the form of terrorist attacks—as the events of September 11 illustrate—whereas the latter, absent some as yet unrealized momentous political action, is more a matter of interpretive degree. In this way, John Ashcroft, as the attorney general, could castigate civil libertarians for purportedly opining over "phantoms of lost liberty."[75] It is this dynamic that institutional changes of the kind Ackerman proposes seek to control. A key question—resolution of which may itself be inseparable from background attitudes—is: Which risk warrants the greater attention: the catastrophic terrorist attack or the creeping change to the constitutional order through heightened security and lessened liberty?

What we see through the examples of Lincoln's suspension and Bush's detention policies is that contingency depends not merely on the accidents of circumstances but also on the strength and content of constitutional commitments. To be clear, neither precedent looks anything like a prerogative power or a "constitutional dictatorship"—both of which I rejected in chapter 1. But both do involve differing views of how to reconcile commitments and necessity through constitutional justifications. Such commitments are not like binding contracts, or even religious covenants whereby external actors can impose punishment for noncompliance. Constitutional commitments are constitutive features of governing practice that internally justify political action in terms of constitutional values. These are inseparable from views about how far necessity can justify either formal or functional claims that constitutional rights be suspended with regard to government policy. One way to avoid the security paradox is by realizing the positive value of security in conjunction with the liberties it protects. If we incorporate libertarian considerations into our very understanding of security, we foreclose asymmetrical appeal of securitarian perspectives through commitment to the values the constitution aims to protect: we "secure the blessings of liberty," as the Constitution's preamble directs.

Under one way of confronting necessity, political actors use preexisting constitutional commitments to shape their understanding of the necessitous circumstances, conforming their responses to settled practices. Necessity can prod changes through public justifications that in time normalize the role of necessity within constitutional practice. Necessity can thus be generative. Under an alternative approach to confronting necessity, political actors use necessity to construct new constitutional meanings and boundaries, altering present understandings to better address claims to urgent action. Necessity can introduce episodic governance led by the accidents of perceived crisis circumstance rather than deliberative governance determined by reflective justification. By avoiding the constitutional constraints habeas represents—a "bulwark of our liberties"—episodic governance can undervalue, or undermine, core constitutional values. Necessity can thus be dangerous.[76] In this way, contingency exists on all sides, for emergencies do not come with their meanings or their required responses enclosed, like instructions for self-assembly goods. We must choose how we normalize necessity in American constitutionalism. And given this choice, only the one way coheres with good government through reflection and choice.

3

Normalizing Necessity: From Scrutiny to Exigency

ADDRESSING PRESIDENTIAL CLAIMS THAT indefinite detention of individuals at the U.S. naval base in Guantánamo, Cuba, pursuant to counterterrorism policy, was justified by appeal to necessitous circumstances, Justice O'Connor, writing for the Supreme Court in *Hamdi v. Rumsfeld,* acknowledged that "the exigencies of the circumstances may demand that" deviations from otherwise applicable due-process standards might be justified.[1] Moreover, rejecting stronger arguments about presidential supremacy when it comes to national security claims, O'Connor admonished that "[s]triking the proper constitutional balance here is of great importance," for "[i]t is during our most challenging and uncertain moments that our Nation's commitment to due process is most severely tested; and it is in those times that we must preserve our commitment at home to the principles for which we fight abroad."[2] President George W. Bush argued first that courts not only had no jurisdiction to hear cases from military detainees, but that even if they did, complete deference was owed to presidential determinations about detention policy in light of the background necessitous circumstances. As we saw in the previous chapter, in making claims to unilateral, unreviewable power to detain individuals for counterterrorism purposes, the president presented stark claims about the exigencies of the situation, to which the Court offered an approach that would strike a balance between necessity and liberty.

There is a long constitutional tradition in seeking to balance the exigencies of the circumstances against prior commitments to legal rules and standards.

This tradition encompasses far more than claims about national security, though it is relevant to questions about the scope of executive power. Chief Justice Marshall, in a case addressing the scope of Congress's power to charter a national bank pursuant to its "necessary and proper" power, reasoned in *McCulloch v. Maryland* that the Constitution afforded latitude for Congress to choose the best means for achieving those ends, for "It would have been an unwise attempt to provide by immutable rules for exigencies which, if foreseen at all, must have been seen dimly, and which can be best provided for as they occur."[3] So long as the means Congress chooses comply with the letter and spirit of constitutional principles, then necessity can be normalized into ordinary constitutional decision-making. Chief Justice Marshall reasoned, "Let the end be legitimate, let it be within the scope of the Constitution, and all means which are appropriate, which are plainly adapted to that end, which are not prohibited, but consist with the letter and spirit of the Constitution, are Constitutional."[4] As a way of articulating in 1819 the view that constitutional governance must "strike a balance" between rigid adherence to rules already laid down and flexible governing practice responsive to exigencies, Marshall's opinion provides a guide for how to think about the "exigencies of circumstances" within American constitutionalism.

As I will explore in this chapter, both the "letter and spirit" of the Constitution shape how unforeseen exigencies are normalized within constitutional practice. Necessity can be constitutionalized through practical and interpretive flexibility. By interpreting both the scope of government powers and the constraints that rights impose, courts and political decision-makers can accommodate necessity within structures of constitutional justification and practice. Chief Justice Marshall argued for a broad understanding of Congress's power to do what is necessary within "a constitution intended to endure for ages to come, and, consequently, to be adapted to the various crises of human affairs."[5] Flexibility of this kind, however, introduces a degree of contingency into American constitutionalism. When governing practices adapt to the various practical necessities that arise within human affairs, constitutional meanings can change. This contingency is not simply a matter of unforeseeable future events, but it is in the "character of human language, that no word conveys to the mind, in all situations, one single definite idea," as Marshall explained. In this way, necessity is normalized within a structure of justification that applies constitutional language to the necessities of human affairs.[6]

There is a further constraint built into this contingent constitutional structure. A proposed course of action and a proffered interpretation of the constitution must have salience. There must be a confluence of background conditions—the political and practical dimensions of a social imaginary—that make a proposed constitutional meaning and government action appear reasonable. For example, even though two justices argued that President Bush must either release Hamdi, try him for a crime, or suspend habeas—that there was no constitutionally authorized indefinite detention alternative—the Suspension Clause in the post–September 11 counterterrorism context has not been a salient option.[7] As we encountered in the previous chapter, suspension served as a background example of the potential scope of presidential power to act unilaterally in times of exigent circumstances. Suspension is one way to constitutionalize necessity. But its use has not arisen as a salient counterterrorism option. That is in large part because other doctrines of constitutional law make available alternative ways to justify adaptive interpretations. Beyond suspension, two additional approaches to internalizing necessity are available: (1) when courts apply the exigent-circumstances doctrine to review executive actions said to violate a constitutional right; and (2) when courts apply a doctrine of "tiered scrutiny" to balance government interests against constitutional rights. Each of these has played a role not only in shaping the legal contours of counterterrorism policy but also in everyday constitutional practice.

A key doctrinal means for executive officials to make necessity arguments before courts, for example, is to argue that exigent circumstances justify deviating from rigid application of a constitutional right that might otherwise forbid a chosen action. In this way, a doctrine of exigent circumstances has the effect of altering baseline protections of civil rights and liberties to provide flexibility for presidential policy choices. As both a doctrine and a conceptual term, an exigency doctrine is a way of constitutionalizing appeals to necessity.

Exigency arises because there is something about the intensity and immediacy in a situation that requires a governmental response with greater flexibility and more urgency than rigid adherence to baseline constitutional constraints would allow. But every governmental response to a collective problem requires actions and policies that impact features of everyday life that constitutional rights protect—from privacy, to speech, to the basic liberties protected by due process. When individuals are made party to a legislative objective through implementation of a regulatory restriction, they have their liberties curtailed when judged from a baseline of what they might have chosen to do otherwise, absent the legislative choice.

Think here, for an example outside the counterterrorism context, of the controversy surrounding the Patient Protection and Affordable Care Act's insurance mandate. All taxpayers who meet statutory criteria are required to purchase health insurance or pay an additional tax. The taxpayers required to purchase or pay might presumably prefer to exercise their basic human freedom in ways other than those mandated by the legislative act. Regulatory effects on individual freedom arise from ordinary collective-action problems (how to make health insurance available to all, or most, Americans) that produce contingent, and therefore revisable, governmental policies (the Affordable Care Act can be repealed subject to future political will). Government justified, and courts upheld, these contingent government policies by claiming in part that they are necessary to further a proper government end.[8] Even when it comes to highly protected rights, such as the right to free speech, government is not absolutely forbidden to regulate speech or speakers, but must do so in relation to the intensity of its need in light of the degree of burden on a speaker's right. Courts review government action in light of a sliding scale that purports to balance the intensity of government need against the degree of intrusion on a protected right in a way that acknowledges the necessity of government action. As I explore in the next section, under such proportionality review, or "tiered scrutiny," necessity becomes a key analytic concept in adjudicating the inevitable conflicts that arise between collective action and individual freedom and equality.

But just as these ordinary necessities produce effects on baseline—or absolute—conceptions of rights, exigent circumstances do the same, even if with greater magnitude. There is thus a continuum from everyday necessity to exigency, for each produces deviations from background rights protections. Within this continuum there is a structure of justifications requiring more compelling reasons for the necessitous action the more protected the right and the more invasive the impact. In this way, constitutional practice

normalizes necessity through justificatory practices that internalize constitutional norms and principles. In the continuum from baseline deviation to
exception, the task is to justify government action in light of the constitutional values and principles accommodating the practice. Through accommodation, the justificatory structure preserves constitutional meanings by
explaining the scope of a right in relation to desired government practices.
This process of meaning preservation through rights transformation is not
without limit, for if the justification for accommodation fails, a right will
function as a prohibitory constraint on government action.

As a doctrine, exigency is a kind of exception that seeks to reshape constitutional practices. Judges at times adapt the application of constitutional rules
protecting civil liberties to the specific exigencies executive officials confront,
internalizing exceptions as part of what the underlying rule means.[9] Because
exigencies arise in more vexed, even emergency, situations, and because exigencies can justify greater legal deviation, the exceptions they implement can
have more pervasive effects on constitutional governance than simple proportionality allows. But in another important respect, while perhaps correctly
thought of as exceptions, exigencies create exceptions no more than any other
deviation from an absolute protection for a right does. All government actions create deviations that effect background constitutional constraints and
meanings. Human freedom and constitutional rights are never so absolute
that balancing is unavoidable. In this way, this chapter seeks to demonstrate
how necessity is internalized into justification structures that ratchet up the
reasoning required when the action is less urgent and when the effects are
more invasive.

To make, and to judge, a claim about exigency or everyday necessity is to
engage in an interpretive practice, the results of which cannot be mechani-
cally determined. Instead, attitudes about commitment and flexibility play a
large role in determining the potential outcomes of interpretive choice. Here
again, as we saw in chapter 2, a background social imaginary, a way of thinking about and prioritizing the relations between security and liberty, is unavoidable when making interpretive choices about exigencies. Whether
securitarian or libertarian logics take priority in decision-making will determine substantive outcomes. The choice between attitudes cannot itself
be determined by a constitution, but it arises as an unavoidable aspect of

constitutionalism itself. Nonetheless, the argumentative discourse required by the exigency exception is one that is constitutional in both form and substance. We ask: What is the meaning and scope of a constitutionally protected right in light of the exigent circumstances to which it is to be applied? Because this form of question reveals that constitutional rights already include the conceptual tools for altering their application, depending on the specific social facts understood in light of salient features of the social imaginary, claims to exigent exceptions are not themselves exceptional in law—at least not in an alarmingly disjunctive way. Indeed, as the judicial doctrines of tiered scrutiny reveal, there is a continuum from ordinary legislative choice over the means of fulfilling policy goals consistent with constitutional constraints to extraordinary executive practice justified by the exigencies of a situation. Though because of their power to redefine the scope of a right or the extent of an executive power, exigencies remain a challenge for constitutionalism, requiring careful attention to the justifications offered for them.

As this chapter seeks to demonstrate, both practices of rights proportionality and doctrines of exigency are part of how constitutionalism overcomes claims of necessity through internalizing and normalizing them. In each case, constitutionalism incorporates necessity through justificatory processes in which government actors must articulate how to resolve necessitous circumstances in ways that honor constitutive commitments. By reasoning within both the letter and spirit of the law, these justificatory processes avoid the arbitrariness of "accident and force" while upholding the "reflection and choice" on which good government depends. These structures of justification do not guarantee optimal rights-protective governing practices, because they too are subject to background attitudes and beliefs about the relation between liberty and security. But they do assure that deviations from baseline rights protections will be justified in ways that incorporate consideration of the meaning and scope of those rights within governing practices.

Proportional Constitutional Rights

Within constitutional processes, necessity is often invoked to describe the urgency or importance of a particular means of achieving an otherwise compelling state purpose. As in the situation of exigency, there is both a temporal and a substantive scale. What is necessary occurs within a temporal setting in which dispatch matters. It also occurs within a substantive setting in which priorities are determined. Necessity depends, however, always on a relevant background that is already given in the situation—a goal, a consequence to be avoided, a value or state of affairs to be preserved. What can be justified as necessary by governing actors depends on background practices and values—particularly constitutional ones—that make salient some actions as conceivably necessary and that foreclose others as imaginatively possible. In the case of everyday legislative process, necessity matches legislative means to ends already chosen. The question to ask is, What means are necessary to achieve a given policy goal? To locate necessity in relation to legislative purpose in this way is to invite scrutiny over whether the relation is proper in light of constitutional constraints embedded in text, structure, practice, and the like. As I will explore, the current judicial doctrine of "tiered scrutiny" segments government action for purposes of constitutional review between three standards that relate necessity to its constitutional effects on a scale of increasing intensity: rational basis review, intermediate scrutiny, and strict scrutiny.[10]

How do we strike a balance preserving constitutional values while allowing flexible transformations in the scope of rights and powers? In first articulating an answer to the question in *McCulloch*, Chief Justice Marshall reasoned that "the powers given to the government imply the ordinary means of execution."[11] He then continued: "The government which has a right to do an act, and has imposed on it the duty of performing that act, must, according to the dictates of reason, be allowed to select the means."[12] Congress need not rely on reason alone, for "the Constitution of the United States has not left the right of Congress to employ the necessary means, for the execution of the powers conferred on the Government, to general reasoning," because "[t]o its enumeration of powers is added that of making 'all laws which shall be necessary and proper, for carrying into execution' "[13] Congress's other constitutional powers. Necessity enters constitutional practice through a textual assignment of power to Congress in Article I. This power entitles Congress to link the ends it may legitimately pursue—regulating interstate commerce, or levying taxes, for instance—to its chosen means: chartering a national bank to enable regulation and receipt of funds. Or, as Justice Marshall explains, the Court's interpretation of the Necessary and Proper Clause should not "impair the right of the legislature to exercise its best judgment in the selection of measures to carry into execution the constitutional powers of the government."[14]

To settle the question regarding the sweep of Congress's "necessary and proper" power, Marshall, as we saw earlier, explained that if the end is legitimate, and within the scope of Congress's powers, then appropriate means are those that "consist with the letter and spirit of the constitution."[15] Necessity has limits. What is necessary must be proper. It must compel action consistent with both constitutional text and spirit. That necessity is constrained by the "spirit of the Constitution" means that political actors must do more than consider "the letter" of the law narrowly construed. The ends necessity pursues must also be within the scope of Congress's constitutional powers. But in requiring a proper fit between means "plainly adapted" and legitimate ends, the Constitution contemplates that necessity will have a continuing role to play in everyday political governance. Necessity encompasses and compels national power.

Since Marshall penned his opinion in *McCulloch*, American constitutional practice has seen an ever increasing expansion of national power. In both wartime and peace, from the addition of the Reconstruction Amendments to the transformations of the New Deal, Congress has been drawn into resolving collective problems that arise not only from the immediate transactions of commerce but also from the aggregate effects of a highly integrated national economy and intricately intertwined social spheres. Especially during the Great Depression and its aftermath, Congress and the president worked together to forestall the dire effects of pressing economic necessity as matters of national security thought no less important than matters of political security.[16] President Franklin Roosevelt's claim that "a clear realization of the fact that true individual freedom cannot exist without economic security and independence" suggests the facilitative role of national power in addressing the needs necessity creates.[17] On this view, individual freedoms are not threatened by, but depend upon, robust exercise of national power to facilitate economic security.

Whether tied directly to interstate economic transactions or more indirectly to activities that have substantial effects on national economic matters,

Congress has power to do what is "necessary and proper" to achieve collective solutions to national problems as a way of promoting the overarching constitutional goals of securing liberty and promoting the general welfare. Here is how the Court has more recently articulated the "necessary and proper" power: "If it can be seen that the means adopted are really calculated to attain the end, the degree of their necessity, the extent to which they conduce to the end, the closeness of the relationship between the means adopted and the end to be attained, are matters for congressional determination alone."[18] The Court will not interpose its own determinations of what might be judged necessary for the decisions Congress makes about how to achieve its legislative ends. In this way, what is necessary takes on a meaning less about the exigency of the circumstance than about the desirability of a means to achieve a legitimate policy goal. If Congress judges a particular program or regulation as particularly efficacious in bringing about the desired end, then they are entitled to claim that it is necessary, and the judiciary will defer, absent some additional worry regarding democratic failure, discrimination, or fundamental rights violations.

Marshall's constitutional tradition produced a doctrinal framework for judicial review of this increased legislative power. This framework of tiered scrutiny employs a sliding scale of justificatory expectations, the most demanding of which is called "strict scrutiny." If a discrete and insular minority group is forced to bear the cost for benefits others enjoy, if individuals are denied access to democratic and social practices constitutive of active citizenship, or if persons are deprived of their other protected rights and liberties, the Court would be committed to interposing constitutional constraints on congressional power. This idea, based on footnote 4 of the Court's decision from 1938 in *Carolene Products,* provides the justification for searching judicial scrutiny of legislative power that has the purpose or effect of depriving persons of equal protection, due process, or other constitutional rights and liberties.[19] If Congress (or a state legislature) targets minority groups to bear the costs for policies that provide benefits to others, or if Congress (or a state legislature) infringes on a fundamental right or liberty, the Court examines legislative claims to necessity strictly. It requires the legislation to be necessary to achieving a compelling government interest. In each of these cases, necessity connects means to ends. But only under what is called "strict scrutiny" does the Court expect government action to provide a close fit between ends that are compelling and means that are truly necessary.

The requirement that government may impose liabilities on members of minority groups in cases of "pressing public necessity" was first articulated in the Supreme Court's review of the Roosevelt administration's policy of excluding individuals of Japanese ancestry from the West Coast during World War II. As we saw in the previous chapter, the administration justified this forced exclusion in terms of military necessity and national security. In *Korematsu v. United States,* the Court upheld the constitutionality of this policy but cautioned that "all legal restrictions which curtail the civil rights of a single racial group are immediately suspect. That is not to say that all such restrictions are unconstitutional. It is to say that courts must subject them to the most rigid scrutiny. *Pressing public necessity* may sometimes justify the existence of such restrictions."[20] Here we find "pressing public necessity" appearing at the heart of the Constitution's protections for equality and due process.

In announcing the basis for developing tiered scrutiny, the majority utterly capitulated to claims of necessity. According to General John DeWitt, military commander of the Western Defense Command, who issued the Japanese exclusion order, "military necessity" paired with the "pressing public necessity" we encountered with President Lincoln in chapter 2 meant that constitutional rules ceased to function normally. The Court licensed deviance, placing a claim of necessity at the heart of the Constitution.

Pressing public necessity is a dangerous principle, occasioning vigorous judicial debate. Justice Jackson's dissent warned the Court not to "rationalize[] the Constitution to show that the Constitution sanctions such an order" excluding persons on the basis of race under claims of "pressing public necessity."[21] Jackson reasoned that exclusion (and detention by implication) "violates constitutional limitations even if it is a reasonable exercise of military authority," and that the Court had no basis for weighing the reasonableness of the military's action against the protections the Constitution affords.[22] Under Jackson's reasoning, necessity provides a political justification for lawless action, not a legal one.[23] Similarly, Justice Murphy's dissent emphasized how the inappropriate deference granted by the Court sanctioned an "erroneous assumption of racial guilt, rather than *bona fide* military necessity."[24]

The missing analytic element in the debate between Justice Black's opinion for the Court and the dissents is consideration of whether, in providing such a sweeping deprivation of constitutional rights, the claim to pressing public necessity fell within the spirit of the Constitution, even as it deviated from the letter. Because *Korematsu* granted too much deference to executive claims of necessity, it is a constitutional outlier, even though it established a principle of strict judicial review over claims of "pressing public necessity." Like other constitutional failures, *Korematsu* serves as an antiprecedent, providing an example of how too great a deference to "pressing public necessity" can lead to constitutional effects too deviant to ever become normalized within constitutional practice.[25]

In the wake of *Korematsu,* a robust doctrine of "strict scrutiny" came to define the Court's review of government actions that classified persons on the basis of race, or that censored protected speech, creating a judicial presumption against the legitimacy of such actions. Precisely how "strict" this scrutiny works in practice is a matter of some debate. One version is that it is "strict in theory, but fatal in fact."[26] But the idea is that government action or legislation that infringes on protected rights falls within permissible constitutional limits only when relying on means that are necessary to achieve ends that are compelling.

In one of its first full articulations of the "strict scrutiny" inquiry in a more entrenched doctrinal form, the Court examined laws that burdened the fundamental right of individuals to move between states, claiming that "any classification which serves to penalize the exercise of that right, unless shown to be necessary to promote a compelling governmental interest, is unconstitutional."[27] "Strict scrutiny" has come to signify the expectation that "pressing public necessity" is a narrow category infrequently satisfied and counterbalanced by the heavy weight of constitutional constraints. The Court applies "strict scrutiny" to government action that burdens equal protection, due-process rights, freedom of speech, and the free exercise of religion—and in each case, sometimes finds government action to be in service of a pressing public necessity. Even restrictions on free speech can be necessary, as in the case of *Burson v. Freemon,* in which the Court upheld prohibitions on campaign speech within one hundred feet of a polling location as necessary to avert the potential for voter intimidation.[28] Thus, the very conceptual framework of "strict scrutiny" means both that courts will examine government action with exceeding care, but also that sometimes government action infringing on protected rights and liberties will be judged necessary. In this way, not only does necessity live within the Constitution to match means to ends when examining congressional power, but it also dwells within the practice of judicial review.

Tiered scrutiny is not a mechanistic practice of constitutional construction. It is an embedded constitutional practice. Courts make judgments about the social meanings of practices claimed necessary on the basis of understandings implicated by those very practices. For example, Americans share a constitutionally protected right to free speech, as do citizens of all liberal constitutional democracies. But what is the meaning of free speech? What practices does this right protect? May persons receive constitutional protection for their speech in furtherance of a conspiracy to overthrow the government? Do persons have the right to occupy Main Street in order to protest Wall Street? Answers to these questions inevitably involve not only inquiries into the central values protected by the First Amendment—be they values of autonomy, collective self-determination, or dissent—but inquiry into the balance between society's desire for openness and its need for order.[29] Necessity enters this inquiry by enabling limitations to unfettered speech only when outweighed by the compelling interests of other values. In this way, necessity plays a role in establishing the scope and meaning of free speech.

When the Supreme Court held that the government could not suppress publication of materials from the classified study "History of U.S. Decision-Making Process on Viet Nam Policy," it had to assess, and reject, claims to "national security" as pressing public necessity having priority over any First Amendment rights.[30] President Richard Nixon argued that publication of this study would cause irreparable damage to national security. Moreover, the president argued that the Supreme Court should defer to his claims and impose a prior restraint on the study's publication. In rejecting this argument, the Court both rejected national security claims of pressing public necessity and upheld the salience of constitutionally protected free speech rights as constraints on claims of necessity. But the Court does not always uphold rights in conflict with claims to necessity. In other instances, however, the temporal urgency of protecting against grave harms from "imminent lawless action" bends the First Amendment's limits back within the domain of necessary government action.[31] During past perceived moments of crisis, the Court has allowed the background political and social circumstance to shape the priority of necessity, lest "[a] single revolutionary spark may kindle a fire that, smouldering for a time, may burst into a sweeping and destructive conflagration."[32] In this alternating way, the meanings of constitutional principles of free speech both foreclose and make available various understandings of what might be necessary.

What the Constitution means—whether principles of equality prohibit race-conscious decision-making, or when free speech can be suppressed to protect national security, for example—depends on how necessity is understood in relation to the constitutional principles and values it seeks to disrupt. Judgments about necessity, in turn, occur within justificatory frameworks of varying levels of scrutiny. This mutual interdependence means that necessity sometimes changes the boundaries and meanings of constitutional constraints through practice. At the same time, constitutional principles shape the meanings that claims of necessity can have—their availability, salience, and content. In this way the meanings and scope of both claims of necessity and constitutional constraints are mutually implicated. But if under the *McCulloch* framework, claims of necessity must cohere with the letter and spirit of the law, there must also be a degree of meaning preservation even if the scope of a right is transformed. In this way, legislatures and courts alternately normalize and overcome necessity by enacting and interpreting ordinary law to solve everyday collective problems.

Does this outcome mean that American constitutional rights are never absolute? Do they yield to a general principle of proportionality? American tiered scrutiny shares close affinities with European approaches to constitutional law that often rely on principles of proportionality. Germany's constitution, for example, is understood to embed a principle of proportionality allowing a general method of principled balancing. In German jurisprudence, if government action is suitable, necessary, and proportionate, then state action can limit the enjoyment of a protected right. The German understanding of necessity is that "the end cannot equally well be achieved by the use of other means less burdensome to the individual."[33] International courts such as the European Court of Justice and the European Court of Human Rights also employ a generalized proportionality review that protects rights by subjecting to close analysis government claims to everyday necessity.[34] Constitutional rights are seldom absolute, because most are subject to the possibility that necessity might empower government action otherwise forbidden.

Although the U.S. Supreme Court has not adopted a general proportionality review, it does at times speak in this manner. In 2012, the Court held in *United States v. Alvarez* that the First Amendment bars Congress from prohibiting false claims to receipt of military decorations or medals. By ruling that the Stolen Valor Act of 2005 was unconstitutional, Justice Breyer claimed that the Court had employed a "proportionality" inquiry. He reasoned that if "the First Amendment is to offer proper protection in the many instances in which a statute adversely affects constitutionally protected interests but warrants neither near-automatic condemnation (as 'strict scrutiny' implies) nor near-automatic approval (as is implicit in 'rational basis' review)," the Court must determine more flexibly "whether the statute works speech-related harm that is out of proportion to its justifications."[35] Viewing claimed necessity in balance with the kind and degree of restrictions to the exercise of protected rights is part of American legal practice, even if it is less systematic than a general proportionality review would imply, and even if contested by some jurists.[36] Justice Breyer's invocation of proportionality recognizes in part the contingency of tiered scrutiny as a judicial method. As Professor Richard Fallon traces, tiered scrutiny has developed into its present form only since the early 1970s.[37]

Under a model of proportionality, or tiered scrutiny, necessity is principally bounded in three important respects. First, it is a concept in service of legislative and judicial rationality. Under the U.S. Constitution, the national government is constitutionally empowered "to promote the general Welfare." Laws must be passed to implement policies and resolve problems. Subject to judicial review, these laws must demonstrate heightened showings of necessity the more the laws affect constitutionally protected interests. But it would be impossible to legislate without impacting, at least to some extent, the liberties or equal standing of some persons. Any law will affect the rights, duties, responsibilities, or conduct of those who fall within its purview.

Because liberty without law is constrained by liberty under law, absolute freedom must give way to "ordered liberty," subject to legislative rationality. All laws must match the means government employs to the legitimate public ends it seeks to achieve, with increasing rationality the more public order supersedes individual liberty. This expectation derives from the relation between the rights and powers the Constitution assigns within which necessity functions. Within constitutional practices, necessity's role in legislative enactments is bounded on all sides by constitutional constraints and is only possible in furtherance of constitutionally conferred powers. Necessity is part of a conversation of justification, subject to background meanings and constraints, and therefore is never a trump. Claims about necessity occasion reflective conversations that probe the rationality and wisdom of the contemplated impacts on constitutional rights and liberties. Neither rights nor necessity have absolute priority in this exchange of reasons. But the method of tiered scrutiny—or an alternative sliding scale—is meant to reflect the fact that the more central and fundamental the right, the greater the justification for deviance will have to be.

Second, necessity is a concept bounded by political and normative conditions of availability. What is cognizable as a possible means necessary to achieving either a rationally legitimate or a compelling end depends on what is socially and politically possible. Particular collective problems have political salience that generates the seeming necessity of pursuing the relevant means to their achievement. Other problems and means do not. Whether an event or goal will generate strong claims to necessity will therefore be a matter contingent on other background beliefs and practices. In this way, a claim to necessity within legislative practice can only arise from what is available as a political possibility.

Third, a claim to necessity must also fit within normative values expressed in and through legal practices. What we have repeatedly encountered as the "social imaginary" captures this idea that legislative necessity is limited by what is available.[38] A social imaginary is the unarticulated background that structures how members of a polity see claims to necessity and the problems they are meant to address. Both normal and extraordinary politics involve contests over how a particular practice or policy fits within this broader narrative of constitutional and political meanings. A policy will not be accepted simply because it is imaginable. At the same time, part of what it means to engage in authentic political action is to attempt to imagine how a new practice might fit within existing normative commitments. American political practice occurs between the tension to do whatever is claimed necessary and the commitment to uphold more pervasive and defining constitutional values.

As the argument so far has demonstrated, tiered scrutiny is a way that interbranch constitutional dialogue resolves this tension and justifies how necessity is normalized in practice. As the next section argues, the use of exigency doctrines is another way of resolving this tension. Moreover, as we will see in the next chapter, nowhere is this tension more manifest than in the claims to unilateral and supreme emergency power to do whatever is necessary in response to the attacks of September 11.

Exigent Circumstances, Special Needs

Another way of normalizing necessity within constitutional practice is through the judicial application of an "exigent circumstance" doctrine to justify government deviation from rights baselines. Exigent circumstances, and the related existence of "special needs," are doctrines that arise under the Fourth Amendment's prohibition against unreasonable searches and seizures that have particular importance to executive claims that actions taken in pursuit of national security are necessary despite their effects on constitutional rights.

Let's begin with the central constitutional problem that exigency creates: the possibility of changing the meanings of constitutional commitments and constraints by prioritizing the needs of exigency without proper regard for the normative political order's constitutive principles. For example, looking back to the prior chapter, what is concerning in the case of alternative frameworks, such as Ackerman's "emergency constitution," is the degree to which mission creep and doctrinal drift can normalize particular practices in ways that invite further suspensions and weaker regard for civil liberties. Indeed, Professor David Cole levied precisely this kind of critique against efforts to control necessity by normalizing deviant practices through legislative means.[39] Specifically, the invitation to engage in mass detention in an emergency neither guarantees against further constitutional deviation, nor assures that such power will be used only in especially dire situations.

A ratchet effect might ensue when decisions that create emergency exceptions produce new norms for which future emergencies create new exceptions, ratcheting up security policies while diminishing liberty.[40] Such a ratchet would move in only one direction—away from liberty, loosening the constraints that would otherwise inhibit executive actions. And indeed, as we shall see, in the case of judicial doctrines regarding policing practices, for example, special needs in one situation rendered normal have grown to cover additional situations. In this way, deviation from prior baselines can become the new normal, altering perceptions about what is appropriate and what is necessary. The concern is that more than ratchet effects, the polity comes to see the very meaning of the right differently, not because we have engaged in a deliberative process about the meanings of American constitutionalism and its relation to privacy, but because episodic claims to necessity have unreflectively changed constitutional meaning. Doctrinal shifts in constitutional criminal procedure illustrate this dynamic.

Let's first canvas some Fourth Amendment basics: unreasonable searches or seizures of both persons and places are forbidden. Possession of a judicial warrant backed by probable cause to believe evidence will be found is sufficient to make a search reasonable. There are other ways to justify a search—for example, a limited search of a person may be conducted based on reasonable suspicion. But a baseline rule of criminal procedure is that the Fourth Amendment requires police officers to obtain a warrant backed by probable cause from a neutral magistrate before entering a person's home to look for evidence of criminal wrongdoing. Baseline rules are not absolute but are subject to exceptions capable of redefining the meaning of the rule.[41]

The Supreme Court has carved out an exception to basic Fourth Amendment rules in situations claimed to be exigent for public safety—for example, when in hot pursuit of a fleeing felon, or when needing to administer "emergency aid."[42] This family of exigent-circumstance exceptions is intended to give constitutional flexibility to police officers faced with rapidly unfolding dangerous situations. Fourth Amendment doctrine constantly negotiates a tension between a right to privacy and the needs of police.[43]

Exigency justifies constitutional deviation. For example, in *Kentucky v. King*, the Supreme Court held that when police have probable cause to believe contraband lies on the other side of a residential door, but have no warrant justifying a search, they may enter anyway if they can articulate a fear that evidence will be imminently destroyed. As the Court proclaimed: "[A] rule that precludes the police from making a warrantless entry to prevent the destruction of evidence whenever their conduct causes the exigency would unreasonably shrink the reach of this well-established exception to the warrant requirement."[44] The reason the exigency might be "police created" is because it is only in response to the police knocking on the door in the first instance, seeking to confront the inhabitants inside, that the behavior behind the door could be construed as creating an exigency. In this way, the exigent-circumstances exception to the rule becomes part of the meaning of the rule.[45] Despite the special protected status of the home, a place where the Supreme Court asserts that the Fourth Amendment draws a firm and bright line, exigent circumstances in light of order-maintenance priorities provide a doctrinal mechanism for necessity to alter constitutional baselines.[46] Thus, even a place of special constitutional protection can be invaded by police absent the normal procedures if the necessitous circumstances can be judged to warrant the intrusion. In this way, claims of necessity constitutionalize privacy invasions otherwise unavailable.

In the context of criminal procedure, exigency, like emergency, supports claims to act free from ordinary constitutional constraints. Consider another example, one that has particular salience for counterterrorism policies and practices. Under normal situations, the Fourth Amendment prohibits suspicionless searches of individuals.[47] In order to have authority to conduct searches of persons or places, state officials must either obtain a warrant from a neutral magistrate legitimated by the requisite individualized suspicion or rely on a specific exigency.[48] Exceptions abound for this requirement.

Recognizing a need for flexibility in police practices, the Supreme Court held that suspicionless searches are sometimes justified as necessary to meet a "special" government need. This "special needs" exception to the ordinary Fourth Amendment warrant requirement lowers the standard that justifies police invasions of privacy in light of the special circumstances said to exist in particular contexts.[49] Responding to a perceived compelling state need, the

Court authorized border patrol agents to conduct suspicionless searches of cars for illegal aliens near the Mexican border.[50] When conducting suspicionless searches, police have neither individualized suspicion nor a warrant. They act on their own discretionary authority. But the circumstances of the potential criminal behavior rendered such searches necessary, the police claimed, and the Supreme Court agreed. Having established the exception by accommodating claims of necessity in one circumstance, similar claims arose. As a result, the courts recognize special needs for suspicionless highway sobriety checkpoints, checkpoints for information gathering, drug testing of student athletes, searches of airline baggage, and, relevant to counterterrorism, random searches of bags in the New York City subway system.[51] In each case, the special need is justified by circumstances that purport to make necessary the searches and temporary seizures employed by state officials, which have the effect of suspending the normal rule.

The right of "the People" to be free from unreasonable searches and seizures was never meant to be an absolute, thereby being ripe for adjustment in light of necessity. What is unreasonable will vary with the circumstances, and the Court's attention to police needs in normal criminal investigation will only increase in the context of national security.[52] Indeed, we can see how flexible standards such as reasonable suspicion—the minimal requirement police must satisfy in order to temporarily detain an individual to ascertain whether criminal activity is afoot—can be applied in ordinary contexts with an eye toward the extraordinary. In *United States v. Arvizu*, the Court accepted an argument that police could aggregate a number of innocent behaviors to justify reasonable suspicion.[53] Obliquely reasoning in light of the possibility of a future, more extraordinary case, the Court concluded that police should be afforded discretion in drawing conclusions based on the "totality of the circumstances." Because what appears as quotidian may in fact be extraordinary, what counts as reasonable suspicion to justify temporary detention and further investigation is a matter to which "due weight" must be given to the needs and inferences of law enforcement officers.[54] When, for example, New York City implemented a policy of random searches of subway travelers' bags, the Second Circuit Court of Appeals upheld this public safety policy by noting that "[w]e have no doubt that concealed explosives are a hidden hazard, that the Program's purpose is prophylactic, and that the nation's busiest subway system implicates the public's safety. Accordingly, preventing a terrorist from bombing the subways constitutes a special need."[55] Asserting that the searches were necessary in order to prevent terrorist attacks, government officials used claims about necessity to alter constitutional baselines.

Similarly, when it comes to claimed law enforcement need to conduct a buccal swab applied to the inside of a person's cheek to obtain DNA information from a person arrested for a serious offense, the Supreme Court in *Maryland v. King* balanced the "need for law enforcement officers" to obtain accurate identification of those they arrest with "the degree to which the search intrudes upon an individual's privacy."[56] Privacy "depends on the context within which a search takes place," which incorporates the special needs the State might have for obtaining nonconsensual information.[57] When privacy is diminished because the intrusion is judged minimal, then law enforcement procedures become reasonable in relation to Fourth Amendment constraints if the state can articulate legitimate reasons for the intrusion. The standard is not high. If the needs of law enforcement justify invasions of a protected right of privacy in ordinary cases, then when the need is claimed as necessary for safety and security, constitutional constraints are all the more susceptible to a light measure in the assessment of balance.

In the case of surveillance, to which I turn in the next section, courts have focused on "the nature of the government intrusion and how the government intrusion is implemented. The more important the government's interest, the greater the intrusion that may be constitutionally tolerated."[58] As this reasoning makes clear, the government interest is first foregrounded, after which a court will turn to a question of balance: "If the protections that are in place for individual privacy interests are sufficient in light of the government interest at stake, the constitutional scales will tilt in favor of upholding the government's actions."[59] The scales tilt toward the government in the presence of special needs or exigent circumstances. In this way, necessity gets incorporated into an analysis of the scope of privacy rights, preserving constitutional meaning even as it transforms the scope of the right.

Necessity, whether through claims to exigency or to "special need," is at home in the Fourth Amendment. It is shaped by the doctrines that normalize it, and it in turn shapes the social and political practices and expectations in which it arises. This observation highlights the potential danger unreflective acquiescence to necessity arguments can have in shaping constitutional meanings around exigency. Rather than requiring claims to exigency to conform to preexisting constitutional commitments and understandings, they can instead transform the right. Such transformation is all the more possible in the context of national security and counterterrorism policy, where claims to special need or exigency are used to justify far-reaching surveillance programs.

National Security as Special Need

Surveillance is a central tool of counterterrorism policy and practice. The government needs information. Privacy is a core value protected by the Constitution. Persons need to be left alone to pursue their lives. Surveillance needs and privacy protections are therefore in inevitable tension. Claims about necessity provide the justifications government officials offer for expanding surveillance at the expense of both privacy and liberty. And, indeed, Americans are exposed. The expansion has been so vast that it is becoming common to claim that we live in a national surveillance state.[60]

To see how necessity has played this role, let's begin with the statutory framework created by Congress that provides basic surveillance authority to executive departments. The Foreign Intelligence Surveillance Act (FISA), established in 1978, provides the statutory authority for obtaining foreign intelligence aimed at non-U.S. persons. FISA created the Foreign Intelligence Surveillance Court (FISC), which reviews government requests for authorization to conduct surveillance targeted at non-U.S. persons to determine whether they comply with statutory and constitutional standards.[61] Enacted in the wake of extensive congressional hearings, led by Senator Frank Church, into executive abuses of surveillance powers during the period 1936–1975, FISA established the exclusive means by which executive officials could acquire electronic foreign intelligence when communications were routed through facilities located in the United States.[62] Executive abuses were legion. Unwarranted monitoring of the communications of hundreds of thousands of Americans suspected of being "subversives" was conducted over a number of years outside the bounds of any statutory authority and in conflict with constitutional limits on executive authority.[63]

By establishing a special court—FISC—to review applications for warrants to conduct electronic surveillance, FISA mandated that the executive must demonstrate probable cause to believe that the person targeted is a "foreign power" or an "agent of a foreign power," and after Congress's 2001 amendments, that obtaining foreign intelligence is "a significant purpose"[64] of the surveillance (rather than "the purpose," as originally enacted). These targets could be located within the United States or could be communicating with U.S. citizens or other persons located within the United States. In this way, FISA is meant to be flexible. Executive officials could even initiate surveillance first and apply to the Foreign Intelligence Surveillance Court later for judicial authorization in special emergency circumstances. But recall the constitutional baseline: if government wished to monitor a U.S. person, ordinary Fourth Amendment principles apply.

This statutory framework has proven unstable in light of continuing presidential efforts either to supersede statutory limits or to build surveillance programs on the basis of tenuous statutory interpretations. The National Security Agency (NSA) has been the chief government body tasked with collecting signals intelligence, which under a recent nine-year stretch was headed by a four-star general, Keith Alexander, whose motto was "Collect it all."[65] Especially after September 11, the NSA has pursued ever more powerful and ever expanding surveillance capabilities, at home and abroad, in a drive to acquire as much information as possible in order to thwart future attacks.

Two significant revelations have unveiled secret government programs that have transgressed statutory limits and relied upon Fourth Amendment exceptions stretched to extremes. In 2005, the New York Times exposed a secret Terrorist Surveillance Program (TSP) that operated outside the FISA framework. And in 2013, Edward Snowden leaked documents exposing the NSA's pervasive monitoring of U.S. citizens' electronic communications, including previously classified details of the legal analysis relied upon by the Foreign Intelligence Surveillance Court.[66]

When Eric Lichtblau and James Risen revealed in the New York Times the existence of the TSP, President Bush claimed the program was "a vital tool in our war against the terrorists," and that it was pursued in a manner "fully consistent with my constitutional responsibilities and authorities."[67] After September 11, President Bush concluded in secret that FISA was not flexible enough, and he authorized an extensive surveillance program that operated outside of its framework. This program authorized the NSA to eavesdrop on international telephone calls made by selected individuals inside the United States in a search for evidence of terrorist activity. Despite the president's contrary claim, there were serious legal deficiencies in the program. Prior to a subsequent amendment designed to bring the TSP within a legal frame-work, a warrant was required from the FISC supported by probable cause to believe the target was a foreign power or its agent. President Bush decided this was too cumbersome for surveillance of potential al-Qaeda operatives and their associates, and authorized a warrantless program that intercepted the content of communications "into and out of the United States of persons reasonably believed to be linked to al Qaeda" even when the party to the conversation was a U.S. person.[68]

President Bush's view had support from memos drafted by Department of Justice (DOJ) lawyers, who argued that the Constitution confers on the president "the primary responsibility, and therefore the power, to ensure the security of the United States in situations of grave and unforeseen emergencies. Intelligence gathering is a necessary function that enables the President to carry out that authority."[69] We have seen this problematic argument already, and will encounter it being repeatedly used to claim expansive presidential authority.[70] Moreover, as a consequence of the president's powers and responsibilities to counter the terrorism threat after September 11, DOJ lawyers argued that if FISA were "interpreted to impede the President's ability to use the traditional tool of electronic surveillance to detect and prevent future attacks by a declared enemy that has already struck at the homeland and is engaged in ongoing operations against the United States, the constitutionality of FISA, as applied to that situation, would be called into very serious doubt."[71] Going a step further, the president's lawyers asserted that "the President has inherent constitutional authority to conduct warrantless searches and surveillance within the United States."[72] Congress or courts do not matter. This unilateral authority follows because "[t]he Constitution gives him all necessary authority to fulfill that responsibility" it assigns to the president to protect the nation from armed attack.[73] Given the gravity of the perceived threat, and the nature of terrorist attacks, the president claimed a primary obligation to respond to circumstances in the manner he perceived as most necessary. This NSA surveillance program was, the DOJ argued, "an indispensable aspect" of national security, constituting a "special need" for purposes of the Fourth Amendment.[74]

The *New York Times* revelations of illegal surveillance prompted legislative reform that led first to the Protect America Act of 2007 as an interim fix. Congress authorized the NSA to engage in warrantless surveillance of foreign targets "reasonably believed" to be outside the United States and did not intentionally target Americans. Confronting a challenge by communications service providers led by Yahoo, who were tasked with turning over the content of communications to the NSA, the U.S. Foreign Intelligence Surveillance Court of Review added a foreign intelligence gathering exception to the Fourth Amendment's individualized suspicion requirement, citing the precedent of "special needs" cases. When the surveillance is "undertaken for national security purposes," imposing an individualized suspicion requirement for a warrant "would impede the vital national security interests that are at stake."[75] In order to trigger the Fourth Amendment exception, the claim of necessity makes reasonable any deprivations of privacy, because the governmental interest in national security "is of the highest order of magnitude."[76] Because the information sought is not part of ordinary crime control, and because the government can show a vital "special need" in discovering information deemed necessary for national security, what is reasonable under the Fourth Amendment changed to accommodate the claims of necessity. As the court described the conclusion it reached, "the reasoning of the special needs cases applies by analogy to justify a foreign intelligence exception to the warrant requirement for surveillance undertaken for national security purposes and directed at a foreign power or an agent of a foreign power reasonably believed to be located outside the United States."[77] Although privacy is implicated, the special needs of government outweigh any intrusions imposed on personal communications, especially since the national security purpose is different from that of ordinary law enforcement. Moreover, as a prior, and the first ever, opinion from the U.S. Foreign Intelligence Surveillance Court of Review reasoned, the purpose of thwarting "an imminent terrorist attack" means that "[t]he nature of the 'emergency,' which is simply another word for threat, takes the matter out of the realm of ordinary crime control," and thus puts it within the scope of reasonableness afforded government surveillance as a "special need."[78]

As a result of the disclosure, we are able to see how executive officials first use necessity arguments in public to justify constitutional deviations and statutory authorizations, and then, second, use these same arguments in secret to justify expansive interpretations of judicial doctrines and statutory provisions. Section 702 of the FISA Amendments Act of 2008 creates a legal framework authorizing surveillance in a similar manner and scale to the secret Terrorist Surveillance Program that the *New York Times* revealed. Maintaining that he needed the "tools necessary to protect the country," President Bush succeeded in using necessity arguments first to transgress the law, and then to change it.[79] As a result, so long as surveillance is targeted at "persons reasonably believed to be located outside the United States," the information sought is only for foreign intelligence purposes, there are no efforts to intentionally target a person known to be in the United States, and efforts are made to avoid intentionally acquiring communications of persons located within the United States, no warrant is now required from the FISA Court.[80] For targeted persons, reasonably believed to be agents of a foreign power, the executive need only show that foreign intelligence gathering is a "significant purpose," rather than a "primary" purpose, as was previously the case. Although authorized intentionally to target only non-U.S. persons, the NSA can incidentally acquire vast amounts of communication content, including the communications of persons inside the United States who are in contact with those targeted.[81]

In another significant disclosure concerning U.S. surveillance practices, Edward Snowden revealed information in 2013 about Obama administration NSA activities, providing insight into the workings of a vast surveillance program called "PRISM," which allows the NSA to read emails, Facebook chats, private messages, internet search histories, and more—all obtained directly from the servers of Google, Microsoft, Facebook, Yahoo, Apple, and other providers of internet services.[82] According to a FISC opinion authored by Judge John Bates and released to the public after the

Snowden leak, the "NSA acquires more than two hundred fifty million Internet communications each year pursuant to Section 702," on which the president relies in pursing this broad program of surveillance.[83] The NSA gathers even more communications from an "upstream" collection of data directly from fiber optic cables and other infrastructure as the data flows past. Each of these programs in fact captures the communications of U.S. persons either because they are in contact with targeted persons abroad or incidentally in the pursuit of targeted communications. Either way, U.S. persons are not supposed to be intentionally targeted, and the NSA must adhere to procedures that minimize incidental surveillance of U.S. persons in order to comply with the Fourth Amendment. Because there is no requirement that each target be individually identified, the judge's role in reviewing the surveillance program is limited. If the government provides all the required information regarding its section 702 data collection, including a demonstration that its minimization procedures are reasonably designed to avoid unintentional acquisition of U.S. persons' communications, then under the statute, a judge may not question the underlying substance of the application. The scope and scale of this suspicionless surveillance is vast, to say the least. *The Guardian* reported that over a thirty-day period in March 2013, the NSA acquired 3 billion pieces of intelligence from its internet monitoring, which included data from U.S. persons.[84] Moreover, the NSA daily collects and stores more than 1.7 billion emails, phone calls, and other communications, or more than 850 billion call events in 2007—and this is through another NSA tool called XKeyscore.[85]

In seeking reauthorization for the program before Congress in 2012, the government argued that this surveillance program constituted "a critical intelligence collection tool that has helped to protect national security."[86] To both Congress and courts, executive officials across both the Bush and Obama administrations consistently invoked necessity claims to justify an ever growing expansion of surveillance. To the extent that the Fourth Amendment provides a limit on these claims to vital need—to necessity—it is already inflected by an understanding that balances the government claims to necessity against the privacy interests at stake.

The constitutional right against unreasonable surveillance, designed to check executive claims to necessity, itself imbeds exceptions for "special need" or exigency in a way that gives executive officials two layers of necessity justification: first, for the statutory authorization or doctrinal principle, and second, for expanded application of each of these. Thus, apart from recognizing a "special need" for a "foreign intelligence exception" for information deemed vital for national security, the Foreign Intelligence Surveillance Court balances these claims against any individual privacy interests invaded. By examining the acquisition, retention, and use of information by the NSA, the reviewing court draws conclusions about the "reasonableness" of the surveillance, though absent any countervailing advocacy on behalf of the privacy interests at stake. Only when there is a deficiency in the procedures minimizing, though not eliminating, the acquisition and retention of information about U.S. persons, as well as purely domestic communications, does the scope of the program violate the Fourth Amendment. In this way, Judge Bates's 2011 FISC opinion reviewing the NSA's section 702 minimization procedures in place at that time concluded that incidentally acquiring tens of thousands of U.S. persons' communications violated the Fourth Amendment, even though this large number of persons affected constituted a small percentage of the overall communications the NSA collected. Even so, the absolute number—tens of thousands—was large, and the NSA could not show that such collection "serve[s] the national security needs underlying the Section 702 collection."[87] When the quantity of data and persons affected becomes sufficiently large, even a program justified by "special needs" can run afoul of the Fourth Amendment. But the magnitude of the intrusions only serves to highlight the distance constitutional constraints can bend in order to accommodate the claimed needs of necessity. Moreover, Judge Bates's ruling is limited not to requiring the NSA to cease acquiring upstream data, but to put in place better procedures for "minimizing" the incidental collection of strictly domestic communications content.

From the development of a category of searches constituting "special needs" in limited circumstances, courts and government actors have expanded the exception to encompass expansive collection of data about U.S. persons, even if only incidental to the targeting of non-U.S. persons. In this way, "balancing" in light of claims to necessity leads to increased loss of privacy. But the loss of privacy is internalized by constitutionalizing necessity through the "national security exception" to the Fourth Amendment.

In addition to monitoring the content of large numbers of internet communications, the Snowden leaks also revealed a secret, comprehensive program that collected the metadata of all Americans' communications—the number from which a call is placed, the number dialed, as well as the time and duration of the call and apparently the location of the phone—and all this information is retained for up to five years.[88] Section 215 of the Patriot Act authorized the collection of "the production of tangible things (including books, records, papers, documents, and other items) for an investigation to obtain foreign intelligence information," which the Bush and Obama administrations interpreted to include bulk telephony metadata.[89] Because information about the potential contacts of a possible terrorism suspect would be of vital importance, and because such information would be lost if not collected, President Obama argued that such collection is necessary for national security. Government needs the data now in case it needs to query it later. Thus, all metadata records are "relevant," and "bulk collections such as these are "necessary to identify the much smaller number of [international terrorist] communications," as a FISC opinion reasoned in upholding the program.[90]

Implementing statutory authorization to acquire "business records" to include all the metadata of U.S. personal communications is staggering in scale, demonstrating that by making claims to national security necessity, executive officials are capable of taking as broad and bold a step as interpretive creativity will allow. In secret the FISC concluded that no constitutional violation occurs in the systemic collection of such data. The Supreme Court in *Smith v. Maryland* had concluded in 1979 that there was no expectation of privacy in the numbers a person dials, because one voluntarily conveys this information to a telecommunications provider in order to complete the call.[91] Under the Supreme Court's reasoning, if one voluntarily conveys information to a third party, then one no longer has a reasonable expectation of privacy in that information. Without a reasonable expectation of privacy—a doctrine the Court adopted in the 1967 decision *Katz v. United States*—one can have no Fourth Amendment protection against government access to the shared information.[92] Following the logic of this "third party doctrine," the Supreme Court in *Smith* authorized police use of a pen-register device without a warrant to obtain records of the numbers a particular suspect dialed. But can a Supreme Court case about a single instance of obtaining analog telecommunications data of a single person apply to the digital telecommunications information of all Americans? Apparently, yes. The FISC agreed with the government that this doctrine applies to bulk metadata collection. Seeing no distinction between the single, limited-duration case for a specific law enforcement end and the bulk collection of every American's call records at all times, Judge Eagan, writing for the FISC, observed that "so long as no individual has a reasonable expectation of privacy in meta data, the large numbers of persons whose communications will be subject[] to the ... surveillance is irrelevant to the issue of whether a Fourth Amendment search or seizure will occur."[93]

This point about the quantity of data is a source of constitutional disagreement subject to future development, for the Supreme Court has clarified that *Smith*'s reach is confined to its technological circumstances. In *Carpenter v. United States,* the Court held that in ordinary criminal investigations police may not access historical cell site data from a person's cellular telecommunications provider without a warrant, rejecting the government's argument that the third-party doctrine limited the Fourth Amendment's reach. Concerning this form of incidental metadata, the Court reasoned that "when the Government tracks the location of a cell phone it achieves near perfect surveillance, as if it had attached an ankle monitor to the phone's user."[94] Although not directly applicable to the NSA metadata program, it at least signals the possibility of shifting constitutional constraints, despite the Court's narrowing claim that "our opinion does not consider other collection techniques involving foreign affairs or national security."[95]

After Snowden revealed the breadth of NSA surveillance, the Obama administration justified its program as a matter of balancing the needs of security with respect for liberty, emphasizing the claim that the program constituted a minimal privacy intrusion, and relying on the "third party doctrine" to conclude that no Fourth Amendment interest was invaded. In a white paper that explained the legal arguments said to support the administration's practice, the DOJ defended the program by reasoning that "any arguable privacy intrusion arising from the collection of telephony metadata would be outweighed by the critical public interest in identifying connections between terrorist operatives and thwarting terrorist plots, rendering the program reasonable within the meaning of the Fourth Amendment."[96] Despite the confidence portrayed in the constitutionality of the program, President Obama gave a speech in January 2014 that simultaneously defended the program and admitted its contested character—all the while promising future reform. He acknowledged, "we have to make some important decisions about how to protect ourselves and sustain our leadership in the world, while upholding the civil liberties and privacy protections that our ideals and our Constitution require."[97]

Many of these "important decisions" were made in nonpublic administrative venues, with limited congressional oversight, that took on a more urgent need for justification and redesign only after Snowden revealed the program's existence. They were also made in a way that gave priority to necessitarian logic, rejecting the very idea of constitutional limits, while also subordinating privacy to security. Even the order of priority within the speech is first about the necessity of privacy-invasive surveillance for national security purposes and secondarily about the need to uphold "our ideals" and "basic values" in compliance with the needs of necessity.[98] Without Snowden's revelations, President Obama was otherwise content to make these "important decisions" unilaterally on the basis of contestable and broad statutory interpretations as well as self-serving claims to broad executive authority unconstrained by constitutional rights.

One feature of the post–September 11 intelligence-gathering imperative is the epistemic belief that an adequately empowered observer can discern the causal pattern revealing the plot to the next attack. This "mosaic theory" claims that hidden in the prosaic details of everyday life—phone records, financial records, internet search histories, and the like—are clues to unlocking, and therefore preventing, a future attack.[99] The adequately empowered observer must have access to vast amounts of data in order to draw the connections and to understand their meaning. Or, as the Obama administration argued, to look for a needle in a haystack, you have to first compile the haystack.[100] But adopting a mosaic approach, U.S. counterterrorism practice depends on pervasive, large-scale surveillance of ordinary life. It is under this theory that President Obama defended a U.S. policy of mining vast amounts of metadata about the communication habits of all Americans, seeing no need for public debate or judicial intervention until Snowden's leaks forced them to the fore. The practical justification for such pervasive surveillance also relies on the claim that such methods are necessary to ful-filling the president's duty to keep America safe. To achieve compliance with congressional authorization, the president relies on strained readings of "business records" in the case of bulk metadata under section 215, or an ex-panded claim of "relevance" under section 702 in the case of PRISM. But in each case, the special needs of national security also lead to additional claims about the priority of executive expertise regarding questions of security over judicial concerns about the impact on liberty that, in their most robust form, are claims to executive unilateralism and supremacy.

When the president's program was publicly challenged, however, federal courts rejected the legal justifications purporting to legitimate such wide-spread surveillance. Indeed, the federal court for the District of Columbia held that, as a case about limited use of analog technology, *Smith* could not govern bulk collection of contemporary digital data. The quantity of data available changed the very nature of the surveillance and thus ran afoul of Fourth Amendment privacy protections.[101] Judge Leon reasoned that "the almost-Orwellian technology that enables the Government to store and analyze the phone metadata of every telephone user in the United States is unlike anything that could have been conceived in 1979."[102] Moreover, the ubiquitous role that cell phones play in contemporary life means that the types of metadata now available are vastly different than what was available in 1979, with the result that Americans very well may expect far more pro-tection for privacy in the amount of information potentially available to government surveillance. The Supreme Court in *Carpenter* acknowledged that the quantity of data is constitutionally significant.

At least in terms of the political understanding of constitutional con-straints, public outcry and congressional skepticism led to passage of the USA Freedom Act in 2015, which among other things ended the NSA bulk metadata program in its unilateral form.[103] Access to Americans' metadata has not been foreclosed, but rather the data is retained by telecommunica-tions companies who must grant NSA access only upon statutorily pre-scribed procedures. Other changes were made as well, such as the number of "hops" analysts can query having been reduced.[104] The Obama administra-tion had claimed the power to query the phone records for the associations of up to three persons removed (the contacts of the contacts of those called by a targeted person), which is a very large number of persons whose associations could be mapped on the basis of one suspicious person. What remains is a vast surveillance capacity claimed consistent with constitutional values even as it transforms both their meaning and the meaning of the "state" charged with upholding them.[105]

How Necessity Challenges Constitutionalism

In both cases—President Bush's Terrorist Surveillance Program, and President Obama's bulk metadata collection program—initial choices about the scope of policy and presidential power were made without public debate or accountability. In the case of the section 702 content program, as we have seen, the FISA Court had some oversight, and even refused to uphold some aspects of the program, but did so in a legal space where privacy interests had no advocate apart from those already committed to the securitarian paradigm.

Necessity within constitutional doctrine is both creative and dangerous. First, necessity can alter our understanding of the scope and meaning of a constitutional rule by expanding exceptions through doctrines designed to give greater flexibility and power to government. Second, by purporting to justify illegal activity said to be necessary in secret, once publicly revealed, the president can push Congress to grant more power with greater intrusion into everyday privacy, citing the purported success or indispensability of the program. And even when procedurally modified, as in the case of the USA Freedom Act, executive officials retain the ability to query substantially similar data to that available under the secret program. Thus, on the basis of claims to necessity on behalf of national security, creative—and yet potentially dangerous from a rights-based perspective—policies and understandings of law become entrenched. In this way, necessity risks undermining the very constitutional doctrines and practices in which it plays a normalizing role.

What is significant about this line of cases, and their use in justifying executive surveillance practices, is the way in which it becomes possible for a "special need" in one circumstance to spread to others. Constitutional doctrine moves by accretive creep from a point of specific "special need" to the blossoming of many different "special needs." What was special becomes ordinary. We thus begin to see the world in terms of terrorist threats and suspicionless searches. The core modern Fourth Amendment doctrine, derived from *Katz*, provides that the Fourth Amendment protects expectations of privacy that society is willing to recognize as reasonable.[106] When the incremental growth of "special need" exceptions leads to suspicionless searches of pedestrians on sidewalks in urban centers, or suspicionless monitoring of everyday electronic communications, expectations to a privacy right to be "left alone" when in public become more difficult to maintain. Many real and potential effects follow.[107] In Justice Brandeis's famous analysis of the right to be left alone, the political sphere must remain free from monitoring in order to allow room for self-government. In an era in which government was tapping new technologies for surveillance purposes, Justice Brandeis argued, "The greatest dangers to liberty lurk in insidious encroachment by men of zeal, well meaning but without understanding."[108] Justice Douglas echoed this sentiment years later, arguing that "monitoring, if prevalent, certainly kills free discourse and spontaneous utterances."[109]

In this way, the concern over intrusive government surveillance is not only about its effects on the private lives of individuals, but on the political practices of free debate and association that are necessary conditions for successful collective self-determination. Invasion of personal liberty is an invasion of the means to democratic government. And if the claim is that in order to protect the conditions for self-government, necessity undermines that liberty in nonreflective, secret decision-making processes, then a paradox follows. Necessity would seem to justify undermining political security in order to protect physical security.

Justice Sotomayor sounded a similar note regarding the need to preserve personal and political spaces free from the potentially stultifying effects of systemic surveillance in her *United States v. Jones* concurrence.[110] In that case, the Court rejected the government's claim that it invaded no protected interest in privacy when it placed a Global Positioning System (GPS) monitoring device on Jones's car to track all of his movements over the course of a month. There was no interest in privacy, and thus this GPS monitoring did not constitute a search for purposes of the Fourth Amendment, the government urged, because it was only monitoring the publicly observable movements of the defendant. In a prior case, *United States v. Karo*, the Supreme Court had reasoned that since a person's movements in public are readily viewed by anyone who cares to look, the Fourth Amendment does not bar police from also tracking these movements, even when they used the assistance of radio technology.[111] The government in *Jones* argued that using GPS technology to track the whole of a person's movements fell within the scope of the Court's prior reasoning. In rejecting this argument, Justice Sotomayor followed the reasoning of Justices Brandeis and Douglas, who preceded her in urging both the personal and the more systemic political consequences of expanded government surveillance. How persons inhabit public space will change, on their view, with the reduced privacy they receive from public search and surveillance practices.[112] The quantity of data available from systemic GPS tracking of the whole of a person's movements would produce substantially greater risk of chilling protected liberty of movement and association.[113]

How judicial doctrine incorporates claims of necessity under the Fourth Amendment shapes the meaning of privacy, which in turn provides the principle through which future claims to necessity will be evaluated. In this way, exigencies and special needs both destabilize and restabilize existing constitutional orders by altering constitutional meanings and governing practices as well as the social practices they impact.

The civil libertarian can argue that the growth of "special needs" fails to weigh the importance of privacy rights, while the national security advocate can argue that security requires these constitutional exceptions. Whether judicial doctrine should create and expand exceptions or uphold privacy baselines, both views agree that necessitarian justifications given in terms of "special needs" fall within ordinary constitutional discourse. Through a doctrinal structure of justification, government actors must demonstrate that their actions are the product of "reflection and choice." Within such a structure of justification, arguments on behalf of necessity calling for some form of overridingness on behalf of "pressing public necessity" outside of normal constitutional discourse should have no traction. Such arguments have the form of "accident and force," urging actions and legal interpretations that could have lasting effect without consideration of their holistic legal consequences.

Attention to tiered scrutiny and exigency within Fourth Amendment doctrine highlights how necessity claims within the Constitution are bound by justificatory frameworks. The Constitution incorporates necessity through justificatory processes. Deviations from rights baselines on claims of necessity must be justified in ways that honor constitutional commitments. "Pressing public necessity" does not jettison constitutional discourse. Rather, it is but one, particularly robust, move in a complex constitutional structure of justification. Assertions of presidential power are incomplete without further institutional and rights-based justifications. From the everyday claim that an incidental burden on a constitutional right serves a legitimate government interest, to the claim that a substantial burden is justified by the overwhelmingly important government interest in national security, necessity is bound by structures of justification. As we have seen, problems emerge either from the attempt to avoid public justification through secret legal transgression or interpretation, or from too much deference to rote claims to executive claims about national security necessity.

Exigency arguments are highly particular and episodic, albeit scalable. They are about particular recurring problems that occur in the exercise of regulatory police powers and the compelling need to deviate from baseline protections for individuals. They are not comprehensive in terms of their governing powers or their effects on individuals. An isolated example of being subjected to a drug test or a warrantless home entry invades privacy and degrades dignity, but it need not affect the polity in a comprehensive way. It is when government practices move from isolated instances to more regularized practices that exigency turns into normality. This generative move—from episode to program—is possible whether the effects on civil liberties and national power are slight or grave. This programmatic possibility requires continuing constitutional vigilance.

A key difference between particular exigencies capable of repetition in everyday life and emergencies is that the latter come already packaged to a greater scale. Emergencies do not have to be aggregated to produce more comprehensive government practices and effects. Because of the potential scale and reach of emergency circumstances, and the demand for governing responses, greater constitutional deviance and destabilization are possible. With both localized exigency and more widespread emergency, necessity can feature both generative and dangerous effects. Controlling these effects is the difficult task for constitutional theory and practice committed to governing through "reflection and choice."

4

Constitutional Emergencies
Inside and Out

AN ADVOCATE FOR STRONG NATIONAL POWER, Alexander Hamilton urged in
Federalist 23:

> The authorities essential to the common defense ... ought to exist without
> limitation, because it is impossible to foresee or define the extent and variety
> of *national exigencies,* or the correspondent extent and variety of the means
> which may be necessary to satisfy them. The circumstances that endanger
> the safety of nations are infinite; and for this reason no *constitutional shackles*
> can wisely be imposed on the power to which the care of it is committed.[1]

Citing to this and similar statements, Department of Justice (DOJ) lawyers
working under the G. W. Bush administration similarly argued, "The text,
structure and history of the Constitution establish that the Founders entrusted the President with the primary responsibility, and therefore the power, to ensure the security of the United States in situations of compelling,
unforeseen, and possibly recurring, threats to the nation's Security."[2] As
prior chapters have similarly noted, lawyers such as John Yoo made these
arguments in the context of a claimed unreviewable and unilateral power to
detain even U.S. citizens indefinitely and without any judicial review on the
claim that they presented grave threats to national security in the "war on
terror." Justice Thomas accepted the Bush administration's position, arguing in his dissenting opinion in *Hamdi v. Rumsfeld* that the president has
"primary responsibility—along with the necessary power—to protect the

national security and to conduct the nation's foreign relations."[3] "Constitutional shackles" on the presidentialist and securitarian view include the Supreme Court's decision in *Hamdi*, which imposed Due Process Clause protections on Bush administration detention practices at Guantánamo Bay in order to protect basic constitutional liberties—a hearing before a neutral body to contest the factual basis of detention. "National exigencies"—emergencies—give these presidentialist arguments greatest salience, for it is under such circumstances that arguments empowering governing officials to do whatever is necessary have greatest force.

Because of this relation between necessity and emergency, American constitutionalism's sliding scale—from ordinary necessity that balances needs against limits to more pressing needs that create exigencies—leads to the extreme situation we conceptualize as emergency. As we saw in the case of Lincoln's unilateral suspension of habeas corpus, emergency arises as a particularly disruptive event in a polity's life. But where the Suspension Clause is an emergency measure, designed to give some latitude to executive power while an emergency situation unfolds, a broader claim about the necessity that emergency creates would sweep away all other governing priorities and constraints. Constitutionalism's ability to incorporate and thereby overcome necessity reaches a limit when it comes to claims about emergency as events that supersede all other legal constraint.

One view might locate the controversy over the extent of emergency powers within the political realm. It is for an electorate and their representatives to hash out the scope of emergency authority and the shape of substantive policy. Law professors Gabriella Blum and Philip Heymann articulate such a view: "At the heart of the question of how to manage the tension between the rule of law and the necessities of emergency action lie political understandings of democratic structures and the allocation of powers among the various branches of government."[4] On the one hand, this claim would seem to be unobjectionable. Managing this tension does require an understanding of the complex structures that allocate powers among governing institutions. Yet, on the other hand, limiting the analysis to "political understandings of democratic structures" fails to acknowledge the importance of constitutive understandings about the complex relations among the values, responsibilities, and constraints that guide and structure the "political understandings" and their application to concrete emergency situations. Constitutive features of the polity—its commitment to securing "the blessings of liberty," for example—both inform political understandings and stand outside of ordinary politics. The tension between law and necessity is at heart a constitutional matter.

American constitutionalism requires that constitutional principles matter to our political decision-making processes. In the prior two chapters, I explored the possibility of suspension as a constitutive feature of U.S. constitutionalism, as well as the use of "exigency" and "special needs" as judicial doctrines providing constitutional deviation from baseline rights protections. In each case, I answered questions about how to manage tension between necessity and constitutional governance through development of contested constitutional understandings. Necessity could not be used to avoid justifying government action in light of applicable constitutional principles and values. Suspending habeas is contemplated by constitutional text, and applying exigency doctrines is consistent with flexible balancing of constitutional liberties. The application of each doctrine might be contested, but the outcome always requires constitutional justification, not constitutional avoidance.

"National exigencies"—real emergencies—are different, the modern-day Hamiltonian might urge. Suspension is one way of unshackling government, but perhaps not the only, nor the most useful. It is too hidebound to constitutional structures, when what might be needed is circumstantial flexibility. Might there instead be an internal and implied constitutional principle of necessity that would ground and legitimate both Hamilton's call for "no constitutional shackles" and Yoo's argument that the president has all the power necessary to fulfill his national security responsibility? Some scholars and public officials say yes, arguing that "the law of necessity is an operative principle of the Constitution"—namely, that the Constitution itself imbeds an implied principle of necessity that gives legal priority to claims of necessity.[5] As constitutional scholar Michael Paulsen argues, an internal principle of constitutional necessity would provide a metarule of construction for understanding how constitutional principles apply, or fail to apply, in crisis situations.[6] This purported unwritten internal principle of necessity constitutionalizes prerogative by assigning power to the president to do whatever is necessary in times of dire national crisis, even if that includes violating the constitution in the name of preserving the nation.[7] The imperative to do whatever is necessary to preserve the nation overrides other, more specific, constitutional constraints. A principle of necessity thereby generates presidential power. Such power would furthermore be unified in the executive and subject to no judicial review, since by definition it is an implied power for the president alone. Thus, under this theory, a necessitarian principle resides deep within the Constitution.

On this view, when President Lincoln referred to "indispensable necessity" under which "measures, otherwise unconstitutional, might become lawful, by becoming indispensable to the preservation of the constitution, through preservation of the nation," he appealed to an implied principle of necessity.[8] When appealing to "indispensable necessity," constitutional constraints do not foreclose constitutional powers to act as necessary when triggering conditions are satisfied. Even if prerogative power, or a "constitutional dictatorship," does not apply within liberal constitutionalism, this view reasons that there is an internal constitutional principle of indispensability that accomplishes a similar end. But even better than residual prerogative, constitutional dictatorship, or another external principle, a principle of "indispensable necessity" exists inside the Constitution implied by structure and text. It is implied as a source of power, perhaps, in the way that "privacy" is a source of constraint on government as a right implied from the liberty protected by the Due Process Clause.[9]

If an action is indispensable to preserving the Constitution, it becomes a precondition for the Constitution's existence, and thus cannot be forbidden by that very Constitution. In this way, Lincoln seemingly could justify actions that would otherwise be illegal as in fact lawful. Lincoln's precedent, in which he unilaterally suspended the writ of habeas corpus, called forth the militia, expended public funds, and took other "emergency" actions in response to Southern seccession, can thus be seen as simultaneously justified by both the Suspension Clause and exigency doctrines, as well as by an internal principle of "pressing public necessity." It is this latter principle— the prospect of an "emergency constitution" inside the Constitution—that opens up new questions about the role of necessity.

In the prior two chapters, the goal was to describe ways that the Constitution internalizes and overcomes necessity through particular legal pathways:

the infrequent and extraordinary suspension, or the episodic judicial use of exigency and special needs doctrines, each of which empowers government with a degree of flexibility while preserving the overall constitutive normative order. And even though I reject the idea that the president has a residual royal prerogative power justified by principles external to a constitution, could there be a functionally similar internal principle of necessity? If there is such an internal principle, then claims about emergency can be untethered from other constitutional commitments or principles to empower a president to do whatever is necessary to protect national security. The lingering intuition is, "We want the President to abide by the law except in truly exigent circumstances of national danger,"[10] as Jack Goldsmith explains.

The fact of the claimed emergency—the "indispensable necessity" that requires a president to act—gives rise to a serious new challenge to constitutional constraints and commitments. For the very idea of the Constitution as a precommitment to principles of government and individual liberty can be challenged by granting certain factual circumstances—those that we label dire emergencies—priority status on the basis of which new powers can be based. To take Hamilton's view from *The Federalist*, Yoo's argument on behalf of the Bush administration, and Paulsen's internal principle of necessity as a family of related claims, together these move beyond the idea that the Constitution facilitates responses to necessity through the ways that it regulates them. Rather, in this family, necessity overcomes—or overwhelms—constitutionalism by attempting to shed the limits to action that constraining norms impose. This new position is one that looks only to relate fact to claimed need in such a way as to find the functional equivalent of executive prerogative masquerading as constitutional license. The implied imperative becomes: do whatever is necessary to resolve the emergency. Constitutional constraints need not constrain. Necessity knows no law. Or necessity is the law.

Emergency powers so understood—authority to match power with circumstance—are further bolstered by two additional arguments: the "not a suicide pact" argument, and the extralegal-measures argument. The former reflects a skeptical attitude about rights' constraints during crisis, while the latter proposes a process of acting illegally first and seeking forgiveness later. The "not a suicide pact" might also support the functional equivalent of a constitutional principle of necessity: "a nonlegal 'law of necessity' that would furnish a moral and political but not legal justification for acting in contravention of the Constitution may trump constitutional rights in extreme situations."[11] The constitutional principle finds the moral and political imperative implied within the Constitution, while the extralegal approach defers judgment until later.

As I will explore in what follows, the problem of torture and the "ticking bomb" hypothetical serve as examples of how far these justifications for emergency powers, as an implied principle of American constitutionalism, might go. If confined to the immediate circumstances, changes wrought by emergency might engender milder concern. But just as there exists the cliché that "necessity is the mother of invention," there is the widespread sentiment, exemplified by Milton Friedman, that "[o]nly a crisis—actual or perceived—produces real change. When that crisis occurs, the actions that are taken depend on the ideas that are lying around."[12] The ideas that are lying around presently include a number that invite the facts of necessitous circumstances to occasion lasting changes to constitutional commitments. Friedman's point is that emergency produces change. The constitutional challenge is to control and legitimate that change.

Against either the "necessity knows no law" view or its functional equivalent, the "internal principle of necessity" view, the Supreme Court explained:

> Emergency does not create power. Emergency does not increase granted power or remove or diminish the restrictions imposed upon power granted or reserved. The Constitution was adopted in a period of grave emergency. Its grants of power to the Federal Government and its limitations of the power of the States were determined in the light of emergency, and they are not altered by emergency. What power was thus granted and what limitations were thus imposed are questions which have always been, and always will be, the subject of close examination under our constitutional system. ... But even the war power does not remove constitutional limitations safeguarding essential liberties.[13]

These sentiments were further explored when the Court considered the scope of Congress's commerce power:

> Extraordinary conditions may call for extraordinary remedies. But the argument necessarily stops short of an attempt to justify action which lies outside the sphere of constitutional authority. Extraordinary conditions do not

create or enlarge constitutional power. The Constitution established a national government with powers deemed to be adequate, as they have proved to be both in war and peace, but these powers of the national government are limited by the constitutional grants. Those who act under these grants are not at liberty to transcend the imposed limits because they believe that more or different power is necessary.[14]

Neither of these judicial statements provides a substantive account of what the liberties that limit power are, or what the limits of constitutional grants of power shall be. But they do remind those who would claim that necessity knows no law, that in fact claims about necessity are subject to limits both on the grants of government power and by protections for individual liberty. And even though the sentiment expressed in the latter case has been overwhelmed by a more flexible approach to congressional power, the idea that emergency does not create or enlarge governing power on a claim, without more, that a course of action is necessary, remains sound.

Necessity's role, I suggest, does not support the existence of an implied internal principle of overridingness giving authority for political actors to act beyond constitutional constraints in ways that constitutionalize prerogative by sleight of hand. For necessity justifies legal deviations, not extralegal action. And deviance must be justified within the terms of constitutionalism. The distinction between deviance and illegality is important and marks the boundary of constitutionalism and highlights the function of justification in legitimating emergency responses. To redefine prerogative as an implied principle of necessity erodes any distinction between deviation and deviance. The more the power to match governing practice to circumstance in extreme situations enters into an understanding about the scope and nature of constitutional constraints during emergency situations, the more it also risks shaping the constitutional imaginary in all circumstances.

The Constitution as Suicide Pact?

Absent a principle of necessity that can override otherwise applicable constitutional constraints during emergencies, we are told, constitutional commitments become a collective "suicide pact."[15] Appearing as the title to a book written by a federal judge, the "not a suicide pact" argument admonishes that no responsible executive official would adhere to constitutional principle come what may. "While the Constitution protects against invasions of individual rights, it is not a suicide pact," Judge Richard Posner argues.[16] No one, the argument goes, is so committed to strict adherence to constitutional rights that they would allow great harms to occur, or for the nation to go to ruin, but for the violation of some constitutional right. Thus, it would constitute a kind of "suicide" to protect rights and liberties, or to follow legal requirements, if doing so would lead to great harm. Lincoln expressed a version of this view in his "Message to Congress" in 1861 when he asked, "Are all the laws but one to go unexecuted, and the Government itself go to pieces lest that one be violated? Even in such a case, would not the official oath be broken if the Government should be overthrown when it was believed that disregarding the single law should tend to preserve it?"[17] Generalizing the point that some law might have to give way to preserve the whole, Eric Posner and Adrian Vermeule argue that "[a] well-functioning government will contract civil liberties as threats increase," and that failure to do so "is pathologically rigid not enlightened, and that rigidity is at least as great a threat to national values or to the nation's existence."[18] On this view, necessitous circumstances make constitutional scruples dangerous. Indeed, Posner and Vermeule argue that "[t]he real risk is that civil libertarian panic about the specter of authoritarianism will constrain government's ability to adopt cost-justified security measures."[19]

This "not a suicide pact" view is a moral argument, at root, grounded in an imagined limit to constitutionalism when confronting particular questions of security. It is also an argument about the limits to rights-based constraints on government officials. Judge Posner makes the moral argument clear when he advocates for across-the-board utilitarian balancing of the harms potentially perpetrated by adherence to a rule against the benefits to be gained from its abrogation. "Constitutional law is intended to be a loose garment; if it binds too tightly, it will not be adaptable to changing circumstances."[20] Moreover, this nonbinding loose garment means that the real danger comes from those who view the Constitution as a source of principled commitments not subject to ready discard. As President Bush's attorney general John Ashcroft admonished, "To those who scare peace-loving people with phantoms of lost liberty, my message is this: Your tactics

only aid terrorists, for they erode our national unity and diminish our resolve."[21] The appeal is not to constitutional text, tradition, or history, but to
a moral sense that the higher duty is to do whatever is necessary to protect
national security, constitutionalism notwithstanding.

The very idea that adhering to constitutional rules could be equivalent to
fulfilling a collective "suicide pact" makes sense only from a perspective
that is skeptical of constitutional commitments absent flexible noncompliance options. It is a perspective manifest through an attitude about constitutional constraints, a claim about the implied constitutional principles,
and a commitment to the flexibility entailed by securitarian logics. Rights
constraints, on the "not a suicide pact" view, risk causing positive national
security harms by hampering actions justified by necessity that executive
officials might otherwise pursue. Indeed, on this view, it is the rights-
adherent who is the danger to the polity, not the unconstrained (and legally
ungoverned) government official. As an attitude, the "not a suicide pact"
view shapes substantive practice, but when combined with a claim to implied constitutional authority, it provides additional reason for acting according to a principle of necessity that overrides rights constraints. For the
idea is that it would be fanatical to adhere rigorously to rights constraints,
especially given the authority licensed by a constitutional principle of necessity. In addition, when thinking about the balance of risks between promoting liberty and protecting security, the "not a suicide pact" view is based
on a securitarian logic that gives priority to security as reflected in its very
understanding of the nature of liberty as a risk to the polity. Protections for
liberty might constitute a collective "suicide pact" if zealously guarded.

Moreover, on such a view, the president is said to be the institutional actor best suited to match action to circumstance to meet pressing "public
necessity" with sufficient dispatch, as Hamilton extolled in *Federalist* 70:
the president can act with "[d]ecision, activity, secrecy, and dispatch."[22] As
we explored in relation to constitutional suspension, the claim that emergency gives rise to the need for the president to act was exemplified by
Lincoln's suspension of habeas and other acts taken in response to Southern secession. Because of the president's superior institutional competence, the deference thesis entails that other institutional actors (as well as
lawyers, scholars, and citizens) should step aside and accept the fact that

security has priority over liberty.[23] When such claims are also tethered to an argument that where the president has responsibility to protect national security, he must have whatever power is required to meet the emergency, then adherence to rights protections seems all the more "suicidal" in the face of security threats.

When claiming that a constitution is not a "suicide pact," securitarian advocates seem to have in mind the need to overcome constitutionalism in the name of necessity. Claims of necessity, like the constitutional norms and practices to which they relate, always require further interpretive articulation in light of the facts of the emergency situation. The securitarian fear that too rigid an adherence to constitutional values and processes leads to a polity's self-destruction is an interpretation that gives priority to discretionary responses over constitutionally constrained responses. Indeed, advocates of this view argue that "[i]t is clear, however, that sometimes tangible security harms do in fact occur when claims of civil liberties are respected."[24] Under this reasoning, libertarian insistence on protecting constitutional rights risks producing a dangerous ratchet effect that does not reflect the need to readjust liberties to provide security. As Judge Posner argues, "Civil libertarians are the ratcheters, insisting that every increase in civil liberties should be treated as a platform for further increases."[25] On this view, if government officials and courts were to follow the directions of civil libertarians, we would have increased protection for civil liberties during emergencies at the expense of security. Moreover, because necessitous circumstances change how we should view the relation between security and liberty, Posner and Vermeule conclude that "a government that refuses to adjust its policies has simply frozen in the face of the threat."[26] By valuing civil rights and liberties, and by sometimes providing structural limitations on the methods and options government has in implementing policies, even security policies, the civil libertarian has become the real danger to the state, according to the securitarian.

With the challenge posed by the "not a suicide pact" view, a question of priority arises. Emergency government relies on necessity to lead law and politics. Constitutionalism, by contrast, requires constitutional principles and practices to lead emergency responses. The degree to which necessity overrides existing constitutional principles and commitments depends not just upon the emergency circumstances themselves (whatever these might be) but also on the attitudes and choices with which officials and citizens respond. The attitudes we adopt toward constitutionalized prerogative could lead to empty promises of principled guidance or substantive commitments to legal constraint.

The attraction of constitutionalizing prerogative and adopting the "not a suicide pact" view is that flexibility might be preferred to legal formality in crisis situations. It may be a basic intuition that many share, that there is reason to fear the straitjacket of legal constraint when decisive action is in order. It is difficult to dispel this intuition.

The danger inherent in adopting this attitude, however, is that by incorporating escape hatches for emergency circumstances within the very conception of legal constraints, we risk weakening or undermining them in all situations. Such an attitude builds into the very conception of constraint a principle of flexible freedom and discretion. Once accepted, exceptions have a way of going in search of the means for bringing them about.

Extralegal-Measures Approach

Perhaps a principle of necessity might overcome the inherent danger in fostering attitudes of lawlessness toward emergency situations by incorporating accountability procedures. To do so would go beyond the claim that adhering to constitutional principles in necessitous circumstances constitutes a collective suicide pact. One widely discussed option is to take the position that the president should act in whatever way is necessary to resolve a crisis (no suicide pacts here), and then be subject to post hoc accountability for the actions taken. Under this "extralegal-measures approach," executive officials would be justified in doing whatever is necessary according to the facts of the emergency situation, even when their actions violate otherwise applicable law. If officials violate the law, then they can be subject to prosecution after the fact, thereby preserving the rule of law. If illegal acts are nonetheless justifiable as necessary and appropriate under the circumstances, then their actions can be ratified after the fact. On this view, illegal actions remain illegal. They are not redefined as "outside" the law, nor are they given the imprimatur of ex ante legality. Legislatures do not ratify the action, nor do courts provide creative interpretations redefining the scope of legality to cover the action. Executive officials take responsibility not only for addressing the crisis situation, but for the claimed necessity of their illegal actions. The operative principle of necessity on this view is: do whatever it takes now, be accountable later.

One key caveat exists for this view: a government official's actions must be pursued for the public good and disclosed in order to make accountability possible. Leading proponents of this view, Oren Gross and Fionnuala Ní Aoláin, argue that "[e]ven when acting to advance the public good under circumstances of great necessity, officials remain answerable to the public for their extra-legal actions."[27] Once these conditions of openly pursuing the public good are met, "It is up to society as a whole, 'the people,' to decide how to respond ex post to extra-legal actions taken by government officials in response to extreme exigencies."[28] One goal of this two-step process—act openly first, face accountability later—is to preserve the ordinary legal system from the taint of exceptional and illegal measures. Illegal actions, on this view, cannot lead to deviant perversions of constitutional practices, because they "are not made legal or constitutional as a result of the necessity of the situation."[29] Necessity justifies actions taken only upon subsequent ratification by the public. Without later affirmation, then necessity would fail to justify the authority assumed and the actions undertaken in its name. But without the possibility of public indemnification, then executive actors would lack the authority or motivation to do what is necessary to address the emergency situation.[30]

The attraction of this view is that it need not accommodate necessity as an internal principle of the Constitution, but instead implements a way of incorporating necessity into an evaluation of government action. The conditions of necessity become the normative basis for subsequent public evaluation of the propriety of those actions. A claimed advantage of the extralegal-measures approach is that it maintains the distinction between what is ordinary and what is extralegal, resisting the temptation to find a principle of necessity internal to the Constitution that would convert what is claimed necessary into what is thought constitutional. Such an approach has affinity with Justice Jackson's admonishments in his *Korematsu v. United States* dissent. There, he argued that in the face of claims that military necessity justified the exclusion of Japanese Americans from their homes on the West Coast, "if we cannot confine military expedients by the Constitution, neither would I distort the Constitution to approve all that the military may deem expedient."[31] When confronting claims that national security necessity requires deprivation of liberty—in this case through racial discrimination— more harm follows from constitutionalizing the practice rather than recognizing it as an extralegal measure. Justice Jackson argued that "once a judicial opinion rationalizes such an order to show that it conforms to the Constitution, or rather rationalizes the Constitution to show that the Constitution sanctions such an order . . . [t]he principle then lies about like a loaded weapon,"[32] ready for officials to use on a claim of pressing public necessity. By distorting the Constitution, Jackson argues, future political practices will change to conform to the new shape. But by keeping necessitarian actions extraordinary and extralegal, Americans avoid establishing legal precedents that can be used and expanded on future occasions. Extralegality thus limits necessity's consequence for the polity. Or does it?

On closer inspection, however, the distinction may in fact be largely illusory. First, the model assumes a practice of actual accountability mechanisms—prosecutions, elections, congressional oversight, and the like. There is good reason to doubt the robust availability of accountability mechanisms. For example, as I will explore below, the Bush administration turned to practices that President Obama later unabashedly labeled as torture. Nonetheless, no government officials who perpetrated such acts were sanctioned or prosecuted for their illegal actions. Moreover, attempts by victims to seek damages through private suits from those who perpetrated or facilitated their torture were rebuffed by both the executive branch and the courts.[33]

To mention only one example, a federal court dismissed legal claims brought to hold the private contractors who transported ("rendered") a Canadian citizen, Maher Arar, to Syria in order to be tortured on behalf of the United States. Federal courts accepted the Obama administration's argument that victim suits seeking to hold their torturers accountable for damages would compromise state secrets.[34] Relying on a judicially created doctrine that shelters executive officials from suits when adjudication might risk revealing state secrets, the Obama administration persuaded courts to foreclose even the possibility of accountability. In this way, government actors who committed illegal acts of kidnapping and torture—on the belief that the victim had vital counterterrorism information necessary to protect national security—were never subject to post hoc evaluation. The first step in the extralegal-measures approach was taken, while the second step that purports to legitimate the first was actively thwarted by the very executive officials subject to accountability. To the extent that it is true that executive officials kidnapped, transported, and tortured individuals, not only did they violate the law, but they escaped accountability. Taking the first step without the second undermines the viability of the extralegal-measures justification for necessitarian executive license. According to legal scholar Heidi Kitrosser, such moves more broadly undermine a constitutional structure of substantive accountability that "reflects a goal of enabling regular and adaptable checks against abuses of executive energy and secrecy."[35]

Relying on judicial doctrines to avoid accountability is merely one example of accountability avoidance that undermines the extralegal-measures approach. Executive secrecy itself is another problem. As we saw in chapter 3, absent Edward Snowden's whistleblower revelations, surveillance practices that exceeded statutory authority were conducted in secret, losing the possibility of the kind of accountability that would legitimate actions taken under claims of necessity. Prior to Snowden's revelations, Senator Christopher Coons of Delaware had warned about the scope of NSA surveillance in relation to the FISA Amendments Act Reauthorization Act of 2012, which expanded government surveillance authority.[36] He admonished that "[t]he law doesn't forbid purely domestic information from being collected. We know that at least one Fisa court has ruled that the surveillance program violated the law. Why? Those who know can't say and average Americans can't know."[37] And when individuals subject to surveillance in ways that likely violate the Constitution filed suit, the Bush and Obama administrations successfully argued that they lacked "standing" to sue, since they could not demonstrate that their communications were actually being monitored.[38] If they could not show a concrete injury—demonstrate that the administration had monitored their communications—then the judicial doctrine of standing means that courts cannot consider the merits of their claim. Of course, they are unable to show the concrete injury because the very officials they seek to hold accountable conduct their surveillance in secret, supported by secret legal justifications.

Secrecy undermines accountability. Were it not for Snowden's revelatory actions, no accountability for surveillance practices would be possible, because "[t]hose who know can't say and average Americans can't know." In this way, the executive branch can reflexively rely upon necessity to justify extralegal measures, while simultaneously taking actions to avoid public accountability. When its actions—as in the cases of rendition and mass surveillance—are made public, executive officials then actively seek to avoid any institutional means of holding illegal actors or actions accountable.

One might readily see how presidents might take step one but seek to avoid step two. If officials incorporate into their thinking the belief that illegal actions would be justified if subjected to subsequent accountability, then the claimed necessity of the actions ex ante remain constant, while the availability of later ratification is highly contingent. This contingency is not merely a matter of the vigilance and integrity of citizens, courts, and other government officials, but recursively subject to executive manipulation. Accountability can be avoided. An illegal act claimed to be clearly in the right (because necessary) need not go through the formal mechanisms of public prosecution—or so a president might argue. If an action is necessary, and if in the world of counterterrorism secrecy is important, why ever willingly proceed to step two?

If the first problem with the extralegal-measures approach is skepticism about its availability in practice, the second problem is the instability in its very conception. Step two's ex post perspective informs how one thinks about step one's ex ante status, regularizing as a feature of constitutional practice the idea of readily justifiable extralegal measures. Because the extralegal-measures approach builds into an understanding of constitutional powers and constraints the conditions of their own abrogation— doing whatever is necessary during an emergency—it undermines the purported strength of the ex ante rule that is supposed to be the basis for ex post accountability.

The extralegal-measures two-step approach is meant to "keep the ordinary legal system clean and distinct from the dirty and messy reality of emergency so as to prevent, or at least minimize, the perversion of that system."[39] But if the ordinary understanding of legal rules incorporates the possibility of their own derogation ex ante, then the conditions of necessity that would justify the rule's abrogation ex post have already infiltrated how one thinks about the rule ex ante. The meaning of a rule that incorporates a necessity exception is different from one that does not. In this way, the extralegal-measures approach would unavoidably change the meaning of those constitutional principles and practices subject to abrogation. How one understands a constitutional rule in the first place is a precondition for later judgments both about what kinds of actions constitute derogations and which ones would require post hoc public indemnification.

Thus, the "act first, be accountable later" model might seem comforting, but it will ultimately prove self-defeating, either because of the practical un-availability of ex post accountability or because of the "perversion" of the ex ante understanding of actions. An additional problem could arise from nor-malizing the extralegal-measures approach. If in practice ex post forgiveness were to become the norm, then the rule would no longer constrain. Public officials would expect forgiveness for rule violations, undermining the ex ante effectiveness of legal constraint. As a result of these three failures, an asym-metry would exist between the ex ante and ex post. Adopting this way of thinking makes certain that extralegal measures will happen—and perhaps more readily than otherwise—because of the false belief that there will be ex post accountability to justify the ex ante action. The practical result of the ex-tralegal-measures approach is to incorporate within a polity's legal under-standing a justification for rights derogations without any framework for evaluating their propriety—either within a constitutional system or without.[40]

On the Ideas That Are Lying Around

By appealing to this family of constitutional theories, executive officials seek to justify taking actions viewed as necessary to resolve a national emer-gency. Following the claimed imperative that the Constitution not be a "sui-cide pact," each grants necessity a priority over rights constraints and over structural limitations. Whether acting on principle or practice, necessity provides its own normative ordering, asking only whether the actions un-dertaken are adequate to meet the emergency circumstances. In each case, there is a possibility of later normative assessment. But the grounds for this assessment remain opaque on each of these positions because securitarian logics take priority over protections for liberty, or practices of republican self-government.

Just as the extralegal-measures approach would have more systemic effects were it to become the operative constitutional practice, adopting any internal principle of necessity as an override to other principles presents similar structural problems. Constitutionalizing prerogative as an implied principle of necessity has effects on the other approaches to taming and over-coming necessity upon which prior chapters have focused—suspension and exigency. First, an implied necessity principle may encourage officials to route around the Suspension Clause, relying on less transparent necessity justifications rather than public suspension. Indeed, Justices Scalia and Ste-vens accused the Bush administration of doing precisely this when deciding that the president did not have authority to detain American citizens at the naval station in Guantánamo Bay, Cuba.[41] Second, appealing to an implied principle of necessity can bolster public justifications for suspending habeas in cases that might otherwise lack merit. By bundling the two arguments together, they may appear stronger, and therefore justify more rights-invasive policies, than either standing alone might do.

Finally, absent suspension, the obligations entailed from an implied principle of necessity can be used to justify acceptance of an exigency justi-fication for intruding on a protected right absent judicial review, and out-side the formal mechanisms of suspending habeas. Executive officials would claim exigency and judge its propriety. Citing a duty to do whatever is necessary, executive officials can claim any action they take is therefore constitutional. Because this view is used to justify actions that would other-wise be illegal, finding an implied principle of necessity at the heart of the Constitution therefore has pervasive effects not only for the justification of policy but also for the separation of powers.

If constitutionalism overcomes necessity by establishing commitments to a reflective normative order, then the problem of "emergency powers," by contrast, is that they invite unreflective and episodic change. We are to imag-ine instead the aftermath from a terrorist's detonating a weapon of mass destruction in a major city, for example. We must react with haste and force. Catastrophic terrorist bombings are thus the kinds of emergency events that are likely to produce rupture, not reflective change. The imagined rupture, as the Bush administration articulated when arguing for the necessity of invading Iraq, could be a "mushroom cloud" over a major U.S. city.[42] Since an emergency event of this kind would produce an existential threat to the nation, the result would be a breakdown in the government's effective provision of security, one of the state's basic functions. In light of such imagery, worries over constitutional commitments becoming "suicide pacts" might seem more salient. And thus, claims that the Constitution provides an internal principle of necessity might appear more attractive.

But the problem with such impassioned imagery is that representative democracy relies on reason and not passion—even during emergencies—and that emergency might be used as a vehicle for liberty deprivations. Panic, born of emergency, can produce pathological tendencies for liberal constitutionalism, threatening ever more repressive laws and executive practices because "[a]fter each successful attack, politicians will come up with a new raft of repressive laws that ease our anxiety by promising greater security—only to find that a different terrorist band manages to strike a few years later."[43] Moreover, unreflective change need not be unintended. As President Obama's chief of staff, Rahm Emanuel, proclaimed, "Never allow a crisis to go to waste. They are opportunities to do big things."[44] In this way, the Obama administration embraced Milton Friedman's observation that responses to emergencies are opportunities that depend upon the ideas we have lying around. They are opportunities to accomplish things that in normal times would not be possible. This sentiment is correct, I think. Our prevailing ideas and attitudes matter when the next crisis hits.

We develop the normative constitutional ideas we have lying around to better shape and analyze what we expect from emergency government within structures of republican self-government. By urging that we must do this conceptual work first, I also lay the groundwork to better preserve liberty in the face of emergency claims to prioritize security. Preserving liberty does not have to be an inflexible exercise, but it does have to be one in which claims to national-security necessity internalize a coordinate concern for their normative implications. The problem to overcome is how emergency leads others, like Judge Posner, to conclude that constitutionalism's "basic flaw is the prioritizing of liberty."[45] The problem is that

Posner's necessitarian thinking does not internalize norms of constitutional justification. We can seek security without undermining liberty.

Indeed, the prospect that the combination of executive prerogative and emergency might lead to liberty-depriving tyranny was an explicit Madisonian concern in *The Federalist Papers:*

> [T]he executive department is very justly regarded as the source of danger, and watched with all the jealousy which a zeal for liberty ought to inspire. In a democracy, where a multitude of people exercise in person the legislative functions, and are continually exposed, by their incapacity for regular deliberation and concerted measures, to the ambitious intrigues of their executive magistrates, tyranny may well be apprehended, on some favorable emergency, to start up in the same quarter.[46]

Moreover, as Madison continues, in a representative democracy, the threat of unconstrained and unconstitutional usurpations is tamed by government "pursuing the objects of its passions, by means which reason prescribes."[47]

The special problem of emergency, in short, is that it presents an occasion that purports to exceed all of the other ways that constitutional principles and practices overcome and tame necessity. Doctrines of exigency and principles of suspended judicial review do not apply to the claim that dire circumstances exceed what the Constitution can guide and govern. Emergencies arise from within a constitutional order yet claim to fall outside what that order can regulate. What makes acting on necessity in light of emergency therefore particularly challenging is the prospect that changes within a constitutional order will be dictated by conditions outside, absent the usual "reflection and choice" that is the hallmark of constitutional transformations. It does not improve matters simply to assert that instead of an external extralegal measure, actions are rather justified by an unwritten, implied internal principle of necessity. Such a result would turn the relationship between constitutionalism and necessity on its head, making the operative practice one in which necessity continually seeks to overcome constitutionalism from within. Emergency—addressed by the family of related claims exemplified by extralegal measures, antisuicide rationales, or implied principles of necessity—makes possible ever expanding claims to executive power that intrude into areas protected by constitutional constraints. The problem at issue here is that each of these approaches fails on any account that seeks to place limits on the one-directional expansion of security policies at the expense of liberty. These approaches fail to internalize the constitutional norms and constraints that would otherwise govern and guide emergency measures. And a failure to internalize is a failure to make a meaningful contribution to American constitutionalism.

Torture and Constitutional Emergency

Whereas chapter 2 considered whether and to what extent the president has authority to detain persons on claims of necessity, emergency also brings to the fore questions about how detainees may be treated. Under emergency conditions government officials may confront an informational deficit. What the best course of action is depends on accurate information and intelligence. As a result of this informational deficit, the question of torture seems to have inevitably arisen. As Jonathan Alter wrote in *Newsweek* shortly following the emergency of September 11, "even a liberal can find his thoughts turning to . . . torture."[48] In order to save lives against the emergencies that acts of terrorism create, law professor Alan Dershowitz argued that torture is morally and constitutionally permissible, so long as judges warrant the practice in particular cases.[49]

The question of whether torture might be necessary in some circumstances entered the national consciousness after September 11,[50] not simply through debate over imaginary "what if" scenarios,[51] as I will examine shortly, but also through government action made iconic through the photos leaked of the torture of Iraqi prisoners at Abu Ghraib,[52] as well as in popular culture.[53] Because it touches core moral, political, and legal conceptions of the proper limits to state power and the obligations owed to other persons, torture is a topic of intense academic debate. Indeed, there may be an academic consensus that in extreme circumstances one could morally justify the practice of torture as a lesser evil to avoid the greater evil of many thousands, or even millions, of innocent deaths.[54]

Emergency, the extreme event, and torture, the extreme response, are closely connected. Like other responses to emergency, torture receives its best justification through the family of claims formed by the implied principle of necessity, the "not a suicide" view, and the "do whatever it takes and ask forgiveness later" theory. Given its central prohibitory place within enlightenment constitutional thinking, torture, as a response to emergency, is the most salient example of how far this family of constitutional theories can go in purporting to justify (or engage in apologetics on behalf of) deviant legal and political practices under claims that they are necessary.

A decision to respond to the September 11 attacks entirely through the framework of war, rather than as a massive criminal conspiracy, not only allowed President Bush to utilize enhanced war powers but also shaped other institutions and practices. Peoria, Illinois, was now possibly a "battlefield," as was any other location from which this book might be read.[55] War power claims led to detention, interrogation, surveillance, and targeted killing policies, each with its own constitutional justifications and claims to both unilateral and unreviewable presidential power.

Importantly, initiating a "war on terror" required a threshold interpretive judgment—that the United States was properly in a state of war. War is a contested—and contingent—choice. Despite claims to the contrary, the president *chose* a war framework, having the effect of triggering enhanced executive powers.[56] Moreover, the enhanced powers claimed necessary to address the aftermath of the attacks shaped the ends to be pursued. Rather than focusing on finding and punishing those persons and organizations responsible for terrible criminal acts, a global "war on terror" provided a far broader end to be pursued, requiring different governing actions, policies, and priorities than would responding to criminal actions.[57] As President Bush proclaimed, "After the chaos and carnage of September the 11th, it is not enough to serve our enemies with legal papers. The terrorists and their supporters declared war on the United States, and war is what they got."[58]

According to President Bush, the attacks not only "changed the way we look at the world" but also "revealed the outlines of a new world."[59] Through a number of decisions and institutional choices, executive officials went to work constructing a "new paradigm" that "renders obsolete" prior understandings of domestic and international law.[60] Necessity required "a new kind of war" for which new institutional practices and enhanced executive powers would be needed. Although presented as if imposed by the circumstances—a task imposed but not chosen—both the response as well as the interpretation of the nature of the crisis required constructive choices. These choices gave priority to a particular way of thinking about necessity as justifying constitutional exigencies and emergencies. Such claims constitute a contingent "mindset," as then candidate Senator Obama proclaimed, subject to change through a change in administrations and the adoption of different ideas.[61]

One of those choices arising out of a securitarian worldview was to initiate interrogation practices that President Obama subsequently acknowledged constituted torture. In advance of the release of a Senate report detailing the abuse and torture involved in U.S. interrogation policy and practice during the "war on terror," President Obama admitted, "We tortured some folks," and "did some things that are contrary to our values."[62] But because some of the folks who perpetrated such acts were, in his assessment, "real patriots," it is easy to understand "why it happened. I think it's important when we look back to recall how afraid people were after the twin towers fell."[63] Other than President Obama's admission that such wrongdoing "crossed a line," no official who either perpetrated, authorized, or legally defended such actions was held accountable—a real-world case study of acting illegally ex ante from claimed necessity, out of fear and "under enormous pressure," as Obama phrased it, in the absence of any formal ex post accountability. Indeed, citing the need to move on and focus on the future, Obama repeatedly refused to pursue accountability for illegal acts of torture.[64] In 2012, the Obama administration completed its inquiries into the torture program, announcing there would be no prosecutions, and thus ended "a contentious three-year investigation by the Justice Department."[65] Moreover, when faced with private suits by individuals who were seized, rendered to third parties, and then tortured, the Obama administration invoked the "state secrets doctrine" to argue that courts should not hear the case.[66] Moreover, in other cases—such as a suit to hold John Yoo accountable for his role in allegedly violating José Padilla's constitutional rights—courts declined accountability on grounds that executive-branch actors had qualified immunity from suits for official actions taken under color of law.[67] In this way, the Obama administration, with the assistance of judicial doctrines, shielded perpetrators and facilitators of illegal acts of torture and rendition against legal accountability.

The Senate Select Committee on Intelligence's extensive report on the Bush-era interrogation practices provided public documentation of the scope of the interrogation program, its frequent mismanagement, and the complete absence of accountability for actions that violated domestic and international law.[68] As a consequence of this lack of accountability, those who were architects and builders of an illegal interrogation program that tortured terrorism detainees have continued to advance in government service, ensuring that a return to torture under a future emergency may remain a viable approach. Indeed, Vice President Cheney continued to defend the Bush-era interrogation practices, and President Trump campaigned on returning to the use of torture. In an early draft of an executive order that was leaked to the press, President Trump considered revoking President Obama's decisions to close the so-called "black sites" and to end any further use of "harsh interrogation" practices.[69] Since current law restricts interrogation procedures for all government actors to those authorized by the Army Field Manual, and since the president has the authority to alter the terms of the field manual, President Trump, through his secretary of defense, has the ability to take steps to realize his campaign assertion that torture works. By nominating Gina Haspel to be director of the CIA, Trump clearly signaled a lack of concern about her central role in the agency's harsh interrogation program, including her role in running a "black site" where detainees were subject to conditions that President Obama later acknowledged constituted torture.[70] Trump seems to have a consistent view that there is nothing wrong with torture—having proclaimed that "torture works"[71]—making both detention and interrogation practices subject to future shifts in directions antithetical to human rights commitments.

This episode alone serves as a powerful response to the viability of the extralegal-measures approach. With no public accountability ex post, the ex ante claims to necessity lack the legitimacy the theory purports to grant.[72] Moreover, it would seem that the indefinite possibility of later accountability already infuses the prior decision to violate the law with an implied appeal to an internal principle of necessity. Ex ante justification based on an ex post accountability that never happens simply inscribes a principle of necessity at the heart of executive decision-making. Moreover, the appeal to necessity ex ante with an absence of accountability serves to normalize the illegal practice for future use. As a result, executive responses to the future emergency event can cite as authority the Bush-era interrogation practices. And, paradoxically, the absence of legal accountability can in turn be used as a source of actual legitimation of the acts undertaken.

Looking backward from the absence of accountability, it is perhaps less surprising that in the very few years following the events of September 11, 2001, the focus on human rights, which included a near universal consensus on the prohibitory norm against torture, could dissipate so quickly. In a series of cases brought under the Alien Tort Statute, U.S. federal courts proclaimed that the prohibition against torture is one of the *jus cogens* norms, such that the "torturer has become like the pirate and the slave trader before him hostis humani generis, an enemy of all mankind."[73] Commentators and international law treatises largely agreed. International treaties to which the United States is a signatory, such as the Covenant on Civil and Political Rights,[74] the Convention Against Torture and Other Cruel, Inhuman or Degrading Treatment or Punishment,[75] and the Geneva Conventions,[76] all prohibit the use of torture. Moreover, the Convention Against Torture contains an explicit nonderogation provision, proclaiming that "[n]o exceptional circumstances whatsoever ... may be invoked as a justification for torture."[77] The Supreme Court declared that the use of torture violates the Due Process Clause.[78] In the words of Justice Kennedy, the "use of torture or its equivalent in an attempt to induce a statement violates an individual's fundamental right to liberty of the person."[79] Presidential statements affirm the unequivocal fact that "America stands against and will not tolerate torture."[80]

Despite its near universal legal condemnation, how did the illegal acts of abuse and torture nonetheless happen? I suggest that emergency arguments following September 11, stripped of their judicial limits within exigency doctrines, prevailed in executive branch practice, giving overriding priority to claims of necessity. What did these justifications look like?

DOJ lawyers concluded in classified memos that executive officials had wide latitude to employ interrogation methods they deemed necessary. "As Commander-in-Chief, the President has the constitutional authority to order interrogations of enemy combatants to gain intelligence information concerning the military plans of the enemy," reasoned DOJ lawyers.[81] This memorandum was credited to John Yoo and signed by Jay Bybee, who later was placed on the U.S. Court of Appeals for the Ninth Circuit. In light of the blanket authority to order interrogation, the memo also claimed that federal statutory prohibitions against torture applied only to interrogation methods that inflict pain "equivalent in intensity to the pain accompanying serious physical injury such as organ failure."[82] Congress implemented its treaty obligations under the Convention Against Torture by outlawing acts "specifically intended to inflict severe physical or mental pain or suffering upon another person."[83] The convention obligates signatories to "prevent acts of torture" and "[n]o exceptional circumstances whatsoever . . . or any other public emergency, may be invoked as a justification for torture."[84] Focusing on the federal torture statute's prohibition against "severe" pain, the memo concluded that "[t]he victim must experience intense pain or suffering of the kind . . . that would be associated with serious physical injury so severe that death, organ failure, or permanent damage resulting in a loss of significant body function would likely result."[85] Even under such a tendentious definition of torture, the president need not comply with the statute "if it impermissibly encroached on the President's constitutional power to conduct a military campaign." More than noncompliance, the DOJ declared, "Any effort to apply . . . [statutory prohibitions against torture] in a manner that interferes with the President's direction of such core war matters as the detention and interrogation of enemy combatants thus would be unconstitutional."[86] And, all other arguments failing, an official who committed an act that might qualify as torture under this exceedingly narrow understanding, and who was subject to post hoc accountability, could invoke the criminal defense of necessity to justify his actions.

Because interrogation was central to the administration's counterterrorism efforts, and "harsh" interrogation was the particular means chosen, a number of additional DOJ memos further outlined the extent and combination of methods legally permitted. Specifically addressing interrogations of "high value" al-Qaeda detainees Abu Zubaydah and Khalid Shaikh Mohammed, additional DOJ memos beginning in August 2002 concluded that use of stress positions, nudity, dietary manipulation, sleep deprivation, cramped confinement boxes (with insects), and waterboarding, among other techniques, were all permissible under statutory prohibitions and treaty obligations.[87] These techniques could be employed individually or in combination. Moreover, no statutory, constitutional, or treaty prohibitions—as construed by the Bush administration—stood in the way of waterboarding Abu Zubaydah 83 times and Shaikh Mohammed 183 times over a single month. In a separate memorandum, Department of Defense general counsel William J. Haynes recommended approval of a number of interrogation techniques, including stress positions, physical isolation, sensory deprivation, nudity, and extended interrogations. After Secretary of Defense Donald Rumsfeld approved the policy, Mohammed al-Qahtani was subjected to sleep deprivation, interrogated more than eighteen hours a day, led around on a leash, deprived of clothing, and threatened by dogs, among other forms of "harsh" treatment for purposes of interrogation.[88] Rumsfeld even added a handwritten note to Haynes's memo, asking, "Why is standing limited to 4 hours?" because after all, "I stand for 8–10 hours a day."[89] Although the DOJ memos do take note that "[t]orture is abhorrent both to American law and values and international norms," the memos also concluded that these enhanced interrogation procedures are not torture under U.S. and international law—a conclusion that facilitated enhanced discretionary executive power to direct the course of counterterrorism policy free from specific legal constraints.[90]

And even when memos purported to justify what could reasonably be classified as torture, they set limits to interrogation practices by carefully drawing up and analyzing a list of authorized techniques. Nonetheless, Central Intelligence Agency officials still exceeded even these permissive limits with no accountability. In the case of Abd al-Rahim al-Nashiri, a detainee suspected of planning the bombing of the USS *Cole*, interrogators not only waterboarded him, but subjected him to a mock execution, started a power drill next to his head, and locked him in a coffin for days at a time. These practices were in addition to those, like walling and sleep deprivation, that the Haynes memo sought to justify.[91] In another memo for John Rizzo, the acting general counsel of the CIA, Jay Bybee authorized interrogation techniques to be applied to Abu Zubaydah that included the combined use of prolonged forced standing and other stress positions, facial slaps, cramped confinement in a box that included an insect, sleep deprivation for more than seventy-two hours, and waterboarding. Because on the unchallenged view of the CIA these techniques taken individually or in combination did not constitute severe pain and suffering, nor did the interrogators specifically intend to cause severe mental or physical pain or suffering, there could be no violation of a domestic statute making it a crime "to commit torture," according to the DOJ.[92] Because of Zubaydah's key role in planning the attacks of September 11 and the possibility that he had knowledge of unfolding plots, the administration believed it necessary to utilize such interrogation techniques to make sure to find out what he knew. Zubaydah, on this view, was like the suspect in a ticking bomb hypothetical.

In the wake of his harsh treatment, reports indicate that al-Nashiri suffers lasting psychological effects—as do others subjected to the interrogation methods the DOJ authorized as legal.[93] The effects are contrary to what the CIA asserted, and DOJ lawyers accepted without further question, would be the lasting effects of these techniques. And even when the Bybee memo authorized enhanced interrogation techniques for Abu Zubaydah that would "not be used with substantial repetition," we find that substantial repetition was in fact applied. These episodes demonstrate how actions justified in one circumstance, according to underlying arguments from necessity, will be exceeded at later times under a claim that the necessities of the situation require going even further because "we" need to know what the detainee knows—or more accurately, what we think or imagine the detainee might know. In this way, the purported legal justifications papered over, rather than constrained, executive action.

Executive officials publicly affirmed the key idea that the necessities of circumstance enhanced the power of the executive to act under wartime detention and interrogation authority. Although shying away from embracing the term "torture," Vice President Dick Cheney stated, concerning the waterboarding of suspected terrorist Khalid Shaikh Mohammed, that "[h]e and others were questioned at a time when another attack on this country was believed to be imminent. It's a good thing we had them in custody, and it's a good thing we found out what they knew."[94] Wielding an unusual amount of government power, Vice President Cheney was ultimately responsible for much post–September 11 policy, as he notoriously described the task: "We also have to work, though, sort of the dark side . . . it's going to be vital for us to use any means at our disposal."[95] According to the vice

president, circumstances rendered necessary the use of "harsh interrogation" in order to ensure protection for national security—"we" need to
know what they know. It's a "good thing" to do whatever is necessary to
protect national security, on this view. Such an approach highlights the fact
that the use of torture is as much about what "we" imagine and fear than it
is about what the detainee actually knows.

Vice President Cheney's arguments about what was necessary are also
mindful of legality, even if law is treated as something to avoid or supersede:

> Now, you can get into a debate about what shocks the conscience and what is
> cruel and inhuman. And to some extent, I suppose, that's in the eye of the
> beholder. But I believe, and we think it's important to remember, that we are
> in a war against a group of individuals and terrorist organizations that did, in
> fact, slaughter 3,000 innocent Americans on 9/11, that it's important for us to
> be able to have effective interrogation of these people when we capture them.[96]

The goal is to obtain information without regard to human rights. The only
normative constraint operative is the claimed duty to do whatever it takes to
enhance security. Investigative reporter Barton Gellman observed about
the vice president and George Tenet, director of the Central Intelligence
Agency, that "Cheney considered the gloves off questioning, as Tenet did,
an absolute necessity."[97] Claiming that the president had made "tough and
courageous" decisions in the war on terrorism, Mr. Cheney asserted that
detention and interrogation programs for high-level detainees had yielded
"information that has saved thousands of lives."[98] In other words, the goal
of saving lives makes it necessary to employ extralegal means, with no ac-
knowledgment that necessity might be constrained by what is appropriate,
and no demonstration that other, legal means might have proven just as
effective. Claiming necessity and expediency sufficed.

One feature of Madisonian constitutionalism is the possibility of interbranch checks to balance against excess power in the president. After the
photographs emerged of detainee abuse at the Abu Ghraib prison in Iraq,
and after Yoo and Bybee's DOJ memos were leaked to the public, Congress
moved to strengthen statutory prohibitions against torture and provided
that no individual under control of the U.S. government be subject to "cruel, inhuman, and degrading treatment" through the Detainee Treatment

Act of 2005 (DTA).[99] The act further specified that Department of Defense personnel were limited by the United States Field Manual guidelines when interrogating detainees, which is a far stricter standard than those allowed under DOJ memos authorizing "harsh" interrogation procedures by the CIA or other government officials. For example, waterboarding is not allowed under the field manual, though permitted by the Bybee/Yoo memos. Whether such harsh techniques would violate prohibitions against "cruel, inhuman, and degrading treatment" was a question left unanswered. Such a prohibition is a commonplace of international human rights treaties to which the United States is a signatory, appearing most applicably in Common Article 3 of the Geneva Conventions. It is clearly a prohibition on treating detainees in ways that fall short of torture. But how short? The Bush administration exploited this indefiniteness.

This institutional dynamic, in light of the emergency circumstances in which the claimed necessity of "harsh interrogation" arises, is not a story about constraints alone. The president sought to limit the reach of the new congressional constraints. When signing the DTA into law, President Bush issued a statement declaring that the executive branch would construe the act "in a manner consistent with the constitutional authority of the President to supervise the unitary executive branch and as Commander in Chief and consistent with the constitutional limitations on the judicial power."[100] The president set about construing the act with assistance from the Office of Legal Counsel (OLC) deputy assistant attorney General Steven Bradbury. In two memoranda issued in 2005 and 2006, Bradbury concluded that none of the CIA interrogation techniques then in use—including waterboarding—violated Article 16 of the Convention Against Torture, which prohibits "cruel, inhuman, and degrading treatment," or the Detainee Treatment Act.[101] Both were governed by the Supreme Court's Fifth Amendment standard prohibiting actions that "shock the conscience," reasoned Bradbury—a standard with very little substantive guidance. Reasoning that there are substantive limits to what state actors can do to a person under their obligation to respect limits of bodily integrity, the Supreme Court employed a malleable, and largely unhelpful, "shock the conscience" standard.[102]

To determine whether actions "shock the conscience," Bradbury reasoned in his May 30, 2005, memo addressing "Certain Techniques That May Be

Used in the Interrogation of High Value al Qaeda Detainees," that conduct must be "arbitrary in the constitutional sense," in that it fails to have "any reasonable justification in service of a legitimate governmental objective."[103] In a subsequent memo on August 31, 2006, addressing the implications of the "Detainee Treatment Act to Conditions of Confinement at Central Intelligence Agency Detention Facilities," Bradbury determined that "the ultimate inquiry [under a 'shock the conscience standard'] is whether ... the hardships associated with a particular condition or set of conditions are out of proportion to a legitimate governmental interest."[104] As a result of this reasoning, harsh interrogation techniques that included waterboarding would not constitute "cruel, inhuman, and degrading treatment," Bradbury concluded. If other methods had not elicited the desired information when the CIA had "credible intelligence that a terrorist attack is imminent," and it also had "substantial and credible indicators that the subject has actionable intelligence that can prevent, disrupt or delay this attack," then use of waterboarding would be permitted.[105] As a result of this reasoning, the DTA was no bar to any of the "harsh" interrogation practices that the CIA had been employing and wished to retain discretion to continue. The necessity of gaining particular information was to be balanced against any prohibition against employing particular techniques, allowing increasing harshness the more pressing the interrogator's interest became.

All of this legal maneuvering occurred against a common background, voiced by the executive branch. Speaking of the interrogation of the "high-value" detainee Abu Zubaydah, whom we now know was repeatedly subjected to waterboarding, President Bush claimed, "I can say the procedures were tough, and they were safe, and lawful, and necessary." In this same speech delivered to advocate the creation of military commissions to try suspected terrorists, the president asserted that the United States does not torture and cited DOJ legal determinations that the administration's policies were legal. The president also made clear that his overriding obligation was "getting vital information necessary to do our jobs, and that's to protect the American people and our allies."[106]

Following President Bush's reasoning, all legal constraints are in a kind of rough balance with claims that necessity guides and governs procedures and policies, given the overriding priority of security. These claims of necessity serve to enhance executive power relative to other institutional actors, and they challenge the role that legal commitments and constraints play in guiding choices. The president both articulated a self-understanding of what it is to "do our jobs" and provided an interpretation of the constitutional context in which the overriding responsibility of his office is to "protect the American people." Both the self-understanding and the interpretive context require "reflection and choice," even if the assertion of will is hidden by the implied compulsion of "public necessity." The president's approach was to appear to make all the correct legal pronouncements, and then do whatever he deemed was necessary.

The conflict between choice in circumstances and compulsion of public necessity masks a contested attitude about legal constraints. When the president claimed that the administration's interrogation policies were reviewed by lawyers who determined that they "complied with our laws," he seemed to adopt the perspective Justice Holmes identified with the "bad man."[107] The "bad man," Holmes explained, simply wants to know from law what will keep him out of jail and cares not for the lofty meanings and principles the law is meant to reflect.[108] The journalist Anthony Lewis described the reasoning of the legal memos on which Bush relied in a way that reflects the "bad man" logic: "The memo reads like the advice of a mob lawyer to a mafia don on how to skirt the law and stay out of prison. Avoiding prosecution is literally a theme of the memoranda."[109] Similarly, Jack Goldsmith described the torture memo's rationale this way: "[V]iolent acts aren't necessarily torture; if you do torture, you probably have a defense; and even if you don't have a defense, the torture law doesn't apply if you act under color of presidential authority."[110] President Bush's initial choice of Guantánamo Bay to detain terrorism suspects, combined with his initial claim that neither U.S. courts nor the Geneva Conventions applied, bolstered his identification with the "bad man" perspective on law. At a Rose Garden news conference, President Bush argued against tighter restrictions on interrogation policies in the wake of the Supreme Court's ruling in *Hamdan v. Rumsfeld*, which held that the Geneva Conventions applied to Guantánamo detainees.[111] At one point he asked of the Geneva Conventions in a skeptical tone, "What does that mean, 'outrages upon human dignity'?"[112] Whatever else, the implication is that the legal constraint is not to be embraced as a meaningful limitation on interrogation policy, but as an obstacle to U.S. interrogation policy. Constitutional commitments and constraints are to be followed only when they cannot be evaded, an implication that prioritizes necessity over norms. And when in May 2018, Gina Haspel, one of the Bush administration CIA officials responsible for oversight of interrogation practices at a black site in Thailand, claimed in a Senate hearing that she would "follow the law" if confirmed as President Trump's pick to be director of the CIA, one cannot but note that those responsible for torture all claimed to be "following the law."[113]

The priority of evasion over compliance reflects the priority of necessity over constraint. This priority, however, is not written into the nature of events or institutions. It is the product of intentional choice and interpretation. It is the manifestation of a way of thinking that gives security priority over other governing values. But more than setting priorities, it entails a disposition toward choosing means. Differing temperaments are possible in relation to how the priorities are realized. The relation between law and necessity cannot be determined by the nature of things, but must be chosen in light of the attitudes and priorities we have—and in light of the ideas we have lying around.

The Bush administration chose to embrace the family of views that necessity knows no law, together with the view that the president was authorized, because obligated, to do whatever he deemed necessary to protect national security. I will focus on the scope of presidential power in chapter 6, but the Bush administration's legal view was that neither Congress nor courts nor the polity's constitutional values—apart from the priority of security—could guide or constrain executive officials in doing what was necessary. In this way, we see that necessity overcomes constitutionalism from within. Under this internal principle of necessity, the Schmittian view that constitutionalism can do no more than assign the power to decide seems to have prevailed within the Bush administration.

So as we see, torture and its justifications were among the ideas we had at hand when the emergency arose. A shared social imaginary informs how we think about emergency and its relation to constitutive constraints. There is one more piece to the story of how internal necessity principles were embraced and animated by background ideas. We cannot leave the topic of emergencies as constitutional exigencies without confronting the resilience of the ticking bomb hypothetical and the work it does within the social imaginary to frame anxiety about constitutionalism. Paired with the claim that the Constitution is "not a suicide pact," the idea is that constitutional commitments have limits that break down in dire circumstances. In the face of existential threats, constitutive commitments become "fanatical" rather than principled or appropriate. Indeed, as Judge Posner argues, "In the era of weapons of mass destruction, torture may sometimes be the *only* means of averting the death of thousands, even millions, of Americans. In such a situation it would be the moral and political duty of the president to authorize torture."[114] He also urges that "if the stakes are high enough torture is permissible. No one who doubts that should be in a position of responsibility."[115] Because we cannot predict future threats and emergencies, binding ourselves to present legal commitments—such as an absolute ban on torture—can produce future harms. We are not like Ulysses binding ourselves to the mast for a specific goal with known risks.[116] Rather, we are vulnerable to future risks of dire harm beset by uncertainty, a situation that can caution legal flexibility rather than rigidity. As we have seen, skeptics of constitutional commitments argue that refusing to adjust constitutional constraints to provide more security is "pathologically rigid."[117] Rigidity produces a real threat to security, on this view, because the risk of constitutive changes presents nothing like the shipwreck certain to follow from heeding the sirens' call. The real threat runs in the opposite direction—not being sufficiently flexible in the face of security threats.

In order to explore this terrain, we must rely on imagination. Imagination, as it turns out, has been more than adequate, weaving together any number of variations on a simple ticking bomb hypothetical.[118]

The "Ticking Bomb" and the Role of Imagination

The standard argument from necessity justifying torture presupposes that harm may be done to a specific person where necessary to protect many people from death. Such a ticking bomb scenario works best when we imagine a whole city, with perhaps hundreds of thousands of potential victims, under immediate threat unless an identified person were to give up the whereabouts of the bomb. Torturing this individual would be justified, as the hypothetical goes, in order to save the lives of many others. The intuition is that the limited act of torture would be clearly justified on consequentialist grounds. As others have noted, the power of the justificatory intuition relies on the simple intuitive appeal of the standard hypothetical—a bomb and a suspect who knows where it is.[119]

Notice three things, however: First, the *justification* for imposing the harm of torture is only incidentally related to the identified particular person. Second, the *scope* of the harm imposed is not bound to a particular person. Third, the hypothetical requires an imaginative commitment to the logic of necessity and a suspension of normal rules in such a way as to set no limits on how far imagination might wander.

First, as to the justification for torture in the ticking bomb case, if a terrorism suspect is the person believed to have planted the bomb or is otherwise believed to know where the bomb is located, and if there were no other means within the temporal limitations of the potentially catastrophic situation to obtain the information, then officials would be justified in torturing the suspect—not for purposes of punishment, official terror, or sadism, but merely for informational purposes. The location of the information necessary to save the lives of thousands is only *contingently* related to a specific suspect.[120] The location of the ticking bomb is what is needed, and any particular torture victim is merely a means to finding it. Apart from interrogation, if there were other means of compelling such a person to reveal the information, those means would be equally justified. In the desperation to prevent catastrophe, the justification for torture already eliminates finer distinctions about the means chosen, because by description, anything becomes permissible to avoid the harm of the impending catastrophe.

Necessitarian logic here also implies that if torturing other persons who matter to the identified person—say family members—might prove effective in avoiding greater harm, then such acts would be similarly justified.[121] The hypothetical's intuitive appeal depends on the proposition that a "little" loathsome harm is justified by the greater good achieved. This proposition combines the intuitions of both the "lesser evil"[122] and the "dirty hands" arguments.[123] Thus, if obtaining information from a terrorism suspect requires the harm of another person, then that harm would also be justified.

The second point to observe is that just as torture justified by necessity need not be person-specific, it need not be narrowly circumscribed. The standard justification need not impose clearly bounded constraints on the scope of the harm or the number of individuals tortured in order to obtain the required information. Imagine a variation of the standard case, a variation that may even be more realistic. Instead of having in custody a single individual whom officials have good reason to believe knows where the bomb is located, officials have, for example, one hundred individuals. They know that one, and only one, of the individuals can identify where the bomb is located, but they do not know which person among the group knows. If the clock is ticking, then officials would claim that it is necessary to torture all of them simultaneously. Would they be justified in torturing all one hundred, or more, persons? Under the logic of the standard justification, the answer must be yes.[124]

Because the necessity argument relies for its justification on weighing the harm to be prevented against the harm perpetrated, the scope of the harm imposed is therefore not merely limited to the person thought to have information, but extends outward to groups of individuals for which there is a high probability that one of them has the desired information. This latter prospect animated the Bush administration's interrogation policy. Proof of the possible was found in the actual. Terrorists had succeeded in pulling off a complex and highly destructive attack on September 11, and thus it was reasonable to think other attacks might follow. Bracing for such a prospect, it was also reasonable to think that any number of suspicious persons with ties to organizations like al-Qaeda, who were responsible for the attacks, might yield information that could thwart the next attack. So when the administration detained such individuals, given the potential for catastrophic harm at stake, resorting to torture in an attempt to gain valuable information followed from the logic of the ticking bomb scenario.

The logic of the ticking bomb scenario tempts us to confuse questions of blame and punishment with justifications for torture. The scenario presupposes that the person to be interrogated is already suspicious, and, if not actually guilty of participating in acts intended to bring harm to us, is at least knowledgeable about such acts or the planning of such acts by others. Therefore, the individual is guilty by association with other persons who do actually intend us harm, and therefore we need not lose any sleep over this individual's torture.[125] He deserves it.

What is interesting about the scope of harm justified by necessity is that it affirms a situation frequently cited as a reason against allowing torture in the first place. Critics of torture argue that abuses, such as those perpetrated against prisoners at Abu Ghraib, are examples of why, as a practice, we should not engage in torture.[126] Once permitted, torture is not easily controlled, and it will quickly spread to other instances, creating a more pervasive practice of official torture.[127] Consequentialists respond to this point by observing that such arguments are about the negative consequences of the practice of torture, not any principled limitations.[128] If the scope of harm must increase, that is only because the scope of potential catastrophe has increased. In the consequentialist's hands, torture will be practiced more or less widely as circumstances prescribe.[129] According to critics, the problem is that circumstances are malleable, and, as in the case of Abu Ghraib, torture will be practiced in situations far removed from the ticking bomb. In this exchange, however, consequentialists and critics agree that under the logic of necessity, the scope of harm perpetrated is not tethered to the particularity of the person thought to have the needed information. Rather, torture is tethered to the perceived necessitous circumstances and the available means for resolving the emergency.

This third implication of the ticking bomb hypothetical is that once imagination justifies torture in the simple case, then we commit ourselves to following our imaginations in the more complex cases—though, perhaps, as with other kinds of tragic choices, we hide this commitment from ourselves.[130] If one is already inclined to fear the perceived rigidity of constitutional commitments, then one will have such a scenario ready at hand as an example of the harms overzealous constitutionalism might produce. This social imaginary already imbeds a particular kind of constitutional skepticism,[131] for it imagines that constitutional rules are set against a background of creative discretion available to match unpredictable circumstance. How one views the risks of future attacks also inflects a view about constitutional principles and institutions. Vice President Cheney made this clear in how his "one percent doctrine" influenced the development of not only interrogation policy, but a range of other counter-terrorism responses.

Cheney's "one percent doctrine" held that if there is even a 1 percent chance of another terrorist attack, given the gravity of the possible harm, that risk must be addressed as if it were a certainty.[132] Imagined possibilities become known policy actualities. Security is of such paramount importance that other values must give way to the perceived needs of counterterrorism policy's goal of eliminating all conceivable risk.

As soon as we announce in advance the justifying principle of necessity based on the ticking bomb hypothetical, all officials with a terrorist suspect in custody will have to ask themselves whether they *ought* to torture.[133] After all, when the suspect is in custody, it may be the case that the suspect has information about an impending attack in which thousands of lives may be at stake. What is to be feared most, as former defense secretary Donald Rumsfeld claimed, is the things we don't know that we don't know (for example, a bomb that is ticking that we neither know is ticking nor know where it is).[134] And in a state of ongoing anxiety about the prospect of the next attack, it becomes reasonable to imagine that each suspect may have the key piece of information to unravel an otherwise unknown and dangerous plot. Following Rumsfeld, officials torture not only to find out what the detainee knows, but they imagine that the results will produce information they think they need. Thus, once officials rely on imagination to justify the practice, at least in emergency situations, they are bound by their imaginations in all other situations. The gap between what they imagine might be possible and what they actually know will always require them to consider the question of torture in any given case. Imagination therefore has perverse impacts in practice. Following their imaginations, officials must now consider the question of torture, not as a hypothetical, but as an omnipresent, pressing question.

Return to Necessity

By exploring the tenor of such hypothetical considerations, I mean to contrast, on the one hand, the supposed fanaticism of commitment to principle in the face of extreme consequences, with the monstrosity of commitment to consequences, no matter how terrible the act, on the other.[135] Rather than engage our moral intuitions, I am suggesting that the "official" justifications, which start small and are said to be limited to "extreme cases," in fact know no boundaries, precisely because such a conception of necessity is unbounded by the rule of law. Such a conception is freed by an imagination that sees risk of catastrophic harm as elevating the obligations to security over all other constitutional values. Even if seemingly unbounded, this conception of necessity's priority is nonetheless an argument about normative ordering. Emergencies, as exigencies both real and imagined, become occasions for executive officials to assert a limit to constitutionalism and to mark the openness of extralegal discretion. Such a conception turns liberal constitutionalism on its head, making it subject to an overriding principle of necessity.

Even though "not a suicide pact" and ticking bomb imagery invoke fear of catastrophic harm, actual existential ruptures are unlikely to occur, affecting very many laws and legal institutions all at once. What the suitcase bomb imagery does, however, is raise the specter of wholesale catastrophe in order to justify a particular local change (or what may seem like merely a specific change). The problem with this wholesale-local equivocation occurs in how necessity works in our constitutional thinking to give salience to "suicide" when what is at stake is usually far less consequential, albeit serious, security threats that at best might require adjustments to more localized constraints. The arguments and the attitude purport to be about the big picture—the death of the Republic—but they work in a specific setting with more limited threats to security (though far from inconsequential ones). But by overstating the stakes and the imagery, the method is to implement a legal or constitutive change without the usual self-governing processes of reflection and choice. To avoid "suicide," the extralegal measures justifies, or the internal principle of necessity authorizes, the authority to detain, surveil, or interrogate, for example, in ways ordinary law would not permit.

In focusing his argument that the Constitution is "not a suicide pact," and in defending consequentialist arguments regarding torture, Judge Richard Posner explains necessity's status in relation to presidential suspension of habeas corpus: "justification for it must be sought in a 'law of necessity' understood not as law but as the trumping of law by necessity."[136] The "trumping" function of necessity is one that purports to remove the justification for action outside the ordinary constraints of law.[137] By speaking of this exceptional situation as itself the "law of necessity," one contem-

plates the "logic of necessity"—that is, actions unconstrained by considerations of law or morality, but fully determined by the contingency of
perceived circumstances and justified by appeal to necessity alone.

Judge Posner's appeal to the "law of necessity" brings us back to where we
began in this chapter—to a conflict between constitutional commitments
and emergency flexibility. What this family of views urges, which Posner's
writing represents, is that in the face of emergency, torture can be justified.
The extralegal-measures approach leaves out accountability in practice, and
the internal principle of necessity and the "not a suicide pact" views undermine constitutionalism altogether.

Necessity justifies too much. Once we are outside the bounds of ordinary
legal and constitutional constraints—in the domain of "necessity's law"—if
the torture of an indefinite number of individuals is permissible, then it
would seem that anything and everything is licensed by the emergency situation. Necessity requires only that officials act to achieve security ends, and
means to those ends depend only upon their effectiveness in bringing about
what necessity requires. There is no requirement that they internalize constitutional commitments to values of protecting the dignity, privacy, and liberty of persons or that they consider the effects on the constitutional order of
actions undertaken inconsistent with other normative commitments.

A problem here is that we create a culture circumstantially committed to
its principles. One need not be so committed to the rule of law that one
rigidly adheres to the principle *fiat justitia, ruat coelum* (let justice be done,
though the heavens fall) to recognize the way in which the argument from
necessity demonstrates the utter contingency of liberal constitutionalism's
deepest commitments. No doubt, in the United States many constitutional
rights are subject to state derogations on an appropriate showing of sufficient need. One safeguard of judicially recognized derogations from constitutional rights is that the government must *justify* its specific need along
a continuum from rational to compelling reason, and it must justify its
means on a continuum from reasonably related to narrowly tailored—as
we explored in the previous chapter. Even if constitutional law has a specifically "dynamic character," as thoroughgoing consequentialists, such as
Judge Posner, suggest, especially on the margins or in the "penumbra" of
a constitutional right, it does not follow that there are not fixed points of

reference—core meanings—regarding the scope of constitutional rights.[138] Military conscription and aggressive questioning are one thing; slavery and torture are quite another.

At this point, Jeremy Waldron argues that the prohibition against torture operates as a "legal archetype."[139] The prohibition against torture "sums up or makes vivid to us the point, purpose, principle, or policy of a whole area of law," in which we express our fundamental belief that "[l]aw is not brutal in its operation. Law is not savage.[140] Law does not rule through abject fear and terror, or by breaking the will of those whom it confronts."[141] Waldron's point illustrates how one legal rule can be so centrally embedded within a larger system of law that to derogate from that rule calls into question the operation of many others. Exemplifying another legal archetype, *Brown v. Board of Education*[142] stands as "an icon of the law's commitment to demolish the structures of de jure (and perhaps also de facto) segregation."[143] The civil rights movement and continuing claims seeking to obtain racial redress and eliminate the last vestiges of segregation in society all seek to fulfill the promise of *Brown*. To call *Brown* into question would be to call into question the entire trajectory of this social movement and body of law.

Likewise, to permit the practice of torture would call into question many other rules against forms of state-sanctioned cruelty. To put the point in due process language, for the state to engage in torture is "to violate a principle of justice so rooted in the tradition and conscience of our people as to be ranked as fundamental."[144] Through a sustained effort over a number of cases and across a spectrum of constitutional protections, the Supreme Court articulated basic principles of human dignity, integrity, and autonomy tied to the avoidance of state-imposed cruelty.[145] Similarly, regarding the purposes of the Eighth Amendment, the Court explained that the framers "feared the imposition of torture and other cruel punishments."[146] Through these and other articulations of the importance of human dignity free from state abuse, the Court placed the prohibition against torture at the foundation of our constitutional culture.

To erode these constitutional commitments under the guise of state necessity is to loosen deeply embedded limitations on state power over individuals. These limitations are essential to preserving not just liberty but also human dignity and decency, which are all key components of our constitutional identity. A conception of the person who grounds sovereign legitimacy—a "We the People"—is placed in unsustainable tension with the person subject to state power. If the latter conception of the person is subject to unconstrained power by the state, the former then loses the ability to serve as a limiting ground of constitutional legitimacy. If the body upon whom the state acts displaces the person by leave of whom the state exists, constitutionalism will be undermined by the claim to emergency power acting to compel thoughts, beliefs, and ideas, in addition to the information the torturer seeks.

Emergency can produce practical and constitutional change. As my appeal to Milton Friedman earlier suggests, emergencies can be opportunities to do things politically that might not otherwise be possible. If the emergency situation were sufficiently dire, or the frequency of September 11–style attacks were to increase, these implied structures of necessity could produce dramatic legal and normative changes. What would justify these changes? The family of "not a suicide pact" views offer no positive account of constitutionalism they seek to supplant by a principle of necessity. Yet there are ample grounds to reject the coherence of these views as both conceptually confused and practically implausible accounts of good government for a constitutional democracy to adopt. If we work backward from the rejection of torture as a failed example of a practice in which necessity can be said to know no law, it is clear that necessity is bound by constitutional principles and values. For these reasons, we reach the limit of how far necessity can be used to alter constitutional practices and reach a point at which the task of constitutionalism is to overcome necessity by remaining true to the commitments constituting our normative order. Having found no reason to accept the "not a suicide pact" view, are there similar reasons to reject the related claims that liberty *must always* be balanced away for more security, and that the president is the one to decide on this balance? The next chapter concludes that the grounds for such balance are likewise unsustainable as an account of American constitutionalism, and that separation-of-powers principles limit claims to presidential unilateralism.

Who Decides? Interpretation, Balance, and the Role of Courts

HAVING SERVED ON THE SUPREME COURT during World War II and served as chief prosecutor at the Nuremberg trials, Justice Jackson had occasion to consider claims of necessity when they were presented as most pressing. In a lecture given in 1951, Justice Jackson posed the question of extralegal government action this way: "The issue as we get it is more nearly this: Measures violative of constitutional rights are claimed to be necessary to security, in the judgment of officials who are best in a position to know, but the necessity is not provable by ordinary evidence and the court is in no position to determine the necessity for itself. What does it do then?"[1] Speaking of the problem of necessity in the Japanese internment case *Korematsu v. United States,* Justice Jackson commented, "It seemed to me . . . that the measure was an unconstitutional one which the Court should not bring within the Constitution by any doctrine of necessity, a doctrine too useful as a precedent."[2] Finally, Justice Jackson also admonished that "[i]t is easy, by giving way to the passion, intolerance and suspicions of wartime, to reduce our liberties to a shadow, often in answer to exaggerated claims of security."[3] In these comments, we find the multifaceted problem of necessity. What constitutional status should necessity have? Who gets to decide on claims of necessity? How far may necessity impact rights and liberties? Are there reasons to doubt the verity or strength of necessity claims? Are there reasons to contain the effects of practices and precedents based on necessity?

I have to this point focused on understanding the status of necessity within American constitutionalism, deflating outsized claims that necessity justifies superseding constitutional commitments and constraints. But Justice Jackson raises the additional issue of who gets to decide how to address necessity, and how far it might justify "reduc[ing] our liberties." If emergencies must inevitably lead to constitutional deviations, as we explored in the previous two chapters, who decides how much liberty must be forgone to achieve adequate security? This chapter turns to these questions, arguing that claims to presidential unilateralism and exclusivity are both wrong and dangerous. Moreover, if we must balance rights in pursuit of security, then we must apply constitutional values and principles to concrete circumstances by attending to details about what we give up and gain. The empty imperative that we must give up liberty to obtain security makes sense only from a perspective that already prioritizes necessity over constitutionalism. Under what conditions would a president ever admit to utilizing this imperative?

The prior three chapters have focused on the constitutional status of necessity claims, first as matters internal to American constitutional practice through the Suspension Clause, proportionality review, and the judicial doctrines of exigency and "special needs." Second, I argued that the family of constitutional theories exemplified by the "not a suicide pact" approach is conceptually and practically incoherent, providing no reason to abandon constitutional constraints, particularly when it comes to rights violations embodied by torture. My overall conclusion so far is that no justified authority exists to act contrary to, or outside of, constitutional structures and principles, or to abandon structures of constitutional justification imbedded in a commitment to good government through reflection and choice. American constitutionalism is in turn capable of addressing, normalizing, and overcoming necessity. But questions remain about who decides on the scope of authority necessity provides and how far one can use necessity to alter the scope of constitutional rights and liberties. The former question is one about comparative institutional competence of the courts, Congress, and the president, while the latter question is one about how security and liberty might trade off. This chapter focuses on these questions.

What makes a discussion of necessity central to the very idea of constitutionalism is that claims of necessity, as I have suggested, organize a way of thinking that gives priority to flexible exits from constitutive commitments and constraints. This way of thinking is motivated by a fear of *unlimited* constitutionalism, because circumstances may present dire, even catastrophic, threats requiring unfettered choice in governing action. To give such moral, political, and legal priority to necessity is to make a claim about what kinds of justifications—and their limits—fit within constitutional theory and practice. To prioritize necessity entails the priority of reasoning from circumstantial flexibility—at least given a threshold trigger like an emergency—over reasoning from constitutive commitment. It is also to inhabit a social imaginary. Both contested constitutional interpretations and contested factual interpretations arise within an imaginary about how government functions in relation to crises.

"Public Necessity," to which President Lincoln appealed,[4] or the "doctrine of necessity," against which Justice Jackson warned, has a rhetorical life of its own. Necessity is both a claim about the status of law and an expression of temperamental attitude. As to legal status, it seems to say that the circumstances of a crisis are sufficient to justify an action without recourse to a governing or guiding legal principle. Principles occur only as imperatives to action—to protect national security or public safety, for example—not as constraints or sources of constitutive norms. The spirit of the laws reduce to their letter, which, in any event, is to be circumvented in the name of urgency and action. As to temperament, necessity invokes an attitude of impatience with guiding legal principles and theory. These are matters for academics or civil libertarians, arm-chair speculators and thinkers, not the matters of doers. The world of action is sufficient in its own right without the need of guidance from principle and precedent, particularly when that guidance constrains.[5]

The problem with this matter of emphasis is that it incoherently suggests that the relationship between the crisis circumstances and the political action that follows is unmediated by norms or principles. No action undertaken to resolve a crisis will be norm-free. But perhaps there is a weaker claim here. John Yoo, for example, in arguing that the G. W. Bush administration had complete and unilateral power to do whatever it deemed necessary to protect national security, need not say that theory has *no* relation to practice.[6] He need only assert that many legal norms—particularly those that constrain choice of action—do not apply. To admit that proposition, however, is inconsistent with the claim that necessity provides the principle of action apart from other background legal norms and principles. For on the strong version of the security lens through which "necessity knows no law," existing norms and constraints fail to apply. Complete discretion will not exist where rules and norms foreclose the range of actions. And if constitutive constraints and norms apply, then we need specific arguments about why particular principles would need to deviate in an emergency.

This is the dilemma: the claim of pressing public necessity is either a claim that action is determined only by the relation between the circumstances and the action claimed necessary to address them, or the claim allows that the legal norms and principles constrain political action relevant to the crisis's resolution. We can reasonably disagree over the scope and application of constitutive principles and constraints, but not over whether they apply at all. The former possibility is one the family of related claims we examined in the last chapter—the internal principle of necessity, the "not a suicide pact" view, and the extralegal-measures approach—each sought to legitimate. But if we reject the first possibility, then how do we determine how constraint functions? If the attempted affirmation of torture is inconsistent with legitimate exercise of state power within a liberal constitution, then law binds necessity. The executive does not have "complete discretion" to say that necessity knows no law. If we turn our attention from these failed theoretical propositions to focus on the ways that necessity is normalized through claims that liberty and security naturally must trade off during crisis, and that claims courts should defer to executive decisions about how that trade-off is to be made, a new problem of legitimating republican self-government arises. This problem is that the claimed power of the executive to interpret facts as emergencies and thereby accrue unilateral power to establish a balance between liberty and security is inconsistent with a balanced approach to American constitutionalism.

Interpretive Priorities

Claims about necessity arise in relation to interpretive choices. Balance, as we have seen in terms of proportionality review and the application of exigency, is a matter of interpretation. But emergencies do not arise prepackaged with interpretations enclosed. Citizens and officials construct events as emergencies. Presidents declare states of emergency. But even then, the nature of the emergency is a contingent factual matter—its size, impact, reach, implications, connection to other events, and so on are all matters to establish and will require varying degrees of interpretive judgment. On the one hand, we might all agree on the basic facts of the attacks of September 11—the Twin Towers, the Pentagon, United Flight 93. But on the other hand, how those events came about and how they are understood, described, and analyzed are all matters of interpretive judgments. Interpretive conclusions about the nature of an emergency, moreover, make available, but do not compel, responses as products of prior normative commitments interacting with present circumstances.

For executive officials, there is a tendency to make political emergency seem more like natural necessity. The hurricane thrusts itself upon us; we do not choose it. The only issue is how best to respond. Likewise, with the response to September 11. As President Bush argued before the United Nations in the immediate aftermath: "It is our task, the task of this generation, to provide the response to aggression and terror. We have no other choice, because there is no other peace. We did not ask for this mission."[7] But the political meaning of terrorist attacks, while wreaking harm upon individual lives, is not the same as natural disaster. Presidents, for example, do not give speeches before the United Nations about American responses to hurricanes that land upon our shores. Officials must choose which apparatus of state to employ in response, which in part will be guided and governed by available legal justifications and frameworks. In this way, public policy choices follow initial factual interpretations, though neither the facts nor the normative frameworks alone can be said to determine any particular response.

Because facts are malleable, so too are declarations of emergency. Failing to achieve funding for his signature campaign promise—to build a "beautiful" wall between the United States and Mexico—President Trump exercised authority granted by the National Emergencies Act (NEA) to declare a national emergency.[8] This purported emergency arose because of Trump's perception that the nation's border was insufficiently secure and that the absence of a wall constituted an emergency. Because Congress conferred complete statutory discretion upon the president to make the relevant factual determinations in the NEA, Trump has control of the triggering determination that an emergency exists. Having the power of interpretive framing is no doubt significant, but it is not without constraints, be they the stubbornness of facts, the need for additional statutory authorization to reallocate funds, or the separation-of-powers structures arrayed in potential political opposition.

Whether and to what extent a response to emergency should follow a criminal law or war-powers model had far-reaching effects on policies such as detention, surveillance, interrogation, and prosecution.[9] Such interpretive framing, as we saw in the previous chapter, is exactly what President Bush provided after the fact in his State of the Union Address in 2004: "The terrorists and their supporters declared war on the United States, and war is what they got."[10] By interpreting the events of September 11 as acts of war, requiring the U.S. government and military to undertake a war footing, a number of consequences followed. First, wartime enhances executive power. If it is necessary to engage in military actions, then the president is the constitutional officer empowered to implement the wartime policies as commander in chief. Second, courts are said to play a diminished role in checking the wartime decisions of executive officials tasked with prioritizing security. One implication of this diminished role is the corresponding claim, to which we will turn shortly, that liberty must be traded in for greater security. Third, congressional power to intervene, despite having the power to declare war and to control expenditures, is likewise diminished, whether in deference to the political power the president accrues when embarking on military action, or in recognition of the consequential nature of wartime actions. Fourth, the public may also alter attitudes, at least for a time, toward greater patriotism and increased support for presidential actions.[11] Wartime is not only about warlike policies, but a restructuring of political time, as Professor Mary Dudziak has argued, having implications for political decision-making and public perceptions.[12]

By choosing war and declaring a state of emergency the president claimed power to engage in enhanced surveillance, interrogation, and detention practices. A choice to address the emergency events through a model of crime would not have produced the same effects. Crime can be handled through doctrines of exigency, whereas emergency initiates the possibility of claims to unilateral and exclusive power, backed by appeal to principles of overriding fear of "suicide pacts," as I diagnosed in the last chapter. Responding under a crime model leaves the balance of constitutional protections in their normal place, whereas war opens the possibility to claim the need to rebalance liberty for more security.

Without deciding whether war or crime was the appropriate model with which the Bush administration should have responded to the attacks, significant for our purposes is that claims about what was necessary were grounded in prior—and contestable—interpretations about the appropriate legal framework to adopt. They are also grounded in initial interpretations of the meaning of the factual circumstances. They are not determined by the circumstances themselves. Reflection and choice are at work. This initial choice of framing—war or crime—has downstream effects. One particularly troubling effect of the war model is that it invites expansive—at times dangerous—claims about the scope of the president's war powers, as we saw in the previous chapter.

Whether administration officials choose war or crime or perhaps a third possibility suggested by Bruce Ackerman—a "state of emergency"—the important point here is that necessitous circumstances do not alone determine interpretive priorities.[13] Actions and legal frameworks have to be chosen. But the dilemma posed by necessity seems to suggest otherwise, creating what seems like a difficulty for liberal constitutionalism. For the claim that "necessity knows no law" (and similar viewpoints) seems to suggest that necessity determines both means and ends. By seeming to determine actions, necessity enhances executive power to do what circumstances demand but dangerously hides both the background choices and present priorities.

Whereas in the prior chapter we confronted accountability-avoidance practices related to the extralegal measures model, here we find responsibility avoidance in the claim that necessity itself determines actions, not reflective choice. Responsibility avoidance is problematic because of its effect on democratic accountability, promoting a kind of false necessity, as Roberto Unger calls it, that implies that matters could not have been otherwise.[14] By hiding the exercise of choice, as well as the values employed in choosing, executive officials avoid democratic accountability while potentially altering legal practices and meanings through interpretations presented as inevitable fact. The mistaken view that appears to follow is that executive officials cannot be responsible for what matters they did not choose but were instead determined by the circumstances.

Interpretations do not occur independently from the political and institutional pressures that have unexpressed reasons for seeing emergencies as opportunities for claims of necessity to exploit.[15] This often hidden dynamic is behind the rhetoric of necessity—that the path taken was dictated by the necessity of the circumstance, and thus not chosen. When the Office of Legal Counsel argues, as we have repeatedly seen, that the president has the responsibility, and therefore must have the requisite power, to protect national security through whatever means the president decides is necessary, it provides a legal interpretation—a highly contestable one at that.[16] The rhetoric of necessity tends to obscure the underlying interpretive choices by making it seem as if not only that no law governs, but that matching policy means to security ends has a logic that is both determined by circumstances and free from background legal norms. Necessity presents its responses as inevitable.

Emergencies do not create exceptions to rules. Emergencies create circumstances in which governing officials claim justification at times to deviate from normal legal rules as necessary considering their commitments to legal rules and norms. These deviations can become entrenched in law and institutions as exceptions—but that is a further step beyond the immediate claim to the necessity of responsive deviation. Perhaps an emergency creates a circumstance in which, for example, responses must deviate from particular baseline civil liberties protections. Perhaps it does not. Whether this is so cannot be known, however, ex ante. And whether deviations are justified will depend on the reasons and arguments given on their behalf. Necessity within constitutionalism does not function as some kind of powers trump card, or a "get out of the Constitution free" card, that governing officials can play when they claim dire circumstances require it. That is, it cannot do so unless we adopt a way of thinking that adheres to this peculiar mixture of determinism and freedom. And it is this point that bears repeating: how we respond to claims about what is necessary depends on ways of thinking that we adopt toward the many forms that necessity takes. We could imagine, for example, a different administration with a different constitutional interpretation invoking minimalist war powers, rejecting the need to make expansive unilateral and exclusivist arguments about the scope of presidential power.

If the meaning of emergencies, and our responses to them, are unavoidably interpretive, then how are these choices made? For one, background ideas and dispositions, the attitudes from which decisions are made, are important. And for another, the institutional allocation of interpretive and decisional authority matters to governing practices, particularly when claims to the priority of security over liberty are used to "rebalance" the scope of constitutional rights. Let's first turn to the matter of temperament.

Temperament as First Premise

As we have observed, attitudes about how to respond arise from within a social imaginary that helps us make sense of features of both our factual and normative world. A social imaginary allows us to make sense of the crisis out of an existing background—how we link our fears and hopes together with our sense of what is both possible and proper in the situation. These attitudes are not themselves always evident to us. Does one self-consciously identify as a national security maximalist or a liberty maximalist, as one scholar carves the relevant landscape?[17] Or, if we take up law and social science research that attempts to map various dispositional orientations to differences in both factual and legal interpretation, do the subjects so categorized understand themselves as more "authoritarian" or more "libertarian," for example? Perhaps sometimes, but the question, and the research, only highlights how ways of thinking about questions of necessity both reside in the background and are causally significant in constructing interpretive outcomes. Research by Dan Kahan and others points to the existence of what they identify as "cognitive illiberalism"—a tendency to conform new information to existing culturally informed values and desires.[18] So if one has a set of cultural commitments, one's interpretation of facts and assessment of alternative normative arguments will be shaped by those existing commitments, undermining a presumed neutrality from which public reason is supposed to operate. One implication of this research is that when viewing controversial events, individuals will see different things without being self-conscious of the ways that their perceptions are shaped by the cultural dispositions they carry.[19]

This insight is not new, however. The American philosopher William James published his lectures on pragmatism in 1907 with an opening insight, claiming that "[t]he history of philosophy is to a great extent that of a certain clash of human temperaments."[20] When engaging in discussion, philosophers seek to hide this first premise of temperament. "Temperament is no conventionally recognized reason, so [the philosopher] urges impersonal reasons only for his conclusions. Yet his temperament really gives him a stronger bias than any of his more strictly objective premises."[21] Within what we have identified as a social imagination resides also a temperament—an attitude toward the law and legal constraints that when confronted by the claims that necessitous circumstances inevitably raise, shapes the kind of response that follows. A pragmatist by disposition, Judge Richard Posner explains how this first premise plays a role within the "not a suicide pact" view he espouses:

> Each judge brings to the balancing process preconceptions that may incline him to give more weight to inroads on personal liberty than to threats to public safety, while another judge, bringing different preconceptions to the case, would reverse the weights. The weights are influenced by personal factors, such as temperament (whether authoritarian or permissive), moral and religious values, life experiences that may have shaped those values and been shaped by temperament, and sensitivities and revulsions of which the judge may be quite unaware.[22]

The temperament seemingly best matched to prioritizing the security lens would seem to be, on Posner's terms, authoritarian. When looking through the security lens, and the interpretive approach it focuses, scholars and officials advocate unfettered executive power to confront emergency situations by curtailing civil liberties in pursuit of national security goals. This attitude is one that supports the priority of decision over reflection, as we saw the debate play out in chapter 1. But this is a significant place to find this way of thinking emerge in relation to the activity that judges have been historically most connected—the practice of legal interpretation. And beyond what we might term as a version of legal realism—a rejection of the idea that law is constituted by formal and mechanized processes of decision-making—these attitudes exist within an imaginary that shapes how we begin to prioritize our understanding of both the facts and the law surrounding emergency situations.

Military Detentions: An Example

Bush administration decisions regarding the detention and possible trial before military commissions established on the president's own authority serve as an example of how framing a crisis situation as constituting an emergency—itself a chosen legal determination—has further interpretive consequences. These consequences are not inevitable, however. Seeking to preserve maximum flexibility, White House counsel Alberto Gonzales advised, and President Bush ultimately agreed, that the Geneva Convention Relative to the Treatment of Prisoners of War did not apply to al-Qaeda and Taliban detainees.[23] The president was in part motivated by the fact that "it is difficult to predict the needs and circumstances that could arise in the course of the war on terrorism."[24] The administration reasoned that because they were not proper soldiers, nor were they civilians, Taliban and al-Qaeda fighters were unlawful enemy combatants unprotected by any of the categories of persons to whom the convention applied. According to the Bush administration, Geneva protections applied only to "High Contracting parties" or states that comply with the convention, not to nonstate actors such as al-Qaeda. Moreover, the administration reasoned, the convention's catch-all category in Common Article 3 covered only persons engaged in a conflict "not of an international character."[25] Since the conflict with al-Qaeda and associated forces was by its nature international, the convention did not apply. Asserting both war powers and foreign affairs powers, the president claimed to have an authoritative interpretation of the convention's meaning and application. "The decision is solely for the Executive," the government argued before the Supreme Court.[26] Left to their own interpretive framework, executive officials were unconstrained when detaining and interrogating opponents in the so-called "global war on terror."

Not so fast, the Supreme Court concluded. A conflict "not of an international nature" means all conflicts that are not between two nations. The meaning and spirit of Common Article 3 is to maximize its coverage, leaving no parties to a conflict uncovered, a condition contemplated by the catchall category of "armed conflict not of an international character." Since the conflict between the United States and members of al-Qaeda and associated forces is an armed conflict not between nation-states, Article 3's provision therefore applies to all such persons. Asserting interpretive authority over the meaning of the Geneva Conventions was on the one hand an exercise in ordinary legal reasoning over the meaning of a treaty provision. But on the other hand, the implications were far broader in recasting the meaning of the emergency situation the Bush administration claimed rendered their view necessary. The enemies the United States confronted were not so extraordinary as to authorize entirely new legal—or extralegal—categories of persons. Nor were the situations executive officials confronted in detaining and interrogating suspected terrorists so extraordinary as to give the officials interpretive discretion to construe laws in a way that facilitated their desired flexibility. Instead of furthering the administration's desire for legal pliability because of the unpredictability of events, the Court construed the treaty to entail the existence of prior commitments that allow no category of persons caught within the purview of armed conflict to fall outside of the legal protections the convention provides.

One implication of the executive's own determination was that executive officials claimed not to be bound by the War Crimes Act (WCA), which made it a criminal offense to violate provisions of Common Article 3. It prohibits acts of "violence to life and person," "cruel treatment and torture," and "outrages upon personal dignity, in particular, humiliating and degrading treatment."[27] But the new, and legally superior, interpretation the Supreme Court provided in *Hamdan* meant that officials who might have acted contrary to the protections afforded by Common Article 3 were now vulnerable to prosecution under the WCA. Prior to the Detainee Treatment Act, the WCA applied to a "grave breach" of any of the international conventions related to the laws of warfare, including Common Article 3. In this way, the president's determination that the Geneva Conventions did not apply was an attempt to avoid the constraints and the accountability the WCA imposed.

This episode illustrates the importance of constructive interpretation over default determinism in two ways. Where the former is self-conscious about the judgments involved in interpretive processes, the latter attempts to mask interpretative choices as circumstantially determined outcomes.

First, appealing to the prerogatives of necessity in the war on terror, executive officials asserted interpretive authority in a way that enhanced executive power by removing legal constraints. The priority of security required, on this view, the removal of human-rights-based legal restraints on executive action. The process of "removal," as I call it, was affected through interpretive means, not by legislative or administrative lawmaking processes. Despite Bush administration protestations to the contrary, however, these claims of necessity that purported to entail legal flexibility were themselves undetermined choices the Supreme Court could analyze and overturn.

If one could use interpretation to elide legal constraints, then correlatively, it could also be used to enhance executive power. In this second way, interpretive practices attempt to use default determinism to construe the dynamics of emergency in such a way as to enhance executive power to address the necessities of circumstance. And again, because this construal was the product of interpretive choice, the Supreme Court had authority to reject the self-serving interpretations the president proffered. Legal interpretation is the provenance of courts, and apart from the special rules of administrative deference to executive agencies that the Supreme Court applies, there is no reason to afford executive officials interpretive deference, particularly when that deference has the effect of enhancing power by removing rights-based constraints.[28]

When executive interpretive practice combines with a constitutional theory about the relative competence of courts and presidents to decide matters of security, then interpretation becomes a method of enhancing power. It is only by giving ex ante priority to any claims about the necessities of security, and thereby granting executive authority over interpretations of fact and law regarding what is necessary, that one can arrive at the seeming inevitability that courts should not be involved, and that policy must be less libertarian, as some scholars suggest. The purported inevitability of security's priority—at the expense of liberty—is itself an interpretive stance not required by any "objective" features of the situation. This is not to deny on the one hand that national security emergencies raise the priorities of security. But it is to deny, on the other hand, that actions taken to enhance security are determined in a way that makes inevitable—without interpretive judgment—the loosening of legal constraints, particularly those designed to protect liberty. Any decision to frame an action as necessary, to construe an event as an emergency, or to understand a rule to require an exception is an interpretive decision about the facts, which considers background norms, principles, and past practices. As the next section will explore further, the possible need to trade off liberty for greater security raises additional questions about how to understand the very conception of trade-off, leading to more questions about who has the ultimate authority and responsibility to decide such matters.

A Trade-off? Liberty and Security, or Liberty Versus Security?

Whether approached as a matter of executive discretion, judicial role, or individual rights, questions about security are never far removed from questions about liberty. We are often told that there must be a trade-off between liberty and security. As Jeremy Waldron described the ubiquity of this claim, "Talk of a liberty/security balance has become so common that many view it as just an ambient feature of our political environment."[29] Despite the purported equivalence of these two values, this trade-off is seldom framed with reasons to adopt policies that make us more insecure to achieve the benefits of greater freedom. If "it has become part of the drinking water in this country that there has been a trade off of liberty for security," this is because talk of trade-offs is unidirectional.[30] Scholarly defenses of national security expertise will argue not that we must take care to preserve civil liberties, but "that the government must make tradeoffs, that policy should become less libertarian during emergencies, and that courts should stay out of the way."[31] On this view, there is something called a balance, but in order to achieve greater security, a polity must give up some liberty.

The trade-off thesis asserts the inevitable existence of conditions under which it will be impossible for policy makers to improve security without curtailing liberty. The thesis begins with the proposition that "[a] national emergency, such as a war, creates a disequilibrium in the existing system of constitutional rights," requiring that the balance between civil liberties and national security be recalibrated in a way that favors security over liberty. Because, on the strong version of the trade-off view, civil liberties impede effective security policy, "[t]here is a straightforward tradeoff between liberty and security."[32] Indeed, two advocates of trade-off, professors Eric Posner and Adrian Vermeule, claim that "[t]here is no reason to think that the constitutional rights and powers appropriate for an emergency are the same as those that prevail during times of normalcy,"[33] whereas there is ample reason to think that increased national security benefits justify relaxing constitutional norms. What compels trade-off, on this view, is the belief that it is unlikely in a modern liberal democracy that governments will have failed to identify ways of increasing security without burdening liberty. Moreover, another reason for thinking that liberty and security must be traded "is that without physical security there is likely to be very little liberty."[34] Security seems to have lexical priority over liberty in that it becomes a necessary condition for the possibility of having liberty—a problem we first confronted in chapter 1.[35] Thus, when there is a question of security, it takes priority over liberty, requiring resolution of security questions in terms of the necessities of the situation, not in terms of the commitments to liberty.

Taken by itself, the trade-off thesis purports to describe a feature of the world devoid of normative evaluation. It just so happens that liberty and security relate in this way. But trade-offs are not mechanical exercises, nor are the values at stake always fungible. Trade-offs require allocative choices implicating institutional actors and normative principles that complicate their seeming simplicity. For the transcendental argument can run the other way, too. If physical security—natural necessity—is a necessary condition for liberty, liberty is in turn a necessary condition of political security, without which there is no free political life to secure.

The trade-off thesis trades on an equivocation. At first glance, the trade-off thesis says that if our allocations are already operating at, in economic terms, a Pareto frontier regarding any two suitably related goods (security and liberty, for example), to have more of the one means necessarily having less of the other. To operate at a Pareto frontier means that any gain in one good must entail a loss in the other.[36] For example, if we have already done as much on behalf of both security and liberty at airports, such that there is nothing more we can do to improve security without further impacting liberties, then there will have to be a trade-off. But notice that under the assumption that we are not operating below the frontier, such that improvements in both liberty and security are possible, the kinds of liberties that might be traded are of the everyday sort. The requirement that the name on our flight reservation match the name on our government identification curtails our freedom to travel with imprecise identification. Such a policy is said to improve security while costing us some of our liberty. But the myriad ways that freedom of movement in an airport, or on a public street, might be impacted by government policy designed to improve everyone's security are not the kinds of issues that are of primary concern to civil libertarians.[37] Rather, the trade-off thesis becomes problematic when it assumes that fundamental liberties are no different than the quotidian.

Under conditions of scarcity, trading security for liberty may be no different than trading guns for butter. Policy decisions have allocative effects not only on the matter at hand—provision of specific security policies—but on other matters affected, like specific liberties. By contrast, trading the freedom from unreasonable searches and seizures or the right to free speech for purported gains in security raises different issues.[38] Or perhaps more generally, losing important features of privacy or suffering dignitary harms in order to improve security are matters very different from minor tweaks to policy, such as bank-reporting regulations designed to prevent money laundering by terrorists or others. The specific constitutional protections afforded fundamental rights means that they have a special status within our politics. They exceed the normal trade-offs.

Judicial review of government policies that impact rights and liberties exemplify this distinction. If government establishes policies that touch on nonfundamental liberties, the Supreme Court reviews government actions under a rational basis standard, asking only whether the policy bears some rational relation to a legitimate government interest.[39] By contrast, if government policy affects fundamental rights, then the Court reviews the government action under strict scrutiny, asking whether government has pursued a compelling interest through narrowly tailored means.[40] We have very many different kinds of constitutive liberties that work in relation to each other and to other values, such as security and equality, in complex ways that might defy any straightforward weighing in the balance. We saw in chapter 3 how our understanding of rights normalizes everyday necessity on a sliding scale that requires more compelling justifications the more invasive the government action. On closer inspection, the trade-off thesis applies not only to the banal trade-offs of everyday policy but also to the contentious derogations of fundamental rights, such as the right to free speech or the right to be free from unreasonable searches and seizures. By ignoring relevant differences, the trade-off thesis trades on losses in liberty to increase security in the quotidian case to justify the more fundamental.[41] Under this equivocation, "[c]onstitutional rules do no good, and some harm, if they block government's attempts to adjust the balance as threats wax and wane."[42] On this argument, the trade-off thesis applies equally to the everyday and the constitutionally significant case.

Trade-offs are inevitable only when goods and values are available for trade. Availability depends on the background values and priorities to which a constitutional polity commits itself. Constitutional values are not absolute and are subject over time to changing circumstances and choices.[43] But at any given moment, particular values and principles will be central to a constitutional polity's self-understanding, and therefore not amenable to trade.[44] For example, under present constitutional understandings, a free and independent press is a good that is unavailable for trade, even if it were true that a less-informed public could be made more secure through censorship. The point of protecting particular rights and liberties under a constitution is to make them unavailable to ordinary trade-offs. Focusing official claims that trade-offs of fundamental liberties are necessary through an analysis of compelling interests and narrow tailoring, as Supreme Court doctrine requires, is a way of incorporating constitutional values into the allocative decision-making of governing officials. A trade-off of a fundamental liberty like the freedom of the press would mean something very different to a constitutional order than would a trade-off of an everyday good such as uninhibited movement through airports. This difference makes some trade-offs that might otherwise appear hypothetically possible, according to the trade-off thesis, practically and constitutionally unavailable. Equivocation regarding this distinction occurs by ignoring the distinctive role that constitutional principles and practice play in the political lives of citizens and officials alike.

Moreover, concerning the necessity of balancing security and liberty, reliance on the priority of security may beg the central question. If one simply posits at the outset that there must be balance between security and liberty, then it would seem to follow that they *ought* to balance to maximize the social welfare that security provides. After all, one ought to do whatever one must to protect security. Much of the normative work exists in the conceptual framework that posits how security and liberty are related—as values that must trade off against each other. What is interesting, however, is that for two values or principles to be relationally defined for purposes of asserting the priority of one over the other under conditions of necessity, they do not seem to be relationally defined in other contexts. But why think, then, that security has such lexical priority in any circumstance? Two considerations undermine the necessity of balance as the priority of the security argument seeks to present it.

First, as we have seen, the real issues are about the nature and degree to which trade-offs are appropriate under a constitutional commitment to the rule of law. Merely asserting necessity does not make everything possible. Even if "law must adjust to necessity born of emergency," constitutional government must always act within constraints, whether the constraints are constitutional, institutional, political, or practical.[45] It is true that we make many decisions under conditions of uncertainty. Even so, government does not ordinarily derogate from constitutional rights without articulating specific reasons for doing so. Tiered scrutiny, as we saw in chapter 3, is the judicial doctrine through which such officials provide reasons.

Even if constitutional law has a specifically "dynamic character," as Judge Posner suggests, that allows it to absorb everyday claims of necessity, there remain core meanings—such as the prohibition against torture.[46] In light of a strong tradition that views rights as constraints not susceptible to utilitarian balancing, the trade-off project does not provide substantive reasons for thinking we should reject accounts of civil liberties and rights as trumps or side constraints that do not (always) answer to consequentialist values, such as efficiency or necessity.[47] If we look at constitutional practice and theory, sometimes liberty will have priority over security, sometimes the two will fail to trade off, and at other times security may have priority. Protecting national security is merely one reason the state might advance to justify an expanded exercise of power. In the face of sufficient justification, particular liberties may give way, but the proof will be in the reasons offered in justification, not a presumptive assumption that we must give up liberty in order to achieve security as necessity requires, especially under claimed emergency circumstances. And the scope of the justifications required will depend on the nature of the government intrusion on liberty. Outside of an analysis of the specific circumstances, the only reason for adhering to the lexical priority of security is because one already views the issues through the security lens, occupying a social imaginary that prioritizes necessity within constitutional thought.

Second, it is not clear how to calculate the trade-offs, and it is unclear what counts as maximizing social welfare in this context.[48] The "emergency" conditions that have given rise to the renewed debate about emergency powers do not present an existential threat—a security threat, no doubt, but not a threat to our very existence as a people and a nation.[49] Attacks of the kind we experienced on September 11 are neither precursors to a potential invasion, as Pearl Harbor might have been, nor harbingers of potential annihilation, as the Cold War threatened. So if one is in the messy world of marginal increases in security against nonexistential threats, it becomes particularly unclear how to calculate trade-offs. Apart from the assumption that one must balance security and liberty, advocates provide no arguments in support of standards of measurement or means of calibrating the scales.[50] Richard Posner admits that "the 'weighing' is usually metaphorical. The consequences that judges consider are imponderables, and the weights assigned to them are therefore inescapably subjective."[51] I would argue that lack of clarity undermines the assumption that liberty and security necessarily must be balanced, particularly since trade-off methodology places a thumb on the side of security, arguing as it does that in times of emergency, liberty must be diminished and security augmented. We are left with no good reasons for thinking that necessarily liberty must be traded away to achieve security.

Who Decides?

This question of trade-offs cannot be approached without asking the question of who decides on the proper allocation of liberty and security.[52] Defenders of unbounded executive power argue that security relies on experts to whom citizens and courts alike must defer.[53] Especially during emergencies, executive officials are presumed to have superior information about what is necessary to preserve security.[54] According to the deference thesis, to impose constitutional limits on executive discretion risks creating security harms rather than enhancing freedoms. Deference to experts means "that the executive branch, not Congress or the judicial branch, should make the trade-off between security and liberty."[55] When citizens, scholars, or judges attempt to intervene in debates over the proper measure of security, defenders of unchecked executive power claim that "they are amateurs playing at security policy, and there is no reason to expect that courts can improve upon government's emergency policies in any systemic way."[56] On this view, citizens and courts lack sufficient specialized knowledge to make optimal decisions about security. According to Judge Richard Posner, critics of executive expertise risk erroneous trade-offs, because "civil libertarians tend to exaggerate the costs . . . and to ignore or slight the benefits" of security policy.[57] To interpose legal principles protecting rights and liberties as barriers to security policy risks producing "tangible harms," while adding nothing relevant to expert decision-making.[58]

Such claims are puzzling in light of the image of balancing exemplified by blindfolded Justitia, who must weigh the relative merits of the competing claims of liberty and security.[59] At the very moment talk of balancing liberty and security becomes salient, the rhetoric shifts to the necessity of security's priority to liberty. We are reminded of the fact that "without physical security there is likely to be very little liberty."[60] Emergency provokes the direction of trade, for under the trade-off thesis: "As threats increase, the value of security increases; a rational and well-motivated government will then trade off some losses in liberty for greater gains in increased security."[61] Moreover, at this point the supposed suicidal nature of rights commitments gets introduced again into the debate, as Judge Richard Posner puts the point: "While the Constitution protects against invasions of individual rights, it is not a suicide pact."[62] Rather than external threats, a polity's own constitutive commitments may be the real source of harm, as advocates of the centrality of trade-offs explain, "It is clear, however, that sometimes tangible security harms do in fact occur when claims of civil liberties are respected."[63]

Although there are reasons for caution in deferring to judgments about balance made by the very officials tasked with giving priority to security, presidential claims to expertise in matters of security are unexceptional. What follows from these assertions are another matter. From the founding, the president has benefited from the claimed advantage that "[d]ecision, activity, secrecy, and dispatch will generally characterize the proceedings of one man," by comparison to larger deliberative bodies when it comes to matters of security.[64] In addition, courts tend to defer to executive expertise under the commander-in-chief and foreign-affairs powers, especially regarding military matters.[65] For example, the Supreme Court defers to executive conclusions in security matters because "national security and foreign policy concerns arise in connection with efforts to confront evolving threats in an area where information can be difficult to obtain and the impact of certain conduct difficult to assess."[66] Executive officials are presumed to have superior institutional capacities to acquire and analyze information too complex and varied to leave to democratic processes. Centralized decision-making, combined with specialized knowledge and institutional capacities, define the conditions for expanded presidential power that Aziz Rana traces from the New Deal to the present.[67] What is most notable is that the meaning of "security" changes during the twentieth century to accommodate the developing capacities of presidential administration.[68] "Security" becomes a matter for experts who have access not only to specialized knowledge but also privileged information, rendering it possible to claim that other academics and even judges are "amateurs" in the field of policy.[69] Expanding presidential power has been a source of political and academic consternation, interrupted by occasional commendation, and driven by never ending large and small crises purporting to require deference to executive expertise.[70] If there is nothing exceptional regarding presidential claims of unique expertise in matters of security in American legal practice, the same cannot be said about matters of individual liberty.

If the trade-off between security and liberty is to be a real weighing of the risks, costs, benefits, burdens, and consequences of various policy decisions, then who has the necessary expertise to decide on liberty? After all, to make decisions about the appropriate balance between security and liberty implies that a decision-maker be an expert not only about security but also about liberty. Otherwise, the idea of a balanced trade-off is empty because it becomes nothing more than an assertion of security's priority over liberty, combined with institutional deference to the security decisions of executive officials. There would be a trade-off—more security and less liberty—but not one that involves balanced consideration of both interests. Thus, the question becomes, Are decisions about the appropriate allocations and distributions of liberty ones that executive officials necessarily have superior knowledge and expertise to determine? To make the claim that some baseline of liberty must give way—if the trade-off is to be more than a rhetorical charade—requires knowledge about how this loss of liberty will affect people's lives through the costs it imposes, in light of the benefits in security expected to accrue. Such knowledge must extend beyond the slogans "security" and "liberty" to examine precisely what is to be gained and what is to be relinquished. Who has this knowledge? Apart from the epistemological question, upon whose moral consent are such decisions premised? Who has the democratic and institutional legitimacy to make these determinations?

If security is said to be the special province of executive expertise, there is an absence of similar claims about liberty. When it comes to decisions about the proper scope and substance of individual liberties, constitutional practice reveals that citizens and courts, in addition to the political branches, have a role to play.[71] Indeed, "We the People" established the Constitution and are the ultimate authors of its transformations, through both formal and informal amendment processes as well as through the intergenerational conversations over constitutional meaning they sustain. Whether it involves the transformations "We the People" fashion, the interventions the people themselves make, or the interpretations courts construct, the protection of liberty is a shared enterprise.[72] From the Constitution's preamble, the goal is not to provide security alone as a matter of "common defence," but to "secure the Blessings of Liberty."[73] This goal is to be realized through a divided structure of government suspicious of concentrated power.

Because of liberty's shared responsibility, there is a problem for the unbound executive: if the relationship between liberty and security entails trade-offs, especially during perceived emergencies, and if liberty is a matter for citizens and courts alike, then security must be as well. Since decisions about security necessarily entail decisions about liberty, for citizens and courts to have a role in the one is for them to have a role in the other. Alternately, we are left with the claim that given the relationship between security and liberty and given the special expertise required in deciding on security, citizens and courts should defer to executive decisions about both security and liberty. In short, the trade-off thesis implies that whoever has authority to decide on liberty must also have authority to decide on security. This correspondence creates a dilemma: either citizens and courts have nonexclusive authority to decide on both, or courts must grant executive officials expansive deference on matters of liberty as well. But the latter proposition is untenable and, therefore, citizens and courts must have nonexclusive authority to make decisions about both national security and individual liberty.

Is there a reason to think that questions about liberty are properly entrusted to executive discretion? Liberty plays such a central role in American constitutional theory and practice that it becomes, at times, the very air in which more substantive values breathe. From the foundational arguments urging ratification of the Constitution, the view has been that "[t]he genius of republican liberty, seems to demand on one side, not only that all power should be derived from the people; but that those entrusted with it should be kept in dependence on the people."[74] Under the Madisonian framework, not only does power ultimately reside in the people, but the separation of powers "is admitted on all hands to be essential to the preservation of liberty."[75] Liberty could be threatened by factions using government to advance their own selfish agendas or by corrupt officials wielding the power of office in defiance of the common good. Madison's design problem then is "not only to guard the society against the oppression of its rules, but to guard one part of the society against the injustice of the other part."[76] Each of these governing problems could be solved through constitutional design. By "giving to those who administer each department the necessary constitutional means and personal motives to resist encroachments of the others," Madison argued that the Constitution could provide "security against a gradual concentration of the several powers."[77] Officeholders were to identify with their offices, jealously guarding them against encroachments from other departments. In this way, legislators would be inclined to identify with the powers and virtues of their office and contest aggrandizement of their power by executive officials. By maintaining a federal structure and a divided national government, "a double security arises to the rights of the people."[78] In turn, an enlarged Republic would "make it less probable that a majority of the whole will have a common motive to invade the rights of other citizens."[79] In these ways, structural design could turn mere "parchment barriers," which by themselves are "not a sufficient guard against those encroachments which lead to a tyrannical concentration of all the powers of government in the same hands," into a means of securing constitutional rights.[80]

These constitutional design features seek to disperse decision-making authority across offices and actors to best preserve and promote liberty. No thought was given to the proposition that liberty would be best preserved in times of crises through concentration of powers over liberty or security in the executive department. In fact, quite the opposite is the case. A theme repeated throughout *The Federalist Papers* is that the "security of liberty" is to be achieved through a constitutional design of separated powers. Constituting government to provide "security for civil rights" suggests, along with the goal to "secure the Blessings of Liberty," that security and liberty are often mutually reinforcing goals subject to dispersed authority.[81] Responsibility for security is shared by Congress—which has the power to declare war, raise, support, and make rules for armies and a navy, and call forth the militia to suppress insurrections or invasions—and by the president, who is the commander in chief with foreign relations powers and duties to faithfully execute the laws.[82] In addition, some responsibility for security resides with "the People" who compose the militias.

Against Madison, some scholars argue that this structural design has failed because it does not adequately constrain executive discretion in the modern administrative state.[83] Particularly in times of crisis, Congress, courts, and citizens are prone to grant great deference to executive decisions, providing oversight, if at all, with minimalist interventions.[84] Whatever Madison may have intended, the complexity of modern government means that Congress no longer has the ability to monitor the executive's implementation of legislation.[85] Add to this complexity the institutional problems of collective action, asymmetry of knowledge, and party identification, and Madisonian checks can seem optimistic at best.[86] Moreover, the presumed incentive structure seems not to be borne out in practice, as officials care less about the interests of their departments than about their own.[87] Recognition of these failures has led to passage of framework statutes meant to cabin executive power, a legislative process always open to further structural reforms.[88] To the critics, the cycle—expanding executive power, leading to new statutory checks, followed by renewed expansion of executive power—demonstrates that the primary check is political, not constitutional.

Whether these criticisms hit their mark or not, they do not establish who decides on liberty. Even if Madisonian structural design has not always succeeded in full, failure to provide adequate oversight of executive administration does not mean that executive officials either do or should make final decisions on matters of liberty. The American constitutional tradition often expects such decisions to involve the judiciary, as the Supreme Court made clear regarding the military detention and trial of civilians in *Ex parte Milligan*: "We all know that it was the intention of the men who founded this Republic to put the life, liberty, and property of every person in it under the protection of a regular and permanent judiciary, separate, apart, distinct, from all other branches of the government."[89] More broadly, the judiciary's role includes oversight of fundamental liberties against legislative majorities when it comes to matters of speech, association, privacy, and marriage, among others.[90]

Even during military actions under emergency conditions, executive authority over the detention of individuals does not remain free from judicial oversight, deferential as it might be at times.[91] In *Boumediene v. Bush*, the Supreme Court retained habeas jurisdiction over "enemy combatant" detainees held at Guantánamo Bay and concluded that the president lacked unilateral powers to try terrorism suspects in military commissions that did not comply with domestic and international legal standards in *Hamdan v. Rumsfeld*.[92] Although the scope and meaning of these judicial interventions are subject to interpretation, what remains clear is that constitutional cases do not recognize an unchecked presidential authority to decide matters of liberty, even during emergencies or wartime. Perhaps during a prior military conflict, the Court's opinion in *Korematsu* might represent a high-water mark of presidential deference, coming closest to upholding a nearly unchecked executive authority over the liberty of persons.[93] Yet, even here, the Court purports to apply "the most rigid scrutiny" in upholding the detention of persons of Japanese ancestry on the basis of military necessity.[94] And at least in dicta when upholding President Trump's "travel ban," Chief Justice Roberts declared that it has not survived the "court of history."[95] Much, however, in the development of domestic and international law has changed since the Court's decision in *Korematsu*, providing a very different context for judicial oversight of executive detention practices.[96] In this context, the Supreme Court recognized that the executive might have an important security interest in establishing detention policies, but that "history and common sense teach us that an unchecked system of detention carries the potential to become a means for oppression and abuse of others who do not present that sort of threat."[97] Contested though they may be, and imperfectly implemented as critics might allege, Madisonian structures continue to provide the framework in which decisions about liberty and security are made.[98]

Background institutional practices that caution courts to adopt minimalist approaches that defer to determinations about security—because of the executive's institutional expertise—themselves provide incentives for executive officials to overvalue security.[99] Invoking threats to national security triggers statutory powers, burnishes political power, and raises barriers to criticism of presidential policy. Once the executive cites emergency, then judicial review shifts toward minimalism, freeing executive decisions from more searching inquiry. As a consequence of this dynamic, rule-of-law critics contend that the resulting legal "grey holes" grant "the façade or form of the rule of law rather than any substantive protections" to unconstrained executive action. Defenders of unbounded executive power respond by arguing that "[j]udges defer because they think the executive has better information than they do, and because this informational asymmetry or gap increases during emergencies."[100] Even while presidents prefer to govern through administration, relying on their own powers and broad readings of congressional delegations, governing through emergency provides still greater prospects for unchecked creativity. Justice Jackson warned that "emergency powers would tend to kindle emergencies."[101] We know this tendency is possible because of the interpretive discretion the executive possesses. In this way, judicial minimalism contributes incentives for the president to govern through emergencies, small and large, because emergencies require the knowledge and expertise over which executive officials claim special prerogative.[102] Security facilitates, whereas liberty constrains, expansive presidential power. In a choice between liberty and security, therefore, one can expect presidential action will gravitate to its least inhibited position.

Charged with keeping America safe, executive officials may find no security risk too small to pursue, despite the costs to liberty.[103] President Obama, for example, claimed that his responsibility for the nation's security is "the first thing that I think about when I wake up in the morning. It's the last thing that I think about when I go to sleep at night."[104] The more a president listens only to those charged with similar responsibilities, the greater the risk that the group of decision-makers collectively will produce more polarized threat assessments and less constrained policies to address them. As Alexander Hamilton warned in *Federalist* 8, "Safety from external danger, is the most powerful director of national conduct. . . . To be more safe, they at length become willing to run the risk of being less free."[105]

These dynamics—a temptation to overinflate security risks, a focus on institutional duties to provide security, and the possibility of cognitive bias—are reasons to think that the executive does not have any particular expertise to decide on liberty. Skepticism, combined with the existence of constitutional constraints, provides reasons to look elsewhere for expertise on questions of liberty. Asserting dispersed authority to decide on liberty, Justice O'Connor's plurality opinion in *Hamdi* claimed that "[w]hatever power the United States Constitution envisions for the Executive in its exchanges with other nations or with enemy organizations in times of conflict, it most assuredly envisions a role for all three branches when individual liberties are at stake."[106] Because decisions about security are often also about liberty, the Court reserves a role in checking the president's claims to decide on questions of individual liberty by deciding on matters of national security.

The problem may be that the question of who decides on security fails because of its own success. Taken in isolation, as a question about specific policies regarding resource allocation, intelligence gathering, military deployments, or diplomatic relations, security can be seen as requiring special expertise of executive officials.[107] But as soon as security decisions become inextricably tied to decisions affecting fundamental liberties through trade-offs, the complex relation between security and liberty undermines executive claims to expertise and deference. If to decide on security is to decide on liberty, then expertise on liberty must entail authority to decide questions of security. In this way, the trade-off runs in both directions, as does the authority to decide matters of liberty and security.

Relational Values

In general, having abandoned the state of nature, human liberty is always constrained by limits imposed by the protections of and participation in civil society. How much liberty we give up from this hypothetical state of pure liberty depends on the collective needs of civil society in providing order and stability. Liberty exists in relation to other values and applies in situations where it is capable of diminishment. But so too does security.

Security is never absolute. Indeed, the pursuit of absolute security is the illusory goal of authoritarianism. But like liberty, "security" is also a family of related values. Physical and social security are two that we have repeatedly discussed in relation to the view that gives primacy to necessity when thinking about future contingencies. But even within physical security, there are so many different contexts in which security might be a salient value. Moreover, we can ask how secure our freedoms themselves are, for one of the principal goals of security is the safeguarding of liberty. In this way, the relation between security and liberty need not be antagonistic but cooperative: security serves liberty. As the Constitution's preamble makes clear, the point of constitutionalism is to "secure the Blessings of Liberty." In this way, rather than opposite on a scale, liberty and security are coordinate values, whereby unjustified deprivation of either produces a loss of public good. As coordinate values, recall from chapter 1 that President Roosevelt connected individual freedom to a broad definition of security as a way of forestalling "the stuff out of which dictatorships are made." Without "economic security, social security, moral security"—as Roosevelt explained—Americans cannot realize the liberty all of this talk of balance is ultimately meant to preserve as a constitutive feature of American constitutionalism.[108]

As Neil Walker and Ian Loader argue, security is an unavoidable human good, which the state is obliged to provide through inclusive deliberative democratic processes.[109] What this means is that neither "security" nor "liberty" can serve as un-examined categories that give priority to a particular governing policy. To engage in a process of balancing, we must also engage in a practice of interpretation. None of the values at stake speak for themselves or determine actions. They require discursive articulation through processes of reflection that lead to choices, not accidental actions forced upon the polity by contingent circumstance. In this way, both liberty and security must be examined with attention to particulars—what liberties, in which contexts, on behalf of what precise gains in safety. Tolerance for risk, whether to security or liberty, will depend on temperament—the beliefs, attitudes, and priorities constituting a particular imaginary. Through a process of "civilizing security," which requires the pursuit of security to avoid undermining the very liberties the state is constituted to secure, these temperaments must be given public articulation within the framework of constitutional institutions and processes that serve as checks against the rule of passions responsive only to episodic necessity.

In the end, balance is familiar, yet misleading. Although some rights may properly be balanced against government need, some civil liberties are so fundamental that it is simply inappropriate to balance them against state interests. My right to my own life and person may make it inappropriate for the state to balance my claim to life against social welfare, or my right to bodily integrity against particular invasive acts for purposes of obtaining information. And although it may be appropriate to balance some aspects of some particular civil liberties, it is inappropriate to balance others. Accordingly, the devil is in the details as to whether, when, and to what degree it is appropriate to balance specific liberties against security. These are interpretive details in which deference to claims of necessity lead to unjustified distortions in constitutional practice. Rather than finding a structure of justification in which necessity must be given overriding priority, we find a messy domain of constitutional argumentation in which providing the appropriate level of particularity about what is to be balanced, and how it is to be measured, is a process of reflective normative ordering. Temperament and interpretation are unavoidable, but in no way does necessity require deference to executive claims that liberty must give way to security under conditions of asserted necessity. Because, as we began this chapter, "[it] is easy . . . to reduce our liberties to a shadow, often in answer to exaggerated claims of security," American constitutionalism requires that we adhere to processes of reflective choice when making fundamental decisions about the normative ordering of liberty and security.[110]

6

Presidential Power and Constitutional Responsibility

IN 1803, DURING THE FIRST TERM OF HIS PRESIDENCY, Thomas Jefferson expanded the American continental presence by purchasing from the French not only the Port of New Orleans but also the vast territory called Louisiana, doubling the national area of the United States. Aiming only at the more modest purchase of New Orleans and West Florida, which had recently been transferred from Spain to France by retrocession, Jefferson sent James Monroe as special envoy to France with authorization to purchase New Orleans and the Floridas. Monroe instead was offered the entire Louisiana territories, and at a bargain price to boot. Jefferson had aimed small and came up big. These events are American history as we all know it, and thus may not elicit any immediate questions of necessity or the need for use of enhanced executive power.

The problem is that Jefferson believed the U.S. government lacked constitutional authority to make the purchase. A strict reading of constitutional text did not reveal to Jefferson any assigned power to acquire new territory. Under Article IV, Section 3, Congress has power to "dispose of and make all needful Rules and Regulations respecting the Territory or other Property belonging to the United States." Left unsaid, however, is whether Congress has the power to add new territory to the United States. Adding potential support for the proposition, the Constitution also provides in Article IV that "new states may be admitted by the Congress into this Union" provided no new state is carved out of the territory of an existing state without its consent. This

Admissions Clause contemplates territorial expansion but does not explicitly grant the power to acquire new territories.[1] But territorial expansion could mean incorporation of new states out of territories already held in 1789 (such as the Northwest Territories), not the acquisition of entirely new territories. As a consequence of the lack of clear textual authorization, Jefferson believed a constitutional amendment was necessary to empower the United States to make the Louisiana Purchase.[2] He urged that it would be necessary to "appeal to *the nation* for an additional article to the Constitution, approving and confirming an act which the nation had not previously authorised. The Constitution has made no provision for our holding foreign territory, still less for incorporating foreign nations into our Union."[3] No such amendment was ever proposed, yet the purchase went through.

Jefferson yielded to the necessities of circumstance. Entering into a treaty with France for the purchase of Louisiana required ratification in the Senate, but no more than that. Completion of the purchase required funds allocated from the House. Fearing that Napoleon might back out of the deal if the United States delayed long enough to do more and formally amend the Constitution, Jefferson kept his further constitutional objections private. After the president set aside his scruples, he presented the treaty to the Senate, which gave its "Advice and Consent," voting by more than the required two-thirds to ratify. The treaty became the supreme law of the land with the president's approval, and the House of Representatives allocated funds to pay for the transaction.

This episode puts into greater context the striking Lockean claims that Jefferson expressed in a letter to John B. Colvin, editor of the *Republican Advocate,* a weekly newspaper in Maryland. Jefferson wrote concerning the exercise of power not strictly authorized by the Constitution:

> A strict observance of the written laws is doubtless *one* of the high duties of a good citizen: but it is not *the highest.* The laws of necessity, of self-preservation, of saving our country when in danger, are of higher obligation. To lose our country by a scrupulous adherence to written law, would be to lose the law itself, with life, liberty, property and all those who are enjoying them with us; thus absurdly sacrificing the end to the means ... the unwritten laws of necessity, of self-preservation, and of the public safety, control the written laws of meum and tuum.[4]

In answering affirmatively the question of "whether circumstances do not sometimes occur, which make it a duty in officers of high trust, to assume authorities beyond the law," Jefferson made a case for Lockean prerogatives in presidential practice. However, he did so with the caveat that the affirmative answer is "easy of solution in principle, but sometimes embarrassing in practice."[5] The embarrassment involved may stem from Jefferson's own belief, expressed to others, that the government lacked power to do what he led it in doing. There is a further ambiguity, in light of the theory of prerogative, that speaks to the possibility of a constitutionally embedded, yet unwritten, law of necessity. On this view, necessity is a source of law, not a source of lawlessness.

Maybe Jefferson believed that the "laws of necessity" were of a "higher obligation" than the duty to comply with ordinary law and could thus provide a post hoc rationalization for abandoning his strict constructionist views of the Constitution when purchasing Louisiana. On his narrow construction of constitutional meaning, he would "rather ask an enlargement of power from the nation, where it is found necessary, than to assume it by a construction which would make our powers boundless. Our peculiar security is in possession of a written Constitution. Let us not make it blank paper by construction."[6] Jefferson expected a written Constitution to provide explicit and narrow enumeration of governing power. That failing, he thought that the temptation to give a broad construction would undermine the limitations imposed by a written Constitution. Rather than broad constructions of constitutional writing, Jefferson instead took comfort in a broad construction of the unwritten laws of necessity. He paired a narrow formalism regarding the written constitution with a broad functionalism regarding the unwritten "higher" laws of necessity.

Jefferson's approach seems to reopen numerous issues we have addressed throughout this book: the idea that necessity requires extralegal action paired with post hoc ratification, the idea that necessity knows no law, the idea that there is an unwritten internal principle of necessity, or that the idea that necessity creates special executive responsibilities and powers. Here, having considered in the prior chapter whether the president is owed special deference when making claims about national security necessity when balanced against intrusions on liberty, I turn to questions about the scope and extent of presidential power. As prior chapters explored, necessity arises both in the ordinary practice of representative lawmaking and in the decisions executive officials make. Both are available for judicial review, though courts have developed a more robust practice of scrutinizing legislative enactments for their fit with constitutional meanings and understandings. And even when the president has discretion over whether to declare an emergency or what security policies to pursue, previous chapters demonstrate that government action must nonetheless comport with constitutional principles and constraints. Here the question becomes, How do normative constitutional constraints function to shape the scope of presidential power and to provide substance to the grammar of presidentialism?

We have also seen that the events following September 11 have challenged how we think about necessity and constraint. They have, more particularly, shaped expectations and understandings of executive power. In the days following the attacks on September 11, Congress granted the president authority to use "all necessary . . . force against those nations, organizations, or persons he determines planned, authorized, committed, or aided the terrorist attacks."[7] With this grant of power, President George W. Bush subsequently undertook a number of actions. He deployed military forces to invade Afghanistan and created a prison camp to detain captured "enemy combatants."[8] He authorized aggressive interrogation practices and established military commissions to try those detained and interrogated. He created surveillance programs that included electronic monitoring of Americans and sought to avoid judicial review of his policies. All of these actions were said to be necessary to protect national security. Many of these policies were later modified and legitimated by congressional acts and continued by subsequent administrations. President Obama authorized broad surveillance of all Americans and greatly expanded the use of unmanned aerial strikes against targeted individuals. "Because the terrorist threat continues, the national emergency declared on September 14, 2001, and the powers and authorities adopted to deal with that emergency must continue in effect," Presidents Obama and Trump continued to proclaim more than a decade later, sustaining a state of emergency continuously in effect since the September attacks.[9]

Indeed, a strong form of the view of the relationship between power and responsibility found its way into official executive branch legal doctrine after

September 11, in Department of Justice memos stating an argument we have seen throughout this project, that "[t]he text, structure and history of the Constitution establish that the Founders entrusted the President with the primary responsibility, and therefore the power, to ensure the security of the United States in situations of compelling, unforeseen, and possibly recurring, threats to the nation's security."[10] This view was given credence by Justice Thomas, who dissented in *Hamdi v. Rumsfeld*, arguing that the president has "primary responsibility—along with the necessary power—to protect the national security and to conduct the Nation's foreign relations."[11]

In short, with great responsibility comes great power. From this presidentialist perspective, this responsibility extends presidential power to such a degree that a former Department of Justice attorney could claim that "[a]ny effort to apply . . . [statutory prohibitions against torture] in a manner that interferes with the President's direction of such core war matters as the detention and interrogation of enemy combatants . . . would be unconstitutional."[12] In the context of the National Security Agency surveillance program revealed by the *New York Times* in 2005, the Bush administration argued to Congress not only that, "[u]nder Article II of the Constitution, including in his capacity as Commander in Chief, the president has the responsibility to protect the Nation from further attacks, and the Constitution gives him all necessary authority to fulfill that duty," but also that contrary statutory provisions "must be construed in harmony to avoid any potential conflict . . . [with] the President's Article II authority as Commander in Chief."[13] Congress is not alone, on this view, in being disabled relative to the power of the president. Courts must also defer to presidential expertise in deciding how best to protect national security.

If an analysis of presidential power went no further, the U.S. Constitution would create a hermetically sealed executive office. Circumstances would create the necessity for which the president has primary responsibility. Responsibility would, in turn, trigger the power to respond as necessity required, notwithstanding other applicable law. And power would be exercised to respond to circumstances in any manner the president deems necessary. On this view, the Constitution confers responsibility and power on the president, who otherwise remains unchecked and unconstrained when ensuring national security.

One problem for this view is that it creates a constitutional paradox. On this view, the constitution matters insofar as it empowers the president, but ceases to matter when it limits presidential power. Why should presidential claims to power have priority over obligations to and for other constitutional values? The strong presidentialist response is that protecting national security, preserving the nation, is the highest constitutional value, and thus, the powers of the president reign supreme in the face of dire necessity.

My goal here is to focus on how the responsibility that is said to create power also serves as a robust constraint on that power. We have confronted these necessitarian claims on behalf of the president's asserted authority to decide questions of security in a trade-off with questions of liberty. I argued that such a conception of trade-offs was poorly conceived, and that no constitutional tradition exists that recognizes unchecked presidential authority to decide questions of liberty in the process of deciding questions of security. Whereas judicial review of legislative enactments is well established through tiered scrutiny, by contrast we saw in the previous chapter that even in reviewing executive actions affecting individual liberties, the Supreme Court struggled to find the right balance of deference and assessment. And apart from balancing, chapter 4 rejected the idea that emergency required superseding constitutional constraints under theories of "suicide," extralegal measures, or internal principles of necessity. While rejecting the notion that the president merits untrammeled discretion to decide questions of security, we have yet to confront the limitations internal to executive power and practice that would guide and constrain responses to necessity.

Here the question becomes, How do we understand the nature and extent of presidential power in relation to claims about what necessity requires? How might constitutional commitments—including the claimed responsibility the president bears—guide and constrain the exercise of executive power? From the presidentialist point of view focused through a security lens, claims about responsibility purport to entail the existence of unilateral, unreviewable power to address necessitous circumstance. In this way, this same dynamic relation between necessity and constraint reemerges within the very conception of the executive office and its powers.

In this chapter, I focus on how constitutional responsibilities constrain executive power, even when the supposed unwritten laws of necessity beckon otherwise. Given that there exists a strong motivation and need to address necessitous circumstances, the question is, What additional considerations internal to constitutional understandings and practices provide reasons for shaping appropriate responses? The "responsibility produces power" view of presidential power does not seem to invite consideration of normative constraints. Indeed, a way of thinking about presidential power that emphasizes necessity produces a way of talking about the nature of the office that has its own grammar.

Once a particular way of talking and thinking about presidential power takes hold in the popular imagination—for example, the view we have labeled as securitarian that prioritizes claims to security above all others—then such a view can seem inevitable. But if we recognize that part of the power of the office is what we can identify as the "grammar" of the office, and that how we envision the constitutive features of the presidential office produces its own grammar, then we are in a better position to judge particular claims that presidential actions are justified because they are said to be necessary. What I mean by grammar here includes the priorities and concepts we use to talk about and implement presidential power. There is a distinctive grammar to presidential practice within constitutionalism— patterns of conceptualizing and talking about our expectations and normative critiques of presidential practice. Against the temptation to say that exercise of presidential power is justified even if it remains unchecked, I argue that there is a normative aspect to executive power that cannot reduce to assertions of power.

I want to examine some of the usual institutional constraint approaches in light of the need for normative guidance. For existing or new institutions must be guided by salient values and by conceptions of propriety. These considerations can be analyzed in three parts. First, presidential responsibility entails its own constraints, derived from the virtues of office and the grammar of presidentialism. Second, there are a cluster of considerations that surround the Constitution's textual command that the president must "take care to faithfully execute the laws," which entail a responsibility to and for the Constitution. Third, presidential vision must be publicly articulated and justified, suggesting that far from episodic discretionary authority, the power of the president derives in part from the ability of officeholders to convey their vision of American constitutionalism as a form of governing practice. Finally, from all of these, and from implied textual understandings, responses to necessity are always tethered to claims of propriety—what it would be appropriate to do in response to necessity. To expect presidential power to be guided and constrained by norms established through a legal practice implementing textual and structural principles is a feature of American constitutionalism itself.

Responsibility, Virtue, and the Grammar of Presidentialism

Structural constraints on the presidential office follow not simply from the division of constitutional powers among coordinate government institutions, according to Madisonian theory, but also from the fact that executive action is responsible for fulfilling a vision of constitutional life. The powers of the president's office contain their own constraints, for built into the ability to exercise power are both principled and practical commitments internal to what it means to exercise executive authority. External constraints through courts or political process also rely on normative conceptions of presidential responsibilities that constitutional meanings make available. Other institutional actors can have competing visions of the proper scope of executive power, bringing internal normative considerations about constitutional principles and values to the fore. Thus, my first argument is that having responsibility—even for national security—within constitutional structure is also a constraint on power. Presidents are responsible not only *to* the Constitution but also *for* the Constitution.

The Bush administration's bold assertion of power derived from a sense of responsibility to national security stands in contrast to Jefferson's somewhat timid, albeit momentous, exercise of power, constrained by a sense of responsibility to constitutional constraints with which he struggled to reconcile his actions. But Jefferson's self-described constitutional dilemma belies the facts of the matter. Other members of his cabinet did not think a constitutional amendment necessary. Neither did Congress, which fulfilled its constitutional powers in ratifying the treaty with France and provisioning funds for the purchase of the Louisiana territories. The president duly executed the law. In practice, Jefferson's views were thus mistaken.

Constitutional form allowed Congress and the president to ratify a treaty and provision funds for its fulfillment. Constitutional text, while not specific in the matter, is not unreasonably construed to permit the purchase of new territory as a means of facilitating admissions of new states to the Union—an implied necessary-and-proper power elsewhere explicitly granted to Congress. Thus, we can avoid appealing to a principle of necessity as a source of power by exercising constitutional flexibility—a practice we examined in chapter 3 regarding tiered scrutiny or exigent circumstances allowing deviations from rights baselines.

In theory, Jefferson's views regarding the priority of unwritten "higher law" are mistaken as well. They privilege a narrow view of constitutional form over function, adhere to a view of continual constitutional amendment that would obviate the need for a "broad construction, by appealing for new power to the people,"[14] and give priority to the unwritten laws of necessity. Regarding the need for amendment, such a theory is consistent with Jefferson's broader view that constitutional upheaval for every generation would be an appropriate path for constitutional governance. Americans should be sitting in constitutional conventions and establishing new constitutional amendments at regular intervals, according to Jefferson. If we reject his general views of continual constitutional revisionism, we have even less reason to adopt his specific claim that necessity was the basis for extralegal action in making the Louisiana Purchase. Plausible understandings of the Admissions Clause, combined with Congress's power to make treaties and implement them domestically, provide a written source of power without the need for even less constrained notions of unwritten laws. Only by adopting an implausible and inflexible understanding of constitutional form can Jefferson render actions fulfilling constitutional functions as privileging the laws of necessity over the laws of the land.

Jefferson wants to avoid making the Constitution "blank paper by Construction," and instead renders it empty paper by strict construction. Jefferson's rigid formalism regarding constitutional text generates the seeming need to appeal to necessity. In turn, the circumstances the nation faced seem to require appeal to Lockean prerogative. Consequently, Jefferson's approach would render all law vulnerable to unbounded and unconstrained appeals to sources of "higher" laws of necessity. If we jettison the rigid formalism, then we have no need for the laws of necessity. In this case, Congress and the president eliminated the rigid formalism, working together to produce a functioning government adaptable to the needs of the people while adhering to broad understandings of enumerated powers and constitutional constraints. This constitutional functionalism overcame necessity through adaptive institutional cooperation and constitutional interpretation that recognized governing limitations, commitments, and values. It did all this without succumbing either to unilateral or exclusivist claims about presidential power. Rather than support the argument that no matter the constraints—either from formal or flexible constitutional interpretations—the president can still claim power from necessity to go beyond the Constitution, this episode highlights presidential responsibility for constitutional justification.

Presidents have responsibility for the presidential office and its role among other constitutional institutions. Madisonian constitutional design, as we considered in the previous chapter, retains the goal, "first to obtain for rulers men who possess most wisdom to discern, and most virtue to pursue, the common good of the society."[15] But a problem arises because "enlightened statesmen will not always be at the helm," as Madison warned.[16] Recognizing that virtue founders on human frailty and necessity, the second goal of constitutional design is to provide institutional checks for the problems of faction and self-interest, "the diseases most incident to republican government."[17] These diseases could be cured in part by ensuring that power does not collect in a single governing department. There must be a "separate and distinct exercise of the different powers of government, which to a certain extent is admitted on all hands to be essential to the preservation of liberty."[18] This much is embedded in constitutional practice. Believing that aggrandizement of power by one branch at the expense of another would be curbed when officeholders identified with their offices, Madison claimed, "Ambition must be made to counteract ambition. The interest of the man must be connected with the constitutional rights of the place."[19] This design feature remains unexplained, for it is not clear why officials would identify with their office rather than with factional allies across the government.[20] And with the rise of party discipline, such identifications are part of normal politics. It is the ambiguity of this design feature that highlights both the fragility and centrality of the virtues and attitudes of those who occupy executive office.

And so here is a too often overlooked feature of the Madisonian structural approach. Constitutional responsibility requires virtue. The Constitution creates a particular institutional framework, yet inescapably relies on the virtue of rulers and the ruled to implement the design to achieve a common good.[21] Although Madison designed institutions for unenlightened statesmen, he also recognized the fundamental role of virtue: "I go on this great republican principle, that the people will have virtue and intelligence to select men of virtue and wisdom. Is there no virtue among us? If there be not, we are in a wretched situation. No theoretical checks, no form of government, can render us secure. To suppose that any form of government will secure liberty or happiness without any virtue in the people, is a chimerical idea."[22]

Virtue in the people leads to virtue and intelligence in the selection of governing representatives, which in turn leads to virtue in fulfilling constitutional responsibilities.[23] Responsibility and virtue are particularly important where governing discretion extends beyond institutional checks. Although enlightenment cannot be expected of all statesmen, no government can survive without some virtuous statesman fulfilling the norms and expectations of the executive office. For "a government ill executed, whatever it may be in theory, must be, in practice, a bad government."[24] Ill-executed government will be unchecked by institutional processes alone, for institutions require priorities and principles with which to implement policy. For that, all eyes are on the particular virtue of the officeholder implementing presidential power.

Officeholders will differ in attitudes and priorities, especially regarding reliance on claims that actions are justified because they are said to be necessary. But virtue in office may have reached its nadir, and the realization that "enlightened statesmen will not always be at the helm" may have its best example in the substance and style of Donald Trump's presidency. From his persistent disregard for truthfulness to his lack of respect for coordinate branches of government, to his attempts to impede the execution of the laws, and to details regarding his failure to take care to implement the body of statutory laws that govern the administrative state, Trump has been not only a norm-altering president but one that alters the practical functions of governing institutions.[25] And despite evidence that one of the more effective checks on President Trump past the midpoint of his first term in office has come from within the executive branch, as White House officials refuse to carry out unlawful and unwise directives, institutional process cannot preclude longer-term institutional changes wrought by an occupant lacking regard for the virtues and responsibilities of the office.[26] For example, President Trump's refusal to comply with congressional sub-poenas subsequent to the midterm elections in 2018 augurs a troubling future for Congress's constitutional oversight role.[27] Additionally, President Trump's demands to subordinates for their personal loyalty or to halt criminal investigations of administration officials are acts that eschew responsibility for the laws and institutions he is bound by oath to uphold.[28] For Madison, virtue is a quality of reflective prudence, dedicated to pursuit of the common good, not the aggrandizement of personal position. For Trump, personal aggrandizement seems to be a primary goal. This conflict has constitutional implications.[29]

Constitutional responsibility might thus plausibly be analyzed differentially in terms of institutional responsibility and substantive responsibility. The former reflects the kind of commitments and attachments that define Madisonian constitutionalism. Here the emphasis is on solving problems about the scope of powers through institution building and institutional identification. The latter includes the often overlooked Madisonian constitutional commitments to the virtues defining a particular vision of executive power. Presidential power must be wielded with particular attitudes and conceptions that reflect commitments to principles and values. Whereas institutional responsibility seeks a more defined relation to legally constructed governing entities and offices, substantive responsibility for policy choices is ineliminably subject to discretion and contingency. When the Bush administration—and later the Obama administration—claimed that it had constitutional responsibility to provide national security, and thus had all the requisite power to fulfill that obligation, it invoked in part a substantive vision of constitutional values and priorities.[30]

Institutional responsibilities and attachments constrain even as they empower. The Bush administration's view focused only upon the ways that responsibility for national security entailed powers to which other

constitutional actors should defer. Such a view fails to consider how normative features of our constitutional system constrain executive authority by
providing a basis for evaluating the content of discretionary executive policy.
Madisonian constitutionalism harnesses both the virtues of office as well as
coordinate institutions to provide constitutive constraints on presidential
power. What is more, to the extent that politics plays a legal role in binding
the executive, the question remains what normative content this politics is
imagined to have. The pure presidentialist approach imagines a political
world separated from the legal. But such a view renders constitutionalism
vacuous as law or as politics. By contrast, Madisonian constitutionalism
understands how constitutional principles and practices help structure
the content of our politics. Whether officers or policies comply with the
Constitution is an important question to American politics. In this way, responsibility for upholding constitutional values is embedded in contested
conceptions of presidential power and policy.

One feature of the particular grammar of presidentialism within democratic self-governance is that the very nature of presidential power establishes boundaries to the scope of claims that are possible. For example, no
matter the emergency, a president will not vote on legislation, a court will
not issue executive orders, and Congress will not represent the nation in
international affairs.[31] In addition to these role-specific constraints, a president is also bound by the virtues and excellences that define what it means
to fulfill the executive office's duties.[32] If there is responsibility for national
security, then there must be grounds to assess its fulfillment in terms other
than the mere physical provision of security, for there will always be multiple means to protect the nation. Conceptions of how to exercise power are
part of the settled grammar of each office.

Perhaps no one would contest the claim that the very conception of the
office of the president entails particular kinds of constraints. If not, then we
are off to a good start based on a shared understanding. By beginning from
this uncontroversial premise, a more robust account of presidential constraint becomes possible. A president empowered by his own responsibility
retains substantive constitutional obligations, no matter the necessity. As I
will explore, these are responsibilities *to* constitutional principles and *for*
the constitutional community that the exercise of presidential power in part

constructs. Whereas the presidentialist argument focuses on the accrual of power, I am interested in how the responsibility that grounds the claim of power acts as a substantive constraint.

To talk about the "grammar" of presidentialism, moreover, returns us to the root of the problems this book confronts: how the ways of thinking, the attitudes we adopt, and the habits of governance into which we fall determine legal and political outcomes under claims that actions are compelled because they are necessary. What binds executive action to constitutional constraints is a shared commitment to responses capable of public justification. These commitments, however, are not compelled but are the products of choices we make within the social and political imaginary we inhabit. Becoming self-conscious of the contingent ways of thinking that we are tempted to turn into habits and then rediscover as seemingly inevitable features of our constitutional understandings is essential to overcoming necessity.

In addition to the nature of the presidential office and the need to provide public justification, a president is also constrained by choice. But if a president is bound by an obligation to do whatever is necessary to protect national security, then what choice exists? This responsibility, paradoxically, seems to undermine choice, because actions are described as compelled. For example, President Lincoln's decision to suspend habeas corpus in the wake of Southern secession makes use of this grammar. Lincoln asked Congress on July 4, 1861, "Is there, in all republics, this inherent, and fatal weakness? Must a government, of necessity, be too strong for the liberties of its own people or too weak to maintain its own existence?"[33] In asking this question, President Lincoln wrestled with the implications of necessity for executive power. A constitution that rigidly constrains the president would render him lacking in sufficient "energy" to deal with the "most critical emergencies of the state."[34] A constitution that permissively enables a president to act as necessary would render "the security of liberty" subject to accident and caprice.[35] In confronting a situation where maintaining the Union's "territorial integrity, against its own domestic foes" was at issue, President Lincoln claimed that "no choice was left but to call out the war power" in a situation that belies his own claim.[36] Perhaps the choice was clear, but nonetheless a choice had to be made. The rhetorical appeal to necessity—that circumstances left no choice—is one way of obfuscating the issue of responsibility, which I confronted as particularly problematic under the extralegal-measures theory. If the president had no choice, how could he be responsible? But responsible he is, so the choice is his to make. The conditions under which a choice is made are central to understanding the tension between necessity and constraint. Even when the executive is caught between rigid formalism and permissive functionalism, as I argue, the choice of action is bound by the normative obligations of care and fidelity to the Constitution and laws.

Taking Care of the Constitution

Constitutional text opens two general pathways to question the normative content of presidential actions. First, the president is required to take an oath, promising to "faithfully execute the office of the President of the United States," and "to the best of my ability, preserve, protect and defend the Constitution of the United States."[37] The oath does not bind the president to the more politically abstract conception of "nation," but to the "Constitution of the United States."[38] The oath is therefore a complex bond. It binds the president both to the document—its meanings, principles, and constraints—and to the political composition of the American polity—its practices, values, and identity. To be committed to a constitutional document is not to be bound merely to an arid text—mere parchment—but one that has purposes set forth in the preamble to "secure the Blessings of Liberty," and one that has a constitutive role to play in organizing the politics that might otherwise constrain the unbound executive. In this way, a president is bound to a normative order for which he is substantively and institutionally responsible.[39]

Second, constitutional text also commands the president to "take care that the laws be faithfully executed."[40] Presidential discretion in executing the laws is inevitable, for it is in the nature of rules that they are never complete, and it is the fate of statutory directives that they are always partial. Nonetheless, this second textual pathway instructs presidents to exercise their executive discretion with both care and fidelity. Responsibility for "faithfully execut[ing] the Office of President," in addition to preserving the Constitution itself, combined with the obligation to "take care" in the execution of the laws, places normative inquiry at the center of the president's powers.[41] Oath and administration therefore entail duties that transcend articulation of the more specific powers of office. A president who claims that necessity requires extraconstitutional action is still bound by the normative constraints of the office, manifest in the duties of care and fidelity. Lincoln was empowered to exercise something recognizable within a system of government as the office of the president only because the Constitution created and constrained that office. In so doing, the Constitution also created the expectation that executive officials would exercise discretion consistent with the ideals of republican virtue.

If the Constitution provides a textual invitation to engage in normative critique of executive decision-making, then another promising approach is to look to how we might construe the Take Care Clause's meaning. Is it an assignment of power, as some argue, or a designation of a duty, as many others argue?[42] Does the duty entail something like a necessary-and-proper power to make possible a faithful implementation of statutory purposes?

Textually, the clause appears in Article II among a list of other duties, each commanding what the president "shall" do.[43] Moreover, language that instructs the president to "take care" and act "faithfully" is contrasted with the very different context of the Necessary and Proper Clause's wording in Article I.[44] The former language suggests constraint. The president's duty to execute the laws is not according to whatever is "necessary," but is restrained by what is faithful. This potential grant of power presents the question, "Is this duty limited to the enforcement of acts of Congress or of treaties of the United States according to their express terms, or does it include the rights, duties and obligations growing out of the Constitution itself, our international relations, and all the protection implied by the nature of the government under the Constitution?"[45] The Supreme Court, in *In re Neagle*, answered that executive officers have the power to protect and enforce the rights, duties, and obligations that arise from the Constitution, not merely those expressly granted by Congress. From these more expansive sources of law, the president is both empowered and constrained by obligations of care and faithfulness. Moreover, the Court has also cautioned, in the context of presidential efforts to enforce the terms of a treaty, the domestic implementation of which had not been directed by Congress, that the president's duty to take care does not extend to what the Court identifies as "making law." As the Court instructed in checking presidential power to seize domestic steel production facilities under a claim of national emergency, "the President's power to see that the laws are faithfully executed refutes the idea that he is to be a lawmaker."[46]

Apart from cases such as *Youngstown Sheet & Tube Co. v. Sawyer,* the steel-seizure case, the Supreme Court has said very little about the Take Care Clause, nor has it relied upon it as an explicit check on executive discretion. Short of making law, executive officials retain a large amount of discretion to address necessitous circumstances as they might arise, often free from judicial or congressional oversight. Especially in times of emergency, the necessities of the situation seem to be significant occasions for the exercise of executive discretion within the bounds of taking care to execute the laws. But taking care does not imply that the president has "complete discretion in exercising" his enumerated powers, as Justice Department lawyers argued on behalf of policies that included torture and pervasive surveillance in conflict with existing statutes. Discretion always occurs within practical and legal contexts that limit its exercise.[47] Such discretion is never "whatever it takes."

Given the ineliminable nature of executive discretion, and the particular problems that necessity raises, institutions are unavoidably guided by normative understandings. Authority must be exercised with an attitude. Indeed, for republican theory, matching solutions to problems required more than institutional design, as John Adams wrote to his wife Abigail Adams, "[T]he new Governments we are assuming, in every Part, will require a Purification from our Vices, and an Augmentation of our Virtues or they will be no Blessings."[48] Responsibilities of care and fidelity therefore particularize the general expectations of virtue in those who govern. They also provide textual sources for developing more specific constraints on executive power. Here's how.

Given the dearth of Supreme Court interpretation, is there room to say something about what the plausible conditions of taking care and being faithful might include? I suggest that care and fidelity in the exercise of laws requires attending to the best practices of interpretation and implementation—whatever more particularly these may include. It does not seem to be a stretch to say that whatever else taking care and being faithful might mean, an obligation to engage in good-faith interpretive practices establishes a minimal floor. First, the executive's actions do not occur in a legal or historical vacuum. Fidelity means remaining faithful to past practices and precedents as well as maintaining continuity across other bodies of law.[49] Engaging in a practice similar to what Dworkin calls "constructive interpretation," a decision-maker seeks to see the law in its best light, considering precedent and present policy to form a coherent view of the law's purpose and content, consistent with a president's constitutional vision.[50]

Second, the executive's actions have broad implications not only for the rights of affected individuals but also for the maintenance of a legal community with priorities and practices that help define the polity's political identity. A president both receives and reflects a constitutional community and identity.[51] A polity that prizes strict adherence to law or prioritizes respect for human rights and dignity in governing practices will expect its president to reflect these values, too. In turn, a president can shape the constitutional community by choosing to pursue policies and practices in keeping with an administration's policy preferences. This dynamic, which I explore further in the next chapter, is a counterpart to the power the president has to shape both policy and legal interpretation around a chosen constitutional vision.

Constitutional attention to obligations of care and fidelity need not be broadly visionary, however. A president can refuse to take responsibility for building a shared political community based on shared constitutional values, as Trump's approach demonstrates.[52] President Trump, who follows few normative traditions of the presidency, shapes his version of the polity through his rhetoric and priorities that personalize power on behalf of a narrowing political base. By denigrating the judiciary when it rules against his administration's policies, and by repeatedly calling a law enforcement investigation into the extent to which an adversarial nation meddled in the American electoral process a "witch hunt," Trump's vision defines his interests as the nation's.[53] Even though the investigation led by former FBI director Robert Mueller led to criminal convictions of numerous associates of the Trump campaign and White House, uncovered significant and troubling efforts by Russia to interfere in the democratic process of the United States, and presented substantial evidence that Trump had obstructed justice, the president's public response was to tweet that he had received "total exoneration."[54] What mattered was not national, but personal, interest. Faithful execution of the laws for Trump seems to be a matter of loyalty to his interests, which in practice alters both norms and institutions around a personal vision of presidential power. The obligation to take care does not compel the manner of its fulfillment but relies upon the quality of virtue and enlightenment in the polity's officials. Because who is at the helm matters to the virtues and obligations of care and fidelity, institutional constraints are not enough without normative articulation of constitutional values. Within this dynamic relation between the polity and the president, there is room for variation, flexibility, and constructive development in both theory and practice of the appropriate scope of executive power backed by public justification.

In this way the duty to take care and be faithful reinforces the idea that presidents have an obligation to interpret, justify, and implement law in a way that fits and coheres with broader community values through the ability to provide public justifications that demonstrate their fit with a national vision and identity. Within this relation, there are constraints, reflected in Adams's and Madison's concern for the virtue of the new officials—that they take care and be faithful, even in the presence of institutional checks. Executing the laws in a manner aimed at avoiding constraints or reaching preferred outcomes, no matter how implausible the interpretation, fails to take proper care of being responsible for the law and fails to be faithful to the task of fulfilling legal mandates. At a minimum, the president should not approach this task seeking to minimize or trivialize statutory constraints or obligations, treating the law as a nuisance to be overcome in pursuit of more pressing, necessary matters. These strategies of legal avoidance are the ones used to justify torture, which we rejected in chapter 4.

How far could the president go, for example, in pursuing information from detained suspects, and what are the limits on the exercise of military authority on U.S. soil? The infamous "Torture Memo" issued by the Office of Legal Counsel we examined in chapter 4 goes to great lengths to free the president from legal constraint.[55] According to the memo, statutes implementing the Convention Against Torture and Other Cruel, Inhuman and Degrading Treatment or Punishment only prohibit acts that are "of an extreme nature," and that the statute "taken as a whole, makes plain that it prohibits only extreme acts," such as infliction of pain with intensity that accompanies "organ failure, impairment of bodily function, or even death."[56] Even if an interrogation method were torture, the memo concluded, "Any effort to apply [the statute] in a manner that interferes with the president's direction of such core war matters as the detention and interrogation of enemy combatants thus would be unconstitutional."[57] From its exceedingly narrow conception of torture to its lack of historical sensitivity to the important role of prohibitions against torture both in the eighteenth century and in the post–World War II development of human rights law, to its entirely self-serving account of an effectively unconstrained and unenumerated executive power, the memo seeks only to enable presidential action, not to take care to be faithful to the law.[58] This tendentious reading of the statute has drawn much criticism and few defenders.[59] It serves as an example of how the obligation to take care can be evaded through implausible, and subsequently disavowed, legal interpretations of the law.[60]

Another example of the strategies a president might use to avoid responsibility for taking care of constitutional promises and constraints is the use of so-called "signing statements" when signing legislation into law. These can usefully articulate how a president understands his duty under the law, and can signal to the public and other political actors what to expect from the president's enforcement priorities. Used in this manner, they can increase transparency and public accountability.[61] But when used to declare opposition to the law or intent not to enforce it, signing statements can call into question the integrity of the president's commitment to take care to faithfully execute the law. Using this latter approach, President Bush, for example, created controversy by his widespread use of statements, leading to an American Bar Association report questioning the practice.[62] What made his use of such statements questionable—besides the frequency or even the specific statutes—was the basis on which he claimed nonenforcement power. A signing statement issued along with the Detainee Treatment Act, which limited interrogation methods used by the military and at Guantánamo Bay, is illustrative: "The executive branch shall construe . . . the Act, relating to detainees, in a manner consistent with the constitutional authority of the President to supervise the unitary executive branch and as Commander in Chief and consistent with the constitutional limitations on the judicial power."[63] Relying on an unspecified notion of the "unitary executive" as well as the catchall power of the commander in chief, the president claimed these statutory limitations do not bind his authority over interrogation techniques. It is doubtful that an assertion of commander in chief power could preclude congressional oversight regarding interrogation methods. But even more, this legislation was the product of intense democratic participation, coming in the wake of public revelations about the severe abuse of detainees in Iraq at Abu Ghraib.

From the perspective of Article II virtues of care and fidelity, nonenforcement conflicts with the president's responsibilities to and for the Constitution, except when a law is clearly unconstitutional. First, the president is not without institutional resources to avoid the implications of policies he might prefer to avoid.[64] For example, the president can veto a bill, negotiate in advance to keep a provision out of a bill, or lobby for its repeal. Second, the president's responsibility is to take care and faithfully execute duly enacted law. The president may have discretion over priorities and resources in addition to how a statute is interpreted and implemented, but it is conceptually incongruous to claim faithful execution by nonenforcement altogether, particularly when the law in question is meant to limit executive discretion regarding matters claimed to be necessary.

Might a president contravene constitutional constraints without encountering a legal check? The most plausible account of President Trump's so-called "Muslim travel ban" is that it was a policy promised on the campaign trail motivated by unconstitutional consideration of religion, but in the final version of the executive order that implemented the policy, reference to religion disappeared.[65] Chief Justice Roberts's opinion for the majority refused to consider material outside of the four corners of the order that cast unconstitutional light on Trump's action, reasoning instead that "searching inquiry is inconsistent with the broad statutory text and the deference traditionally accorded the President in this sphere."[66] As the Court explained, "The Proclamation is expressly premised on legitimate purposes: preventing entry of nationals who cannot be adequately vetted and inducing other nations to improve their practices. The text says nothing about religion."[67] But Justice Sotomayor's dissenting opinion examined "a far more harrowing picture" of Trump's record, in which he called "for a total and complete shutdown of Muslims entering the United States."[68] Moreover, Trump explained, "[W]e can't allow people coming into this country who have this hatred of the United States . . . [a]nd of people that are not Muslim."[69] After signing the first version of his executive order, President Trump commented that "we all know what that means" with a wink and a knowing smile to indicate what was delivered in dry, neutral legal terms was in fact his "Muslim ban." In this way, the president indicated no care or fidelity to the principle of religious nondiscrimination protected by the First Amendment, and made no attempt to argue that his immigration policy was consistent with constitutional values.

Chief Justice Roberts upheld the policy only by remaining blind to the context, even as he was forced to write in dicta that this policy was no precursor to Japanese internment, and that *Korematsu* "was gravely wrong the day it was decided, has been overruled in the court of history, and—to be clear—has no place in law under the Constitution."[70] Such forceful dicta would hardly be in order were the chief justice not aware of how dangerously close "the court of history" might soon be to criticizing his opinion's willful blindness. And in concurrence, Justice Kennedy admonished, "There are numerous instances in which the statements and actions of Government officials are not subject to judicial scrutiny or intervention. That does not mean those officials are free to disregard the Constitution and the rights it proclaims and protects. The oath that all officials take to adhere to the Constitution is not confined to those spheres in which the Judiciary can correct or even comment upon what those officials say or do."[71] Indeed, he emphasizes that where judicial review is unavoidable, presidential obligations to the Constitution's "meaning and its promise" are all the more imperative. The president can shape institutions and practices through both his legal and extralegal attention to constitutional meaning. Were President Trump clearly upholding his responsibility for the Constitution, its meaning and promise, such judicial lecturing would hardly be necessary or appropriate. Its presence indicates that Trump's actions contravene both his responsibility and the Constitution's meaning despite the lack of a structural check on his actions.

Situations that raise the prominence of necessity as both an imperative and a justification for presidential action that avoids, exceeds, or contravenes existing legal and constitutional limitations are those that lead to a claim that responsibility entails power. That claim responds to duties of care and fidelity by emphasizing strategies such as interpretive creativity, nonenforcement, or even legal contravention. In each case, the justifications offered are about the scope of power, not the degree of responsibility to and for constitutional meaning and identity. But only the latter coheres with a conception of taking care to faithfully execute the law. It is difficult to see how taking care of the Constitution entails ignoring, avoiding, or superseding it. Only by conflating physical security with constitutional security—prioritizing the needs of physical necessity over constitutional principle—could a president argue that focusing on the power said to flow from responsibility is a way of taking care. As we saw in chapter 1, physical security is insufficient to guarantee against the stuff out of which dictatorships are made, which motivated FDR to broaden the scope of constitutional values over which the polity should take care.

In this way, many of the considerations in play regarding structural features—the fact that the executive is the branch with the claimed power entailed by responsibility for national security—can be replicated as claims about the meaning of the duties of care and fidelity. Confronting an emergency, a president could argue that actions taken in conflict with the Constitution or laws fulfill a duty to take care to preserve the nation. But notice that the argument in this iteration is transformed into one about the meanings and constraints the specific virtues of care and fidelity textually impose, not one about the structural obligations of the presidential office. Like its structural counterpart, such a textual approach ultimately fails to provide grounds for unilateral power to do whatever is claimed necessary to protect national security.

To approach the issue of a preclusive power to act in conflict with laws or the Constitution, Justice Jackson's tripartite doctrinal analysis provides the relevant discursive framework. President Truman issued an executive order instructing the secretary of commerce to seize steel mills in order to ensure that an ongoing labor dispute did not disrupt steel production during the Korean War.[72] In the 1952 case of *Youngstown Sheet & Tube Co. v. Sawyer*, the president justified this action as necessary to the war effort, asserting before the Supreme Court authority as the commander in chief, authority derived from the Vesting Clause, and a duty under the Take Care Clause.[73] Lacking express congressional authorization, the president asserted inherent power to address a national emergency. The Supreme Court issued six different opinions explaining why President Truman did not have the power he asserted.[74] Among these, Justice Jackson's concurrence has become "the accepted framework for evaluating executive action in this area."[75] Justice Jackson introduced three categories of executive action. First, "When the President acts pursuant to an express or implied authorization of Congress, his authority is at its maximum."[76] Second, "When the President acts in absence of either a congressional grant or denial of authority," there exists a "zone of twilight" that will "depend on the imperatives of events and contemporary imponderables rather than on abstract theories of law" to justify exercise of such authority.[77] Finally, when the president acts in conflict "with the expressed or implied will of Congress, his power is at its lowest ebb."[78]

When the executive acts in conflict with congressional statutes, his power is at its "lowest ebb," but that does not necessarily mean the president lacks power altogether. Justice Jackson does not explain further when the "imperatives of events"—or more simply stated, necessity—allows the president to act in conflict with Congress.[79] But the possibility is clearly contemplated. By what criteria are we to judge when the "imperatives of events" appropriately justify executive action in conflict with congressional statutes?[80] When is the executive permitted to assume "independent presidential responsibility" for the law because of "congressional inertia, indifference or quiescence"?[81]

Justice Jackson does not tell us how to decide when diminished power at its "lowest ebb" is nonetheless sufficient to justify appropriate action. He warns that a "[p]residential claim to a power at once so conclusive and preclusive must be scrutinized with caution, for what is at stake is the equilibrium established by our constitutional system."[82] "Caution" needs content, and appeal to the overriding responsibility for care and fidelity provides a textual opportunity to give meaning to the remaining constraints guiding exercise of constitutional powers, which may come at the price of "disabling the Congress from acting upon the subject."[83]

A claim about necessity, as we have repeatedly seen, functions as a conversation stopper. "I did what was necessary in the circumstances" is a claim that both purports to be an ultimate justification and serves to foreclose further critical inquiry into, or institutional check on, presidential actions. But if we deny, as I have suggested we should, that "because it's necessary" is a sufficient justification, then critical intervention is required, shifting our inquiry to the normative criteria by which to assess executive actions. The question becomes how to assess executive actions, not whether to do so at all. Recall that the presidentialist view attempted to foreclose judicial review of executive action altogether. Actions necessary to protect national security were said to be for the president alone to choose. The prior chapter rejected that view as inconsistent with our constitutional traditions and understandings about how we protect both liberty and security.

The claim that because the president has responsibility for national security he must also have power is a claim that functions the same whether at the zenith or lowest ebb of executive power, for it seeks to replace critical evaluation with unreflective deference to presidential actions. Whereas claims to institutional prerogative are about legal process—who gets to decide questions of security and liberty—claims about the execution of law and policy are substantive claims. They succeed or fail on their merits.

What is interesting about the textual command the Take Care Clause announces is that an executive who assumes "independent presidential responsibility" retains the same responsibility to take care to faithfully execute the laws. Responsibility for national security does not vitiate the obligation to take care. There is no national security exception to the obligation to take care. The constitutional standards of care and fidelity do not change, even if the circumstances of their application do. To import Chief Justice Marshall's considerations in *McCulloch v. Maryland*, it is not just the content of the laws, but their "spirit" over which the executive has responsibility, and from which his power derives. In this way, care and fidelity are not simply constraints. They are also empowering virtues. If a president is going to execute law well, to live up to the promises of excellence in execution, then he must live up to the "spirit" of the task, not merely the letter. Both the letter and the spirit provide grounds for critical examination of presidential uses and assertions of power. But this is also our critical problem. When we shift attention to how to assess presidential choice, the Constitution only provides standards such as "care" and "fidelity" to guide, leaving the responsibility for reflection and choice to us. But that means that we cannot eschew responsibility for necessity.

Because at the "lowest ebb" the president is not only claiming inherent authority but also asserting superior judgment, we should therefore expect the highest attention to virtues of office and policy justifications through public argumentation. Such attention requires more than following necessity's lead. It requires judgment in accord with the constraints of office, care in avoiding legal conflict to the greatest extent possible, and fidelity to other more general constitutional principles such as equality and due process. A president's broader and more inchoate responsibility to the Constitution, not just to the physical security of the polity, follows not only from the Take Care Clause but also from the president's power to shape policy around a constitutional vision. Because a duty to preserve the physical safety of the nation is ever present, convenience in achieving that goal falls far short of demonstrating that acting in conflict with congressional statutes is necessary. That a program might be useful, or even beneficial, in light of other policy constraints, does not elevate usefulness to necessity. Relying on the too-quick inference from responsibility to power without public justification, it becomes too easy for a president to transform usefulness into necessity.

Responsibility and Presidential Vision

Necessitous circumstances do not befall from nowhere. They arise in contexts. A polity's response to crisis depends in large part on its preexisting commitments, values, and ways of seeing that connect imagined possibilities to everyday governance manifest through a constitutional vision. A president has power to shape this vision.[84] But this power, I argue—inverting the responsibility entails power rationale—is constrained by its responsibility to and for the constitution and the political community it constitutes.[85]

To see how circumstances interact with constitutional vision, consider two speeches each delivered by two different presidents in times of crises. Lincoln mobilized great resources to sustain a vision of national unity realized through the people's material sacrifices.[86] In his "First Inaugural Address," the issue he confronted was not only the recent secession of Southern states like South Carolina but also the constitutional justifications proffered in defense of severing the Union. Political acts rely on constitutional vision. As a consequence, Lincoln argued that "the Union of these States is perpetual," and that "[t]he

Union is much older than the Constitution."[87] Secessionist Southerners contested Lincoln's constitutional vision of the indivisible Union. Focusing on the claim that the states have a prior and continuing sovereign status, Jefferson Davis, in his own "Inaugural Address" to the Confederate states two weeks prior, urged a "right of the people to alter or abolish [governments] at will whenever they become destructive of the ends for which they were established."[88] The rights proclaimed in the formation of the United States, confirmed in the Constitution, "undeniably recognize[] in the people the power to resume the authority delegated for the purposes of government. Thus the sovereign States here represented have proceeded to form this Confederacy."[89] The people to which he refers are not "We the People" of a national community, but the people of the several states.[90] Disavowing rational deliberation, Davis claimed that circumstances compelled insurrectionist actions: "As a necessity, not a choice, we have resorted to the remedy of separation."[91] Lincoln would also rely on necessity to justify his actions to preserve the Union, later claiming that "measures otherwise unconstitutional, might become lawful, by becoming indispensable to the preservation of the constitution, through the preservation of the nation."[92] "Indispensable" measures will later become actions that "whether strictly legal or not, were ventured upon under what appeared to be a popular demand, and a public necessity."[93]

Rejecting the argument that the states have sovereign priority over the Union, which exists merely as a contract between states, Lincoln reasoned, "If the United States be not a government proper, but an association of States in the nature of contract merely, can it, as a contract, be peaceably unmade by less than all the parties who made it?"[94] To undo the Union would require the consent of the whole, not the unilateral actions of individual political bodies, and would imply that the "more perfect Union" lacked in perfection because of the supposed superior status of the individual states.[95] Thus, Lincoln concluded that "no State upon its own mere motion can lawfully get out of the Union."[96] This argument has consequences for the president's responsibility to the Constitution.

Because of the constitutional vision he imparted, President Lincoln declared that "to the extent of my ability, I shall take care, as the Constitution itself expressly enjoins upon me, that the laws of the Union be faithfully executed in all the States."[97] Taking care to faithfully execute the laws against states whose acts against the "authority of the United States are insurrectionary or revolutionary" required mobilization of all the president's powers and the adoption of measures sometimes in conflict with the Constitution and laws.[98]

President Lincoln's speech imparted a contested constitutional vision, constructed contrasting civic communities, and mobilized publics on their behalf. Despite later protestations by the Supreme Court to be preeminent in the interpretation of the Constitution, Lincoln's vision had greater immediate, and more lasting, effect than the prevailing view of constitutional structure reflected in Chief Justice Taney's 1857 decision in *Dred Scott v. Sandford*.[99] That vision authorized a permanent civic caste system wherein black Americans—free or unfree—could not be citizens. Taney's constitution, which contemplated permanent racial division and inequality, was not, and did not become, Lincoln's or ours.

What is significant about these contrasting visions—like Jefferson's concern over his power to acquire the Louisiana territories—is how they shape a national community in ways that far exceed the confines of the narrow legal question on which they are grounded. The settler nation the Louisiana Purchase enabled and furthered became possible as a result of contested conceptions of presidential power.[100] The perpetual union Lincoln envisioned was possible because of an interpreted obligation that the Take Care clause imposed.

Constitutional visions can also have pervasive effects, even when the issues are less momentous than territorial expansion or perpetual union. Following the attacks of September 11, President Bush mobilized the country to embark on a war that "will not end until every terrorist group of global reach has been found, stopped and defeated."[101] Americans now live with the consequences of President Bush's legal and practical decisions. Whereas Lincoln confronted a defining constitutional debate over the structure and future of the Union, President Bush faced no such existential crises. Instead, the vision he projected was much more personal, framed in terms of the president's own responsibility to the national community. Speaking days after the attacks, he declared, "I will not yield; I will not rest; I will not relent in waging this struggle for freedom and security for the American people."[102] Above all else, "Our first priority must always be the security of our Nation."[103] On the fifth anniversary of September 11, President Bush reiterated his personal obligation: "In the first days after the 9/11 attacks, I promised to use every element of national power to fight the terrorists, wherever we find them."[104]

And use them he did. Executive officials under President Bush argued for unilateral powers in conflict with congressional mandates when it came to restrictions on surveillance under the Foreign Intelligence Surveillance Act (FISA) and when it came to prohibitions against torture and cruel, inhuman, and degrading treatment of detainees under the antitorture statute, as well as under international covenants.[105] All of these actions are ones we have confronted in prior chapters. A common feature, however, is how they reflect a vision of presidential power that prioritizes a constitutional responsibility and power to address necessity and that minimizes the function of either institutional or principled constraints. This vision not only shapes immediate responses but has enduring consequences not easily altered by subsequent institutional interventions.

Claiming power to pursue an unyielding and unrelenting struggle to secure the homeland enabled the president to conduct the "decisive ideological struggle of the 21st century, and the calling of our generation."[106] This struggle "is a struggle for civilization. We are fighting to maintain the way of life enjoyed by free nations."[107] The president's unyielding struggle and responsibility became the task for the country itself, and—rather than simply capturing and containing defined perpetrators of the September atrocities—civilization itself was at stake, which was something more, it seems, than preserving the Constitution. Although the president admonished that history made it "our responsibility and our privilege to fight freedom's fight," this campaign had constitutional implications because "America will always stand firm for the nonnegotiable demands of human dignity: the rule of law; limits on the power of the state; respect for women; private property; free speech; equal justice; and religious tolerance."[108] Post–September 11 counterterrorism policy, however, did not always match these constitutional aspirations and constraints. Yet the grammar of presidential constitutionalism claims responsibility for preserving and promoting constitutional values such as liberty and dignity at home and abroad. President Bush asserted presidential power to respond to this new world free from judicial or congressional oversight. A personalized presidential responsibility could generate its own power to match the perceived degree of responsibility—a "with great responsibility comes great power" view we have repeatedly encountered, which John Yoo and others urged within the Bush administration.[109] Even so, as Bush acknowledged, presidential power is responsible for constitutional values other than security.

President Roosevelt described his own powers and responsibility when Congress failed to act as he desired during wartime regarding agriculture prices. During a "Fireside Chat" in September 1942, he explained:

> I cannot tell what powers may have to be exercised in order to win this war. The American people can be sure that I will use my powers with a full sense of my responsibility to the Constitution and to my country. The American people can also be sure that I shall not hesitate to use every power vested in me to accomplish the defeat of our enemies in any part of the world where our own safety demands such defeat.[110]

President Roosevelt's appeal was personal and expansive, recognizing his responsibility to the Constitution even in the context of war powers. Although the content of that responsibility is not specified, mere recognition that it exists serves as a normative constraint on how presidential "powers may have to be exercised."[111] Responsibility, for Roosevelt, extended beyond claims about physical security to encompass social security as a prerequisite for American liberty, because, as we have seen, "necessitous men are not free men."[112] Responsibility to the Constitution—even in terms of necessity—includes a vision of how it might secure new protections and empower expanded individual freedoms.

Responsibility has a complicated relation to power. Taking responsibility for the Constitution and for its principles is a matter subject to shifting constitutional visions that bind imagined possibilities to the realities of government, even during times of crisis. Necessity pulls in the direction of executive discretion to do whatever it takes to resolve the crisis and to provide security. Power enables discretion, and "[e]nergy in the Executive" makes possible vigorous responses to emergencies subject to discretion.[113] Responsibility thus raises questions not only about the scope of power but also about the norms that might guide the exercise of discretionary power.

If the presidential office has responsibility for national security, it also has responsibility for the normative vision through which it acts. This normative vision must connect not only ideals of liberty and dignity, but specific obligations to free speech, democratic participation, privacy, and freedom from pervasive surveillance, to name a few fundamental rights. In this way, the attempt to evade normative responsibility by claiming that actions are compelled by necessity—that the president could not have acted otherwise than he did—fails because of its incomplete understanding of the scope of presidential responsibility to and for the Constitution.

Even as a long-standing political theory debate urges the priority of self-preservation over the rule of law, as Jefferson's earlier appeal suggests and as we explored in chapter 1, a consistent theme in presidential constitutional vision has been recognition of the executive's responsibility for constitutional values.[114] The president is tamed by inescapable commitments to constitutional values and the virtues of exercising executive power.[115] If responsibility entails power, then responsibility also functions as a constraint on power. Power and discretion exist only within the already existing confines of this constraint. Each must operate within boundaries defined by the nature of the office, the circumstances that compel action, the limits of available resources, or the reactions of other political institutions or bodies. Constitutionalizing this constraint embeds further limitations according to the specific powers and responsibilities that constitute the executive office. Foremost of those responsibilities are the virtues of care and faithfulness in executing the laws and preserving, through upholding, the Constitution.

Completing the President: How What Is Proper Constrains What Is Necessary

Much of post–September 11 counterterrorism policy obtains its congressional authority from the Authorization for Use of Military Force (AUMF), which empowered the president to take "all necessary . . . actions" to pursue the perpetrators—and their enablers—of the attacks.[116] President Bush thus pursued actions at the "zenith" of his powers, acting out of both inherent power and congressional authorization. President Obama expanded the scope of this authority to engage in lethal, unmanned aerial strikes against targeted individuals in addition to conducting strikes in Syria and elsewhere against a terrorist group, ISIS, that did not exist in 2001.[117] President Trump has not relinquished any of the authority the Obama administration aggrandized under the AUMF. Moreover, it seems that this power is grounded ultimately in a judgment of necessity. But the ellipsis as I have quoted the AUMF invites us to overlook the normative substance and logical structure of this authority. The ellipsis displaces something often absent from the public discourse, but not from the text of the resolution. The AUMF conjoins an evaluative term to the operational imperative to authorize use of "all necessary *and appropriate* force" in responding to the September attacks.[118] Similar language is employed in the 2002 congressional authorization to use force in Iraq, which empowered the president to use armed forces "as he determines to be necessary and appropriate."[119] What is "appropriate" doing in such legislative empowerment of executive officials? What does "appropriate" mean, and what is its source? How does "appropriate" relate to the need to do what is "necessary"?

Such an evaluative conjunction is not novel. The Constitution empowers Congress "[t]o make all Laws which shall be necessary and proper for carrying into Execution the foregoing Powers."[120] "Appropriate" is a cognate to the Constitution's "proper" limit on congressional necessity. The claim here is simple: the term "appropriate" embeds within executive authority normative constraints, just as "proper" limits the means Congress can employ in furthering its enumerated powers. "Proper" constrains "necessary." But what kind of constraint is the requirement of propriety?[121] What is necessary has been the focus of some judicial attention, but what is proper has been little discussed.

Congress has interpreted the Necessary and Proper Clause to expand its powers, not to limit them. Supreme Court opinions have endorsed this view, though the interpretive emphasis since *McCulloch v. Maryland* has been on the meaning of "necessary."[122] Regarding the meaning of the Necessary and Proper Clause, Chief Justice Marshall explained, "Let the end be legitimate, let it be within the scope of the constitution, and all means which are appropriate, which are plainly adopted to that end, which are not prohibited, but consist with the letter and spirit of the constitution, are constitutional."[123] What is necessary is also proper when it is directed to a legitimate end, is not otherwise prohibited, and coheres with the "letter and spirit" of the Constitution. A "proper" exercise of legislative power does more than match means to ends; it also furthers the aims and values of constitutional "letter" as well as the more inchoate "spirit" of the Constitution. Limiting the president's power to what is "appropriate" does not interfere with the need to match means to ends, but it does require the president to conform to broader constitutional principles and values, and perhaps other laws and treaties, when deciding how to execute a specific law or policy. By giving substance to the "appropriate" limit on the president's power under the AUMF, we can begin to sketch both instrumental and deontological obligations. The president has an ethical responsibility to do what is "appropriate" in addition to a practical obligation to do what is necessary.[124]

Taking care to faithfully execute the laws is an imprecise exercise. Multiple concrete instances of policy and practice are consistent with fidelity to statutory directives. Therefore, courts sometimes give executive officials broad deference as interpreters of their legal duties. This deference, articulated in *Chevron U.S.A. Inc. v. Natural Resources Defense Council, Inc.*, means not only that executive officials have a first responsibility to faithfully execute the law but also that they often have the final word in interpreting the law.[125] Recognizing this discretionary structure, Jack Goldsmith and John Manning have developed a theory of the "completion power" that authorizes the president to compose the unwritten details essential to executing legislative programs.[126] Because statutory frameworks are never complete by nature, on this view the president has the constitutional power to bring to fruition the purposes, practices, and processes enacted by Congress. Absent structural restraints, Madisonian design solutions have little to say about how the president completes available legal directives. Goldsmith and Manning draw inspiration from the dissent in the *Youngstown* steel-seizure case.

Providing a basis to support a completion power, Chief Justice Vinson reasoned in his *Youngstown* dissent that "[t]he absence of a specific statute authorizing seizure of the steel mills as a mode of executing the laws" did not preclude the president from acting.[127] Citing to a body of additional laws and the overriding purpose behind the United Nations Charter to render assistance in Korea backed by congressional appropriations, Chief Justice Vinson claimed that "[t]he President has the duty to execute the foregoing legislative programs."[128] In essence, although there was no specific statutory mandate instructing the president to seize steel mills to ensure uninterrupted steel production, such action was necessary to fulfill—that is, to complete—explicit congressional mandates. Chief Justice Vinson concluded that "[f]lexibility as to mode of execution to meet critical situations is a matter of practical necessity."[129] Linking the duty to "take care" with the demands of "practical necessity," Chief Justice Vinson fashioned an account of presidential power that is textually based but attentive to the demands of necessity. Such attention is authorized by a "practical construction of the 'Take Care' clause" holistic in its orientation.[130]

Deviating from Vinson, Goldsmith and Manning seek to ground the completion power not in a power to "take care," but in an implied power analogous to Article I's Necessary and Proper Clause.[131] They find suitable ground by appeal to the implications of the most basic form of executive power—the "authority to carry out congressional commands directed to the President or his or her agents."[132] Because it would be impossible for the legislature to specify all aspects of a law's implementation, the executive must therefore possess a degree of discretion that implies the completion power. Executive completion power is a residuum that exists from the president's administrative responsibility, which in turn seems to follow from his duty under the Take Care Clause.[133] This approach avoids the temptation to find residual executive prerogative in the very existence of an executive power. On the theory of the completion power, "it would be odd to read the constitutional scheme to assign powers without also assigning incidental authority to carry those powers into execution."[134] The question is, What is the nature of this power to complete, construed as an implied power to do whatever is necessary in the circumstances?

The possible existence of a completion power therefore becomes a possible way for the president to respond to necessity while taking care to faithfully execute the laws. It would also provide a way for the executive to coordinate—not conflict—with congressional instructions. Such a theory has powerful explanatory as well as normative prospects. The advantage of this approach is that so long as a president avoids a direct violation of a congressional or constitutional provision, completing existing powers and policies might justify use of all necessary power. Where this authority exists, appeal to the "unwritten laws of necessity, of self-preservation, and of the public safety," as did Jefferson, may prove unproductive.[135] Why appeal to something so evanescent as the unwritten law of necessity, or appeal to a theory of extralegal measures, when a president can infer power from constitutional structure and analogous text? Even where specific statutory instructions directing specific responses to pressing emergencies are lacking, the president can bring to completion their overall purpose—preserving and protecting the American people. Much will depend on how the purpose is described. What is more, within specific domains, congressional statutes themselves invite the president to use discretion to do what is necessary to achieve congressional goals.

A "residual capacity to take the steps necessary to carry out Congress's program" focuses on the language of necessity found in the Article I Necessary and Proper Clause.[136] It does so, however, in a way that looks very much like another version of residual executive prerogative. And unlike the way that Article I tethers the Necessary and Proper Clause to a long list of powers enumerated for Congress, the completion power—were it to exist—seems capable of an almost limitless ability to justify executive action.[137] Focused on necessity, the completion power seems to provide a textual source that empowers the president to do whatever is necessary in the realm of national security. But if we are guided by text, "necessary" is conjoined to "proper," as we have seen, implying that normative constraints are embedded in the very understanding of a power to do what is necessary.

In his separate *Youngstown* concurrence, Justice Jackson cautions that "[t]he appeal, however, that we declare the existence of inherent powers *ex necessitate* to meet an emergency asks us to do what many think would be wise, although it is something the forefathers omitted."[138] The Constitution likewise omits an express necessary-and-proper power from Article II. When "[t]he plea is for a resulting power to deal with a crisis or an emergency according to the necessities of the case," a powerful complement to the claim of inherent power is a claim to a completion power—an implied necessary-and-proper power.[139] Yet this is precisely what the *Youngstown* Court withheld from President Truman. When the president's actions shift from completing a specific statutory scheme to carrying into execution a "mass of legislation," they begin to look more like lawmaking and less like execution. In fact, Justice Black's majority opinion in *Youngstown* suggests, "[T]he President's power to see that the laws are faithfully executed refutes the idea that he is to be a lawmaker."[140]

The completion power therefore struggles against precedent (no Court has adopted Justice Vinson's theory), constitutional source (no solid textual basis), and conceptual grounding (no clarity about whether the spaces are within or between laws). And although it provides some discursive salience to unavoidable executive discretion, it may function as a more nuanced justification for inherent executive power, especially by emphasizing power to complete the spaces in between the laws. To be clear, I think that the arguments supporting the existence of a separate and robust completion power fail, though they do provide a way of conceptualizing executive discretion, with important normative implications. In this way, even a theory of presidential power that may ultimately fail provides an opportunity to consider further how presidential power is constrained by normative obligations—whether by responsibility to the Constitution or through care and fidelity or to conceptions of constitutional propriety.

Nonetheless, there is something useful in thinking about the completion power. For one, it avoids the worst excesses of claiming inherent power based on some dubious notion of prerogative, an implied principle of necessity, or an extralegal-measures theory. For another, it provides a way of organizing something that different areas of presidential discretion might have in common. Discretion is always discretion on behalf of particular statutory schemes or enumerated powers. To talk of the completion power reminds the president that discretionary power is always derivative of practices and purposes that depend on Congress or the Constitution, even if the president is responsible for fulfilling them. Moreover, a completion power suggests that presidents should think holistically about both ends and means. Finally, the completion power invites consideration of another source of constraint on presidential power. With all powers come constraints, and the completion power's basis in a conception of necessary and proper is no different.

If the president has power to do what is necessary in completing statutory directives, then the president has a responsibility to do only what is proper. If Congress enacts legislation that accords "the President broad discretion," then it "may be considered to 'invite' 'measures on independent presidential responsibility.' "[141] When acting independently, or in between statutory directives, the president's imputed necessary power carries with it an implied constraint to do what is proper. The question then is, What kind of constraint might this be? Because the executive completion power retains obligations of care and faithfulness, what is proper must cohere with the president's responsibility to and for the Constitution.

The complete phrase "necessary and proper" appeared in the Constitution without debate or explanation, giving us little insight into founding-era purposes for its inclusion.[142] Whereas "necessary" is a recurring conjunct, "proper" rarely makes a focused showing in judicial reasoning. In *McCulloch,* Justice Marshall does not discuss the meaning of "proper"—in contrast to his focus on "necessary"—but he does provide an important limitation on the combined necessary-and-proper power: "Let the end be legitimate, let it be within the scope of the constitution, and all means which are appropriate, which are plainly adopted to that end, which are not prohibited, but consist with the letter and spirit of the constitution, are constitutional."[143] What is necessary can only be proper if it is addressed to a legitimate end, not otherwise prohibited by law or the Constitution, and if it coheres with both the "letter and spirit" of the Constitution. This limitation on necessity requires more than the rational attachment of means to ends because it requires fit and demands consistency with both constitutional text and "spirit." What Justice Marshall means by "spirit" invites further inquiry, but it must include holistic considerations about the principles, values, and structures that make up a Constitution's "spirit" and through which it has meaning.

Understanding "proper" to constrain necessity helps make sense of why Congress might authorize the president to do only what is "necessary and appropriate" in using force in Iraq or against the perpetrators of the September 11 attacks.[144] If "appropriate" added nothing, then Congress could simply instruct the president to do what is necessary—a pointless exercise if the president were already empowered by an implied necessity power.[145] Legislative license is combined with a reminder of legal restraint. The president has wide latitude but must take responsibility to faithfully execute the laws and not to avoid, or even act against, them. Like all standards and principles, this limitation is unavoidably imprecise.

To say that necessity is constrained by what is proper may serve no other—and perhaps no better—purpose than as a reminder that the Constitution is meant to constrain, and to do so with values reflected by the community it sustains. The vitality of that constraint depends on institutions and circumstances, statesmen and citizens. Necessity provides its own language, matched by the "energy" with which the executive is characterized as acting with a unity conducive to "[d]ecision, activity, secrecy, and dispatch."[146] But "proper" is too often either assumed or ignored. Either way, the language of constraint is at times difficult to articulate in the face of readily available language from executive power advocates such as Alexander Hamilton, wording that can be used to justify "an indefinite power of providing for emergencies as they might arise."[147] "Proper" reminds us that constraints are operative, but they require us to give them articulation, even in times of crisis. Constitutional responsibility, whether by vision, virtue, or necessity's propriety, constrains the president's power. In this way, taking care is also about remaining faithful to the constitutional project. Care and fidelity are two unavoidable constitutional virtues that both empower and constrain a president.

Responsibility and Constitutional Faith

Keeping faith with the Constitution requires not only development of a coherent and comprehensive constitutional vision but also recognition of how that vision fits within tradition and practice. Remaining faithful to the Constitution is another way of engaging the American people in the pursuit of principle and policy. Quotidian political pursuits share a common commitment to values and constraints that define Americans' sense of self.[148] Faithfulness in this sense is a kind of commitment. Like being true to one's own values and projects extended over a life, constitutional commitment requires fulfillment of political projects and adherence to shared values. Writing for the Court in the 2004 decision *Hamdi v. Rumsfeld*, Justice O'Connor reviewed aspects of President Bush's detention of those he unilaterally designated unlawful enemy combatants, and stated:

> Striking the proper constitutional balance here is of great importance to the Nation during this period of ongoing combat. But it is equally vital that our calculus not give short shrift to the values that this country holds dear or to the privilege that is American citizenship. It is during our most challenging and uncertain moments that our Nation's commitment to due process is

most severely tested; and it is in those times that we must preserve our commitment at home to the principles for which we fight abroad.[149]

Faithfulness is easier in the midst of normal and everyday governing.
Heightened temptation to break commitments occurs only when crisis
arises. When that happens, necessity advises abandoning those commitments that make resolution of the crisis more onerous. Like the biblical
Job, faith can only be outwardly proved through crisis, and if it fails under
trial and temptation, then there is reason to doubt its efficacy, rather than
its mere coincidence, during normal times.[150] That is, if readily abandoned
during crisis, then what appears as faithfulness to the Constitution need
not be the product of commitment but rather a consequence of having insufficient occasion to act in conflict with its constraints. The true test of
faithfulness to the laws and Constitution arises when necessity presses for
political priority in times of national security crisis.

Crisis accentuates the president's powers. It provides the occasion for exercising otherwise dormant statutory and constitutional powers.[151] The nature of
necessity being what it is, crisis and emergency are predictable, even expected.
Because we can plan in advance for the authority executive officials will need
in light of the actions they can be expected to take, crisis need be no challenge
to a president's faithfulness to the Constitution.[152] Whether and to what extent
crisis might be a challenge depends in significant part upon the attitudes toward constitutional responsibilities the president and the public adopt.

To emphasize the president's responsibility for the nation's security does
not entail the existence of yet-untapped reserves of power. Outside of Madisonian institutional checks, apart from legal arguments about the scope of
the president's commander-in-chief power, or the scope of "the executive
power," or the existence of inherent war powers, the grammar of presidentialism turns to normative accounts of "good government" achieved through
the virtues of office.

As the Supreme Court made clear regarding Congress's powers, "emergency does not create power."[153] Nor does claimed responsibility for national
security create powers not already provided in recognition of the scope of a
president's unique role within a normative constitutional order. To find an
overriding source of power in a claim of national necessity is to jettison any

constraint found within the letter or spirit of a president's responsibility to take care and be faithful to the polity's laws. The responsibility-entails-power view is not a coherent account of American constitutionalism. Recognizing that the public, just as much as the president, can be subject to rational bias or panic, the point of faithfulness is to settle constitutional commitments in advance of the episodic temptation to impassioned deviation.

Even were a president to have the responsibility, and therefore the power, to respond to emergencies to preserve national security, the president is therefore also responsible to and for the Constitution and laws. "Responsibility to" the Constitution requires compliance with legal rules and the exercise of discretion within appropriate limits. "Responsibility for" the Constitution and laws requires recognition of a president's role within a social imaginary with effects on political and constitutional culture through the care taken in executing the law and exercising discretion. No matter how a president chooses to respond to an emergency, presidential action helps create the political and ethical community Americans occupy.

Even if the president is responsible to and for the Constitution, what ensures continued constitutional commitment? In what way does that commitment work to stabilize policy and practice over time? Recent discussion has focused the question of constitutional commitment, finding a puzzle in "how popular majorities or other powerful political actors successfully commit themselves to constitutional constraints."[154] It is one thing to identify the meaning of softer constitutional constraints, as we have done here; it is quite another to understand why a president would ever commit to fulfilling those virtues. Once elected, a president will have ample opportunity to act, seeking policies and practices that further particular interests no matter the finer points of constitutional form.[155] One solution to the puzzle of constitutional constraint may be to recognize public-choice mechanisms that permit actors to commit themselves to constraining institutional forms even when their self-interest might tempt them otherwise.[156] At bottom, these commitments are contingent social practices that rely on the continued political and social support of citizens and officials.[157] Yet, despite its descriptive usefulness, social and political support through mechanisms described in public-choice theory is insufficient to account for the constitutive role of president and polity that constitutional constraints create. "Our" Constitution requires our shared willingness to continue the project of constitutional governance, a project that is inseparable from the persistence of our shared political identity. It is also a project that relies on more than political entrenchment as a hurdle to formal change that provides constraints against presidential innovation in governing forms.[158]

The Madisonian solution for constitutional constraint both creates institutions for unenlightened statesmen and relies on virtue to make governing possible. Unchecked presidential authority can expand as far as the nature of the office will allow. Recognizing this, the Madisonian tradition supplements the constraint of the office with other institutions, each constituted with powers to check the other. If constitutional constraints went no further, "parchment barriers" may prove insufficient because the Constitution must be embodied and implemented in governing practice. As necessity leads form to give way to function, institutions are malleable. Judges defer to executive officials, and Congress gives way to presidents who, without more, would have only self-interest and constitutional form to guide their actions. But the Madisonian solution provides more. Though unavoidably incomplete, the Constitution imbeds and requires virtue in implementing governing practice. Taking care and being faithful to the laws and Constitution to do only what is proper when acting as necessary are practices in virtue that cannot be resolved by appeal to institutional design.

As the next chapter explores, constitutional commitment is constitutive commitment. To be committed to the principles and values embodied in the document is to be committed to the people it constitutes. It is also to be committed to the offices the Constitution creates. What it means to be a president is to occupy an already constituted office that requires its holder to work within already constituted institutional structures.[159] As we have explored here, the office of president has its own grammar. To inhabit those structures means more than seeking to achieve self-interested goals; it entails fulfilling the responsibilities that define the office, such as the obligations to take care and be faithful to the nation's political constitution. A president has great responsibility, but part of that responsibility is not only to execute the laws with care and fidelity but also to play a role in constituting the community through constitutional practices and commitments. With great power comes great responsibility.

7

Identity, Freedom, and Constitutional Constraint

NECESSITY IS TETHERED TO PROPRIETY. Constitutional text makes this connection explicit. Even apart from the text, a political theory that advocates strong executive power to do whatever is necessary, even to violate legal limitations, nonetheless requires an exercise of virtue. So when contemporary constitutional theorists find an implied textual foundation for executive officials to "complete" the Constitution by acting as necessary in states of emergency or crisis, they must also be committed to inquiry concerning the appropriateness of executive action. Moreover, "completeness" requires justifying claimed powers and their use within a preexisting constitutional context in which they must fit.

But where the justification for the "completion power" rests on finding an implied executive power by analogy with a textual grant to Congress, the normative constraints on necessity need not be so narrowly, and tenuously, justified. As we saw in the last chapter, the obligation to take care that the laws be faithfully executed serves as its own textual imperative, entailing that both care of and fidelity to constitutional norms are constitutive duties of executive power. Even more, the argument that there is an implied "necessity constitution," as we have seen, never succeeds in eliminating questions of propriety in the pursuit of necessity. These questions of propriety ask more than whether the means adopted fit the ends sought. For questions of propriety ask us to analyze the qualities of particular options designed often to meet more generalized ends such as security. Because answers to these questions are not determined by legal rule or past practice, the future meanings of American constitutionalism are open-ended. What American constitutionalism will mean—the values it realizes in the practices it enables—will depend on the understandings we develop that shape our attitudes and commitments before we are called to respond to the next emergency.

From rejecting the idea that the president is owed special deference in balancing liberty and security, to the idea that balance itself is a problematic approach to relating security and liberty, to criticism of the idea that a president has power to do whatever is necessary because he has responsibility for national security, I have argued that there is a way of thinking about emergency and necessity that undermines American constitutionalism through both conceptual and practical mistakes that would empower the president to be an unchecked decider. Such a mistake is the functional equivalent of embedding executive prerogative at the heart of liberal constitutionalism. Moreover, these mistakes undermine the reflection and choice Alexander Hamilton identified as an essential condition for "good government" as democratic self-government, for they short-circuit rational justification in favor of claims to necessity inflamed by passion. By taking seriously the suggestion that the scope of the president's powers is expanded by an implied "completion power" derived from an implied Article II Necessary and Proper Clause, I argued in the previous chapter that institutional and functional approaches to ever expanding presidential power ignored the discursive need for normative argument about the substance of presidential power. To be responsible for the Constitution is to be responsible for doing only what is appropriate in light of a constitutional context into which actions must cohere. If actions are urged as necessary, a practice of reflection and choice requires that they be justified as appropriate.

Questions of propriety are normative questions requiring further articulation that the Constitution provides only in part. As Chief Justice Marshall explained in *McCulloch v. Maryland,* to do what is necessary requires consideration of constitutional content, as we explored in chapter 3. When exercising government power, the Supreme Court instructed, the end to be pursued must be "legitimate," and the means chosen must be "appropriate" and "consistent with the letter and spirit of the Constitution."[1] But questions of content are as contested as the plurality of values with which liberal politics must contend. What is appropriate and consistent with the Constitution need not have self-evident answers. I argue this is a source of constitutional strength, not weakness. Democratic self-governance, and the national identity it empowers, cannot answer questions of propriety by mechanical and predetermined processes. This chapter argues that overcoming necessity requires us to recognize that freedom is achieved through how we articulate and commit to the values that sustain an American constitutional identity. These values, and their application, may be contested, but they are also sources of both freedom and constraint. To illustrate this dynamic, I use the debate over a counterterrorism policy of targeted killing of individuals, including U.S. citizens, by use of unmanned aerial drones.

The absence of determinant answers concerning propriety might seem to invite deference to claims of necessity, which arise within specific situations of need. In a world of open-ended value plurality, but in the face of definite claims of necessity, is not the executive free to do whatever circumstances dictate, because some articulation of value will always be available to defend the response?

We seem to be caught within another paradox: the Constitution provides a basis for holding executive action responsible for doing only what can be judged appropriate when addressing necessity, but, nevertheless, any action that satisfies necessity could count as appropriate. In this case, as some have urged, the only effective constraint is political, not legal or constitutional.[2] Such constitutional skepticism emphasizes the failures of Madisonian institutional design—the identity of party, not office, for example.[3] From such failure, as we have seen, skeptics conclude that constitutional commitments do no work, because "[t]he modern economy, whose complexity creates the demand for administrative governance, also creates wealth, leisure, education, and broad political information, all of which strengthen democracy and make a collapse into authoritarian rule nearly impossible."[4]

On this skeptical view, the Constitution becomes coincidental to the exercise of executive power. As a way of constituting a political structure by empowering and limiting governing officials, constitutions, as precommitment devices—ways of limiting our future decisional freedom—fail in practice to constrain. If any choice in addressing necessity is both free from Madisonian institutional checks and from ex ante value commitments, then when it comes to states of emergency and crisis, the Constitution does no work. On such a view, some precommitments do constrain. But these are precommitments of more ordinary vintage, existing in the form of entrenchments: entrenched budgetary constraints, established military capacities, applicable treaty obligations, enacted statutory frameworks, and the like. These are constraints based on prior political choices subject to revision should the benefits prove sufficiently large in light of the political costs. In an important respect, such entrenchments are indistinguishable from the circumstances in which a claim to necessity arises. For what makes extralegal action necessary on a particular occasion will be a product of the contextual setting in which prior commitments, practical constraints, and factual details determine the available options. Moreover, extralegal responses to today's necessities can give rise to tomorrow's precommitments by entrenching policies and practices that structure future responses to necessities. This form of entrenchment, on the skeptical view, poses only practical constraints. Normative questions about propriety remain subservient to necessity. Politics will provide the requisite consequential judgments about how well action satisfies the demands of necessity. No other normative considerations need inform inquiry into the appropriateness of executive action.

Precommitments take other forms, as we have seen. Precommitments work either by making unavailable to future decision-makers particular choices or by raising the costs of those choices, in some cases so high as to render them unavailable in practice.[5] In the one kind of case, by providing structural checks, for example, constitutional precommitments constrain how laws are made, which institution decides particular questions, and many other aspects of everyday governing practice. Other kinds of constitutional precommitments are absolute barriers to particular options—amendments that prohibit denying persons citizenship or the ability to vote based on race, for example. These forms of precommitment are both self- and other-binding. In this sense, Ulysses tied to the mast becomes a formal position inhabitable by whoever would be in a position to change the ship of state's course toward the Sirens' rocky coast. By use of structural arrangements—the self-binding combined with hearing impairment of the sailors—particular choices are made unavailable.

In the alternative kinds of cases, constitutional rights sometimes function as precommitments that require robust forms of justification, raising the cost of deviation. These justifications must be given in terms of the propriety of adopting a particular means to achieve considered ends that respect the right even when it is overridden. In this way, the protections that rights afford can have priority over the present preferences of a democratic majority but need not create absolute barriers to democratic decision-making. Legislative ends, and the propriety of the means adopted, determine whether deviations from absolute-rights protections are legitimate. These increased costs create barriers of justification that in some kinds of cases will be too high to surmount. It is true that there is a democratic means of repealing the Nineteenth Amendment, for example, just as Americans chose to repeal the Eighteenth. But it is difficult to imagine a political context in which taking away the right for women to vote on an equal basis with men could be justified in the way that removing the prohibition on sale of alcohol was. Precommitments and the values they entrench shape both political practices and options.

Precommitments have another important dimension. Particular constitutional rights provide diachronic commitments establishing national character, culture, and identity. Commitments to upholding rights are not themselves determined by constitutional provisions. Although embedded institutional structures and rights provisions serve as precommitment mechanisms that limit our future decisional freedom, they also require the will to adhere to them. If members of a polity are not committed to respecting rights, to following principles, providing appropriate justifications, and governing within established institutional structures, then constitutionalism is not possible. Episodic governance that depends on no more than the present caprice of a particular majority would have no need of constitutive commitments. But neither would such a polity have an identifiable consistent character.

Diachronic commitments that produce steadfast adherence to fundamental principles and values help define character and maintain identity. It matters to the American polity's self-understanding that we have freedom of speech and free exercise of religion, for example. Our commitments to specific rights and the values that inform them constitute, in important respects, who "We the People" are. For constitutive commitments function only to the extent that self-governing practices implement and exemplify respect for constitutional norms. We establish structures of governance in light of shared values of self-governance, and we limit the exercise of governing institutions by the constitutive norms of limited government and respect of the rights and dignity of persons. The specific ways we implement both these structures and their limits compose a constitutional culture and character. Though it bears repeating: nothing in the nature of law or constitutions compels our adherence to our own commitments.[6]

Given the close connection between constitutional commitments and character, might the initial constitutional paradox be less problematic? The constitutional skeptic must, it would seem, provide an account of the content and meaning of these commitments. Might commitment to constitutional rights and structural limits provide the relevant normative content to judge the propriety of an executive response to necessity? I suggest yes.

Constitutional commitments can take different forms. Judicial enforcement, for example, is one way of vindicating commitments. Even when judicial enforcement of constitutional rights is unavailable, precommitments continue to provide structure and meaning to the available means and ends. In the context of ordinary antidiscrimination law, as we saw in chapters 3 and 4, when government actors choose to treat some persons differently than others on the basis of a suspect category like race or gender, they do so on the basis of an understanding of equality structured by constitutional norms and judicial doctrines. Equality is not abandoned. Rather, it is given meaning through an implementation that clarifies the scope and meaning of equality even as it deviates from one version of rights absolutism (that is, no differences allowed). Constitutional meanings are preserved through rights transformations. In a similar fashion, even when executive officials claim it is necessary to deviate from strict rights protections, might constitutional norms structure, and thereby constrain, action in a way that gives content to the obligation to do only what is appropriate?

In other words, one way out of the paradox of necessity is to understand "appropriate" as having normative constitutional content independent from the success of a chosen action in addressing the emergency situation. My task then is to show how commitments to constitutional norms provide a basis for analyzing the propriety of responses to necessity in terms other than their consequences. In pursuing this task, the aim in this final chapter is to make the case that because constitutional commitments are also constitutive commitments, we cannot give priority to necessitarian logic without also undermining national identity. When officials urge the power and the necessity of doing whatever it takes to resolve a crisis—that "necessity knows no law"—they fail to give appropriate consideration to the identity-constitutive nature of constitutional principles and norms that function both within and apart from situational politics.

Constitutional commitments imply both a temporal identity for whom the commitment can matter in the implementation of policy, and a normative articulation of the values those commitments advance. Adopting temporally extended projects and commitments is one of the central tasks of government. Few projects can be accomplished in a moment. Even "constitutional moments"—occasions of transformational constitutional change outside of the formal Article V amendment process—are temporally extended political processes.[7] Projects commenced by citizens at time T1 can bind and constrain their future selves (and future citizens) at time T2. Some of these commitments take the form of precommitments of the kind exemplified by Ulysses tied to the mast of his ship. From this bound position he hears the Sirens' song but is unable to alter his preferences in light of the experience. Time T2 selves can be quite explicitly "bound" by their (or others') prior choices. These prior choices might bind the processes of decision-making by imposing delaying mechanisms, supermajorities, divided power, veto points, judicial precedents, and other mechanisms designed to check and brake uncontrolled passion and unreflective haste. Prior choices can also entrench institutional design and value commitments against future amendment by either removing some constitutional provisions from the amending process altogether or imposing onerous amendment procedures.[8] Current decisions, even those responding to necessitous circumstances, must be made in the shadow of existing institutional commitments. No matter how the mechanisms of binding work in practice, through commitments to particular practices and values, a polity will sustain a temporally extended political identity that informs its policy choices as well as its self-understandings.

A polity's self-understanding gets articulated through the values its entrenchment mechanisms seek to promote. So when, for example, President Lincoln argues that having made a "more perfect Union," its temporal horizon extends into perpetuity, he invokes not simply the fact of the existing institutional bonds, but the values they protect. For Lincoln, "our national fabric, with all its benefits, its memories, and its hopes" is bound in legal form such that "in contemplation of universal law and of the Constitution the Union of these States is perpetual."[9] Sovereignty of the people as a whole, the principle of democratic government, and the protection of constitutional rights are all values President Lincoln identifies a perpetual union as promoting.

But not all commitments bind to the same degree. Some have the character of contingent, self-chosen obligations that impact identity to a greater or lesser extent. Such a degree of impact depends on the relation between the commitment and the strength and depth of the values it supports. Commitment to more quotidian policy implicating with smaller effect on fundamental values can be more easily altered or abandoned. The identity of the nation as a perpetual union was at stake in the conflict over questions of sovereignty and majority governance. Because some questions of policy and commitment bind less tightly, institutional mechanisms exist to transform national commitments. The commitment to equality, for example, was achieved through Supreme Court precedent and national legislation. Cases beginning with *Brown v. Board of Education*, and legislation such as the Civil Rights Act of 1964 transformed American values and identity through entrenching new constitutional commitments to racial equality and nondiscrimination.[10]

This question of identity produces another problem. If what it means to have a character identified with a particular constitutive set of values—a Constitution—is to be committed to their realization in everyday governing practice, can responses to necessity jettison those values without altering or undermining character? Would it be legitimate to alter a polity's constitutive character through executive decisions determined by contingent circumstances unbound by prior commitments? Unconstrained necessities, our constitutional skeptic might say, are not obligated by constitutional commitments. At least, to be clear, they are obligated by no other constitutive commitment than protecting national security—the end toward which all necessary means are aimed. This problem produces paradoxical results when those commitments we choose are abandoned for an end—security— that loses its meaning when constitutive values no longer bind. A necessity that "knows no law," might seem to have been contemplated by abrogating commitments to constraining values inconsistent with the pursuit of security. But in such a case, it becomes unclear what the content of this value of security is. For what it means to be secure must include security in the character that constitutes our political identity. Threats to our political identity must implicate existential security at least as much as threats to physical integrity. President Roosevelt recognized this implication when proposing a second Bill of Rights. There are many kinds of threats to American political identity apart from those that impact physical security.

In sum, the unbound executive produces both a paradox of constraint and a problem of identity. Within the paradox, constitutional commitments do no work of constraint, for any attempt to impose a substantive norm of propriety can be matched by a claim that any response to necessity satisfies so long as it aims to address the crisis situation. In this way any executive action can be made to coincide with constitutional propriety. Under the problem of identity, claims that adherence to commitments and precommitments are constitutive of constitutional character are undermined by political practices that seek to avoid those very commitments when addressing necessitous circumstances. Because of the unavoidable connection between commitment and identity in constitutional practice, on my view, my task is to show how the constitutional skeptic fails to make sense of how our political practices and their deliberative justifications are structured by constitutional values, even if at times we contest their normative content and scope.

Juxtaposing identity and values is a common rhetorical trope in American politics. Examples from the Obama administration are instructive. In an important speech delivered in 2009 at the National Archives, President Obama outlined his vision of American national security policy.[11] Referencing some form of "our values" fifteen times, President Obama emphasized the fact that "[w]e uphold our most cherished values not only because doing so is right, but because it strengthens our country and it keeps us safe. Time and again, our values have been our best national security asset." Claiming that his "single most important responsibility as President is to keep the American people safe," President Obama emphasized that maintaining fidelity to "our values" is a necessary condition for fulfilling this responsibility, for "in the long run we also cannot keep this country safe unless we enlist the power of our most fundamental values" as exemplified in the Declaration of Independence and the Bill of Rights. These documents "are not simply words written into aging parchment. They are the foundation of liberty and justice in this country, and a light that shines for all who seek freedom, fairness, equality, and dignity around the world."[12]

But the existence and importance of these values does not guarantee consensus on their application. Criticizing the Bush administration, President Obama argued at the National Archives that the prior counterterrorism legal framework was "ad hoc," and thus "failed to rely on our legal traditions and time-tested institutions, and . . . failed to use our values as a compass."[13] By contrast, President Bush had also used claims about values, to describe the counterterrorism approach he initiated. Speaking before a joint session of Congress, President Bush promised "to uphold the values of America, and remember why so many have come here. We are in a fight for our principles, and our first responsibility is to live by them."[14] One of the practices to which President Obama objected was the use of torture on terrorism detainees, a practice that President Bush denied while invoking "our values." Under criticism for his interrogation policies, and under pressure from congressional legislation, President Bush asserted in a speech at the White House, "I want to be absolutely clear with our people and the world. The United States does not torture. It's against our laws, and it's against our values."[15] The truth about torture being otherwise, American policy and practice had relied on policies and practices that led to "our government . . . defending positions that undermined the rule of law" and failed to draw upon "deeply held values and traditions," according to President Obama.[16] Using "our values" as a "compass" does not provide agreement on the content of those values nor the direction that they will point. But in each case, claims about values as both a source of law and as a limit on the exercise of legal authority are interwoven with claims about identity and character.

Rather than detention and torture, the Obama administration relied on targeted airstrikes as a central means of implementing counterterrorism strategy. Justifying the use of unmanned aerial "drones" in armed attacks against individuals whom the president determines are specific threats to national security, Attorney General Eric Holder constructed both a "we" and a set of values said to be consistent with such policy. In his speech at Northwestern he proclaimed:

> Our most sacred principles and values—of security, justice and liberty for all citizens—must continue to unite us, to guide us forward, and to help us build a future that honors our founding documents and advances our ongoing—uniquely American—pursuit of a safer, more just, and more per- fect union. In the continuing effort to keep our people secure, this Admin- istration will remain true to those values that inspired our nation's founding and, over the course of two centuries, have made America an example of strength and a beacon of justice for all the world.[17]

This sentiment echoes the Supreme Court's imposition of limits on the executive's power to balance security with liberty when it comes to deten- tion policies: "[I]t is equally vital that our calculus not give short shrift to the values that this country holds dear . . . [because] [i]t is during our most chal- lenging and uncertain moments . . . that we must preserve our commit- ment at home to the principles for which we fight abroad."[18] In each case, a decision about detention or targeted killing is acknowledged as implicating values constitutive of the character of a "we." These values purport to guide and constrain. They also serve as a basis for judging particular actions and provide an occasion for reminding ourselves of shared commitments to principles partially constitutive of a national identity.

Claims about identity and value also made their way into legal analysis. In a speech before the America Society of International Law, Harold Koh, then legal advisor to the secretary of state, described an "Obama-Clinton" doctrine that relied on a legal analysis in part based on "a commitment to living our values by respecting the rule of law."[19] This respect for the rule of law, and commitment to "our values," as the Department of Justice (DOJ) articulated in a white paper, is consistent with targeted killing of individu- als, including American citizens, in locations outside the United States without trial or due process, on an executive finding that they posed an imminent threat of violent attack.[20] Relying on a threshold legal claim that the United States is engaged in armed conflict with al-Qaeda and related groups, Koh argued that targeted individuals are owed no legal process, and that the administration's practice met the legal requirements of distinction and proportionality, and otherwise complied with domestic law and constitutional norms. A "commitment to living our values," in Koh's analysis, shapes the administration's own internal view of the legality of its policies and practices. These values are questionably realized when U.S. citizens are targeted and the Obama administration successfully argues that courts lack authority to review its lethal decisions regarding targeted killings abroad.[21] For all its value talk, the Obama administration was no less cavalier in its legal analysis, citing national security necessity for a policy that greatly expanded unilateral and unreviewable exercise of lethal discretion. Moreover, the DOJ justified President Obama's policy by arguing that constitutional guarantees that government not kill its citizens without due process of law were satisfied by the administration's internal decision-making process.[22] American constitutionalism ordinarily expects that due process requires the availability of judicial oversight, but the Obama administration argued that "due process is not judicial process," in a "trust us, we're the good guys" logic. Although my aim is not to analyze the U.S. policy of drone strikes, flimsy legal analysis regarding due process cannot justify killing U.S. citizens merely because it appeals to values, no more than grand appeals to executive power based on presidential responsibility suffice to justify torture. To return to a central issue of the prior chapter: enlightened statesmen will not always be in charge of presidential "due process" in deciding whom to kill.[23]

Despite President Obama's criticisms of the predecessor administration, both presidents claimed legal authority, backed by DOJ memos, for the counterterrorism practices they implemented. And each administration made claims about the continuity between their actions and American identity and values. The appeal of making such claims raises questions about the work they do.

As legal analysis, "our values" might function as placeholders either to be given content in future legal reasoning or to serve as normative affirmation of conclusions reached on other grounds. In service of the former,

President Obama's National Archives speech does not give much content to what these values are. He lists liberty, justice, freedom, fairness, equality, and dignity. None of these values are placed within specific legal doctrine or reasoning, though they purport to limit the appropriate exercise of executive authority. By contemplating how commitment to constitutional values might shape legal analysis and executive practice, however, President Obama acknowledges that something more than institutional checks matter to the balance achieved between values such as security and liberty.[24] Reference to "our values" invites legal analysis that seeks to justify the fit between constitutional commitments and chosen executive practice. Given the close connection between value commitments and political identity that "our values" claims entail, the interpretive indeterminacy inherent in justifications of fit can produce both conservative and transformative conclusions. For if the polity's identity and values will be realized in different ways depending on whether, for example, practices such as torture "fit," then who "we" are is both a source of constraint and a locus for narrative reconstruction.

An alternative, skeptical, position is possible. Talk of "our values" might be nothing more than rhetorical cynicism masquerading as constitutional discourse. Such references, on this view, provide normative affirmation for claims of executive power grounded on arguments about inherent executive power or narrow readings of statutory limitations. Political considerations, not an internal view of constitutional commitments, are the object of "our values" discourse. On this view, constitutional commitments, apart from a commitment to protecting national security, do no work. Even so, the rhetoric is intended to have an effect on an audience believed to be reassured to hear that government practices cohere with constitutional values and identity. In this way, constitutional identity and values, even for the skeptic, provide some normative constraint on the justification for governing practices (as seen, for example, by the fact that the Bush administration did not openly admit that its interrogation practices included torture). There are limits to plausible claims of constitutional fit. Because politics is structured by political morality articulated in terms of constitutional values, the skeptical claim that politics alone constrain executive power cannot be a complete account. Even cynical rhetoric has constitutional purpose.

As a source of legal constraint, claims about "our values" are frustratingly imprecise and contingent. That presidents must locate their policies within a space defined by national identity and shared values, without always being required to articulate in more detail the fit, might be weak constraint indeed. Nonetheless, this structure means that the politics of necessity works in the shadow of constitutional norms. Constitutional decision-making grounded in structures of justification require Hamilton's "reflection and choice," as we have seen, not mere reliance on the necessities of "accident and force."[25]

Identity claims have a role in constituting the normative orders of constitutional politics and conversation—what values have salience in light of which ends chosen for a constructed national character. These normative orders construct a national character. Americans have commitments to values of liberty, fairness, and equality, among other values, as President Obama's speech acknowledges. These values have been historically realized through variable priorities, practices, and conceptions. These values can come into conflict or require ordering. As we have seen in prior chapters, the claim that liberty and security must trade off has been used on behalf of arguments giving priority to security over liberty under necessitous circumstances.[26] Giving priority to security over liberty is exemplified by the claim that a constitution is "not a suicide pact," as we have already encountered.[27] Moreover, since the executive has expertise over matters of security, this priority entails an institutional ordering whereby judges and legislators should defer to expert executive decision-making in pursuit of national security. Each claim orders values—security has priority over liberty. And in ordering values, each claim also distributes powers by deciding who has the final word on the means said necessary to achieving security ends.[28] These means are further manifestations of values, the choice among which is often hidden behind claims of practical necessity.

Claims about institutional priorities, and prerogatives, are grounded upon claims about normative priorities. When executive officials claim institutional priority and deference, they do so because when it comes to necessitous circumstances, security outweighs other values. Recall from chapter 5, however, that the image of balance between liberty and security implies that decision-makers must have equivalent expertise over both values to be weighed. But whereas executive claims to have expertise over how best to protect security might be plausible, there is no constitutional tradition of granting deference to executive officials over questions of preserving liberty. If the trade-off between liberty and security is to be a neutral balancing of values, then there is no reason to defer to executive determinations of the relative importance of liberty, or other constitutional values.[29] Because of this asymmetry, talk of trade-offs already reflects a prior normative ordering on behalf of security that the salience of practical necessity compels. Necessitous circumstances seem to require this ordering of values, which in turn orders institutional powers. By giving normative priority to security, executive officials accrue institutional priority to advance policies and pursue practices that can have the effect of shaping the polity's normative identity. Normative ordering, not necessity, determines priorities.

What is a salient means to achieving particular goals depends on background values that give content to what can be claimed appropriate in addition to being necessary. The Authorization to Use Military Force (AUMF), under which Attorney General Holder statutorily justifies the U.S. targeted-killing policy, grants the executive power to use all "necessary and appropriate force" against those persons, organizations, or nations involved with the attacks on September 11, conjoining normative constraints to necessary license.[30] Necessity is tethered to propriety. But the paradox of constitutional commitment appears here again. On the constitutional skeptic's account, the content of these normative constraints disappears behind the claims of necessity said to be consistent with, or guided by, "Our most sacred principles and values," as Holder explained.[31] Again, whatever means officials claim are necessary are said for that very reason—that they aid in providing security—to be appropriate. As I noted in the prior chapter, on this view propriety collapses into necessity. No independent normative analysis is thereby required. Practical necessity produces the paradox of constraint and can create a problem of identity.

Let's examine how such claims to practical necessity work. Claims of practical necessity have this form: we must do X (drone strikes), that is, it is impossible that we act otherwise, because if we do not do X, then the overriding value of Y (security, for example) will be undermined (or other lives will be lost). Because of the priority of their obligations to provide security, officials are incapable of acting otherwise than they do; these acts are necessary in this sense. Circumstances compel the particular response. There is no alternative. In this way, claims of necessity are meant to alleviate moral or political responsibility for the act, because it was not freely chosen but was determined by circumstances. When given institutional prerogative, executive officials can thereby rely on the claim of necessity—understood as an incapacity to do otherwise in light of their responsibility to protect the people—to justify their actions, without reference to other legal commitments or constraints.

But here is the problem with this conception of necessity: there is something dishonest about the claim that executive officials have no alternatives. There is also something dishonest about the implied moral and legal blamelessness that purports to follow from the claimed incapacity to do otherwise. What is perceived as available options for executive action already depends on prior normative commitments. The overriding value that purports to compel a particular action as necessary is itself constructed in part through contingent political processes. These values and commitments function as limits to what one imagines is possible, and thus what one constructs as impossible within the circumstances claimed necessitous. What choices are salient also depend on one's habits of action or the capacities of one's character.

The philosopher Bernard Williams analyzes such claims to practical necessity as claims about incapacities that provide content and set limits to one's character: "The incapacities we are considering here are ones that help to constitute character, and if one acknowledges responsibility for anything, one must acknowledge responsibility for decisions and action which are expressions of character—to be an expression of character is perhaps the most substantial way in which an action can be one's own."[32] So to claim that circumstances require a given action is to make a claim about the capacities of one's character—that is, the choices of actions that are salient in light of the values constitutive of one's character. As Williams argues, "character is revealed by what one chooses within those limits" that define the boundaries of action and deliberation, but character is also "revealed in the location of those limits, and in the very fact that one can determine, sometimes through deliberation itself, that one cannot do certain things, and must do others."[33] Necessity is related to impossibility, and in responding within the boundaries of each, claims about the actors' character are both made and revealed. One of the elements of character, why one cannot do certain things, is that one has made commitments within practices that constitute one's identity.[34] In this way, prior constitutive commitments are not like entrenchment devices or other external means of binding oneself or others to decision frameworks, for they are internal to the institutional practices of governing.

Necessitous actions, as an incapacity of doing otherwise, attempt to eschew responsibility. As Williams notes, the claim to have no alternative has a deceitfulness that lies in the "implication that the speaker cannot be to blame for what he will now do, since there is only one thing for him to do."[35] This feature makes necessity an attractive justification, for it does more than provide a reason for action by providing an excuse against blame. Recall from chapter 4, one of the attractive features of the extralegal-accountability approach was that officials take extralegal actions under the knowledge that their actions would be judged later. Knowledge of post hoc accountability was said to promote ex ante executive deliberation. But extralegal actions would be democratically accountable only if there were institutional mechanisms for taking account. When these mechanisms remain within the purview of the executive, then two problems emerge. First, the executive controls the mechanisms for holding executive officials accountable—from the power to classify information to the ability to shape the public debate, to the discretion over prosecution, to the ability to utilize justiciability doctrines before courts. But, second, if official actions were necessitous because determined by the circumstances, then there would be no room for responsibility, because there was no question of choice. The actions were required. And if no choice, then there would be no basis for ex post accountability either. Under claims of necessity, moreover, the promise of ex post accountability gets folded into ex ante deliberations in such a way as to make salient the prospect of constitutional derogations. In either way, the extralegal-accountability approach functions as a charade, promising a mechanism for officials to internalize an external check that will never materialize and thus never constrain.

The priority of practical necessity produces the paradox of constraint: when necessity compels action, constitutional constraints do no work. And if they do no work, there is no basis for ex post legal accountability. There is only political accountability. Thus, according to Williams, practical necessity is invoked to compel action and thus avoid responsibility. For liberal constitutionalism, such responsibility avoidance is an unacceptable outcome. There are good reasons to reject an understanding of necessity that would license a suspension of responsibility, because responsibility flows from actions that express character. And executive practices are, or can become, expressions of national character, reflections and creations of "our values."

When we recognize the role of character and commitment, the claim that decisions about necessity are matters of will in its obedience to necessity becomes implausible. On the skeptical view I have identified, the claim that executive action coincides with constitutional norms suggests that a decision comes first and then norms align later. It is as if the decision comes from nowhere.[36] Because the legal rule does not, or cannot, provide the answer as to how to respond, officials on the skeptical view exercise their will unbound from constitutive constraints. This Schmittian decision-making is an exercise of will that would give meaning to the rule in its absence. We see that the legal rule only goes so far and that necessitous circumstances require responses that provide meaning to the rule by showing the limits of its application. As Paul Kahn articulates Schmitt's reasoning, "The exception, accordingly, can only be recognized in the decision," because "[o]nce the sovereign decides on the exception, we cannot know what might otherwise have happened."[37] The power to decide what counts as an exception is the power to decide the meaning of the rule.[38] Such a view turns the ordinary understanding of legal rules on its head. It is the background normative rules and understandings that are supposed to shape the meaning of our responses, not vice versa. But this exercise of will—as if from nowhere—Williams suggests, cannot be an accurate portrayal of the facts, because the will must be exercised from a character already formed, even when that character has limited choices of what to do. If decisions about how to respond to emergencies must be made from a character already formed, then even when there is considerable indeterminacy about what a legal rule requires in a particular situation, constraints still bind. These are the constraints provided by the commitments that define one's character. These commitments are in part constituted by the values legal rules implement. If we apply Williams's account of character—as causally related to the choice of action—to constitutive political character, then the skeptical position cannot hold.

Although Williams is focused on the individual acting in his or her own capacity, this analysis applies equally to individuals acting as, or on the behalf of, governing institutions. Having a "set of desires, concerns or . . . projects" helps constitute individual character, according to Williams, and, as I would add, national character as well.[39] For a polity has diachronic aspirations, concerns, and projects that constitute its own character with which it can identify and be identified by others. When Attorney General Holder, or the Supreme Court, or the president, makes reference to shared values constitutive of national character, they are making claims about what choices can be salient in light of the commitments and values that define a shared character. So, first, in constructing a set of values to which actions must conform, the Obama administration made a claim about national character. The content of this character includes commitment to principles of "security, justice and liberty for all citizens." Second, the Obama administration made a claim about practical necessity. Rather than seeing these values as incapacities for certain actions, they are rather constructed as reasons for taking certain actions. What "we" are incapable of doing is acting other than we do in keeping American safe. Our values "guide us forward" in our "continuing effort to keep our people secure," as Attorney General Holder asserted.[40] Or, as President Obama explained, "[O]ur constitution . . . provides a foundation of principles that can be applied pragmatically; it provides a compass that can help us find our way."[41]

This constitutive compass, however, does not have a magnetic north to keep us true to some externally imposed, transcendent source of value. Rather, this constitutive compass gives us the directions on which we have already agreed it may provide. As Williams suggests, "Conclusions of practical necessity . . . constitute, to a greater or lesser degree, discoveries about oneself."[42] The degree to which prior agreements may be the case needs not be self-conscious, and certainly needs not be the product of a synchronic decision-making process. Agreements are constructed over time with overlapping and not always consistent layers, subject to the contingency of circumstances and the vicissitudes of changing political priorities and realized through interpretive practices often purporting to "discover" applicable constitutional meanings. The suppressed conclusion to Holder's argument, therefore, is that in making choices about what is practically necessary in order to "keep our people secure," executive officials provide an interpretive construction, a "discovery," as Williams suggests, about the content of our national character. Through their choices—partially disavowed as chosen because of their claimed determinism—executive officials in part construct the content of the national character of "We the People." But discoveries about our national character do not flow from decisions made as if from nowhere. They are made out of a background body of agreements, judgments, beliefs, and commitments that are further realized and defined through the responses the polity makes. These and other considerations mean that officials have responsibility for the character they create through the decisions they make by appeal to claims of practical necessity.[43]

The content of this character is a contingent matter. What one discovers is not an antecedent fixed identity or character. Rather, one discovers a character that is contested and contingent on changing national projects and priorities. The contested nature is reflected, for example, by the contrast between William Lloyd Garrison's antebellum view of the Constitution as "a covenant with death and an agreement with hell," and Frederick Douglass's commitment to the possibility that "justice, liberty, and humanity were 'final,' not slavery and oppression," believing that self-reconstitution could make possible new conceptions of common humanity.[44] Both of these conceptions have been viewed as being consistent with one and the same constitutional text, but each has formed a different contested conception of the polity's character living through that Constitution. No doubt, a degree of "reconstruction," including passage of constitutional amendments, was required before the polity could begin to make real the possibilities that Douglass identified. This "reconstruction" was not immediate in its effects, either, as the complicated story of constitutional failure through judicial interpretations of these new amendments in cases like *Plessy v. Ferguson* and *Giles v. Harris,* which gave the green light to de jure segregation, attest.[45] Such cases abjured constitutional responsibility for the underlying social practices that created racial segregation and the state legal institutions that entrenched discrimination. This story is not mine to tell here, save this one point: "we" was, and is, always contested. But a "we" is also indispensable.

Schmitt's constitutional skepticism can arise anew here. For if "we" is contested, if practical necessity can generate "discoveries" about ourselves, as Williams suggests, who decides on the content of "our" national character? We do. Does not the shape of this character and the content of our commitments depend in part on decisions that themselves cannot be determined by prior rules?[46] Such contingency is a condition of political freedom. Both the identity of the people and the content of their governing choices provide meaning to their particular manifestation of constitutionalism. What values and norms give content to these principles, as well as which voices contribute to collective deliberations speaking as a "we," are always contested questions. There is always tension between identity and exclusion, rule and exception. Although normative orders are unavoidable, the question of the character of whom "we" constitute is never fixed and final. Diachronic identity is underdetermined. And while a self-constituting "we" may ground itself in a prior act of founding, the reconstitution of a "we" depends on future findings that seek to realize and redeem prior commitments to constitutional self-governance. But in each case of contested identity, of a challenged commitment, questions arise against a background of agreement on "our values." Holistic skepticism does not arise, for whether particular practices such as armed attacks from unmanned aerial drones are justified are questions that occur within a preexisting context of commitments and constitutional understandings.

To have an identity is to have a set of defining commitments, beliefs, and projects that exist within a history. We make decisions within a narrative continuity that gives meaning to our diachronic character.[47] But for decisions to be ours, we have to be able to identify with the actions in a way that we become responsible for the character they reveal and create. Radical disruptions in identity are possible, but not on the mere exercise of executive will. Because of the need for coherence, to be able to identify with decisions as the polity's choices, contingency, or the lack of determinate foundations for decisions does not lead to a form of radical meaning relativism. Contingency still requires justifications for new actions that cohere with the polity's character and make sense of its existing commitments.

Like the issue of the acceptable use of drones to kill those, including U.S. citizens, deemed threats, a similar question about identity exists regarding U.S. detention and interrogation policy. The outcome of the next presidential election could determine the near-term direction of U.S. counterterrorism policy.[48] President Trump's reversals of Obama administration policy made Guantánamo Bay available for new detainees and signaled comfort with torture. Regarding Guantánamo, he promised that "we're gonna load it up with some bad dudes."[49] President Obama explicitly linked the idea of contested meanings to national character: "Waterboarding is torture. It's contrary to America's traditions. It's contrary to our ideals. That's not who we are. That's not how we operate."[50] So far President Trump has made no such connection, despite the inevitable consequences for national character.

This character is realized through commitments to constitutional values such as due process, whereby decisions over life and death require a process of legal governance, which ordinarily requires a separation between the ultimate decider and the determination of the decision's legality. Thus, in order to carry on the "war on terror" detention policy at Guantánamo Bay, determinations about who is an unlawful enemy combatant are ultimately subject to process before a neutral body and to judicial review. But the Obama administration—and the Trump administration that followed—eschewed separation-of-powers constraints in favor of a claim that due process is not "judicial process." Such claims alter the character of our governing practices, and ultimately of the polity, for "we" become acculturated to granting unchecked power over life and death to presidential say-so. Such a possible normative reordering should be subject to far greater public debate than it has received, since the new standard will be applicable to unforeseen future circumstances. And without exploring further the policy details, but reasoning strictly from the question of constitutive values, it is difficult to see how a presidential license to kill citizens outside of ordinary constitutional procedures—even those accused of engaging in terrorist activity—can be justified as consistent with American constitutional values. The burden of persuasion is on the president to do more than assure us of its infrequence and of the presence of internal executive-branch deliberation.

One conclusion Eric Holder's and President Obama's comments seem to foreclose is that no inquiry into propriety is required. By making identity, values, and our commitments to each a central analytic feature of their claim to appropriate action in the face of such threats, they are acknowledging that necessity claims are not sufficient in themselves to justify executive action. Our commitments to constitutive values are part of our identity, and they matter to how we analyze and choose policy, even when it comes to questions of national security.

But our constitutional skeptic might respond by saying that I'm elevating political rhetoric to the level of constitutional discourse. Such rhetoric has no constitutional standing: it does not decide cases or determine interpretations. It simply hangs there unattached from legal practices, serving no other purpose than decorative flourish to policies implemented because of their necessity. After all, President Bush defended his illegal Terrorist Surveillance Program by declaring "constitutional guarantees are in place when it comes to doing what is necessary to protect our homeland, because we value the Constitution."[51]

For the skeptical position, as we have seen, constitutional commitments do no work apart from providing political arguments for executive power and its limits—or lack thereof. Commitments need not matter to the normative self-understanding of the president and executive officials who see their roles as primarily directed by necessities. On this view, majoritarian politics and its economic setting provide all the constraints needed. To be fair, the skeptical position as it is developed by Posner and Vermeule is that "law does little to constrain the modern executive," not that the Constitution does no work in empowering the executive.[52] If American constitutionalism is about the relations between governing practices and institutions to the norms and values embedded in the written Constitution, then perhaps the only relations that matter are the ones that empower the president in particular. As the institution with the "energy" to respond to necessities, the Constitution provides the grounds for empowering the executive with tools required to address whatever circumstances might arise.[53] When combined with skepticism about the role of separation of powers, which the skeptical position does, then to emphasize only one narrow aspect of the Constitution—its grant of executive power—is to deny any recognizable comprehensive account of constitutional practice.[54] Such an à la carte approach to the relation between politics and constitutional constraints is just another way of denying constitutionalism.

Constitutionalism requires commitments. It is not simply a matter of norms governing institutions and practices, but ways of inhabiting those institutions. Commitments arise from taking an internal perspective on the values and norms constitutional practices entail. When Attorney General Holder or President Obama, for example, cites American values as part of the self-understanding of the justifications for their policies, they acknowledge that constitutional values are matters to which they are committed. To have a commitment to constitutional norms means that the norms form part of the justificatory process of deciding how best to respond to circumstances.[55] The Constitution matters because it shapes the very perception of the available options. Prior commitments define what are available options. Nothing about these prior commitments forecloses the possibility of their cynical use or denial.

Claims of practical necessity challenge a polity's diachronic identity by opening opportunities for executive officials to exploit these features of constitutional practice. Transformations in character would follow from necessitous constitutional derogations that change ongoing practices and self-understandings. My response to the constitutional skeptic is to show that the very conception of identity and values cannot avoid being grounded in a diachronic narrative that provides normative constraints on the possibility for constitutional transformations. These constraints take the form of commitments that need not rise to the level of legal entrenchments of separated powers or unamendable constitutional provisions (though these are certainly examples of commitments) or other forms of more rigid mechanisms of legal stability. These commitments are realized in settled constitutional practices and meanings. But they too can be overcome by the cynical use of skeptical arguments that purport to identify a constitutional failure on the basis of which can be asserted unconstrained executive power.[56] Commitments are therefore contingent on citizens and officials making them a part of their practices of legal and political justification.

Commitment is inseparable from character and identity. We adopt constitutive values that give content to our national character through the practices in which we lend them meaning. This character is realized over time, with each successive implementation of constitutional values providing further articulation of their meanings. What has not been made explicit so far is the central role that commitments play in both giving coherence to our identity and in defining a central aspect of constitutionalism. Because who we are is realized over time through our commitments, our identity is subject to change. As we adopt new projects, make new commitments, we develop new understandings of ourselves and give meaning to the continuity of our identity over time. But our identity is also stable. We do not amend or alter many of our constitutive commitments to democratic self-government, to political and religious freedom, to due process, or to equality. Indeed, President Lincoln established a principle of the inalienability of our more perfect, and perpetual, union.[57]

Constitutions do not compel their own practices and characters. They depend upon commitments made through the "reflection and choice" to which we have repeatedly turned.[58] To make our self-constitution depend on "accident and force" in responding to necessities is to deny the role that commitment plays, and subjects the continuity of identity to the whim of circumstance, not the self-evaluating choices and exercises of will. And so, again, the constitutional skeptic would have to deny a background feature on which our actual political practices and self-understandings rely: that is, that we justify our actions by reference to constitutional commitments—be they grants of power or principled constraints—that compose our character. Without these commitments it is difficult to make sense of the possibility for a discontinuous, incoherent politics subject to the episodic demands of accidental circumstance. In Hamilton's phrase, such an approach would not allow a polity to establish its political constitution as "good government through reflection and choice" rather than "accident and force."[59]

This question of the connection between the manner of responding to necessities and the realization of national character through commitments to constitutional norms can be further illuminated by a distinction Harry Frankfurt draws between a person and a wanton. Frankfurt identifies the ability to evaluate first-order desires to act in particular ways as an essential condition for being a person. When evaluating the appropriateness of one's desires, a person forms volitions to identify with particular desires and makes that identity a constitutive feature of the choices one makes. It matters to persons what inclinations and desires they follow. By contrast, a wanton is one who is capable of self-evaluation but does not identify with particular desires as constitutive or salient to his or her identity. A wanton "has no identity apart from his first-order desires" and "does not prefer that one first-order desire rather than the other should constitute his will."[60] The wanton is subject to the caprice of "accident and force" that circumstances present, making no commitments to principled values as constitutive of her identity. On Frankfurt's account, such preferences do matter to persons, because both character and identity matter. I think this account provides a useful analogy to the distinction between the constitutional skeptic and the committed constitutionalist.

The constitutional skeptic is a wanton, on my account. The skeptic does not make commitment to values constitutive of national character and identity. Because of this lack of commitment, skepticism really reduces to cynicism. It does not matter to the skeptic what the content of the constraints that politics provides might be. No doubt, self-evaluation is part of politics, for without it no preference of one policy over another would be possible. On the skeptical position, however, there is no will to commit to particular values and principles that guide and constrain the selection of policies. The skeptic might protest, What about the overriding commitment to security? Does that commitment not count as exactly the kind of identification with a particular desire constitutive of nonwantonness? I think not. The desire for self-preservation is so basic and singular a desire that to do no more than identify one's will with security provides no grounds for assessing how a polity might best thrive apart from questions of security. If we affirm Henry Shue's argument that security is a necessary condition for the enjoyment of all other rights, or Ian Loader and Neil Walker's argument that security "is an indispensable constituent of any good society," then to identify with this background condition for constitutional politics to the exclusion of all other considerations is to fail to engage in the kind of strong evaluations constitutive of identity commitments.[61] Security is valuable for its role in supporting and sustaining communities and the trust and openness necessary for democratic self-determination, not merely for its role in preventing or responding to physical attack. Commitment to security isolated from the community it supports provides no other basis for sustaining a comprehensive identity with all of its practices, purposes, and values. Security is a constitutional value but not an overriding value that subsumes all others.

Self-preservation is necessary for the realization of constitutional commitments, but not sufficient to sustain a national character. Self-preservation is a background condition of government, one of its central purposes, no doubt. On the social contract story as it is often told, individuals give up their "natural liberty" that obtains in a state of nature to an organized political body in exchange for sovereign provision of security.[62] This origin gives a kind of ordinal priority to security among the possible values of governing institutions. But it does not provide any basis for the polity having a distinctive identity, apart from being *that* political body that happens to be secured by *this* sovereign. Nor does it give the polity positive principles, projects, and commitments to achieve that would constitute a unique national character. In Williams's terms, there would be nothing further to discover about ourselves through the values we hold dear and to which we remain committed. To put the point one additional way: there is nothing distinctive about the commitment to security, for this is the overriding value that the authoritarian or dystopian government can equally prioritize.[63] To sacrifice the other values essential for liberal self-government that security policy is meant to protect in order to obtain that very security would get the liberal contract the wrong way around. No plausible social contract is formed that makes security the end in itself rather than a means to the achievement of other values—the "Blessings of Liberty," for example, as the Constitution's preamble provides.

On the liberal institutional ideal, we seek security in order to facilitate the virtues and values of self-government. More than focusing on rights limitations as a source for evaluating the propriety of the means of achieving this security, one way of organizing the thought that our commitments matter to the achievement of security is to focus on these background values necessary for self-government. Those government actions that further these values under necessitous circumstances are proper.

In this way we return to the question of propriety as a limitation on necessity. "We the People" have a national identity with its own character consisting in part in its diachronic commitments to particular values, principles, and practices. These values may be politically contested at times, but they nonetheless help structure political practice. Without them, politics becomes nothing more than a matter of episodic majoritarian preference. "Accident and force," the basis of self-constitution that Hamilton contrasted with "good government," would guide political practice. American constitutionalism as a practice of self-government means more than majoritarianism, however. Americans appeal to the Constitution when contesting deeply held moral convictions, just as much as when they seek to implement limits on governing power or to reinforce particular institutional arrangements. When it comes to the impulse to do whatever is necessary to address necessitous circumstances, the skeptical claim was that nothing more than the limits of imagination and politics constrained executive decisions. Constitutional commitments cease to matter. To take such a view is to argue that executive officials would make us a wanton people—forever incapable of asserting our will to make our commitments effective in our political lives. This is implausible.

We are left then with the view that the content of our commitments provides a basis for assessing whether responses to necessity are appropriate. The Constitution's assignment of a necessary-and-proper power to Congress provides a textual mechanism for limiting responses to necessity according to questions of propriety.[64] But text is not required. As we explored in chapter 6, Jack Goldsmith and John Manning found an implied necessary-and-proper power for the president in Article II, opening an unintended door to limiting executive power by propriety. But we need not affirm that there is any such necessary-and-proper executive power in order to justify the normative limitation on presidential power that propriety imposes. These questions of propriety arise out of the constitutive commitments that define the character of American constitutional practice. Naked appeals to security provide an insufficient basis—even when policies are successful in addressing threats—to form and define a national character. In this way, responses to necessity are constrained by the character of our constitutional commitments. And it is the presence of diachronic commitments that make the identity to which presidents and executive officials appeal in exercising their discretion to shape policy and execute the laws.

The skeptic's challenge is to argue that in a deliberative democracy we talk the talk of commitments, and even sometimes walk the walk, but that does not show that these commitments actually do work in justifying and motivating action that is consistent with those commitments. We talk the talk because we wish, as with many tragic choices, to hide the fact that we are willing to get our hands dirty, to commit evil, or at least to violate rights and dignities, in pursuit of particular consequences.[65] We walk the walk when it is convenient to do so, when the appearance of adhering to commitments does not pinch too much. In addition, given the insufficiency of commitments as justifications for actions, there is no showing that we normatively *should* be attached to the commitments when compelling circumstances point in a different direction. This is the meaning of the "suicide pact" argument that we repeatedly encounter.

As the argument of this chapter has unfolded, my response to the skeptic is to say that the commitments are constitutive of what we do in a self-governing constitutional democracy. They are constitutive in the way that the rules of chess, for example, are constitutive of what it means to play chess.[66] One can adopt different rules, but then one at some point will be playing a different game—that is, doing something different. If we abandon the commitments constitutive of our constitutional identity, then we do something else, and in the case of national character and identity, we become something different. Thus, my response is a modest transcendental argument: if we are committed to certain constitutive practices and meanings, then the skeptic's position cannot be maintained. Or one remains a skeptic only at the cost of denying what should be undeniable—that constitutions matter to our political practices and national identity in particular ways that are inconsistent with the skeptical position. What it means to have a constitutional government is to be committed to governing within the terms and norms of a constitution. It means that these values, principles, and practices play a role in structuring how we think about and how we respond to the inevitable crises of human affairs.

To say this—that constitutions play a constitutive role in our thinking and therefore in our identity—does not foreclose the important questions about what the content of these commitments will, or should, be. In so doing, we can open the space for the discussion about the meanings of

American constitutionalism. In this way, the response that constitutionalism offers to constitutional skepticism will always be local, in the way that constituent power has to always be located in a political space for a particular people. The fact that values matter to the language Americans use in their politics suggests not only, as I have urged, that values *do* matter, but also that language matters. Language derives its meaning from the practices in which it is embedded. So to employ the language of "our values" invokes the practices in which they have meaning. "Values" do not float disconnected above our practices like a "brooding omnipresence," but have meaning because of their constitutive role in those practices.[67]

A residual issue about contingency and identity remains unresolved. If the skeptic is wrong, why is it that we seem to be able to be anything, to do anything, so long as we attend to the background conditions of narrative coherence with past decisions—conditions that are as open as our interpretive tolerance can withstand?

If national character is constructed through the priorities, practices, and projects by which values are formed and implemented, what is the source of these values that give meaning to the "we" so constituted? What are we to make of so much constitutional dissonance existing over the content and scope of fundamental values? As the politics of presidential elections makes clear, there exists disagreement over the propriety of torture, for example, among many other fundamental differences in constitutional values. If American constitutionalism depends on agreements in values said to be constitutive of identity, then it would seem to be a very fractured identity.

In the case of the American experience, the source of values resides in part in the self-constituting act of ratifying and committing to a written Constitution and the framework for self-governance it establishes. Sanford Levinson identifies an important aspect of American constitutionalism to consist in our practices of fidelity to contingent understandings of our written Constitution as central to our political life. Constitutional faith sustains our national identity, textually articulated as "We the People."[68] We seek through constitutional understandings and practice to achieve that "more perfect Union" and to secure "the Blessings of Liberty" that the preamble establishes as the principal points of the Constitution. But covenants in writing are contracts, and the "we" is more than a legal construct created through contract. Unlike a contract, this writing is notoriously open-ended, providing the grounding for multiple possible ways of implementing a national identity—as the past slave-owning and the present equality-expanding constitutional cultures attest. But because of this written Constitution, the content of "our" character must be in part constituted through our relation to that writing and its language.

We live our experience of commitment and contestation through the language we construct, both through constitutional text and through the constitutional conversations it sustains. There is a point on how language works as the means of expressing these commitments about which Ludwig Wittgenstein's thought is relevant. Wittgenstein comments that "to imagine a language is to imagine a form of life."[69] Stanley Cavell, glossing Wittgenstein, adds, "To imagine a language means to imagine a modified form of talking life."[70] This form of talking life is, in the context of self-constitution, a life in which an intergenerational conversation about national character is in part constitutive of that character. Set against the background of particular contested contingencies are agreements of the following kind: our actions must accord with our values, and our values must have some relation to a founding and continuing commitment to a constitutive act and a constitutional text.[71] To imagine a certain kind of constitutive language is to imagine a shared form of conversational life—a conversational life of (re) constituting the politically foundational "we." This conversational life is one in which we embed structures of justification into constitutional practice. How a constitutive commitment maintains vitality is through its justificatory use in response to episodic necessitarian claims.

In the context of constitutional practice—we inherit background agreement in the basic constitutional form of the conversation: actions must be justified by reference to powers conferred by the Constitution, must conform to past practices and understandings of how those powers get implemented, and must not conflict with other rights-based or separation-of-powers limitations. Commitments to particular values—such as liberty, equality, fairness, privacy, and dignity—define our character and guide our actions. Within the basic framework of agreement there is much contingency. Governing practices could be different than they are. Two different understandings of values and normative commitments could give rise to very different interrogation policies—though not plausibly and legitimately ones that include torture. Within bounds, each side is able to draw on an inherited background to claim that their policy is consistent with foundational values. But each side is obligated to justify their policy by reference to an inherited background.

At the limit, if we differ too much relative to the shared background agreement, we then, in some sense, will no longer occupy the same world. In terms of constitutive character, we would cease to be the same polity. Thus, like persons, narrative continuity implicates diachronic identity understood through the commitments to particular projects we make and the future choices in light of the contingent circumstances we face. Thus, the question of sameness of worlds, in light of shared agreements, does not lead to a strong relativist conclusion. Rather, it demonstrates that the future direction of a "we" constituted through and sustained by a continuing constitutional conversation is not already fixed and final. It is a product of choices "we" will have to make using the conversational resources reflected in our background agreement in values and meanings. In this way, the choices we make both constitute our character and sustain an identity in a way that belies any attempt to hide the choice behind purported structures of "practical necessity." We constitute ourselves through the commitments we make.

So can we take the inherited background as a necessary condition for the possibility of the constitutional language game to say that although there will be contested meanings and values, contestation is not perfectly elastic? There are limits and constraints, one of which is another necessary condition—that the Constitution and the constraints it imposes must play a meaningful role in our politics. Our constitutive commitments both exist and matter to how we define available policy choices and responses to necessitous circumstances.

One role the Constitution plays is to provide commitments that are more robust than consequentialist pursuits of security and self-preservation. Another role is in articulating how political morality matters to both our self-understandings and our political practices. Mere majoritarian-interest politics cannot be understood to dominate governing decisions about national security apart from the constitutive values of equality, justice, liberty, dignity, and fairness that give constitutional practices their point and by which they are justified.

A primary goal of this book is to understand how the values and meanings of American constitutionalism provide internal checks on necessity. American constitutionalism is inconsistent with granting necessity priority over the commitments that constitute practices of good government. Questions of propriety circumscribe the available responses to necessity. As we have seen, the so-called "war on terror" provided multiple fresh opportunities for necessitous thinking to pervade our political lives, sometimes with pernicious results. The continuing prevalence of consequentialist justifications for torture as a means of interrogation serves as the primary example. But others exist, including the use of drones, as we have seen in this chapter, providing the occasion for executive claims to be guided by American values. If value talk is to be more than empty, then the content of these values must be connected to the commitments that comprise the practices of American constitutionalism. What can we say about the content of these values that give propriety purchase against necessity? They are also contested and contingent, but neither arbitrary nor narrowly relativistic. They develop through text and tradition and require reflection and choice. For purposes of my argument, I need not rely on any particular version of the content of these values, for the central point is that necessity must be analyzed in terms of propriety given content from these values. This procedural requirement alone opens the door to the centrality of questions of propriety that range beyond consideration of consequences in achieving security objectives. More than procedure, however, a demand that governing decisions be justified in terms of constitutional values and principles is also a substantive claim. Justifications that a counterterrorism policy is not legally proscribed on some possible reading of a legal constraint are insufficient. Rather, such justifications involve core questions about identity, character, and the meanings of American constitutionalism that make self-government possible. Confronting these questions is a constitutive element of constitutionalism, foreclosing reliance on unreflective and episodic responses to necessitous circumstances. And to confront these questions with a thick normative self-evaluation is to sustain and transform the meanings of American constitutionalism through a continuing process of overcoming necessity.

NOTES

Introduction

1. Korematsu v. United States, 323 U.S. 214 (1944). The president also relies on the Alien Enemies Act, 50 U.S.C. §§ 21 et seq. (1918).
2. Thomas Jefferson to John B. Colvin, September 20, 1810, in *The Papers of Thomas Jefferson: Retirement Series,* vol. 3, ed. J. Jefferson Looney (Princeton, N.J.: Princeton University Press, 2006), 99.
3. Ibid.
4. Protecting the Nation from Foreign Terrorist Entry into the United States, 82 Fed. Reg. 8, 977–78 (March 6, 2017).
5. Jenna Johnson, "Trump Calls for 'Total and Complete Shutdown of Muslims Entering the United States," *Washington Post,* December 7, 2015.
6. Washington v. Trump, 847 F.3d 1151, 1161 (9th Cir. 2017).
7. Donald Trump, Twitter post, February 5, 2017, 12:39 p.m., https://twitter.com/realdonaldtrump/status/828342202174668800?lang=en.
8. Donald Trump, Twitter post, February 4, 2017, 12:44 p.m., https://twitter.com/realdonaldtrump/status/827981079042805761?lang=en.
9. Trump v. Hawaii, 138 S. Ct. 2392, 2401 (June 26, 2018).
10. See Daniel J. Solove, *Nothing to Hide: The False Tradeoff Between Privacy and Security* (New Haven, Conn.: Yale University Press, 2011).
11. *Federalist* No. 34 (Hamilton), in *The Federalist Papers,* ed. Clinton Rossiter (New York: New American Library, 1961), 207.
12. John Locke, *Two Treatises on Government,* ed. Peter Laslett (Cambridge: Cambridge University Press, 2013), bk. II, § 160, p. 375.
13. *Federalist* No. 23 (Hamilton), in *The Federalist Papers,* 153.
14. Ibid., 152.
15. *Federalist* No. 41 (Madison), in *The Federalist Papers,* 257.

16. Abraham Lincoln to Erastus Corning and Others, June 12, 1863, in *Abraham Lincoln: Speeches and Writings, 1859–1865,* ed. Don E. Fehrenbacher (New York: Library of America, 1989), 460.

17. Abraham Lincoln to Albert G. Hodges, 4 April 1864, in ibid., 585.

18. Carl Schmitt, *Political Theology: Four Chapters on the Concept of Sovereignty,* trans. George Schwab (Chicago: University of Chicago Press, 2005), 6–7.

19. Ibid., 7.

20. Giorgio Agamben, *State of Exception,* trans. Kevin Attell (Chicago: University of Chicago Press, 2005), 39.

21. Paul W. Kahn, *Political Theology: Four New Chapters on the Concept of Sovereignty* (New York: Columbia University Press, 2011), 45.

22. As Adrian Vermeule argues, "The exception, the unforeseen circumstance that creates an emergency, will always overhang the system of liberal legalism and potentially disrupt it." Adrian Vermeule, "Our Schmittian Administrative Law," *Harvard Law Review* 122 (2009): 1103.

23. For more on constitutional skepticism, see Thomas P. Crocker and Michael P. Hodges, "Constitutions, Rule-Following, and the Crisis of Constraint," *Legal Theory* 24 (2018): 3–39.

24. Schmitt, *Political Theology,* 5.

25. McCulloch v. Maryland, 17 U.S. (4 Wheat.) 316, 421 (1819).

26. With this idea, I begin from the premise that necessity is a matter of how we think, not in the nature of things themselves, as the philosopher W. V. Quine suggested in a different context: "Necessity resides in the way we talk about things, not in the things we talk about." W. V. Quine, *Ways of Paradox and Other Essays* (Cambridge, Mass.: Harvard University Press, 1976), 174. That certain ways of thinking have a way of captivating us outside of our critical reflection is an idea about which Ludwig Wittgenstein reminds us: "A picture held us captive. And we could not get outside it, for it lay in our language and language seemed only to repeat it to us inexorably." Ludwig Wittgenstein, *Philosophical Investigations,* trans. G. E. M. Anscombe (Oxford: Basil Blackwell, 1958), § 115.

27. Franklin D. Roosevelt, "Message to the Congress on the State of the Union," January 11, 1944, in *The Public Papers and Addresses of Franklin D. Roosevelt,* comp. Samuel I. Rosenman, vol. 13 (1944–1945) (New York: Harper & Brothers, 1950), 41.

28. Hannah Arendt, *The Human Condition* (Chicago: University of Chicago Press, 1958).

29. Jefferson to Colvin, September 20, 1810, in *The Papers of Thomas Jefferson,* 99.

30. Schmitt, *Political Theology,* 12.

31. David Hume, *Enquiries Concerning Human Understanding and Concerning the Principles of Morals,* 3rd ed., ed. P. H. Nidditch (New York: Oxford University Press, 1975), 80–93.

32. See generally Akhil Reed Amar, *America's Unwritten Constitution: The Precedents and Principles We Live By* (New York: Basic Books, 2012).

33. Jay S. Bybee, Assistant Attorney General, U.S. Department of Justice Office of Legal Counsel, to Alberto R. Gonzales, Counsel to the President, August 1, 2002, Re: Standards of Conduct for Interrogation Under 18 U.S.C. §§ 2340–2340A, 38, https://www.justice.gov/olc/file/886061/download.

34. Schmitt, *Political Theology*, 13.

35. See "Bush: 'I'm the decider' on Rumsfeld; Defense secretary: Changes in military meet resistance," CNN, April 18, 2006, http://www.cnn.com/2006/POLITICS/04/18/rumsfeld/.

36. "Transcript of Frost-Nixon Interview," *New York Times*, May 20, 1977, A16.

37. John Wagner, "Trump Says He Has 'Absolute Right' to Pardon Himself of Federal Crimes but Denies Any Wrongdoing," *Washington Post*, June 4, 2018.

38. Abraham Lincoln to Matthew Birchard and Others, June 29, 1863, in *Abraham Lincoln: Speeches and Writings*, 467.

39. Attorney General Eric Holder on National Security (speech, Northwestern University Law School, March 5, 2012), U.S. Department of Justice, https://www.justice.gov/opa/speech/attorney-general-eric-holder-speaks-northwestern-university-school-law.

40. See Richard H. Fallon, Jr., "Legitimacy and the Constitution," *Harvard Law Review* 118 (2005): 1787–1853.

41. Hamdi v. Rumsfeld, 542 U.S. 507, 545 (2004) (Souter, J., concurring).

42. A. L. A. Schechter Poultry Corp. v. United States, 295 U.S. 495, 528–29 (1935).

43. Capturing the overall sentiment in perhaps less liberty-challenging circumstances, Rahm Emanuel, chief of staff to President Obama, stated, "Never allow a crisis to go to waste. They are opportunities to do big things." Jeff Zeleny, "Obama Weighs Quick Undoing of Bush Policy," *New York Times*, November 8, 2008. Milton Friedman advanced a similar doctrine: "Only a crisis—actual or perceived—produces real change. When that crisis occurs, the actions that are taken depend on the ideas that are lying around." Milton Friedman, *Capitalism and Freedom* (Chicago: University of Chicago Press, 2002), xiv.

44. See generally Geoffrey R. Stone, *Perilous Times: Free Speech in Wartime from the Sedition Act of 1789 to the War on Terrorism* (New York: W. W. Norton, 2004).

45. Civil Liberties Act of 1988, 50 U.S.C. § 1989 et seq., Pub. L. 100–383, title I, August 10, 1988, 102 Stat. 904.

46. Korematsu v. United States, 323 U.S. 214, 246 (1944) (Jackson, J., dissenting).

47. Steven G. Bradbury, Principal Deputy Assistant Attorney General, to John A. Rizzo, Senior Deputy General Counsel, Central Intelligence Agency, May 30, 2005, Re: Application of United States Obligations Under Article 16 of the Convention Against Torture to Certain Techniques That May Be Used in the Interrogation of High Value al Qaeda Detainees, 37, https://www.justice.gov/sites/default/files/olc/legacy/2013/10/21/memo-bradbury2005.pdf. The memo describes waterboarding of Abu Zubaydah 83 times and of Khalid Shaikh Mohammed 183 times during their respective interrogations. See also Steven G. Bradbury, Principal Deputy Assistant Attorney General, to John A. Rizzo, Senior Deputy General

Counsel, Central Intelligence Agency, May 10, 2005, Re: Application of 18 U.S.C. §§ 2340–2340A to Certain Techniques That May Be Used in the Interrogation of a High Value al Qaeda Detainee, https://www.justice.gov/sites/default/files/olc/legacy/2013/10/21/memo-bradbury2005-2.pdf. This latter memo details many techniques used individually and in combination, with questionable legal authority. But even then, authority was exceeded against high-value detainees such as Abd al-Rahim al-Nashiri, who is alleged to have planned the attack on the USS *Cole*. In addition to waterboarding, "the C.I.A. inspector general determined that Mr. Nashiri's was the 'most significant' case of a detainee's being brutalized in unauthorized ways, including being threatened with a power drill and a handgun." Charlie Savage, "Cole Attack Trial Will Test Tribunal System," *New York Times*, November 30, 2009. See Central Intelligence Agency Inspector General, *Special Review: Counterterrorism Detention and Interrogation Activities (September 2001–October 2003* (May 7, 2004), 47.

48. Eric Posner and Adrian Vermeule, "Should Coercive Interrogation Be Legal?" *Michigan Law Review* 104 (2006): 676–77.

49. As one federal court explained, "the right to be free from official torture is fundamental and universal, a right deserving of the highest status under international law, a norm of *jus cogens*." Siderman v. Republic of Argentina, 965 F.2d 699, 717 (9th Cir. 1992). See also Filartiga v. Pena-Irala, 630 F.2d 876, 890 (2d Cir. 1980) (the "torturer has become—like the pirate and the slave trader before him—*hostis humani generis*, an enemy of all mankind.").

50. International Covenant on Civil and Political Rights, art. 7, December 19, 1966, 999 U.N.T.S. 171; Convention Against Torture and Other Cruel, Inhuman or Degrading Treatment or Punishment, art. 2, December 10, 1984, 108 Stat. 382, 85 U.N.T.S. 1465.

51. Convention Against Torture, art. 2.

52. See, e.g., Jenna Johnson, "Trump Says 'Torture Works,' Backs Waterboarding and 'Much Worse,' " *Washington Post*, February 17, 2016.

53. *Federalist* No. 1 (Hamilton), in *The Federalist Papers*, 33.

54. For further discussion of the contingency of constitutional choice, see Thomas P. Crocker, "Envisioning the Constitution," *American University Law Review* 57 (2007): 1–71.

55. For more on the related idea that social forces present themselves falsely as necessary, see Roberto Mangabeira Unger, *False Necessity: Anti-Necessitarian Social Theory in the Service of Radical Democracy* (New York: Verso, 2004).

56. Marbury v. Madison, 5 U.S. 137, 178 (1 Cranch) (1803). Exploring these and related issues of constructing constitutional meanings, see Paul W. Kahn, *The Reign of Law: Marbury v. Madison and the Construction of America* (New Haven, Conn.: Yale University Press, 2002).

57. President George W. Bush, "Address to a Joint Session of Congress and the American People" (speech, September 20, 2001), The White House, https://georgewbush-whitehouse.archives.gov/news/releases/2001/09/20010920-8.html.

58. Ibid.

59. President George W. Bush, "President's Address to the Nation" (speech, September 11, 2006), The White House, https://georgewbush-whitehouse.archives.gov/news/releases/2006/09/20060911-3.html.

60. See Eric Lichtblau, *Bush's War: The Remaking of American Justice* (New York: Anchor Books, 2008), 44. Lichtblau describes the involvement of ordinary citizens in providing over ninety-six thousand "tips" to FBI in the wake of 9/11. Ibid.

61. President George W. Bush, "President Discusses War on Terror" (speech, March 8, 2005), The White House, https://georgewbush-whitehouse.archives.gov/news/releases/2005/03/text/20050308-3.html. See also remarks by the vice president: "The attacks of September 11th, 2001, signaled the arrival of an entirely different era." Vice President Richard B. Cheney, "Remarks by the Vice President at the Ronald Reagan Presidential Library and Museum" (speech, March 17, 2004), The White House, https://georgewbush-whitehouse.archives.gov/news/releases/2004/03/text/20040317-3.html.

62. President George W. Bush, "The State of the Union" (speech, January 31, 2006), The White House, https://georgewbush-whitehouse.archives.gov/stateoftheunion/2006/.

63. See, e.g., Philip Bobbitt, *Terror and Consent: The Wars for the Twenty-First Century* (New York: Anchor Books, 2008); John Lewis Gaddis, *Surprise, Security, and the American Experience* (Cambridge, Mass.: Harvard University Press, 2004).

64. "Terrorism was obviously not new with 9/11, nor were attacks by al Qaeda against Americans new on that day. What changed was the framework through which they were seen." Kim Lane Scheppele, "Law in a Time of Emergency: States of Exception and the Temptations of 9/11," *University of Pennsylvania Journal of Constitutional Law* 6 (2004): 1023.

65. Bush, "President's Address to the Nation" (September 11, 2006).

66. President George W. Bush, "The State of the Union" (speech, January 20, 2004), The White House, https://georgewbush-whitehouse.archives.gov/stateoftheunion/2004/.

67. John Yoo, "Courts at War," *Cornell Law Review* 91 (2006): 574.

68. David Luban suggests that the United States "has simply chosen the bits of the law model and the bits of the war model that are most convenient for American interests, and ignored the rest." David Luban, "The War on Terrorism and the End of Human Rights," *Philosophy and Public Policy Quarterly* 22 (2002): 12.

69. As Agamben suggests, "Not only does necessity ultimately come down to a decision, but that on which it decides is, in truth, something undecidable in fact and law." Agamben, *State of Exception*, 30.

70. The White House, *National Security Strategy* (May 2010), 20, https://obamawhitehouse.archives.gov/sites/default/files/rss_viewer/national_security_strategy.pdf.

71. Karen DeYoung, "National Security Strategy Looks Beyond Military Might," *Washington Post*, May 27, 2010, A4.

72. Contrast President George W. Bush's description of U.S. strategy: "Finally, while maintaining near-term readiness and the ability to fight the war on terrorism, the

goal must be to provide the President with a wider range of military options to discourage aggression or any form of coercion against the United States, our allies, and our friends." The White House, *National Security Strategy of the United States of America* (September 2002), 30, https://georgewbush-whitehouse. archives.gov/nsc/nss/2002/.

73. *Federalist* No. 10 (Madison), in *The Federalist Papers*, 80 (asserting that "enlightened statesmen will not always be at the helm").

74. I have in mind here Charles Taylor's description of the social imaginary that "incorporates a sense of the normal expectations we have of each other, the kind of common understanding that enables us to carry out the collective practices that make up our social life." Charles Taylor, *Modern Social Imaginaries* (Durham, N.C.: Duke University Press, 2004), 24.

75. Harold D. Lasswell, *National Security and Individual Liberty* (New York: McGraw-Hill, 1950), 23.

76. See Peter Baker, "Trump Declares a National Emergency and Provokes a Constitutional Clash," *New York Times*, February 15, 2019.

77. Ibid.

78. Donald Trump, Twitter post, February 4, 2017, 9:12 a.m., https://twitter.com/realdonaldtrump/status/827867311054974976?lang=en.

79. See Katie Rogers and Sheryl Gay Stolberg, "Trump Calls for Depriving Immigrants Who Illegally Cross Border of Due Process Rights," *New York Times*, June 24, 2018.

80. Donald Trump, Twitter post, February 4, 2017, 4:59 a.m., https://twitter.com/realdonaldtrump/status/827864176043376640?lang=en.

81. Donald Trump, Twitter post, June 24, 2018, 8:02 a.m., https://twitter.com/realdonaldtrump/status/1010900865602019329?lang=en.

82. Plyler v. Doe, 457 U.S. 202, 210 (1982). See also Shaughnessy v. Mezei, 345 U.S. 206, 212 (1953).

83. Hannah Arendt, *Between Past and Future* (London: Penguin Books, 1977), 231. For further discussion, see Thomas P. Crocker, "Still Waiting for the Barbarians," *Law and Literature* 19 (2007): 303–26.

84. See H. Jefferson Powell, *A Community Built on Words: The Constitution in History and Politics* (Chicago: University of Chicago Press, 2002).

85. *Federalist* No. 1 (Hamilton), in *The Federalist Papers*, 33.

86. Lasswell, *National Security and Individual Freedom*, 29.

87. U.S. Const. art. I, § 9, cl. 2.

Chapter 1. Can "Necessitous Men" Ever Be Politically Free?

1. See National Emergencies Act of 1976, 90 Stat. 1255, 50 U.S.C. §§ 1601–1651. See generally Stephen Holmes, "In Case of Emergency: Misunderstanding Tradeoffs in the War on Terror," *California Law Review* 97 (2009): 301–55.

2. See, e.g., International Emergency Economic Powers Act, 50 U.S.C. §§ 1701–1706. National Emergencies Act, 50 U.S.C. § 1601. See generally Harold C. Rely-

ea, *National Emergency Powers* (CRS Report for Congress, 98–505, August 30, 2007). For an overview of the constitutional issues, see Harold Hongju Koh, *The National Security Constitution: Sharing Power After the Iran-Contra Affair* (New Haven, Conn.: Yale University Press, 1990).

3. In Germany, for example, parliamentary involvement is required in emergencies but limited by judicial protection of rights. The German Constitutional Court held unconstitutional the Air Security Act, which authorized shooting down a civilian aircraft if it was being used by terrorists as a weapon threatening other lives. See Bundesverfassungsgericht [BVerfG], February 15, 2006, 1 BvR 357/05, http://www.bverfg.de/entscheidungen/rs20060215_1bvr035705.html.

4. See, e.g., Emergency Economic Stabilization Act of 2008, Pub. L. No. 110-343, 122 Stat. 3765. For a related discussion, see William E. Scheuerman, "Exception and Emergency Powers: The Economic State of Emergency," *Cardozo Law Review* 21 (2000): 1883–84.

5. John Locke, "Second Treatise," in *Two Treatises on Government*, ed. Peter Laslett (Cambridge: Cambridge University Press, 2013), § 160, p. 375.

6. John C. Yoo, Deputy Assistant Attorney General, U.S. Department of Justice Office of Legal Counsel, to William Haynes II, General Counsel, U.S. Department of Defense, March 14, 2003, Re: Military Interrogation of Alien Unlawful Combatants Held Outside the United States, https://fas.org/irp/agency/doj/olc-interrogation.pdf, 19.

7. See Richard A. Posner, *Not a Suicide Pact: The Constitution in a Time of National Emergency* (New York: Oxford University Press, 2006). Posner derives the phrase "not a suicide pact" from *Terminiello v. Chicago*, 337 U.S. 1, 37 (1949) (Jackson, J., dissenting) ("There is danger that, if the Court does not temper its doctrinaire logic with a little practical wisdom, it will convert the constitutional Bill of Rights into a suicide pact.").

8. Carl Schmitt, *Political Theology: Four Chapters on the Concept of Sovereignty*, trans. George Schwab (Chicago: University of Chicago Press, 2005), 7. For further discussion of Schmitt's critique, see John P. McCormick, *Carl Schmitt's Critique of Liberalism* (Cambridge: Cambridge University Press, 1997).

9. Ibid., 12.

10. Locke, "Second Treatise," § 158, p. 373.

11. Schmitt, *Political Theology*, 12.

12. See Eric A. Posner and Adrian Vermeule, *The Executive Unbound: After the Madisonian Republic* (New York: Oxford University Press, 2010), 14–15.

13. Paul Kahn, *Political Theology: Four New Chapters on the Concept of Sovereignty* (New York: Columbia University Press, 2011), 55, 90.

14. Clinton L. Rossiter, *Constitutional Dictatorship: Crisis Government in the Modern Democracies* (Princeton, N.J.: Princeton University Press, 1948).

15. Giorgio Agamben, *State of Exception*, trans. Kevin Attell (Chicago: University of Chicago Press, 2005), 40.

16. In response, as one scholar explains, "liberalism seeks to separate emergency rule from the normal constitutional order, thereby preserving the Constitution in

its pristine form while providing the executive with the power, but not legal authority, to act in an emergency." Jules Lobel, "Emergency Power and the Decline of Liberalism," *Yale Law Journal* 98 (1989): 1390.

17. See Posner and Vermeule, *The Executive Unbound*, 5.

18. Franklin D. Roosevelt, "Message to the Congress on the State of the Union," January 11, 1944, in *The Public Papers and Addresses of Franklin D. Roosevelt*, comp. Samuel I. Rosenman, vol. 13 (1944–1945) (New York: Harper & Brothers, 1950), 41.

19. Hannah Arendt, *On Revolution* (New York: Penguin Books, 1963), 112.

20. Hannah Arendt, *The Human Condition* (Chicago: University of Chicago Press, 1958), 7.

21. Ibid., 83. Aristotle argues "for without the necessaries even life, as well as the good life, is impossible." Aristotle, *Politics*, trans. H. Rackham (Cambridge, Mass.: Harvard University Press, 1990), 1253b25, p. 15.

22. Arendt, *The Human Condition*, 118.

23. Ibid., 7–21.

24. Arendt recognizes that alleviation of suffering is a precondition for achieving the goal of revolution—to establish space for political liberty. Arendt, *On Revolution*, 112–14, 255. Here too is where protecting and disciplining persons as members of populations gives rise to "biopolitics" (which is not yet politics for Arendt), whose aim is also providing security against natural necessity. See Michel Foucault, *The History of Sexuality*, vol. 1, trans. Robert Hurley (New York: Pantheon Books, 1978), 136. Biopolitics "protects the security of the whole from internal dangers." Michel Foucault, *Society Must Be Defended: Lectures at the Collège de France, 1975–76*, trans. David Macey (New York: Pan Books, 2003), 243.

25. *Federalist* No. 8 (Hamilton), in *The Federalist Papers*, ed. Clinton Rossiter (New York: New American Library, 1961), 67.

26. Schmitt, *Political Theology*, 13.

27. Schmitt writes, "The exception is more interesting than the rule. The rule proves nothing; the exception proves everything." Ibid., 15.

28. Niccolò Machiavelli, *Discourses on Livy*, trans. Harvey C. Mansfield and Nathan Tarcov (Chicago: University of Chicago Press, 1996), bk. 3, chap. 41, p. 301.

29. David Hume, *Enquiries Concerning Human Understanding and Concerning the Principles of Morals*, 3rd ed., ed. P. H. Nidditch (New York: Oxford University Press, 1975), 186.

30. Thomas Jefferson to John B. Colvin, September 20, 1810, in *The Papers of Thomas Jefferson: Retirement Series*, vol. 3, ed. J. Jefferson Looney (Princeton, N.J.: Princeton University Press, 2006), 99.

31. Ibid.

32. Henry Shue, *Basic Rights: Subsistence, Affluence, and U.S. Foreign Policy* (Princeton, N.J.: Princeton University Press, 1980), 21–22. But if security is a basic right, one thing is ruled out, as Jeremy Waldron argues: "If security is the condition of the effective enjoyment of rights, then sacrificing anyone's security for the sake of others' is absolutely ruled out." Jeremy Waldron, *Torture, Terror, and Trade-Offs: Philosophy for the White House* (New York: Oxford University Press, 2010), 185.

33. Thomas Hobbes, *Leviathan*, ed. Richard Tuck (Cambridge, Mass.: Harvard University Press, 1996), chap. 17, p. 188.
34. Shue, *Basic Rights*, 21.
35. Ibid.
36. See Bruce Ackerman, *Before the Next Attack: Preserving Civil Liberties in an Age of Terrorism* (New Haven, Conn.: Yale University Press, 2006).
37. Ian Loader and Neil Walker, *Civilizing Security* (Cambridge: Cambridge University Press, 2007), 7.
38. Judge Richard Posner reasons, for example, that there must be trade-offs, because "without physical security there is likely to be very little liberty." Posner, *Not a Suicide Pact*, 47.
39. Ron Suskind, *One Percent Doctrine: Deep Inside America's Pursuit of Its Enemies Since 9/11* (New York: Simon & Schuster, 2006), 18. The "one percent doctrine" was Vice President Cheney's, and it holds that if there is even a 1 percent chance of another terrorist attack, given the gravity of the possible harm, that risk must be addressed as if it were a certainty.
40. See, e.g., Steven G. Bradbury, Principal Deputy Assistant Attorney General, U.S. Department of Justice Office of Legal Counsel, to John A. Rizzo, Senior Deputy General Counsel, CIA, May 30, 2005, Application of United States Obligations Under Article 16 of the Convention Against Torture to Certain Techniques That May Be Used in the Interrogation of High Value al Qaeda Detainees, 37, https://www.justice.gov/sites/default/files/olc/legacy/2013/10/21/memo-bradbury2005.pdf. See also Philippe Sands, *Torture Team: Rumsfeld's Memo and the Betrayal of American Values* (New York: St. Martin's Press, 2008), which details the torture of Guantánamo detainee al-Qahtani and its war-crime implications. As a general matter, these cases might appear as cases of rights opposed to other rights until we remember that the torture victims' right to security is being violated to provide security for others. This is not the case of everyone giving up some freedom of movement at a security checkpoint so that all will be made safer. These are cases of one person being made very insecure so that others may feel more secure.
41. See my discussion of trade-offs in chapter 5. Eric Posner and Adrian Vermeule are confident "that the government must make tradeoffs, that policy should become less libertarian during emergencies, and that courts should stay out of the way." Eric A. Posner and Adrian Vermeule, *Terror in the Balance: Security, Liberty, and the Courts* (New York: Oxford University Press, 2007), 158.
42. See Waldron, *Torture, Terror, and Trade-Offs*, 111–65.
43. As Hobbes writes, "the security of individuals and consequently the common peace, necessarily require that the right of using the sword to punish be transferred to some man or assembly; that man or that assembly therefore is necessarily understood to hold sovereign power in the commonwealth by right." Thomas Hobbes, *On the Citizen*, ed. Richard Tuck and Michael Silverthorne (Cambridge: Cambridge University Press, 1998), 77–78.
44. Arendt, *On Revolution*, 114.

45. For further discussion of the meanings of safety and security, see Waldron, *Torture, Terror, and Trade-Offs*, 111–65.

46. Roosevelt, "Message to the Congress on the State of the Union," 40. Cass Sunstein provides a remarkable study of Roosevelt's proposal and exploration of why we still do not have social and economic rights of this kind. Cass R. Sunstein, *The Second Bill of Rights: FDR's Unfinished Revolution and Why We Need It More Than Ever* (Cambridge, Mass.: Basic Books, 2004).

47. Roosevelt, "Message to the Congress on the State of the Union," 41.

48. Ibid.

49. Ibid.

50. Ibid., 40.

51. Ibid.

52. Ibid., 41.

53. Ibid.

54. Ibid.

55. Ibid., 33.

56. Ibid., 41.

57. Ibid.

58. Mere rebellion against or liberation from necessity is insufficient, as Arendt argues, "unless they are followed by the constitution of the newly won freedom." Arendt, *On Revolution*, 143.

59. See Bruce Ackerman, *We the People: Transformations*, vol. 2 (Cambridge, Mass.: Harvard University Press, 1998).

60. The choice to commit to constitutional processes creates the power by which the polity will respond to future challenges. Arendt describes the American experience this way: "To them, power came into being when and where people would get together and bind themselves through promises, covenants, and mutual pledges; only such power, which rested on reciprocity and mutuality, was real power and legitimate." Arendt, *On Revolution*, 181.

61. Schmitt, *Political Theology*, 11. This thought also introduces the ambivalence over sovereignty that runs through Schmitt's critique: "It is precisely the exception that makes relevant the subject of sovereignty, that is, the whole question of sovereignty." Ibid., 6.

62. Posner and Vermeule, *The Executive Unbound*, 34.

63. Kim Lane Scheppele, "Small Emergencies," *Georgia Law Review* 40 (2006): 856. Scheppele observes, "Emergencies have become so common that hardly anyone notices them." Ibid.

64. *Federalist* No. 1 (Hamilton), in *The Federalist Papers*, 33.

65. *Federalist* No. 70 (Hamilton), in *The Federalist Papers*, 424.

66. John C. Yoo, "War and the Constitutional Text," *University of Chicago Law Review* 69 (2002): 1676. See, e.g., Posner and Vermeule, *Terror in the Balance*, 18; Oren Gross, "Chaos and Rules: Should Responses to Violent Crises Always Be Constitutional?," *Yale Law Journal* 112 (2003): 1029.

67. As the Bush administration argued, Article II "vests in the President an unenumerated 'executive power,' " which implies "that national security decisions require the unity in purpose and energy in action that characterize the Presidency" and its power to do what is necessary to protect national security. See Jay S. Bybee, Assistant Attorney General Department of Justice Office of Legal Counsel, to Alberto R. Gonzales, Counsel to the President, August 1, 2002, Re: Standards of Conduct for Interrogation Under 18 U.S.C. §§ 2340–2340A, 36–37, https://www.justice.gov/olc/file/886061/download [hereinafter "Torture Memo"].

68. See Posner and Vermeule, *The Executive Unbound,* 176–205; Aziz Rana, "Who Decides on Security?," *Connecticut Law Review* 44 (2012): 1417–90; see also Thomas P. Crocker, "Who Decides on Liberty?," *Connecticut Law Review* 44 (2012): 1511–44.

69. John C. Yoo, Deputy Assistant Attorney General, U.S. Department of Justice Office of Legal Counsel, Memorandum for Alberto R. Gonzales, Counsel to the President, October 23, 2001, Re: Authority for Use of Military Force to Combat Terrorist Activities Within the United States, 4, https://www.justice.gov/sites/default/files/opa/legacy/2009/03/09/memomilitaryforcecombatus10232001.pdf [hereinafter "Military Force Memo"].

70. Torture Memo, 31.

71. Ibid., 33. See also Military Force Memo, 2.

72. Machiavelli, *Discourses,* bk. 1, chap. 1, p. 8.

73. Ibid., bk. 3, chap. 41, p. 301.

74. 18 U.S.C. §§ 2340–2340A.

75. Convention Against Torture and Other Cruel, Inhuman or Degrading Treatment or Punishment, art. 2, adopted December 10, 1984, S. Treaty Doc. No. 100-20 (1988), 108 Stat. 382, 1465 U.N.T.S. 113.

76. Cesare Beccaria, *On Crimes and Punishments,* trans. David Young (Indianapolis, Ind.: Hackett, 1986), 29.

77. Filartiga v. Pena-Irala, 630 F.2d 876, 890 (2d Cir. 1980). See also Kadic v. Karadžic, 70 F.3d 232, 243 (2d Cir. 1995). See also President Bush's statement: "Freedom from torture is an inalienable human right, and we are committed to building a world where human rights are respected and protected by the rule of law." Statement on United Nations International Day in Support of Victims of Torture, in Public Papers of the Presidents of the United States: George W. Bush, bk. 1, January 1 to June 30, 2004 (June 26, 2004), 1141, https://www.govinfo.gov/content/pkg/PPP-2004-book1/pdf/PPP-2004-book1-doc-pg1141.pdf.

78. Torture Memo, 38.

79. Former head of the Office of Legal Counsel Jack Goldsmith described Yoo's advice as follows: "Violent acts aren't necessarily torture; if you do torture, you probably have a defense; and even if you don't have a defense, the torture law doesn't apply if you act under the color of presidential authority." Jack Goldsmith, *The Terror Presidency: Law and Judgment Inside the Bush Administration* (New York: W.W. Norton, 2007), 144.

80. A continuing state of emergency has been in effect since September 2001. See, e.g., Continuation of the National Emergency with Respect to Certain Terrorist Attacks, 83 Fed. Reg. 46,067 (September 12, 2018).

81. David Dyzenhaus calls this a legal gray hole. See David Dyzenhaus, *The Constitution of Law: Legality in a Time of Emergency* (New York: Cambridge University Press, 2006), 3.

82. Rossiter, *Constitutional Dictatorship,* 4. Alexander Hamilton also invoked the idea of dictatorship to defend a "vigorous Executive," writing, "Every man the least conversant in Roman story, knows how often that republic was obliged to take refuge in the absolute power of a single man, under the formidable title of Dictator." *Federalist* No. 70 (Hamilton), in *The Federalist Papers,* 423.

83. Sanford Levinson and Jack Balkin write concerning the ambivalent status of a prospective dictatorship in the American republic: "It is an institutional framework for emergency government that may be valuable and even necessary to constitutional republics; nevertheless, it contains troublesome tendencies that, if allowed to develop unchecked, pose serious threats to democratic government." Sanford Levinson and Jack Balkin, "Constitutional Dictatorship: Its Dangers and Its Design," *Minnesota Law Review* 94 (2010): 1793. For further critique of the misuse of the idea of a Roman dictatorship, see Nomi Claire Lazar, *States of Emergency in Liberal Democracies* (Cambridge: Cambridge University Press, 2009), 113–35.

84. Rossiter, *Constitutional Dictatorship,* 298.

85. Ibid., 5.

86. McCulloch v. Maryland, 17 U.S. (4 Wheat.) 316, 415 (1819).

87. Rossiter, *Constitutional Dictatorship,* 5.

88. President George W. Bush, "President's Address to the Nation" (speech, September 11, 2006), The White House, https://georgewbush-whitehouse.archives.gov/news/releases/2006/09/20060911-3.html.

89. Even President Bush admitted that the old normal would never return: "It is my hope that in the months and years ahead, life will return almost to normal." President George W. Bush, "Address to a Joint Session of Congress and the American People" (September 20, 2001), The White House, http://georgewbush-whitehouse.archives.gov/news/releases/2001/09/20010920-8.html.

90. Rossiter, *Constitutional Dictatorship,* 295. Rossiter recognizes a potential problem with his presentation, noting that his position may exhibit "a glib assumption that constitutional democracy can use dictatorial powers . . . without making those powers and readjustments a permanent part of the constitutional scheme." Ibid., 13.

91. Ibid., 5.

92. See Ackerman, *Before the Next Attack,* 77–121.

93. I make no pretense of contributing to the free-will debate. Regarding Hume, Locke, and others, see, e.g., James A. Harris, *Of Liberty and Necessity: The Free Will Debate in Eighteenth-Century British Philosophy* (New York: Oxford University Press, 2005).

94. Yoo, Military Force Memo, 4.

95. George W. Bush, "Address to a Joint Session of Congress" (September 20, 2001).

96. Bruce Ackerman, *The Decline and Fall of the American Republic* (Cambridge, Mass.: Harvard University Press, 2010), 67–85.

97. One problem under the Bush administration was the lack of internal interagency deliberation about counterterrorism policy. See, e.g., Benjamin Wittes, *Law and the Long War: The Future of Justice in the Age of Terror* (New York: Penguin Books, 2008), 19–71; Jane Mayer, *The Dark Side* (New York: Doubleday, 2008), 44–71. For a contrary view, see Jack Goldsmith, *Power and Constraint: The Accountable Presidency After 9/11* (New York: Norton, 2012), 99–140.

98. For an overview of the related social science, see Cass R. Sunstein, *The Laws of Fear: Beyond the Precautionary Principle* (New York: Cambridge University Press, 2005); Cass R. Sunstein, *Why Societies Need Dissent* (Cambridge, Mass.: Harvard University Press, 2003).

99. Gitlow v. New York, 268 U.S. 652, 669 (1925). The Court admonished that the state may seek "to extinguish the spark without waiting until it has enkindled the flame or blazed into the conflagration." Ibid.

100. Dennis v. United States, 341 U.S. 494, 509 (1951).

101. See Brandenburg v. Ohio, 395 U.S. 444 (1969); Scales v. United States, 367 U.S. 203 (1961).

102. Military Force Memo, 5 (quoting *Federalist* No. 36 (Hamilton), in *The Federalist Papers*, 223).

103. Jean-Jacques Rousseau, "The Social Contract," in *The Social Contract and Other Later Political Writings*, trans. Victor Gourevitch (Cambridge: Cambridge University Press, 1997), bk. 4, chap. 6.

104. *Federalist* No. 23 (Hamilton), in *The Federalist Papers*, 153.

105. Arendt, *The Human Condition*, 121.

Chapter 2. Constitutionalizing Necessity Through Suspension

1. Abraham Lincoln, "Message to Congress in Special Session (July 4, 1861)," in *Collected Works of Abraham Lincoln*, vol. 4, ed. Roy P. Basler et al. (New Brunswick, N.J.: Rutgers University Press, 1953), 430.

2. Ibid., 429.

3. Thomas Hobbes, *Leviathan*, ed. Richard Tuck (Cambridge, Mass.: Harvard University Press, 1996), 6; Corey Robin, *Fear: The History of a Political Idea* (New York: Oxford University Press 2004), 45.

4. See *Federalist* No. 48 (Madison), in *The Federalist Papers*, ed. Clinton Rossiter (New York: New American Library, 1961), 313. Madison asked, "Will it be sufficient to mark, with precision, the boundaries of these departments, in the constitution of the government, and to trust to these parchment barriers against the encroaching spirit of power?" And Madison warned "that a mere demarcation on parchment of the constitutional limits of the several departments, is not a

sufficient guard against those encroachments which lead to a tyrannical concentration of all the powers of government in the same hands." Ibid.

5. U.S. Const. art. I, § 9, cl. 2. For historical context, see Paul D. Halliday and G. Edward White, "The Suspension Clause: English Text, Imperial Contexts, and American Implications," *Virginia Law Review* 94 (2008): 575–714.

6. Lincoln, "Message to Congress (July 4, 1861)," 423.

7. Ibid., 426.

8. Abraham Lincoln to Albert G. Hodges, U.S. Senator, April 4, 1864, in *Abraham Lincoln: Speeches and Writings, 1859–1865*, ed. Don E. Fehrenbacher (New York: Library of America, 1989), 585.

9. Edward Bates, "Suspension of the Privilege of the Writ of Habeas Corpus," *Opinions of the Attorney General*, vol. 10 (1861), 84.

10. William Blackstone, *Commentaries on the Laws of England*, vol. 1 (Chicago: University of Chicago Press, 2008; 1765–1769), 136.

11. See Larry May, *Global Justice and Due Process* (New York: Cambridge University Press, 2011).

12. Bates, "Suspension of the Privilege of the Writ of Habeas Corpus," 74.

13. Abraham Lincoln to Erastus Corning and Others, June 12, 1863, in *Abraham Lincoln: Speeches and Writings, 1859–1865*, 457–58.

14. Ibid., 458, 459, 460.

15. Ex parte Milligan, 71 U.S. (4 Wall.) 2, 125–27 (1866).

16. Ibid.

17. Lincoln to Erastus Corning and Others, June 12, 1863, in *Abraham Lincoln: Speeches and Writings, 1859–1865*, 458.

18. Lincoln, "Message to Congress (July 4, 1861)," 430–31.

19. Chief Justice Taney, now seeking to limit Lincoln's power, was the one who added fuel to the future secessionist fire by ruling in *Dred Scott v. Sandford*, 60 U.S 393 (1857), that even free blacks were not persons protected by the Constitution.

20. Ex parte Merryman, 17 F. Cas. 144, 149 (C.C.D. Md. 1861).

21. Bates, "Suspension of the Privilege of the Writ of Habeas Corpus," 84.

22. Ibid.

23. Lincoln, "Message to Congress (July 4, 1861)," 429.

24. See Amanda L. Tyler, "Suspension as Emergency Power," *Yale Law Journal* 118 (2009): 667–70.

25. Blackstone, *Commentaries*, 136.

26. Apart from treatment of detainees, the Suspension Clause does not empower the president to shut down the press, to suppress free exercise of religion, or to deny persons equal protection of the law. Though, in practice, the exercise of free speech, for example, has been used as an indicia of dangerousness for purpose of arrest and detention. See Geoffrey R. Stone, *Perilous Times: Free Speech in Wartime from the Sedition Act of 1789 to the War on Terrorism* (New York: W. W. Norton, 2004). In this way, even if with some irregularity in practice, the Constitution remains in force even when the power of judicial review over arrests and detentions is temporarily removed.

27. See Trevor W. Morrison, "Suspension and the Extrajudicial Constitution," *Columbia Law Review* 107 (2007): 1533–1616; Trevor W. Morrison, "*Hamdi*'s Habeas Puzzle: Suspension as Authorization?," *Cornell Law Review* 91 (2006): 411–57.

28. Moyer v. Peabody, 212 U.S. 78, 85 (1909).

29. Ibid., 84.

30. Ibid. Statutory authorization for calling forth the militia is found at 10 U.S.C. § 251 (2016). For further background, see Daniel Farber, *Lincoln's Constitution* (Chicago: University of Chicago Press, 2003), 162–63; Stephen I. Vladeck, "The Field Theory: Martial Law, the Suspension Power, and the Insurrection Act," *Temple Law Review* 80 (2007): 415–30; Stephen I. Vladeck, "Emergency Power and the Militia Acts," *Yale Law Journal* 114 (2004): 156–69.

31. Even then, it took until 1863 for Congress to give the president broad powers to suspend the writ. See Act of March 3, 1863, chap. 81, § 1, 12 Stat. 755. For more on this period, see Richard H. Fallon, Jr., "Executive Power and the Political Constitution," *Utah Law Review* 2007: 1–23; David P. Currie, "The Civil War Congress," *University of Chicago Law Review* 73 (2006): 1131–1226.

32. Since the Suspension Clause is the only "express provision for exercise of extraordinary authority because of a crisis"—Youngstown Sheet & Tube Co. v. Sawyer (*Steel Seizure*), 343 U.S. 579, 650 (1952) (Jackson J., concurring)—we have no other constitutional source to turn to in order to find a Constitution-suspending authority.

33. See, e.g., *Federalist* No. 49 (Madison), in *The Federalist Papers*, 317 ("But it is the reason, alone, of the public, that ought to control and regulate the government. The passions ought to be controlled and regulated by the government."); *Federalist* No. 55 (Madison), in *The Federalist Papers*, 342 (urging that "passion never fails to wrest the sceptre from reason"). For discussion of the relation between precommitment devices and the problem of passion, see Jon Elster, *Ulysses Unbound* (New York: Cambridge University Press, 2000), 115–46; Stephen Holmes, *Passions and Constraint: On the Theory of Liberal Democracy* (Chicago: University of Chicago Press, 1995).

34. Ex parte Milligan, 71 U.S. at 120.

35. Ibid., 120–21.

36. Military Order of November 13, 2001: Detention, Treatment, and Trial of Certain Non-Citizens in the War Against Terrorism, 66 Fed. Reg. 57,883 (November 16, 2001), http://www.fas.org/irp/offdocs/eo/mo-111301.htm.

37. Patrick F. Philbin, Deputy Assistant Attorney General, and John C. Yoo, Deputy Assistant Attorney General, U.S. Department of Justice Office of Legal Counsel, to William J. Haynes, II, General Counsel, Department of Defense, December 28, 2001, Re: Possible Habeas Jurisdiction Over Aliens Held at Guantánamo Bay, Cuba, 8, https://nsarchive2.gwu.edu/torturingdemocracy/documents/20011228.pdf.

38. See John C. Yoo, Deputy Assistant Attorney General, and Robert Delahunty, Special Counsel, U.S. Department of Justice Office of Legal Counsel, to William J. Haynes, II, General Counsel, Department of Defense, January 9, 2002, Re: Application of

Treaties and Laws to al Qaeda and Taliban Detainees, 1, http://hrlibrary.umn.edu/OathBetrayed/Yoo-Delahunty%201-9-02.pdf; Jay S. Bybee, Assistant Attorney General, U.S. Department of Justice Office of Legal Counsel, Memorandum for Alberto R. Gonzales, Counsel to the President, and William J. Haynes, II, General Counsel, Department of Defense, January 22, 2002, Re: Application of Treaties and Laws to al Qaeda and Taliban Detainees, 1, https://www.justice.gov/sites/default/files/olc/legacy/2009/08/24/memo-laws-taliban-detainees.pdf; see also Alberto R. Gonzales, White House Counsel, to President George W. Bush, January 25, 2002, Decision Re: Application of the Geneva Convention on Prisoners of War to the Conflict with Al Qaeda and the Taliban, https://nsarchive2.gwu.edu/NSAEBB/NSAEBB127/02.01.25.pdf.

39. Gonzales to President Bush, January 25, 2002, 2.

40. Brief for Respondents at 25, Hamdi v. Rumsfeld, 542 U.S. 507 (2004) (No. 03-6696).

41. Ibid., 25.

42. John C. Yoo, Deputy Assistant Attorney General, U.S. Department of Justice Office of Legal Counsel, Memorandum for Daniel J. Bryant, Assistant Attorney General, Office of Legislative Affairs, June 27, 2002, Re: Applicability of 18 U.S.C. § 4001(a) to Military Detention of United States Citizens, 10, https://www.justice.gov/sites/default/files/olc/legacy/2009/08/24/memodetentionuscitizens06272002.pdf.

43. There is a large literature criticizing the Bush administration's use of Guantánamo and other counterterrorism policies. See, for instance, Joseph Margulies, *Guantánamo and the Abuse of Presidential Power* (New York: Simon & Schuster, 2006); Stephen Holmes, *The Matador's Cape: America's Reckless Response to Terror* (New York: Cambridge University Press, 2007).

44. See Brief for Respondents at 21, Rasul v. Bush, 542 U.S. 466 (Nos. 03-335, 03-343); Johnson v. Eisentrager, 339 U.S. 763 (1950).

45. Rasul v. Bush, 542 U.S. 466, 485 (2004).

46. Hamdi v. Rumsfeld, 542 U.S. 507, 509 (2004).

47. Ibid., 536–38.

48. Ibid., 536.

49. Ibid.

50. Geneva Convention Relative to the Treatment of Prisoners of War, art. 3, August 12, 1949, 6 U.S.T. 3316, 75 U.N.T.S. 135. See also Hamdan v. Rumsfeld, 548 U.S. 557, 642 (2006).

51. Pub. L. No. 109-366, 120 Stat. 2600, codified at chap. 47A of Title 10, U.S.C. (2006).

52. Boumediene v. Bush, 553 U.S. 723, 797 (2008).

53. Ibid., 798.

54. Ibid., 765.

55. Deborah Sontag, "Video Is a Window Into a Terror Suspect's Isolation," *New York Times*, December 4, 2006.

56. Al-Marri v. Pucciarelli, 534 F.3d 213 (4th Cir. 2008) (en banc).

57. Exec. Order No. 13823, 83 Fed. Reg. 4831 (January 30, 2018), sec. 2(c) (Protecting America Through Lawful Detention of Terrorists), https://www.federalregister.gov/documents/2018/02/02/2018-02261/protecting-america-through-lawful-detention-of-terrorists.

58. See Bruce Ackerman, *Before the Next Attack: Preserving Civil Liberties in an Age of Terrorism* (New Haven, Conn.: Yale University Press, 2006); Bruce Ackerman, "The Emergency Constitution," *Yale Law Journal* 113 (2004): 1029–91.

59. See, e.g., David Cole, "The Priority of Morality: The Emergency Constitution's Blind Spot," *Yale Law Journal* 113 (2004): 1753–1800; David Cole, "In Case of Emergency," *New York Review of Books* 53 (July 13, 2006), 40.

60. See Korematsu v. United States, 323 U.S. 214, 216 (1944).

61. Ibid.

62. *Korematsu*, 323 U.S. at 244 (Jackson, J., dissenting).

63. Ibid., 246.

64. Jenna Johnson, "Trump Calls for Total and Complete Shutdown of Muslims Entering the United States," *Washington Post*, December 7, 2015.

65. Quoted in Trump v. Hawaii, 138 S. Ct. 2392, 2436 (2018) (Sotomayor, J., dissenting). See also Jenna Johnson and Abigail Hauslohner, " 'I Think Islam Hates Us': A Timeline of Trump's Comments About Islam and Muslims," *Washington Post*, May 20, 2017.

66. Jenna Johnson, "Donald Trump Says He Is Not Bothered by Comparisons to Hitler," *Washington Post*, December 8, 2015.

67. Trump v. Hawaii, 138 S. Ct. 2419–20.

68. Ibid., 2423.

69. See Lon L. Fuller, *The Morality of Law* (New Haven, Conn.: Yale University Press, 1969).

70. For discussion of related tensions with security, see Ian Loader and Neil Walker, *Civilizing Security* (Cambridge: Cambridge University Press, 2007). See also Aziz Rana, "Constitutionalism and the Foundations of the Security State," *California Law Review* 103 (2015): 335–85.

71. Cecilia Kang and Alan Rappeport, "Trump Blocks Broadcom's Bid for Qualcomm," *New York Times*, March 12, 2018. Such claims to the primacy of "doing whatever is necessary to protect national security" appear even when there is some distance from the usual setting, such as the issue of the nation's technology sector, from which this statement by the treasury secretary derives.

72. McCulloch v. Maryland, 17 U.S. (4 Wheat.) 316, 415 (1819).

73. See Charles Taylor, *Modern Social Imaginaries* (Durham, N.C.: Duke University Press, 2004).

74. For a more detailed analysis of the different approaches to security, see Loader and Walker, *Civilizing Security*, 7–31.

75. Neil A. Lewis, "Ashcroft Defends Antiterror Plan and Says Criticism May Aid Foes," *New York Times*, December 7, 2001.

76. Blackstone, *Commentaries*, 136.

Chapter 3. Normalizing Necessity

1. Hamdi v. Rumsfeld, 542 U.S. 507, 533 (2004).

2. Ibid., 532.

3. McCulloch v. Maryland, 17 U.S. (4 Wheat.) 316, 415 (1819).

4. Ibid., 421.

5. Ibid., 415.

6. Ibid., 414. On the idea that a political order is organized according to its forms of justification, see Rainer Forst, *Normativity and Power: Analyzing Social Orders of Justification,* trans. Ciaran Cronin (Oxford: Oxford University Press, 2017); Rainer Forst, *The Right to Justification,* trans. Jeffrey Flynn (New York: Columbia University Press, 2012).

7. *Hamdi,* 542 U.S. at 554 (Scalia, J., dissenting).

8. See National Federation of Independent Business v. Sebelius, 567 U.S. 519 (2012).

9. See Frederick Schauer, "Exceptions," *University of Chicago Law Review* 58 (1991): 880. "The presence of an explicit exception, therefore, is once again a signal that the law is operating less to reflect and reinforce existing practice than to attempt to modify it." Ibid.

10. See Romer v. Evans, 517 U.S. 620, 631-36 (1996) (rational basis); Craig v. Boren, 429 U.S. 190, 197-99 (1976) (intermediate scrutiny); Adarand Constructors, Inc. v. Pena, 515 U.S. 200, 201-2 (1995) (strict scrutiny).

11. *McCulloch,* 17 U.S. (4 Wheat.) at 409.

12. Ibid., 409-10.

13. Ibid., 411-12.

14. Ibid., 420.

15. Ibid., 421.

16. See Bruce A. Ackerman, *We the People: Transformations,* vol. 2 (Cambridge, Mass.: Harvard University Press, 1998).

17. Franklin D. Roosevelt, "Message to the Congress on the State of the Union," January 11, 1944, in *The Public Papers and Addresses of Franklin D. Roosevelt,* comp. Samuel I. Rosenman, vol. 13 (1944-1945) (New York: Harper & Brothers, 1950), 41.

18. United States v. Comstock, 560 U.S. 126, 135 (2010). For a helpful analysis of the Necessary and Proper Clause holding in *Comstock,* see H. Jefferson Powell, "The Regrettable Clause: *United States v. Comstock* and the Powers of Congress," *San Diego Law Review* 48 (2011): 713-72.

19. See United States v. Carolene Prods. Co., 304 U.S. 144, 152 4n (1938). Ackerman, *We the People,* 368-75; Bruce Ackerman, "Beyond *Carolene Products,*" *Harvard Law Review* 98 (1985): 713-46; John Hart Ely, *Democracy and Distrust: A Theory of Judicial Review* (Cambridge, Mass.: Harvard University Press, 1980); Reva B. Siegel, "The Supreme Court 2012 Term Forward: Equality Divided," *Harvard Law Review* 127 (2013): 6-7.

20. Korematsu v. United States, 323 U.S. 214, 216 (1944) (emphasis added).

21. Ibid., 246 (Jackson, J., dissenting).

22. Ibid., 247.
23. Justice Jackson reasoned, "If the people ever let command of the war power fall into irresponsible and unscrupulous hands, the courts wield no power equal to its restraint." Ibid., 248 (Jackson, J., dissenting).
24. Ibid., 235–36 (Murphy, J., dissenting).
25. See Jamal Greene, "The AntiCanon," *Harvard Law Review* 125 (2011): 422–27.
26. *Adarand Constructors,* 515 U.S. at 237.
27. Shapiro v. Thompson, 394 U.S. 618, 634 (1969). I have greatly benefited from Richard H. Fallon, Jr., "Strict Judicial Scrutiny," *UCLA Law Review* 54 (2007): 1267–1337.
28. Burson v. Freemon, 504 U.S. 191 (1992).
29. See, e.g., Owen Fiss, *The Irony of Free Speech* (Cambridge, Mass.: Harvard University Press, 1996). See also Thomas P. Crocker, "Displacing Dissent: The Role of 'Place' in First Amendment Jurisprudence," *Fordham Law Review* 85 (2007): 2601–8.
30. New York Times, Inc. v. United States, 403 U.S. 713 (1971). See generally Geoffrey R. Stone, *Perilous Times: Free Speech in Wartime from the Sedition Act of 1789 to the War on Terrorism* (New York: W. W. Norton, 2004).
31. See Holder v. Humanitarian Law Project, 561 U.S. 1 (2010).
32. Gitlow v. New York, 268 U.S. 652, 669 (1925). See also Schenk v. United States, 249 U.S. 47 (1919) (World War I); Dennis v. United States, 341 U.S. 494 (1951) (communist threat). For more on the Court's mixed record of protecting speech during times of war or national crisis, see Stone, *Perilous Times: Free Speech in Wartime*; see also David Cole, *Enemy Aliens: Double Standards and Constitutional Freedoms in the War on Terrorism* (New York: The New Press, 2003), 228–29.
33. Robert Alexy, *A Theory of Constitutional Rights,* trans. Julian Rivers (New York: Oxford University Press, 2002), 68.
34. These courts are part of a broader developing understanding of judicial protections for rights through proportionality review. See Vicki C. Jackson, "Constitutional Law in an Age of Proportionality," *Yale Law Journal* 124 (2015): 3094–3196; Alec Stone Sweet and Jud Mathews, "Proportionality Balancing and Global Constitutionalism," *Columbia Journal of Transnational Law* 47 (2008): 73–165; Jud Matthews and Alec Stone Sweet, "All Things in Proportion? American Rights Review and the Problem of Balancing," *Emory Law Journal* 60 (2011): 797–875.
35. United States v. Alvarez, 567 U.S. 709, 730 (2012) (Breyer, J., concurring).
36. When deciding the meaning of the Second Amendment, Justice Breyer's dissent advocated for a " 'proportionality' approach" used in "various constitutional contexts, including election law cases, speech cases, and due process cases," to conclude that the government regulation was "proportionate." District of Columbia v. Heller, 554 U.S. 570, 690 (2008) (Breyer, J., dissenting). By contrast, Justice Scalia's majority opinion claimed that "[w]e know of no other enumerated constitutional right whose core protection has been subjected to a freestanding 'interest-balancing' approach." Ibid., 634.

37. See Fallon, "Strict Judicial Scrutiny"; see also G. Edward White, "Historicizing Judicial Scrutiny," *South Carolina Law Review* 57 (2005): 1–83.

38. See Charles Taylor, *Modern Social Imaginaries* (Durham, N.C.: Duke University Press, 2004), 24.

39. David Cole, "The Priority of Morality: The Emergency Constitution's Blind Spot," *Yale Law Journal* 113 (2004): 1753–1800.

40. See Eric A. Posner and Adrian Vermeule, *Terror in the Balance: Security, Liberty, and the Courts* (New York: Oxford University Press, 2007): 131–60.

41. See Katz v. United States, 389 U.S. 347, 351 (1967) for the Court's treatment of searches; Payton v. New York, 445 U.S. 573, 601 (1980) for the warrant requirement; and Terry v. Ohio, 392 U.S. 1, 19 (1968) for reasonable suspicion.

42. See United States v. Santana, 427 U.S. 38, 42–43 (1976) (hot pursuit); Brigham City v. Stuart, 547 U.S. 398 (2006) (emergency aid).

43. See Thomas P. Crocker, "The Political Fourth Amendment," *Washington University Law Review* 88 (2010): 303–79.

44. Kentucky v. King, 563 U.S. 452, 461–62 (2011).

45. See Thomas P. Crocker, "Order, Technology, and the Constitutional Meanings of Criminal Procedure," *Journal of Criminal Law & Criminology* 103 (2013): 685–744.

46. Kyllo v. United States, 533 U.S. 27, 40 (2001) explains the baseline: "We have said that the Fourth Amendment draws 'a firm line at the entrance to the house.' That line, we think, must be not only firm but also bright."

47. U.S. Const. amend. IV.

48. Ibid.

49. New Jersey v. T.L.O., 469 U.S. 325, 351 (1985) (Blackmun, J., concurring) ("Only in those exceptional circumstances in which special needs, beyond the normal need for law enforcement, make the warrant and probable-cause requirement impracticable, is a court entitled to substitute its balancing of interests for that of the Framers."); see also Skinner v. Railway Labor Exec.'s Ass'n, 489 U.S. 602 (1989).

50. United States v. Martinez-Fuerte, 428 U.S. 543, 545, 551–53 (1976).

51. Mich. Dep't of State Police v. Sitz, 496 U.S. 444, 455 (1990) (highway sobriety); Illinois v. Lidster, 540 U.S. 419, 427–28 (2004) (information); Vernonia Sch. Dist. 47J v. Acton, 515 U.S. 646, 653–54 (1995) (school searches); United States v. Edwards, 498 F.2d 496, 499–500 (2d Cir. 1974) (airline baggage); MacWade v. Kelly, 460 F.3d 260, 263 (2d Cir. 2006) (subway bags).

52. See Crocker, "The Political Fourth Amendment." The Court considers the effect of national security on the Fourth Amendment in United States v. U.S. District Court (Keith), 407 U.S. 297, 313 (1972).

53. United States v. Arvizu, 534 U.S. 266 (2002).

54. Ibid., 277.

55. *MacWade*, 460 F.3d at 271.

56. Maryland v. King, 569 U.S. 435, 448–49 (2013).

57. Ibid., 462 (citing "special needs" cases). The Court goes on to explain that the "special needs cases [are] in full accord with the result reached here." Ibid., 463.

58. Redacted, 2011 WL 10945618, at *24 (F.I.S.C., October 3, 2011) (quoting *In re Directives*, 551 F.3d 1004, 1012 (2008)).

59. Ibid.

60. See, e.g., Bernard E. Harcourt, *Exposed: Desire and Disobedience in the Digital Age* (Cambridge, Mass.: Harvard University Press, 2015), 54–79; Jack M. Balkin, "The Constitution in the National Surveillance State," *Minnesota Law Review* 93 (2008): 1–25.

61. The Foreign Intelligence Surveillance Act of 1978, Pub. L. No. 95-511, § 101, 92 Stat. 1783 (codified as amended at 50 U.S.C. §§ 1801–11 (2000)).

62. For the Church Committee Report, see *Intelligence Activities and the Rights of Americans: Final Report of the Select Committee to Study Governmental Operations with Respect to Intelligence Activities*, S. Rep. No. 94-755 (2d Sess. 1976).

63. See Seymour M. Hersh, "Huge C.I.A. Operation Reported in U.S. Against Antiwar Forces, Other Dissidents in Nixon Years," *New York Times*, December 22, 1974.

64. Uniting and Strengthening America by Providing Appropriate Tools Required to Intercept and Obstruct Terrorism (USA PATRIOT ACT) Act of 2001, Pub. L. No. 107-56, 115 Stat. 272 (codified in scattered sections). "A significant purpose" is found in § 218 (codified at 50 U.S.C. § 1804(a)(7)(B) (2001)).

65. Ellen Nakashima and Joby Warrick, "For NSA Chief, Terrorist Threat Drives Passion to 'Collect It All,' Observers Say," *Washington Post*, July 14, 2013.

66. See Eric Lichtblau, "In Secret, Court Vastly Broadens Powers of NSA," *New York Times*, July 6, 2013, A1. Using "special needs" as a doctrinal "concept more broadly, the FISA judges have ruled that the N.S.A.'s collection and examination of Americans' communications data to track possible terrorists does not run afoul of the Fourth Amendment, the officials said." Ibid.

67. David E. Sanger, "Bush Says He Ordered Domestic Spying," *New York Times*, December 18, 2005, A1. For the initial story revealing the program, see James Risen and Eric Lichtblau, "Bush Lets U.S. Spy on Callers Without Courts," *New York Times*, December 16, 2005, A1. For the full story of the program, see Eric Lichtblau, *Bush's War: The Remaking of American Justice* (New York: Anchor Books, 2008).

68. U.S. Department of Justice, *Legal Authorities Supporting the Activities of the National Security Agency Described by the President* (January 19, 2006), 1, https://www.justice.gov/archive/opa/docs/whitepaperonnsalegalauthorities.pdf.

69. John C. Yoo, Deputy Assistant Attorney General, to David S. Kris, Associate Attorney General, September 25, 2001, Re: Constitutionality of Amending Foreign Intelligence Surveillance Act to Change the "Purpose" Standard for Searches, 6.

70. It is one of John Yoo's signature arguments, but others employed it as well. See William E. Moschella, Assistant Attorney General, to Members of Congress, December 22, 2005, https://www.justice.gov/sites/default/files/ag/legacy/2007/01/11/surveillance6.pdf ("[T]he President has the responsibility to protect the Nation from further attacks, and the Constitution gives him all necessary authority to fulfill that duty.").

71. U.S. Department of Justice, *Legal Authorities*, 3.

72. Ibid., 7.

73. Ibid., 9.

74. Ibid., 1, 37.

75. *In re* Directives Pursuant to Section 105B of the Foreign Intelligence Surveillance Act, 551 F.3d 1004, 1011 (F.I.S.C., 2008).

76. Ibid., 1012.

77. Ibid., 1011.

78. *In re* Sealed Case, 310 F.3d 717, 746 (F.I.S.C., 2002).

79. "President Bush's News Conference," *New York Times,* September 15, 2006, http://www.nytimes.com/2006/09/15/washington/15bush_transcript.html?pagewanted=print; FISA Amendments Act of 2008, Pub. L. No. 110-261, 122 Stat. 2436. See also the temporary amendments enacted in the aftermath of the public revelation of the warrantless Terrorist Surveillance Program. Protect America Act of 2007, Pub. L. No. 110-55, 121 Stat. 552.

80. FISA Amendments Act of 2008, 50 U.S.C. § 1881a(a)-(g) (2008).

81. And even within a statutory framework that enables vast surveillance so long as there are procedures in place to minimize the unintentional acquisition of U.S. persons' communications, the deferential FISA Court still had occasion to strike down aspects of the program in an October 2011 opinion. See Redacted, 2011 WL 10945618, at *24–*26 (F.I.S.C., October 3, 2011).

82. Glenn Greenwald and Ewen MacAskill, "NSA Prism Program Taps in to User Data of Apple, Google and Others," *The Guardian,* June, 7, 2013.

83. Redacted, 2011 WL 10945618, at *9 (F.I.S.C., October 3, 2011). See also Charlie Savage and Scott Shane, "Secret Court Rebuked N.S.A. on Surveillance," *New York Times,* August 21, 2013.

84. Glenn Greenwald and Ewen MacAskill, "Boundless Informant: The NSA's Secret Tool to Track Global Surveillance Data," *The Guardian,* June 11, 2013.

85. Glenn Greenwald, "XKeyscore: NSA Tool Collects 'Nearly Everything a User Does on the Internet,' " *The Guardian,* July 31, 2013.

86. U.S. Department of Justice white paper, *The Intelligence Community's Collection Programs Under Title VII of the Foreign Intelligence Surveillance Act* (May 4, 2012), 9, https://www.dni.gov/files/documents/Ltr%20to%20HPSCI%20Chairman%20Rogers%20and%20Ranking%20Member%20Ruppersberger_Scan.pdf.

87. Redacted, 2011 WL 10945618, at *29 (F.I.S.C., October 3, 2011).

88. Glen Greenwald, "NSA Collecting Phone Records of Millions of Verizon Customers Daily," *The Guardian,* June 6, 2013.

89. USA PATRIOT Act, 50 U.S.C. § 1861(a)(1). The relevant full text states: "the production of tangible things (including books, records, papers, documents, and other items) for an investigation to obtain foreign intelligence information not concerning a United States person or to protect against international terrorism or clandestine intelligence activities, provided that such investigation of a United States person is not conducted solely upon the basis of activities protected by the first amendment to the Constitution."

90. *In re* Application of the F.B.I. for an Order Requiring the Production of Tangible Things From [REDACTED], 2013 WL 5741573, at *6 (F.I.S.C., August 29, 2013).

91. Smith v. Maryland, 42 U.S. 735 (1979).

92. Katz v. United States, 389 U.S. 347, 351 (1967). I discuss the implications of this view of sharing in Thomas P. Crocker, "From Privacy to Liberty: The Fourth Amendment After Lawrence," *UCLA Law Review* 57 (2009): 1.

93. *In re* Application of the F.B.I., 2013 WL 5741573, at *2 (F.I.S.C., August 29, 2013).

94. Carpenter v. United States, 138 S. Ct. 2206, 2218 (2018).

95. Ibid., 2220.

96. Administration white paper, *Bulk Collection of Telephony Metadata Under Section 215 of the USA Patriot Act* (August 9, 2013), 19, https://perma.cc/8RJN-EDB7.

97. President Barack Obama, "Remarks by the President on Review of Signals Intelligence" (speech, January 17, 2014), The White House, https://obamawhitehouse. archives.gov/the-press-office/2014/01/17/remarks-president-review-signals-intelligence.

98. Ibid.

99. See United States v. Maynard, 615 F.3d 544, 562 (D.C. Cir. 2010). "As with the 'mosaic theory' often invoked by the Government in cases involving national security information, 'What may seem trivial to the uninformed, may appear of great moment to one who has a broad view of the scene.' " Ibid.

100. The needle-and-haystack reference was made by General Alexander, NSA director, in 2013 while defending NSA practices of pervasive surveillance. See Barton Gellman and Ashkan Soltani, "NSA Collects Millions of E-mail Address Books Globally," *Washington Post,* October 14, 2013; Nakashima and Warrick, "For NSA Chief, Terrorist Threat Drives Passion to 'Collect It All.' "

101. Klayman v. Obama, 957 F. Supp. 2d 1 (D.D.C. 2013).

102. Ibid., 33.

103. Uniting and Strengthening America by Fulfilling Rights and Ensuring Effective Discipline over Monitoring Act (USA FREEDOM Act) of 2015, Pub. L. No. 114-23, 129 Stat. 268 (codified as amended in scattered sections of 18 and 50 U.S.C.).

104. See Charlie Savage, "Reined-In N.S.A. Still Collected 151 Million Phone Records in '16," *New York Times,* May 2, 2017.

105. See Harcourt, *Exposed,* 61–66.

106. Katz v. United States, 389 U.S. 347, 359 (1967).

107. Olmstead v. United States, 277 U.S. 438, 478 (1928) (Brandeis, J., dissenting). Brandeis wrote, "The makers of our Constitution . . . conferred, as against the government, the right to be left alone—the most comprehensive of rights and the right most valued by civilized men." Ibid.

108. Ibid.

109. United States v. White, 401 U.S. 745, 762 (1971) (Douglas, J., dissenting).

110. United States v. Jones, 565 U.S. 400, 416 (2012) (Sotomayor, J., concurring).

111. United States v. Karo, 468 U.S. 705 (1984).

112. For further analysis of the effects on the personal and political identities of individuals, see Crocker, "The Political Fourth Amendment"; Thomas P. Crocker, "Ubiquitous Privacy," *Oklahoma Law Review* 66 (2014): 791–829.

113. See David Gray and Danielle Citron, "The Right to Quantitative Privacy," *Minnesota Law Review* 98 (2013): 62–144.

Chapter 4. Constitutional Emergencies Inside and Out

1. *Federalist* No. 23 (Hamilton) in *The Federalist Papers,* ed. Clinton Rossiter (New York: New American Library, 1961), 153 (emphasis added).

2. John C. Yoo, Deputy Assistant Attorney General, U.S. Department of Justice Office of Legal Counsel, Memorandum for Alberto R. Gonzales, Counsel to the President, October 23, 2001, Authority for Use of Military Force to Combat Terrorist Activities Within the United States, 4, https://www.justice.gov/sites/default/files/opa/legacy/2009/03/09/memomilitaryforcecombatus10232001.pdf. This "responsibility entails power" argument appears in a number of U.S. Department of Justice memos purporting to justify expanded executive power to conduct counterterrorism operations.

3. Hamdi v. Rumsfeld, 542 U.S. 507, 580 (2004) (Thomas, J., dissenting).

4. Gabriella Blum and Philip B. Heymann, *Laws, Outlaws, and Terrorists: Lessons from the War on Terrorism* (Cambridge, Mass.: MIT Press, 2013), 28.

5. Michael Stokes Paulsen, "The Constitution of Necessity," *Notre Dame Law Review* 79 (2004): 1267.

6. "The Constitution itself embraces an overriding principle of constitutional and national self-preservation that operates as a meta-rule of construction for the document's specific provisions and that may even, in cases of extraordinary necessity, trump specific constitutional requirements." Ibid., 1257.

7. Ibid., 1257–58.

8. Abraham Lincoln to Albert G. Hodges, U.S. Senator, April 4, 1864, in *Abraham Lincoln: Speeches and Writings, 1859–1865,* ed. Don E. Fehrenbacher (New York: Library of America, 1989), 585.

9. See Griswold v. Connecticut, 381 U.S. 479 (1965); Thomas P. Crocker, "From Privacy to Liberty: The Fourth Amendment After *Lawrence,*" *UCLA Law Review* 57 (2009): 1–69.

10. Jack Goldsmith, *Power and Constraint: The Accountable Presidency After 9/11* (New York: W. W. Norton, 2012), 211. This intuition is also the source of positive theories of modern prerogative. See Julian Davis Mortenson, "A Theory of Republican Prerogative," *Southern California Law Review* 88 (2014): 95.

11. Richard A. Posner, *Not a Suicide Pact: The Constitution in a Time of National Emergency* (New York: Oxford University Press, 2006), 12.

12. Milton Friedman, *Capitalism and Freedom* (Chicago: University of Chicago Press, 2002), xiv.

13. Home Bldg. & Loan Ass'n v. Blaisdell, 290 U.S. 398, 425–26 (1934).

14. A. L. A. Schechter Poultry Corp. v. United States, 295 U.S. 495, 528–29 (1935).

15. This statement originates in *Terminiello v. Chicago*, 337 U.S. 1, 37 (1949) (Jackson, J., dissenting). Justice Jackson warned, "There is danger that, if the Court does not temper its doctrinaire logic with a little practical wisdom, it will convert the constitutional Bill of Rights into a suicide pact." Ibid. See also Kennedy v. Mendoza-Martinez, 372 U.S. 144, 160 (1963). The Court wrote, "[W]hile the Constitution protects against invasions of individual rights, it is not a suicide pact." Ibid. However, the suicide pact could run the other way: "Constitutions are chains with which men bind themselves in their sane moments that they may not die by a suicidal hand in the day of their frenzy." Jon Elster, *Ulysses Unbound* (New York: Cambridge University Press, 2000), 89.

16. Posner, *Not a Suicide Pact*, v.

17. Abraham Lincoln, "Message to Congress in Special Session (July 4, 1861)," in *Collected Works of Abraham Lincoln*, vol. 4, ed. Roy P. Basler et al. (New Brunswick, N.J.: Rutgers University Press, 1953), 430.

18. Eric A. Posner and Adrian Vermeule, *Terror in the Balance: Security, Liberty, and the Courts* (New York: Oxford University Press, 2007), 155.

19. Ibid., 39.

20. Posner, *Not a Suicide Pact*, 7–8.

21. See Neil A. Lewis, "Ashcroft Defends Antiterror Plan and Says Criticism May Aid Foes," *New York Times*, December 7, 2001.

22. *Federalist No. 70* (Hamilton), in *The Federalist Papers*, 424.

23. See, e.g., Posner and Vermeule, *Terror in the Balance*, 15–16, 30–31.

24. Ibid., 24.

25. Posner, *Not a Suicide Pact*, 45.

26. Posner and Vermeule, *Terror in the Balance*, 155.

27. Oren Gross and Fionnuala Ní Aoláin, *Law in Times of Crisis: Emergency Powers in Theory and Practice* (New York: Cambridge University Press, 2006), 137.

28. Ibid.

29. Ibid., 141–42.

30. This view is also attributable to the great British constitutionalist A. V. Dicey, who explained, "There are times of tumult or invasion when for the sake of legality itself the rules of law must be broken. The course which the government must then take is clear. The Ministry must break the law and trust for protection to an Act of Indemnity." Albert Venn Dicey, *Introduction to the Study of the Law of the Constitution*, 8th ed. (Carmel, Ind.: Liberty Fund Press, 1982), 272.

31. Korematsu v. United States, 33 U.S. 214, 244 (1944) (Jackson, J., dissenting).

32. Ibid., 246.

33. See, e.g., Arar v. Ashcroft, 585 F.3d 559 (2d Cir. 2008); Padilla v. Yoo, 678 F.3d 748 (9th Cir. 2012).

34. See Mohamed v. Jeppesen Dataplan, Inc., 563 U.S. 1002 (2011).

35. Heidi Kitrosser, *Reclaiming Accountability: Transparency, Executive Power, and the U.S. Constitution* (Chicago: University of Chicago Press, 2015), 46.

36. Pub. L. No. 112-238, 126 Stat. 1631 (50 U.S.C. 1801 et seq. (2012 & Supp. 2015)).

37. Quoted in Glenn Greenwald and Ewen MacAskill, "NSA Prism Program Taps in to User Data of Apple, Google and Others," *The Guardian,* June, 7, 2013.

38. See Clapper v. Amnesty Int'l, 568 U.S. 398 (2013).

39. Gross and Ní Aoláin, *Law in Times of Crisis,* 161.

40. "[T]he relationship between means and ends must govern the decisions. If, for the public official whose role has been authorized by the consent of the governed, anything else trumps this relationship, he or she should resign. A pacifist should not be asked (or allowed) to be a general." Philip Bobbitt, *Terror and Consent: The Wars for the Twenty-First Century* (New York: Knopf, 2008), 363. The possibility of bad-faith arguments to avoid responsibility is ever present, too. See, e.g., David E. Pozen, "Constitutional Bad Faith," *Harvard Law Review* 129 (2016): 934–39.

41. Hamdi v. Rumsfeld, 542 U.S. 507 (2004) (Scalia, J., dissenting)

42. See, e.g., David Barstow et al., "The Nuclear Card: The Aluminum Tube Story—A special report.; [sic] How White House Embraced Suspect Iraq Arms Intelligence," *New York Times,* October 3, 2004. President Bush's National Security Advisor, Condoleezza Rice, used this imagery on CNN, September 8, 2002. See Wolf Blitzer, "Search for the 'Smoking Gun,' " CNN.com, January 10, 2003.

43. Bruce Ackerman, *Before the Next Attack: Preserving Civil Liberties in an Age of Terrorism* (New Haven, Conn.: Yale University Press, 2006), 2.

44. Jeff Zeleny, "Obama Weighs Quick Undoing of Bush Policy," *New York Times,* November 8, 2008.

45. Richard A. Posner, *Law, Pragmatism, and Democracy* (Cambridge, Mass.: Harvard University Press, 2003), 296.

46. *Federalist* No. 48 (Madison), in *The Federalist Papers,* 309.

47. Ibid.

48. Jonathan Alter, "Time to Think About Torture," *Newsweek,* November 4, 2001.

49. Alan Dershowitz, *Why Terrorism Works: Understanding the Threat, Responding to the Challenge* (Chicago: R. R. Donnelley & Sons, 2002), 132–63.

50. See, e.g., Jim Rutenberg, "Torture Seeps into Discussion by News Media," *New York Times,* November 5, 2001; Mark Bowden, "The Dark Art of Interrogation," *Atlantic Monthly,* October 2003, 51.

51. "For the U.S., most cases for permitting harsh treatment of detainees on moral grounds begin with variants of the 'ticking time bomb' scenario." *Final Report of the Independent Panel to Review DoD Detention Operations* (the Schlesinger report), August 2004, in Mark Danner, *Torture and Truth: America, Abu Ghraib, and the War on Terror* (New York: New York Review Books, 2004), 401. A substantial academic literature criticizes use of the hypothetical (and torture). For one example, see Henry Shue, "Torture," *Philosophy and Public Affairs* 7 (1978): 141–42. For an excellent discussion of the moral dimensions of torture, see J. M. Bernstein, *Torture and Dignity: An Essay on Moral Injury* (Chicago: University of Chicago Press, 2015). See also Christopher Kutz, "Torture, Necessity, and Existential Politics," *California Law Review* 95 (2007) 235–76.

52. See Danner, "Torture and Truth," in *Torture and Truth*, 1–9; Danner, "The Logic of Torture," in *Torture and Truth*, 10–25. As Harold Koh observed, "[E]veryone seems to acknowledge that the U.S. government continues to torture. . . . Before, we treated torture as absolutely forbidden. Now, we accept that even as we speak, our government is engaged in a widespread set of shadowy cruel practices on ghost detainees held abroad." Harold Hongju Koh, "Can the President Be Torturer in Chief?," *Indiana Law Journal* 81 (2005): 1151.

53. Perhaps the most relevant to the threat of terrorism was the popular Fox network show 24. See Jane Mayer, "Whatever It Takes: The Politics of the Man Behind '24,' " *New Yorker*, February 19, 2007, 66; see also Teresa Wilz, "Torture's Tortured Cultural Roots," *Washington Post*, May 3, 2005, C1.

54. See generally Michael Ignatieff, *The Lesser Evil: Political Ethics in an Age of Terror* (Princeton N.J.: Princeton University Press, 2004); see also Cass R. Sunstein, *Laws of Fear: Beyond the Precautionary Principle* (New York: Cambridge University Press, 2005), 221 ("In imaginable circumstances, torture is indeed justifiable.").

55. The government implied that Peoria, Illinois, should be counted as a battlefield in the war on terror for purposes of the president's detention authority over "enemy combatants." Al-Marri v. Pucciarelli, 534 F.3d 213, 219–21 (4th Cir. 2008) (en banc).

56. "Terrorism was obviously not new with 9/11 . . . [;] what changed was the framework through which they were seen." Kim Lane Scheppele, "Law in a Time of Emergency: States of Exception and the Temptations of 9/11," *University of Pennsylvania Journal of Constitutional Law* 6 (2004): 1023.

57. See Ackerman, *Before the Next Attack*, 13–73, for the argument that neither crime nor war were sufficient models; John Yoo, "Courts at War," *Cornell Law Review* 91 (2006): 574 (terrorism is not merely a law enforcement problem). Another view is that government has adopted a "hybrid" model of war and crime. David Luban, "The War on Terrorism and the End of Human Rights," *Philosophy and Public Policy Quarterly* 22 (2002): 12.

58. President George W. Bush, "The State of the Union" (speech, January 20, 2004), The White House, https://georgewbush-whitehouse.archives.gov/stateoftheunion/2004/.

59. President George W. Bush, "President's Address to the Nation" (speech, September 11, 2006), The White House, https://georgewbush-whitehouse.archives.gov/news/releases/2006/09/20060911-3.html.

60. Alberto R. Gonzales, White House Counsel, to President George W. Bush, January 25, 2002, Decision Re: Application of the Geneva Convention on Prisoners of War to the Conflict with Al Qaeda and the Taliban, 2, https://nsarchive2.gwu.edu/NSAEBB/NSAEBB127/02.01.25.pdf.

61. On the campaign trail Barack Obama, then a senator, urged the need for a change in outlook: "That's what happens when we use 9/11 to scare up votes, and that's why we need to do more than end a war—we need to end the mindset that got us into war." Transcript, "Barack Obama's February 12 Speech," *New York Times*,

February 12, 2008, https://www.nytimes.com/2008/02/12/us/politics/12text-obama.html.

62. Michael D. Shear, "Obama Expresses Confidence in CIA Director," *New York Times,* August 1, 2014. See Senate Select Committee on Intelligence, *Committee Study of the Central Intelligence Agency's Detention and Interrogation Program* (December 13, 2012), https://fas.org/irp/congress/2014_rpt/ssci-rdi.pdf.

63. Shear, "Obama Expresses Confidence in CIA Director."

64. Prior to inauguration, President-Elect Obama expressed a "belief that we need to look forward as opposed to looking backwards" regarding accountability for torture. David Johnston and Charlie Savage, "Obama Reluctant to Look into Bush Programs," *New York Times,* January 11, 2009.

65. Scott Shane, "No Charges Filed on Harsh Tactics Used by the C.I.A.," *New York Times,* August 30, 2012.

66. The Obama administration argued that despite public knowledge of the "extraordinary rendition," litigating the issue would involve "state secrets." Mohamed v. Jeppesen Dataplan, Inc., 614 F.3d 1070 (9th Cir. 2010). See also El-Masri v. United States, 479 F.3d 296 (4th Cir. 2007). See generally Jane Mayer, "Outsourcing Torture: The Secret History of America's 'Extraordinary Rendition' Program," *New Yorker,* February 14, 2005.

67. Padilla v. Yoo, 678 F.3d 748 (9th Cir. 2012). Padilla was subject to prolonged isolation, sensory deprivation, stress positions, and other "torture light" techniques.

68. *Report of the Senate Select Committee on Intelligence, Committee Study of the Central Intelligence Agency's Detention and Interrogation Program,* December 9, 2014. See also Mark Mazzetti, "Panel Faults C.I.A. Over Brutality and Deceit in Terrorism Interrogations," *New York Times,* December 9, 2014.

69. See, e.g., Mark Mazzetti and Charlie Savage, "Leaked Draft of Executive Order Could Revive C.I.A. Prisons," *New York Times,* January 25, 2017.

70. See Nicholas Fandos, "Senate Confirms Gina Haspel to Lead C.I.A. Despite Torture Concerns," *New York Times,* May 17, 2018.

71. Jenna Johnson, "Trump Says 'Torture Works,' Backs Waterboarding and 'Much Worse,' " *Washington Post,* February 17, 2016.

72. For more on the importance of "substantive accountability" from external sources, see Kitrosser, *Reclaiming Accountability,* 41–66.

73. Filartiga v. Pena-Irala, 630 F.2d 876, 890 (2d Cir. 1980). See also Kadic v. Karadzic, 70 F.3d 232, 243 (2d Cir. 1995); Hilao v. Estate of Ferdinand Marcos, 25 F.3d 1467, 1475 (9th Cir. 1994) (stating that the right to be free from torture is a norm of *jus cogens*); Sosa v. Alvarez-Machain, 542 U.S. 692, 732 (2004).

74. International Covenant on Civil and Political Rights, art. 7, December 19, 1966, 999 U.N.T.S. 171.

75. Convention Against Torture and Other Cruel, Inhuman or Degrading Treatment or Punishment, art. 2, December 10, 1984, 108 Stat. 382, 85 U.N.T.S. 1465 [hereinafter "Convention Against Torture"].

76. Geneva Convention for the Amelioration of the Condition of the Wounded and Sick in Armed Forces in the Field, art. 3, § 1(a) and art. 12, August 12, 1947, 6 U.S.T. 3114, 75 U.N.T.S. 31; Geneva Convention Relative to the Protection of Civilian Persons in Time of War, art. 32, August 12, 1949, 6 U.S.T. 3516, 75 U.N.T.S. 287.

77. Convention Against Torture, art. 2.

78. See, e.g., Brown v. Mississippi, 297 U.S. 278, 286 (1936) (overturning convictions based on confessions elicited by torture).

79. Chavez v. Martinez, 538 U.S. 760, 796 (2003) (Kennedy, J., concurring in part and dissenting in part).

80. Statement on United Nations International Day in Support of Victims of Torture, in Public Papers of the Presidents of the United States: George W. Bush, bk. 1, January 1 to June 30, 2004 (June 26, 2004), 1141, https://www.govinfo.gov/content/pkg/PPP-2004-book1/pdf/PPP-2004-book1-doc-pg1141.pdf.

81. Jay S. Bybee, Assistant Attorney General, U.S. Department of Justice Office of Legal Counsel, to Alberto R. Gonzales, Counsel to the President, August 1, 2002, Re: Standards of Conduct for Interrogation Under 18 U.S.C. §§ 2340–2340A, at 31, https://www.justice.gov/olc/file/886061/download [hereinafter "Torture Memo"].

82. Ibid., 46.

83. Ronald W. Reagan National Defense Authorization Act for FY2005, 18 U.S.C. § 2340(1) (2004).

84. Convention Against Torture, entered into force June 26, 1987.

85. Torture Memo, 13.

86. Ibid., 31.

87. Jay S. Bybee, Assistant Attorney General, U.S. Department of Justice Office of Legal Counsel, to John Rizzo, Acting General Counsel of the Central Intelligence Agency, August 1, 2002, Re: Interrogation of al Qaeda Operative, https://www.justice.gov/sites/default/files/olc/legacy/2010/08/05/memo-bybee2002.pdf [hereinafter "Interrogation of Operative Memo"]. Later memos confirmed initial conclusions regarding "increased pressure." See Steven G. Bradbury, Principal Deputy Assistant Attorney General, to John A. Rizzo, Senior Deputy General Counsel, Central Intelligence Agency, May 30, 2005, Re: Application of United States Obligations Under Article 16 of the Convention Against Torture to Certain Techniques That May Be Used in the Interrogation of High Value al Qaeda Detainees, 37, https://www.justice.gov/sites/default/files/olc/legacy/2013/10/21/memo-bradbury2005.pdf [hereinafter "CAT High-Value Interrogation Memo"]. See also Steven G. Bradbury, Principal Deputy Assistant Attorney General, to John A. Rizzo, Senior Deputy General Counsel, Central Intelligence Agency, May 10, 2005, Re: Application of 18 U.S.C. §§ 2340–2340A to Certain Techniques That May Be Used in the Interrogation of a High Value al Qaeda Detainee, https://www.justice.gov/sites/default/files/olc/legacy/2013/10/21/memo-bradbury2005-2.pdf [hereinafter "Torture Statute Interrogation Techniques Memo"]. See generally Scott Shane, "Waterboarding Used 266 Times on 2 Suspects," *New York Times*, April 20, 2009, A1.

88. William J. Haynes, II, General Counsel, Department of Defense, to Donald Rumsfeld, Secretary of Defense, November 27, 2002, repr. in *The Torture Papers: The Road to Abu Ghraib*, ed. Karen J. Greenberg and Joshua L. Dratel (New York: Cambridge University Press, 2005), 236–37. For the public details of al-Qahtani's interrogation, see Adam Zagorin and Michael Duffy, "Inside the Interrogation of Detainee 063," *Time*, June 12, 2005. For an in-depth case analysis about the commission of war crimes, see Philippe Sands, *Torture Team: Rumsfeld's Memo and the Betrayal of American Values* (New York: Palgrave Macmillan, 2008).

89. See Mark Danner, "Donald Rumsfeld Revealed," *New York Review of Books*, January 9, 2014; Zagorin and Duffy, "Inside the Interrogation of Detainee 063."

90. Torture Statute Interrogation Techniques Memo, 1.

91. See Mark Mazzetti, "Report Provides New Details on C.I.A. Prisoner Abuse," *New York Times*, August 23, 2009; Central Intelligence Agency Inspector General, Special Review: Counterterrorism Detention and Interrogation Activities (September 2001–October 2003), May 7, 2004, https://www.nytimes.com/interactive/projects/documents/c-i-a-reports-on-interrogation-methods.

92. The Interrogation of Operative Memo accepts a number of factual claims made by the CIA about the physical and mental effects on Abu Zubaydah, leading Bybee to "conclude that on the facts in this case the use of these methods separately or a course of conduct," would not violate the antitorture statute. Interrogation of Operative Memo, 18.

93. See Charlie Savage, "C.I.A. Torture Left Scars on Guantánamo Prisoner's Psyche for Years," *New York Times*, March 17, 2017. See also Matt Apuzo et al., "U.S. Torture Leaves a Legacy of Detainees with Damaged Minds," *New York Times*, October 9, 2016, A1; Matt Apuzo and Sheri Fink, "Secret Documents Show a Tortured Prisoner's Descent," *New York Times*, November 12, 2016; Deborah Sontag, "Video Is a Window Into a Terror Suspect's Isolation," *New York Times*, December 4, 2006 (detailing effects on José Padilla).

94. David Stout and Scott Shane, "Cheney Defends Use of Harsh Interrogations," *New York Times*, February 7, 2008.

95. Quoted in Barton Gellman, *Angler: The Cheney Vice Presidency* (New York: Penguin Press, 2008), 160.

96. *Nightline: Cheney Roars Back* (ABC television broadcast, December 19, 2005), excerpt available at http://abcnews.go.com/Nightline/IraqCoverage/story?id=1419206 (interview by Terry Moran with Vice President Dick Cheney); see also Dan Eggen, "Cheney's Remarks Fuel Torture Debate," *Washington Post*, October 27, 2006, A9 (discussing the vice president's remarks that a "dunk in water" is a no-brainer).

97. Gellman, *Angler*, 178.

98. Scott Shane, "C.I.A. Chief Doubts Tactic to Interrogate Is Still Legal," *New York Times*, February 8, 2008, A9.

99. Pub. L. No. 109-148, § 1003, 119 Stat. 2680, 2739–40 (2005).

100. Presidential Statement on Signing the Department of Defense, Emergency Supplemental Appropriations to Address Hurricanes in the Gulf Mexico, and

Pandemic Influenza Act of 2006, 42 U.S.C. § 2000dd-0 (1) (West Supp. 2007), https://georgewbush-whitehouse.archives.gov/news/releases/2005/12/20051230-8.html.

101. "In the end, Mr. Bradbury's opinion delivered what the White House wanted: a statement that the standard imposed by Mr. McCain's Detainee Treatment Act would not force any change in the C.I.A.'s practices, according to officials familiar with the memo." Scott Shane, David Johnston, and James Risen, "Secret U.S. Endorsement of Severe Interrogations," *New York Times,* October 4, 2007, A1.

102. See, e.g., Rochin v. California, 342 U.S. 165 (1952).

103. CAT High-Value Interrogation Memo, 2–3.

104. Steven G. Bradbury, Principal Deputy Assistant Attorney General, U.S. Department of Justice Office of Legal Counsel, to John A. Rizzo, Senior Deputy General Counsel, Central Intelligence Agency, August 31, 2006, Re: Application of the Detainee Treatment Act to Conditions of Confinement at Central Intelligence Agency Detention Facilities, 1, https://www.justice.gov/sites/default/files/olc/legacy/2010/08/05/memo-rizzo2006.pdf.

105. CAT High-Value Interrogation Memo, 5.

106. President George W. Bush, "President Discusses Creation of Military Commissions to Try Suspected Terrorists," The White House, news release, September 6, 2006, http://georgewbush-whitehouse.archives.gov/news/releases/2006/09/20060906-3.html.

107. Oliver Wendell Holmes, "The Path of the Law," *Harvard Law Review* 10 (1897): 459. Holmes further explained, "A man who cares nothing for an ethical rule which is believed and practised [sic] by his neighbors is likely nevertheless to care a good deal to avoid being made to pay money, and will want to keep out of jail if he can." Ibid.

108. President Bush claimed that the administration's policies, including the practice of extraordinary rendition, in which "a small number of suspected terrorist leaders and operatives captured during the war have been held and questioned outside the United States, in a separate program operated by the Central Intelligence Agency," have been "subject to multiple legal reviews by the Department of Justice and CIA lawyers; they've determined it complied with our laws." "President Discusses Creation of Military Commissions," September 6, 2006, The White House, https://georgewbush-whitehouse.archives.gov/news/releases/2006/09/20060906-3.html.

109. Anthony Lewis, "Making Torture Legal," *New York Review of Books,* July 15, 2004, 4.

110. Jack Goldsmith, *The Terror Presidency: Law and Judgment Inside the Bush Administration* (New York: W. W. Norton, 2007), 144.

111. Hamdan v. Rumsfeld, 548 U.S. 557 (2006).

112. Jim Rutenberg and Sheryl Gay Stolberg, "Bush Says G.O.P. Rebels Are Putting the Nation at Risk," *New York Times,* September 16, 2006.

113. Matthew Rosenberg et al., "Gina Haspel Vows at Confirmation Hearing That She Would Not Allow Torture at C.I.A.," *New York Times,* May 9, 2018.

114. Posner, *Not a Suicide Pact*, 85–86.

115. Richard A. Posner, "Torture, Terrorism, and Interrogation," in *Torture: A Collection*, ed. Sanford Levinson (New York: Oxford University Press, 2005), 295.

116. See Elster, *Ulysses Unbound*, 1–87.

117. Posner and Vermeule, *Terror in the Balance*, 155.

118. See, e.g., Dershowitz, *Why Terrorism Works*, 140; Bob Brecher, *Torture and the Ticking Bomb* (Oxford: Blackwell Publishing, 2007), 1; Shue, "Torture," 142–43.

119. David Luban, "Liberalism, Torture, and the Ticking Bomb," *Virginia Law Review* 91 (2005): 1440–44.

120. By contrast, when we make judgments of guilt, it is highly relevant that the person judged guilty be the same person on whom we impose punishment.

121. See John Conroy, *Unspeakable Acts, Ordinary People: The Dynamics of Torture* (New York: Alfred A. Knopf, 2000), 92 (describing practices of torturing children to get relatives to talk). See also "Introduction," in *Consequentialism and Its Critics*, ed. Samuel Scheffler (New York: Oxford University Press, 1988), 3 (considering such a scenario of torturing a child, and concluding that "utilitarianism seems to imply not only that you may but that you *must* torture the child").

122. See Michael Ignatieff, *The Lesser Evil: Political Ethics in the Age of Terror* (Princeton, N.J.: Princeton University Press, 2004), 140–41.

123. Michael Walzer, "Political Action: The Problem of Dirty Hands," in *Torture: A Collection*, ed. Sanford Levinson (New York: Oxford University Press, 2005), 61. See also John T. Parry and Welsh S. White, "Interrogating Suspected Terrorists: Should Torture Be an Option?," *University of Pittsburgh Law Review* 63 (2002): 763–65.

124. Having introduced the ticking-bomb hypothetical, the variations multiply. See, e.g., Philippa Foot, "The Problem of Abortion and the Doctrine of Double Effect," *Oxford Review* 5 (1967): 15; see also Judith Thompson, "The Trolley Problem," *Yale Law Journal* 94 (1985): 1395–1401; Bernard Williams, *A Critique of Utilitarianism*, in J. J. C. Smart and Bernard Williams, *Utilitarianism: For and Against* (New York: Cambridge University Press, 1973), 75, 93.

125. Penalizing "guilt by association" through laws prohibiting "material support" for terrorists has become a new strategy in the "war on terror." See David Cole, "The New McCarthyism: Repeating History in the War on Terrorism," *Harvard Civil Rights–Civil Liberties Law Review* 38 (2003): 10.

126. See, e.g., Marcy Strauss, "The Lessons of Abu Ghraib," *Ohio State Law Journal* 66 (2005): 1271; Danner, *Torture and Truth*, 23–24.

127. See Shue, "Torture," 142–43.

128. Posner and Vermeule, *Terror in the Balance*, 200–203.

129. Posner and Vermeule argue on consequentialist grounds that torture should be allowed. "[T]he best presumption is that coercive interrogation . . . will be used, or not used, as circumstances warrant." Ibid., 203.

130. See Guido Calabresi and Philip Bobbitt, *Tragic Choices* (New York: W. W. Norton, 1978).

131. See Thomas P. Crocker and Michael Hodges, "Constitutions, Rule Following, and the Crisis of Constraint," *Legal Theory* 24 (2018): 3–39.

132. Ron Suskind, *The One Percent Doctrine: Deep Inside America's Pursuit of Its Enemies Since 9/11* (New York: Simon & Schuster, 2006), 150.

133. See, e.g., Martha Minow, "Which Question? Which Lie? Reflections on the Physician-Assisted Suicide Cases," *Supreme Court Review* 1997: 29–30. Here the idea is that once the issue of assisted suicide becomes permissible, the question "Ought I to seek assisted suicide?" also becomes normalized.

134. Rumsfeld's comments during a press conference have generated much commentary. See, e.g., Errol Morris, "The Certainty of Donald Rumsfeld (pt. 1)," *New York Times*, March 25, 2014.

135. There may be no morally acceptable common frame in which to resolve this dilemma. See Thomas Nagel, "War and Massacre," *Philosophy & Public Affairs* 1 (1972): 143–44.

136. Posner, *Not a Suicide Pact*, 158.

137. Posner suggests, "Even torture may sometimes be justified in the struggle against terrorism, but it should not be considered *legally* justified. A recurrent theme . . . is that a nonlegal law of necessity that would furnish a moral and political but not legal justification for acting in contravention of the Constitution may trump constitutional rights in extreme circumstances." Ibid., 12.

138. See generally Posner, *Not a Suicide Pact*; Richard A. Posner, *Law, Pragmatism, and Democracy* (Cambridge, Mass.: Harvard University Press, 2003).

139. Jeremy Waldron, "Torture and Positive Law: Jurisprudence for the White House," *Columbia Law Review* 105 (2005): 1722–23.

140. Ibid., 1723.

141. Ibid., 1726.

142. Brown v. Board of Education, 347 U.S. 483 (1954).

143. Waldron, "Torture and Positive Law," 1725; see also Ronald Dworkin, *Taking Rights Seriously* (London: Gerald Duckworth, 1977), 111 (noting that precedents also work when "the earlier decision exerts a gravitational force on later decisions").

144. Palko v. Connecticut, 302 U.S. 319, 325 (1937).

145. The Eighth Amendment, for example, protects "concepts of decency, human dignity, and precepts of civilization which we profess to possess." Hope v. Pelzer, 536 U.S. 730, 737 n.6 (2002).

146. Ingraham v. Wright, 430 U.S. 651, 665 (1977).

Chapter 5. Who Decides?

1. Robert H. Jackson, "Wartime Security and Liberty Under Law," *Buffalo Law Review* 1 (1951): 115.

2. Ibid., 116.

3. Ibid.

4. Abraham Lincoln, "Message to Congress in Special Session (July 4, 1861)," in *Collected Works of Abraham Lincoln,* vol. 4, ed. Roy P. Basler et al. (New Brunswick, N.J.: Rutgers University Press, 1953), 429.

5. By contrast, see Immanuel Kant, "On the Common Saying: 'This May Be True in Theory, But It Does Not Apply in Practice,' " trans. H. B. Nisbet, in *Kant: Political Writings,* ed. Hans Reiss (Cambridge: Cambridge University Press, 1970), 61–63. Kant comments, "Thus no-one can pretend to be practically versed in a branch of knowledge and yet treat theory with scorn, without exposing the fact that he is an ignoramus in his subject." Ibid., 62.

6. These are arguments we first encountered in chapter 2. See John C. Yoo, Deputy Assistant Attorney General, to Daniel J. Bryant, Assistant Attorney General, Office of Legislative Affairs, June 27, 2002, Re: Applicability of 18 U.S.C. § 4001(a) to Military Detention of United States Citizens, 10, https://www.justice.gov/sites/default/files/olc/legacy/2009/08/24/memodetentionuscitizens06272002.pdf.

7. President George W. Bush, "Remarks by the President to the United Nations General Assembly," U.N. Headquarters, New York (speech, November 10, 2001), The White House, https://georgewbush-whitehouse.archives.gov/news/releases/2001/11/20011110-3.html.

8. See Peter Baker, "Trump Declares a National Emergency and Provokes a Constitutional Clash," *New York Times,* February 15, 2019. National Emergencies Act, Pub. L. No. 94-412, 90 Stat. 1255 (1976) (codified in scattered sections of 50 U.S.C. 1601 et seq.).

9. By contrast, see John Yoo, *The Powers of War and Peace: The Constitution and Foreign Affairs After 9/11* (Chicago: University of Chicago Press, 2005).

10. President George W. Bush, "Address Before a Joint Session of the Congress on the State of the Union," January 20, 2004, The White House, https://georgewbush-whitehouse.archives.gov/stateoftheunion/2004/.

11. See, e.g., Stephen M. Griffin, *Long Wars and the Constitution* (Cambridge, Mass.: Harvard University Press, 2013).

12. Mary L. Dudziak, *War Time: An Idea, Its History, Its Consequences* (New York: Oxford University Press, 2013).

13. Bruce Ackerman, *Before the Next Attack: Preserving Civil Liberties in an Age of Terrorism* (New Haven, Conn.: Yale University Press, 2006). See also Mary Ellen O'Connell, "The Choice of Law Against Terrorism," *Journal of National Security Law & Policy* 4 (2010): 343–68.

14. Roberto Mangabeira Unger, *False Necessity: Anti-Necessitarian Social Theory in the Service of Radical Democracy* (New York: Verso, 2004).

15. We discussed this dynamic in the prior chapter: "When that crisis occurs, the actions that are taken depend on the ideas that are lying around." Milton Friedman, *Capitalism and Freedom* (Chicago: University of Chicago Press, 2002), xiv. This dynamic also implicates questions of good or bad faith. See David E. Pozen, "Constitutional Bad Faith," *Harvard Law Review* 129 (2016): 934–39.

16. This claim is repeated in a number of Department of Justice memos, including John C. Yoo, Deputy Assistant Attorney General, U.S. Department of Justice Of-

fice of Legal Counsel, and John C. Delahunty, Special Counsel, Memorandum for Alberto R. Gonzales, Counsel to the President, October 23, 2001, Re: Authority for Use of Military Force to Combat Terrorist Activities Within the United States, 4, https://www.justice.gov/sites/default/files/opa/legacy/2009/03/09/memomilitaryforcecombatus10232001.pdf.

17. Cass R. Sunstein, "Minimalism at War," *Supreme Court Review* 2004: 47–109.

18. See Dan M. Kahan, "The Cognitively Illiberal State," *Stanford Law Review* 60 (2007): 115.

19. See Dan M. Kahan et al., " 'They Saw a Protest': Cognitive Illiberalism and the Speech-Conduct Distinction," *Stanford Law Review* 64 (2012): 851–906. What one sees can also be a matter of good or bad faith. See Pozen, "Constitutional Bad Faith," 934–39.

20. William James, *Pragmatism*, ed. Bruce Kuklick (Indianapolis, Ind.: Hackett, 1907), 8.

21. Ibid.

22. Richard A. Posner, *Not a Suicide Pact: The Constitution in a Time of National Emergency* (New York: Oxford University Press, 2006), 24–25.

23. Alberto R. Gonzales to the President of the United States, January 25, 2002, Decision Re: Application of the Geneva Convention on Prisoners of War to the Conflict with al Qaeda and the Taliban, https://nsarchive2.gwu.edu/NSAEBB/NSAEBB127/02.01.25.pdf.

24. Ibid.

25. Geneva Convention Relative to the Treatment of Prisoners of War, art. 3, August 12, 1949, 6 U.S.T. 3316, 75 U.N.T.S. 135.

26. Brief for Respondents at 38, Hamdan v. Rumsfeld, 548 U.S. 557 (2006) (No. 05-184).

27. Geneva Convention Relative to the Treatment of Prisoners of War, art. 3.

28. For administrative deference, see Chevron, U.S.A., Inc. v. Natural Resources Defense Council, Inc., 467 U.S. 837, 842–45 (1984).

29. Jeremy Waldron, *Torture, Terror, and Trade-Offs: Philosophy for the White House* (New York: Oxford University Press, 2010), 111; see also David Cole and Jules Lobel, *Less Safe, Less Free: Why America Is Losing the War on Terror* (New York: The New Press, 2007), 17.

30. James B. Comey, "Fighting Terrorism and Preserving Civil Liberties," *University of Richmond Law Review* 40 (2006): 403.

31. Eric A. Posner and Adrian Vermeule, *Terror in the Balance: Security, Liberty, and the Courts* (New York: Oxford University Press, 2007), 158.

32. Posner, *Not a Suicide Pact*, 147; Posner and Vermeule, *Terror in the Balance*, 12.

33. Posner and Vermeule, *Terror in the Balance*, 16.

34. Ibid., 47.

35. I am borrowing this way of analyzing the relation between principles from John Rawls, *A Theory of Justice*, rev. ed. (Cambridge, Mass.: Harvard University Press, 1999): 214–20. For the argument that security is the necessary condition for the possibility of liberty, see Henry Shue, *Basic Rights: Subsistence, Affluence, and U.S. Foreign Policy* (Princeton, N.J.: Princeton University Press, 1980), 21–22.

36. The Pareto frontier "identifies a range of points at which no win-win improvements are possible: any change in policies that makes A better off must make B worse off." Posner and Vermeule, *Terror in the Balance*, 26.

37. Jeremy Waldron makes a related point about the fact that "liberty could be a matter of more or less." Waldron, *Torture, Terror, and Trade-Offs*, 30.

38. Although the distribution of burdens under a trade-off can produce inequalities—often the lost liberties are those of others, as David Cole suggests—the equivocation occurs in treating all liberties alike. See David Cole, *Enemy Aliens: Double Standards and Constitutional Freedoms in the War on Terrorism* (New York: The New Press, 2003), 21.

39. See Williamson v. Lee Optical of Okla., Inc., 348 U.S. 483, 487–88 (1955); United States v. Carolene Prods. Co., 304 U.S. 144, 152 (1938).

40. See Loving v. Virginia, 388 U.S. 1, 11 (1967); Griswold v. Connecticut, 381 U.S. 479, 497 (1965) (Goldberg, J., concurring).

41. Stephen Holmes notes that the selective focus on liberty has an additional partisan political valence, as "[a]dvocates of unconstrained executive discretion . . . selectively emphasize some forms of liberty while neglecting others, effectively advocating a sharp reduction of the liberties prized by their liberal opponents, while passing over in silence the liberties dear to conservatives." Stephen Holmes, "In Case of Emergency: Misunderstanding Tradeoffs in the War on Terror," *California Law Review* 97 (2009): 314.

42. Posner and Vermeule, *Terror in the Balance*, 31.

43. As Balkin notes, "The content and features of the constitutional system are constantly changing." Jack M. Balkin, *Constitutional Redemption: Political Faith in an Unjust World* (Cambridge, Mass.: Harvard University Press, 2011), 62.

44. See Sanford Levinson, *Constitutional Faith* (Princeton, N.J.: Princeton University Press, 1988). See also Reva Siegel, "Constitutional Culture, Social Movement Conflict and Constitutional Change: The Case of the de facto ERA," *California Law Review* 94 (2006), 1327.

45. Posner, *Not a Suicide Pact*, 158.

46. See ibid., 40.

47. See Ronald Dworkin, "Rights as Trumps," in *Theories of Rights*, ed. Jeremy Waldron (New York: Oxford University Press, 1984), 153–67.

48. Richard Posner writes, "It is true that in the present setting [the risks and harms] cannot be quantified." Posner, *Not a Suicide Pact*, 41.

49. Ackerman, *Before the Next Attack*, 170–71.

50. Posner and Vermeule simply state, "The claim that security and liberty trade off against one another implies that respecting civil liberties often has real costs in the form of reduced security." Posner and Vermeule, *Terror in the Balance*, 24.

51. Posner, *Not a Suicide Pact*, 24.

52. See Aziz Rana, "Who Decides on Security?," *Connecticut Law Review* 44 (2012): 3–9.

53. See, e.g., Posner and Vermeule, *Terror in the Balance*, 26–38.

54. The deferential view . . . rests on "a claim about relative institutional competence." Ibid., 17.
55. Ibid., 5.
56. Ibid., 31.
57. Posner, *Not a Suicide Pact*, 51.
58. Posner and Vermeule, *Terror in the Balance*, 24.
59. See Dennis E. Curtis and Judith Resnik, "Images of Justice," *Yale Law Journal* 96 (1986): 1729–33.
60. Posner, *Not a Suicide Pact*, 47. The philosopher Henry Shue makes a similar point: "Being physically secure is a necessary condition for the exercise of any other right." Shue, *Basic Rights*, 21–22.
61. Posner and Vermeule, *Terror in the Balance*, 27.
62. Posner, *Not a Suicide Pact*, v.
63. Posner and Vermeule, *Terror in the Balance*, 24.
64. *Federalist* No. 70 (Hamilton), in *The Federalist Papers*, ed. Clinton Rossiter (New York: New American Library, 1961), 424.
65. See, e.g., The Prize Cases, 67 U.S (2 Black) 635, 670 (1863); United States v. Curtiss-Wright Export Corp., 299 U.S. 304, 319–20 (1936).
66. Holder v. Humanitarian Law Project, 561 U.S. 1, 34 (2010).
67. Rana, "Who Decides," 1451–58. This genealogy cuts across the political divide, finding advocates for expanded executive power among both progressives and conservatives. Stephen Skowronek, "The Conservative Insurgency and Presidential Power: A Developmental Perspective on the Unitary Executive," *Harvard Law Review* 122 (2009): 2074–75.
68. A consequence of the shifting meanings of "national security," Rana observes, is that "[t]he modern security discourse presented an image of politics marked by uncertainty, public ignorance, and the near continuous condition of threat or crisis." Rana, "Who Decides," 1458.
69. Posner and Vermeule, *Terror in the Balance*, 31.
70. On the part of consternation, see, e.g., Bruce Ackerman, *The Decline and Fall of the American Republic* (Cambridge, Mass.: Harvard University Press, 2010), 11; see also Harold Hongju Koh, *The National Security Constitution: Sharing Power After the Iran-Contra Affair* (New Haven, Conn.: Yale University Press, 1990), 7–8. On the part of commendation, see, e.g., Eric A. Posner and Adrian Vermeule, *The Executive Unbound: After the Madisonian Republic* (New York: Oxford University Press, 2010), 14–15. See also Yoo, *The Powers of War and Peace*, 13. On the influence of emergencies, see, e.g., Kim Lane Scheppele, "Exceptions that Prove the Rule: Embedding Emergency Government in Everyday Constitutional Life," in *The Limits of Constitutional Democracy*, ed. Jeffrey K. Tulis and Stephen Macedo (Princeton, N.J.: Princeton University Press, 2010), 143.
71. John Hart Ely, *Democracy and Distrust: A Theory of Judicial Review* (Cambridge, Mass.: Harvard University Press, 1980), 73–104 (arguing courts should reinforce democratic representation).

72. See Bruce Ackerman, *We the People: Transformations*, vol. 2 (Cambridge, Mass.: Harvard University Press, 1998), 384; Larry D. Kramer, *The People Themselves: Popular Constitutionalism and Judicial Review* (New York: Oxford University Press, 2004), 8; "Security subsists, too, in fidelity to freedom's first principles." Boumediene v. Bush, 553 U.S. 723, 797 (2008); "Whatever power the United States Constitution envisions for the Executive in its exchanges with other nations or with enemy organizations in times of conflict, it most assuredly envisions a role for all three branches when individual liberties are at stake." Hamdi v. Rumsfeld, 542 U.S. 507, 536 (2004).

73. U.S. Const. pmbl.

74. *Federalist* No. 37 (Madison), in *The Federalist Papers*, 227.

75. *Federalist* No. 51 (Madison), in *The Federalist Papers*, 321.

76. Ibid., 323.

77. Ibid., 321.

78. Ibid., 323.

79. *Federalist* No. 10 (Madison), in *The Federalist Papers*, 83.

80. *Federalist* No. 48 (Madison), in *The Federalist Papers*, 308; ibid., 313.

81. *Federalist* No. 1 (Hamilton), in *The Federalist Papers*, 35; *Federalist* No. 51 (Madison), in *The Federalist Papers*, 324; U.S. Const. pmbl.

82. U.S. Const. art. I, § 8, cl. 11–15; U.S. Const. art. II, § 2, cl. 1.

83. See Daryl J. Levinson, "Parchment and Politics: The Positive Puzzle of Constitutional Commitment," *Harvard Law Review* 124 (2011): 671 ("Madison's theory of constitutional design was thus incomplete, and in some important respects mistaken."); see also Posner and Vermeule, *Executive Unbound*, 17 ("Madisonian separation of powers is obsolete."). But see Peter M. Shane, *Madison's Nightmare: How Executive Power Threatens American Democracy* (Chicago: University of Chicago Press, 2009), 5; Josh Chafetz, "The Political Animal and the Ethics of Constitutional Commitment," *Harvard Law Review Forum* 124 (2011): 9.

84. See, e.g., Sunstein, "Minimalism at War," 76.

85. See Adrian Vermeule, "Our Schmittian Administrative Law," *Harvard Law Review* 122 (2009): 1133; Josh Chafetz, "Congress's Constitution," *University of Pennsylvania Law Review* 160 (2012): 723.

86. See Posner and Vermeule, *Executive Unbound*, 25–29.

87. Levinson, "Parchment and Politics," 729.

88. See, e.g., War Powers Resolution of 1973, Pub. L. No. 93-148, 87 Stat. 555 (1973) (codified at 50 U.S.C. 1541–48 (2006)); National Emergencies Act, Pub. L. No. 94-412, 90 Stat. 1255 (1976) (codified in scattered sections of 50 U.S.C.); Inspector General Act of 1978, Pub. L. No. 95-452, Stat. 1101 (1978) (codified at 5 U.S.C. app. § 466–98 (2006)).

89. Ex parte Milligan, 71 U.S. (4 Wall.) 2, 63 (1866).

90. See Brandenburg v. Ohio, 395 U.S. 444, 447 (1969); NAACP v. Alabama, 357 U.S. 449, 461 (1958); Griswold v. Connecticut, 381 U.S. 479, 484 (1965); Loving v. Virginia, 388 U.S. 1, 12 (1967).

91. Even deferential holdings during wartime reviewed whether executive decisions adequately safeguarded individual liberties. See Ex parte Quirin, 317 U.S. 1, 21 (1942).

92. Boumediene v. Bush, 553 U.S. 723 (2008); 548 U.S. 557 (2006).

93. Korematsu v. United States, 323 U.S. 214, 223–24 (1944).

94. Ibid., 216.

95. Trump v. Hawaii, 138 S. Ct. 2392, 2423 (2018).

96. Jack Goldsmith, *Power and Constraint: The Accountable Presidency After 9/11* (New York: W. W. Norton, 2012), xvi.

97. Hamdi v. Rumsfeld, 542 U.S. 507, 530 (2004).

98. "The word 'security' is a broad, vague generality whose contours should not be invoked to abrogate the fundamental law embodied in the First Amendment." New York Times v. United States, 403 U.S. 713, 719 (1971).

99. See Sunstein, "Minimalism at War."

100. David Dyzenhaus, *The Constitution of Law: Legality in a Time of Emergency* (Cambridge: Cambridge University Press, 2006), 3; Vermeule, "Our Schmittian Constitution," 1135.

101. See Elena Kagan, "Presidential Administration," *Harvard Law Review* 114 (2001): 2248; Youngstown Sheet & Tube Co. v. Sawyer, 343 U.S. 579, 650 (1952) (Jackson, J., concurring).

102. See Kim Lane Scheppele, "Small Emergencies," *Georgia Law Review* 40 (2006): 836.

103. Vice President Cheney made clear that "it's going to be vital for us to use any means at our disposal, basically, to achieve our objective." Ron Suskind, *The One Percent Doctrine: Deep Inside America's Pursuit of Its Enemies Since 9/11* (New York: Simon & Schuster, 2006), 18.

104. President Barack Obama, "Remarks by the President on National Security" (speech, May 21, 2009), The White House, https://obamawhitehouse.archives.gov/the-press-office/remarks-president-national-security-5-21-09.

105. *Federalist* No. 8 (Hamilton), in *The Federalist Papers*, 67.

106. *Hamdi*, 542 U.S. at 536.

107. See United States v. Curtiss-Wright Export Corp., 299 U.S. 304, 319 (1936). The Court explained, "In this vast external realm [of foreign affairs], with its important, complicated, delicate and manifold problems, the President alone has the power to speak or listen as a representative of the nation." See also Curtis A. Bradley and Jack L. Goldsmith, "Congressional Authorization and the War on Terrorism," *Harvard Law Review* 118 (2005): 2086. They argue, "The President has significant concurrent constitutional authority in the foreign affairs (and especially the war powers) field."

108. Franklin D. Roosevelt, "Message to the Congress on the State of the Union," January 11, 1944, in *The Public Papers and Addresses of Franklin D. Roosevelt*, comp. Samuel I. Rosenman, vol. 13 (1944–1945) (New York: Harper & Brothers, 1950), 41, 33. Roosevelt further argued, "individual freedom cannot exist without economic security and independence." Ibid., 41.

109. Ian Loader and Neil Walker, *Civilizing Security* (Cambridge: Cambridge University Press, 2007), 195–233.

110. Jackson, "Wartime Security," 116.

Chapter 6. Presidential Power and Constitutional Responsibility

1. See generally Gary Lawson and Guy Seidman, "The First 'Incorporation' Debate," in *The Louisiana Purchase and American Expansion, 1803–1898,* ed. Sanford Levinson and Bartholomew H. Sparrow (Lanham, Md.: Rowman & Littlefield, 2010), 20–21.

2. Jefferson wrote, "Our confederation is certainly confined to the limits established by the revolution. The general government has no powers but such as the constitution has given it; and it has not given it a power of holding foreign territory, & still less of incorporating it into the Union." Thomas Jefferson to John Dickinson, August 9, 1803, in *The Papers of Thomas Jefferson,* vol. 41, ed. Barbara B. Oberg (Princeton, N.J.: Princeton University Press, 2014), 170.

3. Thomas Jefferson to John C. Breckinridge, August 12, 1803, in *The Papers of Thomas Jefferson,* vol. 41, 186 (emphasis original).

4. Thomas Jefferson to John B. Colvin, September 20, 1810, in *The Papers of Thomas Jefferson: Retirement Series,* vol. 3, ed. J. Jefferson Looney (Princeton, N.J.: Princeton University Press, 2006), 99 (emphasis original).

5. Ibid.

6. Thomas Jefferson to William Cary Nicholas, September 7, 1803, in *The Papers of Thomas Jefferson,* vol. 41, 347.

7. Authorization for Use of Military Force, Pub. L. No. 107-40, § 2, 115 Stat. 224, 224 (2001) [hereinafter AUMF, 2001].

8. Ibid.

9. Continuation of the National Emergency with Respect to Certain Terrorist Attacks, 75 Fed. Reg. 55,658, 55,661 (September 13, 2010); Continuation of the National Emergency with Respect to Certain Terrorist Attacks, 83 Fed. Reg. 46,067 (September 12, 2018).

10. John C. Yoo, Deputy Assistant Attorney General, U.S. Department of Justice Office of Legal Counsel, Memorandum for Alberto R. Gonzales, Counsel to the President, October 23, 2001, Re: Authority for Use of Military Force to Combat Terrorist Activities Within the United States, 4 [hereinafter "Military Force Memo"], http://www.justice.gov/olc/docs/memomilitaryforcecombatus10232001.pdf.

11. Hamdi v. Rumsfeld, 542 U.S. 507, 580 (2004) (Thomas, J., dissenting).

12. Jay S. Bybee, Assistant Attorney General, U.S. Department of Justice Office of Legal Counsel, to Alberto R. Gonzales, Counsel to the President, August 1, 2002, Re: Standards of Conduct for Interrogation Under 18 U.S.C. §§ 2340–2340A, 36–37, https://www.justice.gov/olc/file/886061/download [hereinafter "Torture Memo"].

13. Letter from William E. Moschella, Assistant Attorney General, U.S. Department of Justice, to Chairman Pat Roberts, Senate Select Committee on Intelligence,

December 22, 2005, https://www.justice.gov/sites/default/files/ag/legacy/2007/01/11/surveillance6.pdf.

14. Jefferson to Nichols, in *The Papers of Thomas Jefferson*, 10.

15. *Federalist* No. 57 (Madison), in *The Federalist Papers*, ed. Clinton Rossiter (New York: New American Library, 1961), 350.

16. *Federalist* No. 10 (Madison), in *The Federalist Papers*, 80.

17. Ibid., 84.

18. *Federalist* No. 51 (Madison), in *The Federalist Papers*, 321.

19. Ibid., 322.

20. See Daryl J. Levinson, "Empire-Building Government in Constitutional Law," *Harvard Law Review* 118 (2005): 951; Daryl J. Levinson and Richard H. Pildes, "Separation of Parties, Not Powers," *Harvard Law Review* 119 (2006): 2317.

21. See Gordon S. Wood, *The Creation of the American Republic, 1776–1787* (Chapel Hill, N.C.: University of North Carolina Press, 1969), 65–70. The founders believed that "The strength and spring of every free government, is the virtue of the people"; ibid., 120 (Wood quoting Moses Mather, *America's Appeal to the Impartial World* [Hartford, Conn.: Ebenezer Watson, 1775, 67]).

22. Jonathan Elliot, comp., *The Debates in the Several State Conventions on the Adoption of the Federal Constitution*, vol. 3 (Indianapolis: Liberty Fund Press, repr., 1996, 2d ed. 1836), 536–37.

23. These requirements of virtue were not uncontested. See Aziz Rana, *The Two Faces of American Freedom* (Cambridge, Mass.: Harvard University Press, 2010), 121–29.

24. *Federalist* No. 70 (Hamilton), in *The Federalist Papers*, 423.

25. Regarding truthfulness, see, e.g., Glenn Kessler, "A Year of Unprecedented Deception: Trump Averaged 15 False Claims a Day in 2018," *Washington Post*, December 30, 2018; regarding lack of respect for coordinate branches, see Donald Trump, Twitter post, February 5, 2017, 12:39 p.m., https://twitter.com/realdonaldtrump/status/828342202174668800?lang=en., and Charlie Savage, "Trump Vows Stonewall of 'All' House Subpoenas, Setting Up Fight Over Powers," *New York Times*, April 24, 2019; regarding obstruction, see U.S. Department of Justice, Special Counsel Robert S. Mueller III, *Report on the Investigation Into Russian Interference in the 2016 Presidential Election*, March 2019, https://www.justice.gov/storage/report.pdf; Charlie Savage, "Did Trump Obstruct Justice? Mueller Didn't Say, but Left a Trail to the Answer," *New York Times*, April 23, 2019; Carol D. Leonnig, Devlin Barrett, and Josh Dawsey, "Mueller Laid Out 'Thorough and Compelling' Case of Obstruction, but Barr Decided Trump Wasn't Guilty of a Crime," *Washington Post*, April 18, 2019.

26. See Daniel Hemel and Eric Posner, "The Surprising Place Mueller Found Resistance to Trump," *New York Times*, April 23, 2019; Anonymous, "I Am Part of the Resistance Inside the Trump Administration," *New York Times*, September 5, 2018.

27. See Rachael Bade and Tom Hamburger, "House Democrats Grapple with How to Respond to Trump's Refusal to Cooperate with Investigations," *Washington Post*, April 25, 2019.

28. See, e.g., Ashley Parker, Rosalind S. Helderman, and Matt Zapotosky, "Stymied by Aides, Trump Sought Out Loyalist to Curtail Special Counsel—and Drew Mueller's Glare," *Washington Post*, April 25, 2018; Michael S. Schmidt, "Comey Memo Says Trump Asked Him to End Flynn Investigation," *New York Times*, May 16, 2017; Michael S. Schmidt, "In a Private Dinner, Trump Demanded Loyalty. Comey Demurred," *New York Times*, May 11, 2017.

29. Bruce Ackerman warned of institutional decline through failure to preserve republican values, "most notably, the threat posed by the transformation of the White House into a platform for charismatic extremism and bureaucratic lawlessness," in *The Decline and Fall of the American Republic* (New Haven, Conn.: Yale University Press, 2010), 11.

30. See Military Force Memo, 4; U.S. Department of Justice white paper, *Lawfulness of a Lethal Operation Directed Against a U.S. Citizen Who Is a Senior Operational Leader of Al Qa'ida or an Associated Force* (November 8, 2011), 1, https://fas.org/irp/eprint/doj-lethal.pdf. In this white paper, the Obama administration echoed prior Bush-era arguments, reasoning regarding extrajudicial killing of a U.S. citizen that "The President has authority to respond to the imminent threat posed by al-Qa'ida and its associated forces, arising from his constitutional responsibility to protect the country." Ibid.

31. See Richard H. Fallon, Jr., "Constitutional Constraints," *California Law Review* 97 (2009): 979.

32. This thought echoes Alasdair MacIntyre's conception of a practice. See Alasdair MacIntyre, *After Virtue* (Notre Dame, Ind.: Notre Dame University Press, 1981 [1850]), 191. He writes, "A virtue is an acquired human quality the possession and the exercise of which tends to enable us to achieve those goods which are internal to practices and the lack of which effectively prevents us from achieving any such goods."

33. Abraham Lincoln, "Message to Congress in Special Session (July 4, 1861)," in *Collected Works of Abraham Lincoln*, vol. 4, ed. Roy P. Basler et al. (New Brunswick, N.J.: Rutgers University Press, 1953), 426.

34. *Federalist* No. 70 (Hamilton), in *The Federalist Papers*, 424, 426.

35. Ibid., 423.

36. Lincoln, "Message to Congress (July 4, 1861)," 426.

37. U.S. Const. art. II, § 1, cl. 8; see Paul Horwitz, "Honor's Constitutional Moment: The Oath and Presidential Transitions," *Northwestern University Law Review* 103 (2009): 1068.

38. U.S. Const. art. II, § 1, cl. 8.

39. President George Washington acknowledged this binding in his short second inaugural address: "That if it shall be found during my administration of the Government I have in any instance violated willingly or knowingly the injunctions thereof, I may (besides incurring constitutional punishment) be subject to the upbraidings of all who are now witnesses of the present solemn ceremony." George Washington, "Second Inaugural Address of George Washington," The Avalon Project, 1973, http://avalon.law.yale.edu/18th_century/art2.asp. See gen-

erally Corey Brettschneider, *The Oath and the Office: A Guide to the Constitution for Future Presidents* (New York: W. W. Norton, 2018), ix–xxvi.

40. U.S. Const. art. II, § 3.

41. Ibid., art. II, §§ 1, 3.

42. One presidential version holds, "The widest power and the broadest duty which the President has is conferred and imposed by the Take Care Clause." William Howard Taft, *Our Chief Magistrate and His Powers*, ed. H. Jefferson Powell (London: Forgotten Books, 2002 [1916]), 78. Justice Oliver Wendell Holmes states the minimalist, almost tautological, view of the Take Care Clause succinctly: "The duty of the President to see that the laws be executed is a duty that does not go beyond the laws or require him to achieve more than Congress sees fit to leave within his power." Myers v. United States, 272 U.S. 52, 177 (1926) (Holmes, J., dissenting); see also Lawrence Lessig and Cass R. Sunstein, "The President and the Administration," *Columbia Law Review* 94 (1994): 61–70.

43. U.S. Const. art. II, § 3.

44. U.S. Const. art. I, § 8, cl. 18.

45. *In re* Neagle, 135 U.S. 1, 64 (1890).

46. Youngstown Sheet & Tube Co. v. Sawyer, 343 U.S. 579, 587 (1952).

47. Torture Memo, 38. Nor does the memo's citation to *The Brig Amy Warwick* (*The Prize Cases*), 67 U.S. (2 Black) 635, 670 (1862), support the claim that the president has "complete discretion" in exercising presidential powers. In *The Prize Cases*, the Court discussed the president's power to decide under the laws of war who was an enemy belligerent. The Court made no general claim about the president's discretion under the commander-in-chief power. Moreover, examination of other liberal democracies reveals consistent constraint of executive discretion, even in emergencies. See Jenny S. Martinez, "Inherent Executive Power: A Comparative Perspective," *Yale Law Journal* 115 (2006): 2495.

48. John Adams to Abigail Adams, July 3, 1776, in *My Dearest Friend, Letters of Abigail and John Adams*, ed. Margaret A. Hogan and C. James Taylor (Cambridge, Mass.: Belknap Press of Harvard University Press, 2007), 121, 123.

49. Something like Ronald Dworkin's Herculean judge may provide a rough guide here, whereby any interpretation "must fit and justify the most basic arrangements of political power in the community." Ronald Dworkin, *Law's Empire* (Cambridge, Mass.: Belknap Press of Harvard University Press, 1986), 380. See also, David E. Pozen, "Constitutional Bad Faith," *Harvard Law Review* 129 (2016): 885–955.

50. Ibid., 211.

51. On the significance of constitutional culture, see Robert C. Post, "Foreword: Fashioning the Legal Constitution: Culture, Courts, and Law," *Harvard Law Review*, 117 (2003): 76; Reva B. Siegel, "Constitutional Culture, Social Movement Conflict and Constitutional Change: The Case of the De Facto ERA," *California Law Review* 94 (2006): 1342.

52. There is much contemporaneous reporting on Trump's campaign-style rallies, where the focus is himself and his boasts, his preference for appealing to the

viewership of a particular cable news network, and his use of Twitter to personalize both domestic and foreign policy. See, e.g., Jenna Johnson, " 'Life Is a Campaign': After a Difficult First Month, Trump Returns to His Comfort Zone," *Washington Post,* February 18, 2017; Jane Mayer, "The Making of the Fox News White House," *New Yorker,* March 4, 2019; Michael McFaul, "Why Trump's Personalized Approach to Diplomacy Is Bad for America," *Washington Post,* June 28, 2018.

53. By April 2019, Trump had tweeted the phrase "witch hunt" in excess of 190 times, most often in reference to the Mueller investigation. To cite one example after the report was issued: "The end result of the greatest Witch Hunt in U.S. political history is No Collusion with Russia (and No Obstruction). Pretty Amazing!" Donald Trump, Twitter post, April 20, 2019, 7:15 a.m. Trump also called out the judiciary for blocking his Muslim "travel ban": "Just cannot believe a judge would put our country in such peril. If something happens blame him and court system. People pouring in. Bad!" Donald Trump, Twitter post, February 5, 2017, 12:39 p.m., https://twitter.com/realdonaldtrump/status/828342202174668800?lang=en.

54. "No Collusion, No Obstruction, Complete and Total EXONERATION. KEEP AMERICA GREAT!" Donald Trump, Twitter post, March 24, 2019, 3:42 p.m.

55. Jay S. Bybee, Assistant Attorney General, U.S. Department of Justice Office of Legal Counsel, to Alberto R. Gonzales, Counsel to the President, August 1, 2002, Re: Standards of Conduct for Interrogation Under 18 U.S.C. §§ 2340–2340A, at 1, https://www.justice.gov/olc/file/886061/download.

56. Ibid.

57. Ibid., 31.

58. See Cesare Beccaria, *On Crimes and Punishments,* trans. David Young (Indianapolis, Ind.: Hackett Publishing, 1986 [1764]), 29. See generally Lynn Hunt, *Inventing Human Rights* (New York: W. W. Norton, 2007). On the role of constraints in execution, see Dawn E. Johnsen, "Faithfully Executing the Laws: Internal Legal Constraints on Executive Power," *UCLA Law Review* 54 (2007): 1583.

59. Among the critics, see, e.g., David Luban, *Torture, Power, and the Law* (New York: Cambridge University Press, 2014); Harold Hongju Koh, "Can the President Be Torturer in Chief?," *Indiana Law Journal* 81 (2006): 1155–56; Jeremy Waldron, "Torture and Positive Law: Jurisprudence for the White House," *Columbia Law Review* 105 (2005): 1681–1750; Sanford Levinson, " 'Precommitment' and 'Postcommitment' ": The Ban on Torture in the Wake of September 11," *Texas Law Review* 81 (2003): 2017.

60. The Department of Justice eventually withdrew and replaced the Bybee/Yoo Torture Memo, along with others. See Memorandum from David J. Barron, Acting Assistant Attorney General, U.S. Department of Justice Office of Legal Counsel, to the Attorney General, Withdrawal of Office of Legal Counsel CIA Interrogation Opinions, April 15, 2009, 1, https://www.justice.gov/file/18511/download.

61. See Curtis A. Bradley and Eric A. Posner, "Presidential Signing Statements and Executive Power," *Constitutional Commentary* 23 (2006): 310.

62. American Bar Association, *Task Force on Presidential Signing Statements and the Separation of Powers Doctrine,* report (August, 2006), 5, https://www.americanbar.org/content/dam/aba/publishing/abanews/1273179616signstatereport.authcheckdam.pdf. Charlie Savage, "Bush Challenges Hundreds of Laws: President Cites Powers of His Office," *Boston Globe,* April 30, 2006, A1. The internal justification for this practice is contained in Memorandum from Walter Dellinger, Assistant Attorney General, U.S. Department of Justice Office of Legal Counsel, to Bernard N. Nussbaum, Counsel to the President, Re: The Legal Significance of Signing Statements (November 3, 1993), https://www.justice.gov/file/20446/download.

63. President George W. Bush, "President's Statement on Signing of H.R. 2863, the Department of Defense, Emergency Supplemental Appropriations to Address Hurricanes in the Gulf of Mexico, and Pandemic Influenza Act, 2006," in Public Papers of the Presidents of the United States: George W. Bush, bk. 2 (December 30, 2005), 1902, https://www.govinfo.gov/content/pkg/PPP-2005-book2/pdf/PPP-2005-book2-doc-pg1901.pdf.

64. See, e.g., Trevor W. Morrison, "Constitutional Avoidance in the Executive Branch," *Columbia Law Review* 106 (2006): 1189–1259; H. Jefferson Powell, "The Executive and the Avoidance Canon," *Indiana Law Journal* 81 (2006): 1313–18.

65. Protecting the Nation from Foreign Terrorist Entry into the United States, 82 Fed. Reg. 8, 977–78 (March 6, 2017).

66. Trump v. Hawaii, 138 S. Ct. 2392, 2401 (June 26, 2018).

67. Ibid., 2421.

68. Ibid., 2435 (Sotomayor, J., dissenting).

69. Ibid., 2436.

70. Ibid., 2423.

71. Ibid., 2424.

72. Exec. Order No. 10,340, 17 Fed. Reg. 3139 (April 8, 1952).

73. *Youngstown,* 343 U.S. at 587.

74. As a consequence of the fractured opinion, Stephen Vladeck comments that "*Youngstown* . . . was a mess of a case." Stephen I. Vladeck, "Foreign Affairs Originalism in *Youngstown*'s Shadow," *Saint Louis University Law Journal* 53 (2008): 31.

75. Medellin v. Texas, 552 U.S. 491, 524 (2008).

76. *Youngstown,* 343 U.S. at 635 (Jackson, J., concurring).

77. Ibid., 637.

78. Ibid.

79. A general basis for preclusive power to act in conflict with Congress is difficult to justify on either textual or in founding-era precedents and understandings. See David J. Barron and Martin S. Lederman, "The Commander in Chief at the Lowest Ebb—Framing the Problem, Doctrine, and Original Understanding," *Harvard Law Review* 121 (2008): 800.

80. See Neal Katyal and Richard Caplan, "The Surprisingly Stronger Case for the Legality of the NSA Surveillance Program: The FDR Precedent," *Stanford Law Review* 60 (2008): 1028.

81. *Youngstown*, 343 U.S. at 637 (Jackson, J., concurring).

82. Ibid., 638.

83. Ibid., 637–38.

84. See generally Bruce Ackerman, *We the People: Transformations*, vol. 2 (Cambridge, Mass.: Harvard University Press, 1998); Larry D. Kramer, *The People Themselves: Popular Constitutionalism and Judicial Review* (New York: Oxford University Press, 2004); H. Jefferson Powell, *A Community Built on Words: The Constitution in History and Practice* (Chicago: The University of Chicago Press, 2002); Robert Post and Reva Siegel, "*Roe* Rage: Democratic Constitutionalism and Backlash," *Harvard Civil Rights—Civil Liberties Law Review* 42 (2007): 374.

85. Fallon argues that "the Constitution performs part of its constraining function by constituting, empowering, and supporting a network of mutually reinforcing institutions." Fallon, "Constitutional Constraints," 985; Daryl J. Levinson, "Parchment and Politics: The Positive Puzzle of Constitutional Commitment," *Harvard Law Review* 124 (2011): 662; Frederick Schauer, "When and How (If at All) Does Law Constrain Official Action?," *Georgia Law Review* 44 (2010): 769.

86. See, e.g., Daniel Farber, *Lincoln's Constitution* (Chicago: University of Chicago Press, 2003), 7–25.

87. President Abraham Lincoln, "First Inaugural Address (March 4, 1861)," in *Collected Works of Abraham Lincoln*, vol. 4, 265.

88. Jefferson Davis, "Inaugural Address of the President of the Provisional Government (February 18, 1861)," in *Jefferson Davis, Constitutionalist*, vol. 5, ed. Dunbar Rowland (Jackson, Miss.: Mississippi Department of Archives and History, 1923), 49–50.

89. Ibid.

90. U.S. Const. pmbl.

91. Davis, "Inaugural Address," 51.

92. Abraham Lincoln to Albert G. Hodges, U.S. Senator, April 4, 1864, in *Abraham Lincoln: Speeches and Writings, 1859–1865*, ed. Don E. Fehrenbacher (New York: Library of America, 1989), 585.

93. Lincoln, "Message to Congress (July 4, 1861)," in *Collected Works*, 429.

94. Lincoln, "First Inaugural Address," in *Collected Works*, 265.

95. Ibid.

96. Ibid.

97. Ibid.

98. Ibid.

99. Dred Scott v. Sandford, 60 U.S. (19 How.) 393, 426 (1857), held that blacks could not be citizens under the Constitution. The Supreme Court's later assertion, in the wake of Brown v. Bd. of Educ., 347 U.S. 483 (1954), that its interpretations of the Constitution were not only final but supreme, came in Cooper v. Aaron, 358 U.S. 1, 18 (1958), a case enforcing a school desegregation order in Arkansas.

100. See Rana, *Two Faces of American Freedom*, 236–325.

101. President George W. Bush, "Address to a Joint Session of Congress and the American People" (speech, September 20, 2001), The White House, https://

georgewbush-whitehouse.archives.gov/news/releases/2001/09/20010920-8.
html.

102. Ibid.

103. President George W. Bush, "President Delivers State of the Union" (speech, January 29, 2002), The White House, https://georgewbush-whitehouse.archives.gov/news/releases/2002/01/20020129-11.html.

104. President George W. Bush, "President's Address to the Nation" (speech, September 11, 2006), The White House, https://georgewbush-whitehouse.archives.gov/news/releases/2006/09/20060911-3.html.

105. Pub. L. No. 95-511, 92 Stat. 1783 (1978) (codified in scattered sections of 50 U.S.C.); 18 U.S.C. §§ 2340–2340A (2006); Convention Against Torture and Other Cruel, Inhuman and Degrading Treatment or Punishment, art. x, *adopted* December 10, 1984, S. Treaty Doc. No. 100-20 (1988), 1465 U.N.T.S. 85, 113 (entered into force June 26, 1987); Geneva Convention Relative to the Treatment of Prisoners of War, art. 3, *adopted* August 12, 1949, 6 U.S.T. 3316, 75 U.N.T.S. 135.

106. Bush, "Address to the Nation," September 11, 2006.

107. Ibid.

108. Bush, "State of the Union," January 29, 2002.

109. John Yoo's reasoning here has antecedents in defenses of the Unitarian conception of executive power. See, e.g., Steven G. Calabresi and Saikrishna B. Prakash, "The President's Power to Execute the Laws," *Yale Law Journal* 104 (1994): 549. The president also relies on personal power in exercising office. See Richard E. Neustadt, *Presidential Power and the Modern Presidents: The Politics of Leadership from Roosevelt to Reagan* (New York: The Free Press, 1990).

110. September 7, 1942.

111. Ibid.

112. Franklin D. Roosevelt, "Message to the Congress on the State of the Union," January 11, 1944, in *The Public Papers and Addresses of Franklin D. Roosevelt*, comp. Samuel I. Rosenman, vol. 13 (1944–1945) (New York: Harper & Brothers, 1950), 41.

113. *Federalist* No. 70 (Hamilton), in *The Federalist Papers*, 423.

114. See, e.g., John Locke, *The Second Treatise of Civil Government* (London: 1690), § 160 (arguing that the executive has "[p]ower to act according to discretion, for the public good, without the prescription of the Law, and sometimes even against it").

115. See Harvey C. Mansfield, Jr., *Taming the Prince: The Ambivalence of Modern Executive Power* (New York: The Free Press, 1989), 1–22.

116. AUMF, 2001, § 2.

117. President Barack Obama, "Remarks by the President at the National Defense University" (speech, May 23, 2013), The White House, https://obamawhitehouse.archives.gov/the-press-office/2013/05/23/remarks-president-national-defense-university; White House, *Report on the Legal and Policy Frameworks Guiding the United States' Use of Military Force and Related National Security*

Operations (Washington, D.C.: White House, December 2016); Harold Hongju Koh, "The Obama Administration and International Law" (speech, American Society of International Law Annual Meeting, March 25, 2010).

118. See text of AUMF, 2001.

119. Authorization for Use of Military Force Against Iraq Resolution of 2002, Pub. L. No. 107-243, § 3, 116 Stat. 1498, 1501 (2002).

120. U.S. Const. art. I, § 8, cl. 18.

121. For the contrary view, that the "necessary and appropriate" clause in the AUMF does not constrain executive power but expands it, see Curtis A. Bradley and Jack L. Goldsmith, "Congressional Authorization and the War on Terrorism," *Harvard Law Review* 118 (2005): 2081.

122. McCulloch v. Maryland, 17 U.S. (4 Wheat.) 316, 413–23 (1819).

123. Ibid.

124. This discussion will build on the idea of the completion power presented by Jack Goldsmith and John F. Manning, "The President's Completion Power," *Yale Law Journal* 115 (2006): 2280–2312.

125. Chevron, U.S.A., Inc. v. Natural Resources Defense Council, Inc., 467 U.S. 837, 842–45 (1984).

126. Goldsmith and Manning, "The President's Completion Power," 2280.

127. *Youngstown* 343 U.S. at 701 (Vinson, C.J., dissenting).

128. Ibid., 672.

129. Ibid., 702.

130. Ibid. Chief Justice Vinson's theory, unlike that of Goldsmith and Manning, is explicitly based on the Take Care Clause. Ibid., 701; see also *In re* Debs, 158 U.S. 564, 578–79 (1895); Cunningham v. Neagle, 135 U.S. 1, 63–64 (1890).

131. Article I empowers Congress "[t]o make all Laws which shall be necessary and proper for carrying into Execution the foregoing Powers, and all other Powers vested by this Constitution in the Government of the United States, or in any Department or Officer thereof." U.S. Const. art. I, § 8, cl. 18.

132. Goldsmith and Manning, "Completion Power," 2305. Chief Justice Vinson labeled this basic authority, if presented as the whole of the executive power, as the "messenger-boy concept of the Office." *Youngstown*, 343 U.S. at 708–9 (Vinson, C.J., dissenting).

133. Goldsmith and Manning tie this thought to the modern nondelegation doctrine. Goldsmith and Manning, "Completion Power," 2305; see Whitman v. Am. Trucking Ass'n, 531 U.S. 457, 475 (2001).

134. Goldsmith and Manning, "Completion Power," 2306.

135. Thomas Jefferson to John B. Colvin, September 20, 1810, in *The Papers of Thomas Jefferson: Retirement Series*, vol. 3, 99.

136. Goldsmith and Manning, "Completion Power," 2285.

137. The key constitutional language refers to "the foregoing Powers, and all other Powers vested." U.S. Const. art. I, § 8, cl. 18.

138. *Youngstown*, 343 U.S. at 649–50 (Jackson, J., concurring).

139. Ibid., 646.

140. *Youngstown*, 343 U.S. at 587; see also Harold Hongju Koh, "Setting the World Right," *Yale Law Journal* 115 (2006): 2372–73.

141. Dames & Moore v. Regan, 453 U.S. 654, 678 (1981).

142. See Randy E. Barnett, "The Original Meaning of the Necessary and Proper Clause," *University of Pennsylvania Journal of Constitutional Law* 6 (2003): 185; Geoffrey P. Miller, "The Corporate Law Background of the Necessary and Proper Clause," *George Washington Law Review* 79 (2010): 2.

143. *McCulloch*, 17 U.S. (4 Wheat.) at 421.

144. AUMF, 2001.

145. Bradley and Goldsmith argue, by contrast, that "there is no reason to think that 'necessary and appropriate' was meant as an independent and additional restriction." Bradley and Goldsmith, "Congressional Authorization," 2082.

146. Federalist No. 70 (Hamilton), in *The Federalist Papers*, 424.

147. Federalist No. 34 (Hamilton), in *The Federalist Papers*, 207.

148. Sanford Levinson, *Constitutional Faith* (Princeton, N.J.: Princeton University Press, 1988), 75.

149. *Hamdi*, 542 U.S. at 532.

150. See Job 1:6–2:13, which describes God's testing of Job; see also Robert Cover, "The Supreme Court, 1982 Term—Foreword: Nomos and Narrative," *Harvard Law Review* 97 (1983): 9.

151. See National Emergencies Act, Pub. L. No. 94-412, 90 Stat. 1255 (1976); International Emergency Economic Powers Act, Pub. L. No. 95-223, 91 Stat. 1625 (1977).

152. See, e.g., Bruce Ackerman, *Before the Next Attack: Preserving Civil Liberties in an Age of Terrorism* (New Haven, Conn.: Yale University Press, 2006), 77–100.

153. Home Bldg. & Loan Ass'n v. Blaisdell, 290 U.S. 398, 425–26 (1934).

154. Levinson, *Constitutional Faith*, 660.

155. It may be, however, that "the institutional environment in which officials function may influence their psychological apprehensions of the normative constraints to which they are subject." Fallon, "Constitutional Constraints," 1026.

156. Levinson, *Constitutional Faith*, 681–91.

157. Ibid., 699.

158. Presidents will innovate when possible. See Elena Kagan, "Presidential Administration," *Harvard Law Review* 114 (2001): 2248.

159. Fallon, "Constitutional Constraints," 987.

Chapter 7. Identity, Freedom, and Constitutional Constraint

1. McCulloch v. Maryland, 17 U.S. (4 Wheat.) 316, 421 (1819).

2. Eric A. Posner and Adrian Vermeule, *The Executive Unbound: After the Madisonian Republic* (New York: Oxford University Press, 2010). Posner and Vermeule argue that the only effective constraints are, and should be, merely political. Ibid., 12–15. See also Adrian Vermeule, "Our Schmittian Administrative Law," *Harvard Law Review* 122 (2009): 1101–3.

3. See, e.g., Daryl J. Levinson and Richard H. Pildes, "Separation of Parties, Not Powers," *Harvard Law Review* 119 (2006): 2312.

4. Posner and Vermeule, *Executive Unbound,* 201.

5. See Jon Elster, *Ulysses Unbound* (New York: Cambridge University Press, 2000), 1–87.

6. For an important related inquiry, see Joseph Margulies, *What Changed When Everything Changed: 9/11 and the Making of National Identity* (New Haven, Conn.: Yale University Press, 2013).

7. See Bruce Ackerman, *We the People: Transformations,* vol. 2 (Cambridge, Mass.: Harvard University Press, 1998), 3–31, 409–14.

8. See Elster, *Ulysses Unbound,* 105–18.

9. President Abraham Lincoln, "First Inaugural Address (March 4, 1861)," in *Collected Works of Abraham Lincoln,* vol. 4, ed. Roy P. Basler et al. (New Brunswick, N.J.: Rutgers University Press, 1953), 266, 264.

10. Brown v. Board of Education, 347 U.S. 483 (1954). On the idea that law forms archetypes not easily overturned, Jeremy Waldron, "Torture and Positive Law: Jurisprudence for the White House," *Columbia Law Review* 105 (2005): 1681–1750. And not all precedents are alike, Michael J. Gerhardt, "Super Precedent," *Minnesota Law Review* 90 (2006): 1204–31. See generally Bruce Ackerman, *We the People: The Civil Rights Revolution,* vol. 3 (Cambridge, Mass.: Harvard University Press, 2014).

11. President Barack Obama, "Remarks by the President on National Security" (speech, May 21, 2009), The White House, https://obamawhitehouse.archives.gov/the-press-office/remarks-president-national-security-5-21-09.

12. Ibid.

13. Ibid.

14. President George W. Bush, "Address to a Joint Session of Congress and the American People" (speech, September 20, 2001), The White House, https://georgewbush-whitehouse.archives.gov/news/releases/2001/09/20010920-8.html.

15. President George W. Bush, "President Discusses Creation of Military Commissions to Try Suspected Terrorists," September 6, 2006, The White House, news release, http://georgewbush-whitehouse.archives.gov/news/releases/2006/09/20060906-3.html.

16. Obama, "Remarks," May 21, 2009.

17. Attorney General Eric Holder, "On National Security" (speech, Northwestern University Law School, March 5, 2012), U.S. Department of Justice (DOJ), https://www.justice.gov/opa/speech/attorney-general-eric-holder-speaks-northwestern-university-school-law [hereinafter "National Security Speech"].

18. Hamdi v. Rumsfeld, 542 U.S. 507, 532 (2004).

19. Harold Hongju Koh, "The Obama Administration and International Law" (speech, American Society of International Law Annual Meeting, March 25, 2010).

20. U.S. Department of Justice white paper, *Lawfulness of a Lethal Operation Directed Against a U.S. Citizen Who Is a Senior Operational Leader of Al Qa'ida or an Associated Force* (November 8, 2011), https://fas.org/irp/eprint/doj-lethal.pdf.

21. Al-Aulaqi v. Obama, 727 F. Supp. 2d 1 (D.D.C. 2010).
22. DOJ white paper, *Lawfulness of a Lethal Operation,* 5–9.
23. For a brief history of past executive abuses that should caution blind trust in presidential leadership, see David Cole, *Enemy Aliens: Double Standards and Constitutional Freedoms in the War on Terrorism* (New York: The New Press, 2003): 85–179. Nor from press accounts of additional U.S. citizens targeted, beyond the case of Al-Aulaqi, who was targeted because of his continuing role in fomenting terrorist plots against the United States, did the Obama administration seem to constrain its authority. See Mark Mazzetti, "Killing of Americans Deepens Debate over Use of Drone Strikes," *New York Times,* April 23, 2015. For a defense of targeted killing, see Gabriella Blum and Philip B. Heymann, *Laws, Outlaws, and Terrorists: Lessons from the War on Terrorism* (Cambridge, Mass.: The MIT Press, 2010): 69–92.
24. President Obama admonished that "we need not sacrifice our security for our values, nor sacrifice our values for our security." Obama, "Remarks," May 21, 2009.
25. *Federalist* No. 1 (Hamilton), in *The Federalist Papers,* ed. Clinton Rossiter (New York: New American Library, 1961), 33.
26. See also Jeremy Waldron, "Security and Liberty: The Image of Balance," *Journal of Political Philosophy* 11 (2003): 191.
27. See, e.g., Richard A. Posner, *Not a Suicide Pact: The Constitution in a Time of National Emergency* (New York: Oxford University Press, 2006).
28. See Henry Shue, *Basic Rights: Subsistence, Affluence, and U.S. Foreign Policy* (Princeton, N.J.: Princeton University Press, 1980). The place of security within a state's governing priorities is a complicated issue, for American constitutionalism aims, in part, "to secure the Blessings of Liberty," U.S. Const. pmbl.; see also Ian Loader and Neil Walker, *Civilizing Security* (Cambridge: Cambridge University Press, 2007).
29. I pursue this argument at length in Thomas P. Crocker, "Who Decides on Liberty?," *Connecticut Law Review* 44 (2012): 1511.
30. Authorization for Use of Military Force, Pub. L. No. 107-40, § 2, 115 Stat. 224, 224 (2001).
31. Holder, "National Security Speech."
32. Bernard Williams, "Practical Necessity," in *Moral Luck: Philosophical Papers, 1973–1980* (Cambridge: Cambridge University Press, 1981), 130. In this claim and what follows, I rely much on the argument that Williams advances in this essay.
33. Ibid.
34. See Elster, *Ulysses Unbound,* 7–24.
35. Ibid.
36. See Paul Kahn, *Political Theology: Four New Chapters on the Concept of Sovereignty* (New York: Columbia University Press, 2011), 83. He argues, "There must be a decision before we can understand what the norms require." Ibid.
37. Ibid., 45.
38. Again, as Kahn articulates Schmitt's view: "The exception, accordingly, can only be recognized in the decision. More precisely, it is constituted in the decision itself. The truth of the matter is not something apart from the decision." Ibid., 45.

39. Bernard Williams, "Persons, Character and Morality," in *Moral Luck*, 5. Williams also claims that these points about the relation between practical necessity and character apply "to a group or to a tradition." Williams, "Practical Necessity," 130.
40. Holder, "National Security Speech."
41. Obama, "Remarks," May 21, 2009.
42. Williams, "Practical Necessity," 130.
43. Williams articulates the point this way: "Conclusions of practical necessity seriously arrived at in serious matters are indeed the paradigm of what one takes responsibility for." Ibid., 130.
44. William Lloyd Garrison, "Address to the Friends of Freedom and Emancipation in the United States," in *The American Intellectual Tradition*, vol. 1, 1630–1865, ed. David A. Hollinger and Charles Capper (Oxford: Oxford University Press, 1997), 438; Frederick Douglass, "What to the Slave Is the Fourth of July?," in Hollinger and Capper, 447.
45. Plessy v. Ferguson, 163 U.S. 537 (1896); Giles v. Harris, 189 U.S. 475 (1903). An excellent account of the story of constitutional failure and constitutional remaking is told in Mark E. Brandon, *Free in the World: American Slavery and Constitutional Failure* (Princeton, N.J.: Princeton University Press, 1998). The diachronic and difficult process of constitutional transformation from Reconstruction to the civil rights revolution is explored in Ackerman, *We the People*, vols. 2 and 3.
46. These questions evoke the problem of constituent power, which for Schmitt is the product of pure decision, and for others, like Hans Kelsen, is the product of a system of norms. See Martin Loughlin, "The Concept of Constituent Power," *European Journal of Political Theory* 13 (2014): 218–37. See also essays in Martin Loughlin and Neil Walker, *The Paradox of Constitutionalism: Constituent Power and Constitutional Form* (Oxford: Oxford University Press, 2008).
47. See, e.g., Alasdair MacIntyre, *After Virtue* (Notre Dame, Ind.: Notre Dame University Press, 1981); Derek Parfit, *Reasons and Persons* (Oxford: Oxford University Press, 1984); Paul Ricoeur, "Narrative Identity," *Philosophy Today* 35 (1991): 73–81.
48. Charlie Savage, "Election to Decide Future Interrogation Methods in Terrorism Cases," *New York Times*, September 27, 2012.
49. David Welna, "Trump Has Vowed to Fill Guantanamo With 'Some Bad Dudes'— But Who?," National Public Radio, November 14, 2016.
50. Savage, "Election to Decide."
51. Quoted in Eric Lichtblau, *Bush's War: The Remaking of American Justice* (New York: Anchor Books, 2008), 159.
52. Posner and Vermeule, *Executive Unbound*, 15.
53. "Energy in the executive is a leading character in the definition of good government. It is essential to the protection of the community against foreign attacks." This is said to be important, because "[d]ecision, activity, secrecy, and dispatch

will generally characterise the proceedings of one man, in a much more eminent degree, than the proceedings of any greater number." *Federalist* No. 70 (Hamilton), in *The Federalist Papers,* 424.

54. See, e.g., the following additional claims: "Liberal legalism's essential failing is that it overestimates the need for the separation of powers and even the rule of law." Posner and Vermeule, *Executive Unbound,* 15; and "One of our main claims, for example, is that the Madisonian separation of powers is obsolete." Ibid., 17.

55. See also Jed Rubenfeld, *Revolution by Judiciary: The Structure of American Constitutional Law* (Cambridge, Mass.: Harvard University Press, 2005).

56. I analyze the reduction of constitutional skepticism to cynicism in Thomas Crocker and Michael Hodges, "Constitutions, Rule-Following, and the Crisis of Constraint," *Legal Theory* 24 (2018): 3–39.

57. Brandon, *Free in the World,* 175–89; Sanford Levinson, *Constitutional Faith* (Princeton, N.J.: Princeton University Press, 1988), 75.

58. *Federalist* No. 1 (Hamilton), in *The Federalist Papers,* 33.

59. Ibid.

60. Harry G. Frankfurt, "Freedom of the Will and the Concept of a Person," *Journal of Philosophy* 68 (1971): 12, 13.

61. Shue, *Basic Rights,* 21–22; Loader and Walker, *Civilizing Security,* 4. I have in mind also the kind of strong evaluations Charles Taylor argues are constitutive of personhood. See Charles Taylor, *Sources of the Self: The Making of Modern Identity* (Cambridge, Mass.: Harvard University Press, 1989), 3–52.

62. See, e.g., Thomas Hobbes, *Leviathan,* ed. Richard Tuck (Cambridge, Mass.: Harvard University Press, 1996). But also see Stephen Holmes, who calls into question whether we can conceive of such a natural state of liberty, or whether the formation of government is actually the condition for the possibility of liberty itself. Stephen Holmes, *Passions and Constraint: On the Theory of Liberal Democracy* (Chicago: University of Chicago Press, 1995), 18–31.

63. See Thomas P. Crocker, "Dystopian Constitutionalism," *University of Pennsylvania Journal of Constitutional Law* 18 (2015): 593–655.

64. See Jack Goldsmith and John F. Manning, "The President's Completion Power," *Yale Law Journal* 115 (2006): 2280–2312.

65. See Guido Calabresi and Philip Bobbitt, *Tragic Choices* (New York: W. W. Norton, 1978); Michael Walzer, "Political Action: The Problem of Dirty Hands, *Philosophy & Public Affairs* 2 (1973): 160–80.

66. See John Rawls, "Two Concepts of Rules," *Philosophical Review* 64 (1955): 3–32.

67. Neither does the common law, as Justice Holmes explained in Southern Pacific Company v. Jensen, 244 U.S. 205, 222 (1917) (Holmes, J., dissenting).

68. "When Americans talk about American constitutional law, they are necessarily talking about themselves and, ultimately, what kind of persons they wish to be." Levinson, *Constitutional Faith,* 75.

69. Ludwig Wittgenstein, *Philosophical Investigations,* trans. G. E. M. Anscombe (Oxford: Basil Blackwell, 1958), § 19.

70. Stanley Cavell, *This New Yet Unapproachable America: Lectures After Emerson After Wittgenstein* (Chicago: University of Chicago Press, 1989), 48.
71. Wittgenstein suggests, "It is what human beings say that is true and false; and they agree in the language they use. That is not agreement in opinions but in form of life." Wittgenstein, *Philosophical Investigations*, § 240.

INDEX